우루과이라운드

법제화 그룹 회의

_____

우루과이라운드

법제화 그룹 회의

한국학술정보

| 머리말

우루과이라운드는 국제적 교역 질서를 수립하려는 다각적 무역 교섭으로서, 각국의 보호무역 추세를 보다 완화하고 다자무역체제를 강화하기 위해 출범되었다. 1986년 9월 개시가 선언되었으며, 15개 분야의 교섭을 1990년 말까지 진행하기로 했다. 그러나 각 분야의 중간 교섭이 이루어진 1989년 이후에도 농산물, 지적소유권, 서비스무역, 섬유, 긴급수입제한 등 많은 분야에서 대립하며 1992년이 돼서야 타결에 이를 수 있었다. 한국은 특히 농산물 분야에서 기존 수입 제한 품목 대부분을 개방해야 했기에 큰 경쟁력 하락을 겪었고, 관세와 기술 장벽 완화, 보조금 및 수입 규제 정책의 변화로 제조업 수출입에도 많은 변화가 있었다.

본 총서는 우루과이라운드 협상이 막바지에 다다랐던 1991~1992년 사이 외교부에서 작성한 관련 자료를 담고 있다. 관련 협상의 치열했던 후반기 동향과 관계부처회의, 무역협상위원회 회의, 실무대책회의, 규범 및 제도, 투자회의, 특히나 가장 많은 논란이 있었던 농산물과 서비스 분야 협상 등의 자료를 포함해 총 28권으로 구성되었다. 전체 분량은 약 1만 3천여 쪽에 이른다.

2024년 3월
한국학술정보(주)

| 일러두기

· 본 총서에 실린 자료는 2022년 4월과 2023년 4월에 각각 공개한 외교문서 4,827권, 76만여 쪽 가운데 일부를 발췌한 것이다.

· 각 권의 제목과 순서는 공개된 원본을 최대한 반영하였으나, 주제에 따라 일부는 적절히 변경하였다.

· 원본 자료는 A4 판형에 맞게 축소하거나 원본 비율을 유지한 채 A4 페이지 안에 삽입하였다. 또한 현재 시점에선 공개되지 않아 '공란'이란 표기만 있는 페이지 역시 그대로 실었다.

· 외교부가 공개한 문서 각 권의 첫 페이지에는 '정리 보존 문서 목록'이란 이름으로 기록물 종류, 일자, 명칭, 간단한 내용 등의 정보가 수록되어 있으며, 이를 기준으로 0001번부터 번호가 매겨져 있다. 이는 삭제하지 않고 총서에 그대로 수록하였다.

· 보고서 내용에 관한 더 자세한 정보가 필요하다면, 외교부가 온라인상에 제공하는 『대한민국 외교사료요약집』 1991년과 1992년 자료를 참조할 수 있다.

| 차례

정 리 보 존 문 서 목 록

기록물종류	일반공문서철		등록번호	2020030052	등록일자	2020-03-09
분류번호	764.51		국가코드		보존기간	영구
명 칭	UR(우루과이라운드) / 법제화 그룹회의, 1992. 전2권					
생 산 과	통상기구과		생산년도	1992~1992	담당그룹	
권 차 명	V.1 1-3월					
내용목차						

0001

UR 대책 실무회의(91.12.24) 관련 자료

1991. 12. 23.

외 무 부 통 상 기 구 과

0002

- 목   차 -

1. 제도분야 의장 협정문(안) 주요쟁점 및 아국 입장

주요쟁점	의장 협정문 초안	아국 입장 반영 여부 및 대응 방안	비 고
1. 일방조치 억제	○ 여타국의 무역조치의 갓트 위반 여부 판정, 합리적 이행기간 결정, 보복의 수준 결정 및 보복조치 발동과 관련 체약국은 반드시 갓트 분쟁해결 절차를 준수해야 함(일방조치라는 표현 불사용)	○ 분쟁해결과 관련, 일방조치를 발동 해서는 안된다는 아국 입장 반영	○ 모든 협상 참가국이 이의없이 동의
2. 무역관련 법령의 갓트일치	○ 분쟁해결 text에서 언급하는 대신 MTO 협정 문안 제16조 (Final provision) 4항에 "수정이 필요한 경우 이를 위하여 모든 조치를 취하기 위하여 노력해야 한다"고 규정	○ 아국의 입장이 무역 관련 법령의 갓트 일치 의무화인데 반해 의장 협정문 초안은 이를 임의 사항으로 남겨둠 으로써 아국 입장의 반영 정도가 미흡하나 미국의 강한 입장 때문에 현실적으로 관철이 어려움.	○ 국내무역 법령의 갓트일치를 임의 사항으로 하는데 모든 협상 참가국이 이의 없이 동의
3. 교차보복	○ 원칙적으로 동일분야에서 보복 허용 ○ 동일분야에서의 보복이 비현실적이거나 비효과적일 경우 동일 협정하의 다른 분야에서의 보복 허용 ○ 동일 협정하에서의 보복이 비현실적이거나 비효과적일 경우 여타 협정하에서의 보복 허용	○ 엄격한 기준하에 교차보복이 허용 되어야 한다는 아국 fall-back position에 비추어 큰 문제 없음.	○ 모든 참가국이 합의된 것으로 양해
4. MTO 협정 발효 및 가입시한	○ 각료회의(Implementing Conference)를 개최하여 MTO 협정 발효 시점 결정	○ MTO 설립에 원칙적 으로 반대치 않는 입장이므로 각료 회의에서 MTO 협정 발효 시점을 결정 하도록 한것은 별다른 문제가 없음	○ 모든 참가국간에 합의가 이루어진 것으로 양해

주요쟁점	의장 협정문 초안	아국 입장 반영 여부 및 대응 방안	비 고
	ㅇ갓트체약국의 MTO 협정 가입시한은 동 각료회의에서 달리 정하지 않는한 95.1.1까지로 함.	ㅇMTO 협정 가입 시한에 대해서는 신중한 입장이나 컨센서스가 이루어 지는 경우 이에따름	ㅇUR 협상 결과에 대한 참가국들의 평가에 따라, 논란의 여지가 있을 것으로 분석됨.
5.Single Under- taking (일괄수락)	ㅇMTO 협정문 11조에 "UR 협상 결과를 전체로서 수락하는 갓트체약국을 원회원국으로 한다"고 규정함으로써 UR 협상 결과의 선별 수락 가능성 배제	ㅇUR 협상 결과를 일괄 수락하는데 대해 아국은 반대치 않는다는 입장	ㅇ인도, 브라질이 일괄 수락에 반대 입장인바, 향후 논란의 대상이 될 소지가 있음
6.최종 의정서 (Final Act)	ㅇUR 협상 결과의 국제적 이행 여부에 관한 결정을 위한 각료급 갓트 특별총회를 92년말 이전에 개최	ㅇ푼타 델 에스테 각료선언에 의거한 것인바, 별다른 문제가 없음.	ㅇ협상 참가국간에 별다른 이의가 없음
	ㅇ제반 UR 협정의 발효일자 결정을 위한 각료급 회의를 92년말 이전에 개최	ㅇUR 협상 참가국의 국내 수락 절차 완료 상황을 고려하여 UR 협정 발효일자를 결정하게 되므로 별다른 문제가 없음	ㅇ협상 참가국간에 별다른 이의가 없음.
	ㅇ제반 UR 협정의 발효일자 : 93.1.1	ㅇUR 협상 결과에 대한 아국의 전반적인 평가가 이루어 진후 결정할 문제	ㅇ일본은 93.7.1 스위스는 94.1.1, 미국은 협상 종료후 가장 빠른 시점을 주장하는등 협상 참가국간에 의견이 일치하지 않고 있음.

2

0005

2. 최종의정서

1. 91.12.20 이후 UR 협상 추진 일정 (예상)

91.12.20   UR 협상 최종 draft package (Dunkel paper) 배포

92. 1.13   TNC 회의 개최

- UR 협상 참가국, Dunkel paper에 대한 원칙적인 수락
  여부 표명

92.1-3   하기 분야에서 UR 최종 마무리 협상 진행

(분야별 양허 schedule 작성)

- 시장접근

- 농 산 물 (국내보조, 수출경쟁)

- 서 비 스

92.4월경   마무리 협상 종료후 Final Act(UR 협상 최종 package) 채택

92년말 이전
(Final Act 채택   각료급 갓트 특별총회 개최
회의와 동시
개최하는 것으로   - UR 협상 결과의 국제적 이행 문제 결정
양해)
         (푼타 델 에스테 각료선언에 의거)

92년말 이전   제반 UR 협정 및 MTO 설립 협정 발효일자 결정을 위한

각료회의 개최 (Implementing Conference)

- 동 결정시 각국의 국내 비준 상황 고려

(93.1.1)   제반 UR 협정(MTO 설립 협정 포함) 발효

- 상기 UR 협정 발효일자 결정을 위한 각료회의의 결정에
  따라 변경 가능

3

0006

(95.1.1)　　　　　MTO 설립 협정 수락 시한

　　　　　　　　　- 94년말까지 MTO 설립 협정 수락을 통해 UR 협상 결과를
　　　　　　　　　　일괄 수락치 못하는 갓트 체약국은 갓트 체약국으로서
　　　　　　　　　　가입 조건 협상없이 MTO 회원국 지위를 획득할 수 있는
　　　　　　　　　　권리 상실

2. 대 책

o 최종의정서 협의 과정에서 바람직한 Final Act 발효일과 관련하여 일본이
　93.7.1, 스위스가 94.1.1을 제의 하였으나, 미.EC등 다수국 희망대로
　93.1.1로 결정될 가능성이 가장 클 것으로 예상됨.

o 발효일 문제는 정치적인 약속으로서 실질적인 사항은 MTO 설립과 관련하여
　논의될 것이므로 특별한 대책 마련 불요.　　　　　　　　　　끝.

4

0007

3. UR/제도분야 최종 협정문 내용 및 평가

I. 분쟁해결

> 모든 참가국간 합의 또는 대체적 양해하에 작성 되었으며
> Final Act 채택 시점까지 기술적 협상을 거쳐 단일 분쟁해결 절차
> (IDS : Integrated Dispute Settlement System) 형태로의 궁극적인
> 통합을 상정하고 있음.

1. 주요내용

가. 통합 text

o 하기 사항을 주요 내용으로 하고 있으며, 발효후 4년 이내에
전반적인 재검토 예정
- 분쟁해결의 매단계 자동화
- 66년 절차 적용에 관한 규정 존치 (2-Tier System)
- 분쟁해결의 전체 및 단계별 시한 설정 (전체 18개월)
- 상소제도 및 합리적 이행기간 개념 신규 도입
- 보상, 보복과 관련 중재 제도 도입
- 일방조치 배제 (갓트 분쟁해결 절차 준수)
- Non-violation 분쟁에 관한 별도 규정 신설

나. 단일 분쟁해결 절차(IDS) text
- 분쟁해결 기구(Dispute Settlement Body) 설치, 표준 TOR, 협정간
절차 규정 상충시의 적용절차, 협정간 실질규정 상충시의 처리
방법등 UR 협상 종료후 상품, 서비스 협정을 총괄하여 통일적으로
적용될 IDS 문안에 포함될 요소를 나열

5

0008

다. 교차보복 관련 별도 문안
  - 궁극적으로 IDS 문안에 포함될 사항인 교차보복의 기준 및 절차등을
    규정

2. 분석 및 평가

가. 절차 자동화
  - 분쟁해결 매단계별 및 전체시한 설정, 매단계 이사회 결정 방식의
    완전 자동화 등을 통해 분쟁해결 절차 과정에서의 봉쇄(blockage)
    요소가 완전 제거된 반면, 상소제도 도입, 합리적 이행기간 개념의
    도입, 보상, 보복관련 중재 제도 도입등 완전 자동화에 따라 있을 수
    있는 부작용에 대한 견제장치도 아울러 마련

나. 일방조치 억제 공약
  - 상기 분쟁해결 절차 자동화와 연계된 쟁점인 일방조치 억제 공약과
    관련, 분쟁의 판정, 합리적 이행기간 결정, 불이행시의 보복의 수준
    결정 및 보복조치 발동등 GATT 관련 모든 분쟁을 새로운 분쟁해결
    규율에 따라서만 해결토록 한다는 문안에 대해 합의가 이루어짐으로써
    일방적 무역 조치에 대한 억제가 가능하게 됨. 다만 무역관련
    국내법령의 갓트 일치 문제와 관련, 이를 의무사항이 아닌 임의
    사항으로 MTO 설립 협정 제 16조 4항에 규정함으로써 당초 목표보다는
    다소 미흡하나, 미국 입장에서는 최대한의 양보선이라고 판단됨.

다. 통합절차
  - 또한 92.4까지 분쟁해결 관련 단일절차(IDS)가 마련될 전망이며,
    이에 따라 지금까지 GATT내 다수 분쟁해결 절차의 병존에 따라
    발생되어 오던 문제점(Fragmentation 및 Forum shopping)이 해소될
    것으로 전망됨.

6   0009

라. 교차보복

- 다만 아국에 대해 다소 불리하게 작용될 소지가 있는 교차보복이 도입됨으로써 부담이 되는 면은 있으나, 이는 UR 협상 결과 다자간 무역규범이 상품 분야뿐만 아니라 써비스, 지적소유권등 여타 모든 분야로 확대됨에 따른 불가피한 결과임.

3. 전망 및 대책

- 1.13 이후 92.4월중순까지를 목표로 IDS 마련을 위한 실무, 기술적 협상이 진행될 것임.

- 특별한 어려움은 예견되지 않으나, 각 협정간의 절차적 또는 실질적인 상충 가능성을 해소하기 위한 작업에 다소 시일이 걸릴 것으로 예상되며, 이를 위해 기본적으로 사무국이 기초자료를 제공하게 될 것이나, 아국으로서도 UR 협상 전분야 협상 결과 형성될 제반 규범에 대한 면밀한 비교 검토가 필요함.

II. MTO

1. 문서의 성격

- MTO 설립 협정안은 EC, 카나다가 제안하여 91.11.6부터 본격 논의하기 시작 하였으며, 논의 과정에서 참여국의 의견을 반영하여 의장이 작성함. MTO 문제는 1.13이후 추가 협의가 필요한 분야로서 의장의 주석에도 언급되어 있음.

2. 주요내용

가. MTO의 범위(2조)와 관련 상품 협정, 서비스 협정, TRIPs 협정을 개도국의 입장을 반영, 별도 category로 분류

7

0010

나. MTO의 기능(3조)중의 하나로서, 통합 분쟁해결 절차 포함

(선진국 입장 반영)

다. MTO의 구조와 관련 일반 이사회 산하에 상품, 서비스 및 TRIPs

이사회를 각각 설립 (개도국 입장 반영)

라. 특정 회원간의 협약 부적용 규정(13조)와 관련 개도국 주장을 반영

분야별 부적용을 허용

마. 수락, 발효

- UR 참여 갓트체약국은 92.11.1부터 가입 가능

- 각료회의를 개최하여 MTO 협정 발효시점 결정 (93.1.1 예정)

- MTO 협정 발효일로부터 2년이내에 UR 협상 결과를 일괄 수락하여

MTO 협정을 수락치 않는 갓트체약국은 갓트체약국으로서 가입 조건

협상없이 MTO 회원국 지위를 획득할 수 있는 권리 상실

바. 최종 조항 (16조)

- 유보 불가 문제는 PPA 관련 협상 결과에 따름 (미국 입장 반영)

- UR 협상 결과 이행을 위한 국내법 개정 최대 노력

(일방조치 억제 차원)

3. 대 책

- 1.13 이후 추후 협의에 대비, UR 협상 결과를 전반적으로 검토하여

아국 입장 점검.

8

0011

Ⅲ. 갓트 기능

1. 주요내용

가. 갓트의 감시기능 강화

1) 각국 무역정책검토(TPRM)

- 88.12 중간평가 결과 89.4부터 시행중인 TPRM 실시 재확인

- 갓트이사회가 TPRM 실시 상황을 재검토하여 92 갓트 정규총회에
  검토 결과 보고

2) 국제무역환경 검토

- 88.12 중간평가 결과 89.4부터 시행중인 연례 국제무역환경 검토
  제도 재확인 및 계속 실시 권고

3) Domestic transparency

- 각국의 무역정책 결정과 관련한 명료성을 자발적으로 제고하는데
  합의

4) 통고제도 개선

- 기존의 갓트상의 통고 공약 재확인

- 중앙통고문 기탁소를 갓트사무국에 설치

- 기존 갓트상의 통고 의무 및 절차 재검토 (이를 위한 작업반을
  UR 협상 종료직후 설치)

나. 세계경제 정책 결정시 일관성 제고

- 갓트가 통화 및 금융관련 국제기구와의 협력 관계를 추구하고
  발전시켜 나가야 함. (이 경우 각 국제기구의 권한, 비밀준수
  의무 및 독립성을 존중하여 각국에 cross-conditionality나 여타
  추가적인 의무를 부여하는 것을 피해야 함)

9

0012

- 국제경제 정책 수립시 일관성(coherence) 제고를 위하여 갓트
  사무총장이 IMF 및 World Bank 총재와 함께 이들 국제기구간의
  협력 방안을 검토할 것을 권고함.

2. 평 가

- 갓트기능 분야에서 상기와 같이 합의가 이루어짐으로써 TPRM이 갓트의
  주요기능으로서 정착하는 계기 마련

- 또한 TPRM과 함께 연례 국제무역환경 검토 연례화, 갓트사무국내 중앙
  통고문 기탁소 설치, 기존 갓트상의 통고 의무 및 통고절차 검토를 위한
  작업반의 UR 협상 종료직후 설치에 합의가 이루어짐으로써 갓트의 감시
  기능(surveillence)이 현저하게 강화됨.

- 통화, 금융 및 무역정책간의 일관성 제고 문제와 관련 각 기구의
  mandate나 독자적인 지위에 영향을 미치지 않고 또한 각국에 추가적인
  의무를 지우지 않는 범위내에서 GATT, IMF 및 World Bank간의 협력
  관계를 강화하도록 권고함으로써 무난하게 합의가 이루어짐.

3. 대 책

- 갓트기능 강화와 관련하여 합의된 사항은 아국 입장에서 특별한 이해
  관계가 없는 분야이므로 별도 대책이 불필요함.

외 무 부

원 본

종 별 :

번 호 : GVW-2787

일 시 : 91 1223 1850

수 신 : 장관(통상국 최혁심의관)

발 신 : 주 제네바 대사(오행겸참사관)

제 목 : 업연(P.P.A 문제)

연: GVW-2705

1. 미국이 P.P.A 조부조항 원용근거를 계속 보유키 위해 이미 합의한 PPA 철폐에 반대함으로써(MACIEL 의장앞 편지 및 12.17 회의) 결국 최종협상문서에서PPA 철폐 합의가 삭제됨.

2. 또한 MTO 설립 협정과 관련 UR 협상에 참여하는 모든 GATT 회원국은 GATT 규정을 DEFINITIVE BASIS 로 받아들이기로 하되 PPA 상 조부조항은 UR 협상 결과에 따르기로 하여 MTO 가 설립되는 경우 PPA 는 없어지더라도 조부조항 원용근거(PPA 1(B)항)는 살아있게됨.

3. 미국의 조부조항 원용의도는 JOHNS ACT 에서 연안해운 운항에는 미국내 건조선박만 사용토록한 것을 계속 가능토록 하기 위함인바, 농산물을 조부부조항에의거 규제해온 나라들도 이를 원용규제할 수 있겠는가 하는 것이 의문으로 제기될수 있음.

4. 동건관련, 12.23(월) LINDEN 보좌관에 확인한바 PPA 조부조항 원용은 UR협상에서 특정품목과 관련한 별도 협정을 마련한 경우(예:농산물)에는 이를 원용할 수 없는 것이며, 미국의 상기 선박문제는 다른 협상그룹에서 별도로 협상이이루어져 합의된것이 없으므로 원용 가능할것 이라는 의견이었음.

5. 농산물 협상의 경우 별첨 ANNEX 3 에서 모든바와 같이 갓트 12 조, 18 조, 19 조,20 조, 21 조를 제외한 모든 수량규제가 TARIFFICATION COVERAGE(대상)이 되어있기 때문에 동 협정내용이 조부조항을 원용할 수 없게 하는 것임을 참고하시기 바람. 끝

첨부: ANNEX 3

(GVW(F)-0680)

통상국 장관

예고:92.6.30 까지

주 제 네 바 대 표 부

번 호 : GVW(F) - 0680   년월일 : 1223   시간 : 1850
수 신 : 장   관 (통상국 최적 심의관)
발 신 : 주 제네바대사 (오행점)
제 목 : 첨부

총   2 매(표지포함)

보 안 통 제	

외신과 통 제	

680-2-1

0016

Annex 3

MARKET ACCESS: AGRICULTURAL PRODUCTS SUBJECT TO BORDER MEASURES OTHER THAN ORDINARY CUSTOMS DUTIES

Section A: The calculation of tariff equivalents and related provisions

1.   The policy coverage of tariffication shall include all border measures other than ordinary customs duties[*] such as: quantitative import restrictions, variable import levies, minimum import prices, discretionary import licensing, non-tariff measures maintained through state trading enterprises, voluntary export restraints and any other schemes similar to those listed above, whether or not the measures are maintained under country-specific derogations from the provisions of the General Agreement.

2.   The calculation of the tariff equivalents, whether expressed as ad valorem or specific rates, shall be made using the actual difference between internal and external prices in a transparent manner using data, data sources and definitions as specified in Annex 2. Data used shall be for the years 1986 to 1988.

3.   Tariff equivalents shall be established for all agricultural products subject to border measures other than ordinary customs duties:

   (i)   tariff equivalents shall primarily be established at the four-digit level of the HS;

   (ii)   tariff equivalents shall be established at the six-digit or a more detailed level of the HS wherever appropriate, as in the case of certain fruits and vegetables;

   (iii) for transformed and processed agricultural products, tariff equivalents shall generally be established by multiplying the specific tariff equivalent(s) for the agricultural input(s) by the proportion(s) in value terms or in physical terms as appropriate of the agricultural input(s) in the transformed and processed agricultural products, and take account, where necessary, of any additional elements currently providing protection to industry.

---

[*]Excluding measures maintained for balance-of-payments reasons or under general safeguard and exception provisions (Articles XII, XVIII, XIX, XX and XXI of the General Agreement).

0017

UR/제도분야 최종 협정안 평가

1992. 1. 6.

외 무 부 통 상 국

0018

1. 분쟁해결

가. 협정안 주요내용

1) 분쟁해결 절차의 개선 및 강화

○ 분쟁해결의 매단계 자동화

(2번째 이사회에서 패널설치, 패널보고서 60일이내 채택, 상소 패널
보고서 30일이내에 채택, 패널 권고사항 불이행시 합리적 이행 기간
종료후 30일이내에 이사회가 보복 승인등)

○ 66년 절차 적용에 관한 규정 존치 (2-Tier System)

: 개도국 제소시 66년 절차 원용 가능

○ 분쟁해결의 전체 시한 설정 (패널설치로부터 합리적 이행기간
결정시까지 최장 18개월)

○ 상소제도 및 합리적 이행기간 개념 신규 도입

○ 보상, 보복과 관련 중재 제도 도입

○ 일방조치 배제 (갓트 분쟁해결 절차 준수)

○ Non-violation 분쟁에 관한 별도 항목 신설

2) 통합 분쟁해결 절차 수립 (분쟁해결 절차의 제도적 정비)

가) 분쟁해결 기구(Dispute Settlement Body) 설치

- 기존 이사회의 소관사항이던 분쟁해결 기능을 전담할 분쟁해결
기구를 MTO 산하에 신설하여 상품분야뿐 아니라 서비스 및 TRIPs
분야에서의 분쟁등 모든 무역분쟁에 대하여 총괄적으로 분쟁해결
기능을 수행토록 함.

4) 교차보복 인정

○ 원칙적으로 동일분야에서 보복 허용

○ 동일분야에서의 보복이 비현실적이거나 비효과적일 경우 동일
협정하의 다른분야에서 보복 허용

1

0019

o 동일 협정하에서의 보복이 비현실적이거나 비효과적일 경우 여타
  협정하에서의 보복 허용

o 교차보복의 정당성 및 보복의 수준에 대한 판정은 중재 절차애 회부

나. 평   가

o 분쟁해결 절차가 자동화 되고 체약국이 무역분쟁시 갓트 분쟁해결
  절차를 준수키로 약속함에 따라 분쟁해결 절차 강화에 있어서 상당한
  성과를 이룩함.

o 또한 통합 분쟁해결 절차를 도입함으로써 갓트내에 다수의 분쟁해결
  절차의 병존에 따라 발생되어 오던 문제점(forum shopping)이 해소된
  것도 진전

o 다만 무역관련 국내법령의 갓트일치를 의무사항이 아닌 임의 사항으로
  한것은 다자간 무역체제 강화라는 목표를 달성하는데 미흡한 부분임.

o 또한 교차보복 허용 문제와 관련 교차보복의 정당성 및 수준에 대한
  판정을 중재절차에 회부토록 함으로써 자의적인 교차보복 발동을
  용이하게 한다는 문제점이 있는바, 교차보복 허용 문제가 일차적으로
  관련 이사회에서 다루어지도록 하는등 이에 대한 절차 요건을 강화할
  필요가 있음.

2. MTO (다자간무역기구)

가. 설립 협정안 주요내용

1) 범위 (scope)

o 관할 대상의 범위를 상품분야뿐 아니라 서비스 및 TRIPs 분야로
  확대함으로서 모든 무역분야를 관장

2) 기 능 (functions)

  o 상품, 서비스 및 TRIPs 분야 협정의 운용 및 MTO 설립 협정상의
    목적 추진

  o UR 협상 결과 및 향후 협상 결과 이행을 위한 framework 제공

  o 향후 다자간 무역협상을 위한 forum 제공

  o 통합 분쟁해결 절차 및 TPRM 관장

  o IMF, IBRD와의 협력을 통해 세계경제 정책상의 일관성 제고

3) MTO의 구조와 관련 일반 이사회 산하에 상품, 서비스 및 TRIPs
   이사회를 각각 설립

4) 수락 및 발효(14조)

  o UR 참여 갓트체약국은 92.11.1부터 MTO 설립 협정 수락 가능

  o 각료급 Implementing Conference를 개최하여 MTO 협정 발효시점
    결정 (93.1.1 잠정 예정)

  o MTO 협정 발효일로부터 2년이내에 UR 협상 결과를 일괄 수락하여
    MTO 협정을 수락치 않는 갓트체약국은 갓트체약국으로서(가입 조건
    협상없이) MTO 회원국 지위를 획득할 수 있는 권리 상실

  o MTO 설립협정이 발효한 이후에 동 협정을 수락하더라도 UR 협정상의
    의무는 MTO 설립협정의 발효일로부터 발생하므로 소급하여 동 의무를
    이행해야 함 (2항)

5) 최종 조항 (16조)

  o Annex 1에 포함된 협정에 대해 유보 불가 (단, 이 문제는 PPA 관련
    협상(갓트조문) 결과에 따름)

  o UR 협상 결과 이행을 위해 필요한 경우 국내법 개정을 위해
    최대한 노력

나. 평 가

o UR 협상 결과의 이행을 위한 administrative infrastructure를 제공하고 향후 다자간무역체제의 기초가 될 MTO를 설립키로 한것은 다자간 무역체제의 강화에 도움이 될 것임.

o 특히 동 기구가 통합 분쟁해결체제(IDSS) 및 국별무역정책 검토 제도 (TPRM)의 운용을 통해 국제무역에 있어서의 안정성 및 투명성을 제고하게 된것을 환영함.

o 단, MTO 설립협정이 single undertaking을 전제 조건으로 한데는 원칙적으로 동의하나, 동경라운드 MTN 협정중 Annex 4에 수록된 4개의 협정 이외의 5개 협정 (반덤핑, 보조금.상계관세, TBT, 수입허가, 관세평가 협정)에 의무적으로 가입해야 하는 결과를 초래하는바, 개도국들의 반발이 예상됨. 또한 아국도 현재 수입허가 협정에 가입치 않고 있는 상태인바, 이러한 관점에서 16조 2항상의 유보 불가조항은 재검토를 요함.

3. 최종의정서

가. 의정서안 주요내용

o 93.1.1. 이전 발효를 목표로 UR 협정의 수락이 바람직함.

o UR 협정의 국제적 이행을 위한 하부구조(administrative infrastructure) 로서 MTO 설립

o UR 협상 결과의 국제적 이행 여부에 대한 결정을 위해 각료급 갓트 특별총회를 92년말 이전에 개최

o 제반 UR 협정의 발효일자 결정을 위한 각료급 회의를 92년말 이전에 개최

o 제반 UR 협정은 전체로서(as a whole) 수락되어야 함 (5항)

4

나. 평 가

o 최종의정서안 제5항에 규정된 single undertaking과 관련, MTO
   항목하에서와 동일한 논거로 추가 검토가 필요함.

o 최종의정서 발효일자와 관련, 향후 시장접근 및 서비스 분야 양허협상에
   상당한 시일이 소요될 것이며, 각국이 국내적 절차를 완료하는데
   소요되는 시간이 각기 다르다는 점을 감안할때, 발효시점 문제에
   대해서는 신중한 검토가 필요함.   끝.

외 무 부

종 별 :

번 호 : GVW-0157   일 시 : 92 0122 2050

수 신 : 장관(봉기,경기원,재무부,농림수산부,상공부,특허청)

발 신 : 주 제네바대사

제 목 : UR/협상초안 법적준비 작업

대: WGV-0122

1. 오참사관이 1.21. LINDEN 사무총장 보좌관을 접촉, 던켈총장이 1.13.TNC회의에서 밝힌 TRACK 3(법적정비작업) 운영문제에 대해 협의한 동인 언급 요지아래 보고함(이성주 참사관 동석)

가. 법적 정비 작업반 구성

- MATHUR 전 갓트 사무차장이 책임을 맡고 갓트 사무국의 CROOM 국장(지역협정 및 무역, 재정 담당)이 SECRETARIAT 의 역할을 하게될 것이며, ROSSLER 법률국장 및 LINDEN 보좌관도 동작업반에 참여할 예정임.

- 동 법적 정비작업은 모든 UR 협상 참여국에 개방됨.

나. 작업계획

- 1.23(목) UR 협상 참여국들과 1 차 비공식협의를 갖고 앞으로의 작업계획을 논의할 예정이며, 본격적인 작업은 2.5 경 부터 시작할 수 있을 것으로 전망됨.

- 동작업반이 UR 협상 전분야에 걸친 법제화 작업을 하게될 것임.

- 동법적 정비 작업은 비교적 기술적인 작업이 될것이나 경우에 따라서는 실질적인 문제와 연관이 될 가능성이 있다는 점에서 그 구분문제에 있어 논란의 여지가 있을수 있음.

2. 동 보좌관은 MTO 에 관한 추가 협의는 모든 분야에 대한 협상결과가 나오는 단계에 가서 이루어 지게될 것으로 전망한다고 하였음을 참고 바람.

3. 대호 TRACK 3 과 관련 대책관련 사항은 1.23. 회의 결과 및 동 회의 이후의 경과를 본후 추보하겠음. 끝

(대사 박수길-국장)

예고:92.6.30 까지

	계 □ 래 의기 재무부 (1/6. 3.)	
직위	성 김□(서□)	

통상국	장관	차관	1차보	2차보	경제국	외정실	분석관	청와대
안기부	경기원	재무부	농수부	상공부	특허청			

PAGE 1   92.01.23   07:27

외신 2과 통제관 BD

0024

발 신 전 보

<table>
<tr><td></td><td>분류번호</td><td>보존기간</td></tr>
<tr><td></td><td></td><td></td></tr>
</table>

번   호 : WGV-0128   920123 1517 CG   종별 : _____

수   신 : 주   제네바   대사. 총영사/

발   신 : 장 관 (통 기)

제   목 : UR 법제화 작업

        1.13 TNC 회의시 던켈 사무총장이 제시한 협정 초안 법적 정비작업(TRACK 3)과
본부건토결과와 측정   22로 사무국과-자정측 문제를 제기하고 "받응
관련, 하기 문제점이 있는 것으로 보이는바, 관련 협의시 제기하고 동향을 파악,
보고바람.

1.   최종의정서안중 Section C(UR '92 의정서) para. 7과 MTO 설립 협정문 14조 2항

    - UR '92 의정서의 수락시한(93.6.30)과 MTO 설립 의정서의 수락 시한이(MTO 설립

        협정 발효일(93.1.1 예정)로부터 2년) 상이한 바, 93.6.30까지 국내사정상

        MTO 설립 협정을 수락치 못하는 경우 UR '92 의정서 수락 시한 준수를 위하여

        동 의정서만을 위한 수락서를 기탁하여야 할 것인지 여부

2.   MTO 설립 협정 14조 2항에 의하면 MTO 설립 협정 발효(93.1.1 예정) 이후에

        동 협정을 수락하더라도 제반 MTO 관련 협정상의 의무가 MTO 설립 협정 발효일로

        소급하여 발생하도록 되어 있는바, 특히 비관세 분야의 경우(예 : 농산물

        분야에서의 최소 시장접근등) 구체적인 적용방법.   끝.

                                            (통상국장   김 용 규)

<table>
<tr><td></td><td>보 안
통 제</td><td>Mr</td></tr>
</table>

<table>
<tr><td rowspan="2">앙
고
재</td><td>92
년1
월
23
일</td><td>통
상
기
3
과</td><td>기안자
성명</td><td>과 장</td><td>국 장</td><td></td><td>차 관</td><td>장 관</td><td rowspan="2">외신과통제</td></tr>
<tr><td></td><td>이병종</td><td>Mr</td><td>최</td><td>정래</td><td></td><td>4H</td></tr>
</table>

                                            0025

외 무 부

종 별 :

번 호 : GVW-0168   일 시 : 92 0123 2000

수 신 : 장관(봉기,경기원,재무부,농림수산부,상공부)

발 신 : 주 제네바대사

제 목 : UR 법제화그룹

　　연: GVW-0126

　　대: WGV-0122

　　1. 표제그룹 최초회의가 금 1.23. MATHUR 전 GATT 사무차장의 주재하에 개최된바, 동 결과 아래 보고함.(이성주 참사관 참석)

　　O MATHUR 의장은 회의벽두 동그룹은 1.13.TNC 에서 부여된 MANDATE 에 따라참가국간의 권리, 의무의 균형 변경을 가져와서는 안된다는 대전제하에 MTN.TNC/W/FA 상의 모든 TEXT 를 대상으로 동 내부적 일관성과 법적합치성을 확보하기위한 작업을 TRACK 4 와 병행하여 진행하되, TRACK 4 작업이 끝나는 대로 동 GROUP 의 작업도 종결할수 있도록 해야 한다고 언급하고 자신이 판단하는 동 그룹의 과제로서 아래사항을 열거하고 동 작업을 위해 관련 자료를 준비토록 사무국에 요청할 예정임을 밝힌후 이에대한 참가국의 의견개진을 요청함.

　　- MTO 협정과 FA 상의 재협정간의 관계 정립 및 일반 분쟁해결 TEXT 와 재협정상의 분쟁해결 관련 규정과의 관계 정립

　　- 각 협정의 법적 형태(협정, 양해, 결정등) 결정

　　- 용어상의 일관성 확보(예: MEMBERS, PARTIES, PARTICIPANTS 등)

　　- 분쟁해결 관련 3 개 TEXT 를 봉합한 SINGLE TEXT 마련 및 동 TEXT 와 각 협정 분쟁해결 관련 규정과의 관계

　　- 모든 TEXT 에 대한 개별(TEXT BY TEXT) 검토

　　- 단순한 편집 차원의 수정(명백한 FACTUAL ERROR 등)

　　O 선두 발언에 나선 미국은 상기 MATHUR 의장의 제안에 전반적으로 동의한다고 전제한후, 향후의 회의 방식으로 INTENSIVE SESSION(한번 개최될 때마다 최소한 1 주 이상 계속 회의) 및 그룹을 세분함이 없이 전체회의 형식으로 진행할것과 MTO, IDSS

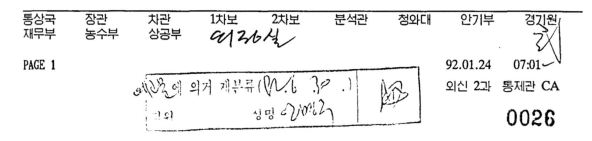

통상국	장관	차관	1차보	2차보	분석관	청와대	안기부	경기원
재무부	농수부	상공부	이강서					

PAGE 1

등 ANNOTATION 에 명기된 사항, S AND D, 분쟁해결, 예외(EXCEPTIONS AND DEROGATIONS) 지방정부등 공통(CROSS-CUTTING) 잇슈, 실질내용(SUBSTANCE) 면에서 차이가 있을 잠재력이 있는 사항, TEXT-BY-TEXT 별 검토의 작업순서를 제의함.

- 대부분의 국가들도 MATHUR 의장의 제의를 대체적으로 지지하고 특히 TRANSPARENCY 확보, 동 작업의 중립적 성격(권리, 의무 변경 불가) 및 사무국 작업의 유용성등에 관하여 발언하였으며 일부 국가(인도, 카나다, EC)는 MTO, IDSS 의 우선 취급 필요성을 언급함.

- 미국은 상기 발언시 CROSS-CUTTING 잇슈의 예로서 개도국과 최빈개도국의정의 명확화 필요성을 언급한바, 이에 대해 다수 개도국(아국, 알젠틴, 브라질, 홍콩, 싱가폴, 멕시코등)은 이문제는 동 GROUP 의 MANDATE 를 벗어나는 사항(UN 및 CTD 등에서 취급되어야 할 문제등) 이라는 이유로 반대입장을 표명(아국은 TRANSPARENCY 확보, 작업의 중립적 성격을 특히 강조하면서, 이에 어긋나는 개도국, 최빈개도국 정의 설정은 MANDATE 를 벗어나는 사항이므로 반대하는 입장표명) 함에 따라, 미국 대표는 자신의 의도는 여러 협정상에 등장하는 개도국 및 최빈개도국이 라는 표현이 모두 같은 의미로 씌여져야 한다는 뜻이 었다고 일단 해명 발언을 함.

O MATHUR 의장은 금일 회의 결과를 아래와 같이 종합함.

- 전체회의로서의 작업진행, TRANSPANENCY 유지, 권리, 의무관계의 균형에 변경을 가하지 않는다는 TRACK 3 작업 추진상의 원칙에 대한 의견의 일치가 있었음.

- 향후 작업은 MTO, IDSS(개별 협정상의 분쟁해결 규정과의 관계 포함) 를 우선적으로 다루어 나가되, 순서 문제는 다소의 융통성이 필요함

- 사무국은 내주(1.27 시작주) 말까지 사실적 오류에 관한 LIST, 본그룹의 과제에 관한 예시적 LIST 및 IDSS 시안을 작성

- 차기회의는 2.5 소집하며, 동 회의에서 INTENSIVE SESSION 을 포함한 향후 협상일정을 결정짓고 가능하면 2.6-7 까지 회의를 연장 본격 토의도 착수할 수 있음.

2. 상기에 비추어 TRACK 3 작업은 2 월중순부터 대체로 미국이 제안한 순서에 따라 집중적으로 전개될 전망인바, 이와 관련 아래와같은 준비가 필요할 것으로 사료됨.

✓ O IDSS 단일 TEXT 작성은 비교적 단순한 기술적 작업이 될 것으로 전망되나, IDSS TEXT 와 각 협정상의 분쟁해결 절차와의 관계설정관련 협정별 특수성 반영필요 및 동 정도에 대한 검토

✓ O MTO 협정과 제협정과의 관계설정 관련, 동 협정 ANNEX 로 첨부될 제협정의 법적

형태 및 FINAL PROVISION 내용 조화 필요성등에 대한 검토

    O 개도국 우대, 분쟁해결, NON-APPLICATION, 지방정부에 대한 중앙정부의 책임, 재검토조항, 봉고의무, 세이프가드규정, 경과규정등 공통 잇슈에 대한 일관성 유지 또는 특수성 반영 필요성등 검토

    3. 상기 작업은 법적, 기술적 작업에 국한한다는 전제가 있음에도 불국하고사안에 따라서는 기술적 사항인지 본질적 내용과 관련된 사항인지 불분명할 가능성도 없지않고(GATT 사무국도 이점에 대해 우려 표명), 27 개 TEXT 를 면밀히 검토하여 작업에 참여해야 할것이므로, 2.5 회의시 부터는 가능한한 본부 과장 또는 서기관급 직원이 당지에 상주하면서 당관 관계관과 함께 참여하는 것이 바람직할 것으로 사료됨. 끝

    (대사 박수길-국장)

    예고:92.6.30 까지

외 무 부

110-760 서울 종로구 세종로 77번지 / (02)720-2188 / (02)725-1737 (FAX)

문서번호 통기 20644-160

시행일자 1992. 1.27.( )

취급		장 관	
보존		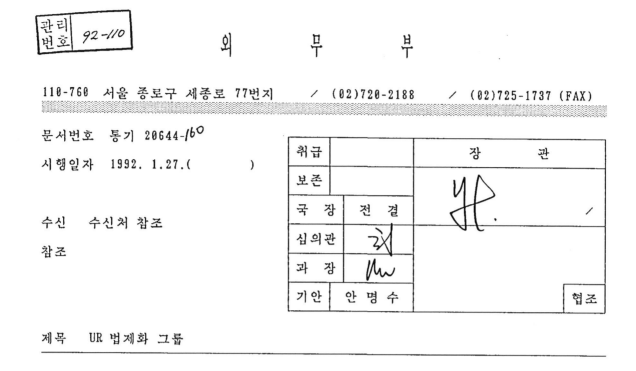	
국 장	전 결		
심의관			
과 장			
기안	안 명 수		협조

수신 수신처 참조

참조

제목 UR 법제화 그룹

관련 : GVW-0168

　　1.23 개최된 UR 법제화 그룹회의 결정에 따라 2.5부터 작업을 개시할 예정인 표제 그룹회의에서는 권리.의무 관계의 균형에 변경을 가하지 않는다는 원칙하에 최종의정서 초안에 포함된 27개 text를 검토할 예정인바, 귀부 소관 text중 최종의정서 초안의 내부적인 일관성과 법적 합치성을 위하여 수정이 필요하거나 기타 검토를 요하는 사항을 2.1까지 당부로 회시하여 주시기 바랍니다.

이 있는경우 이를

수신처 : 경제기획원장관, 재무부장관, 농림수산부장관, 상공부장관

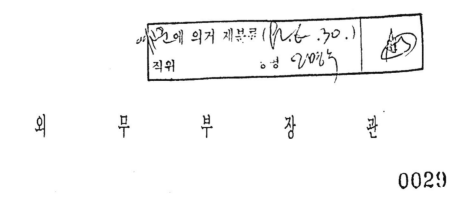

외 무 부 장 관

0029

외 무 부

종 별 :

번 호 : GVW-0198   일 시 : 92 0128 1430

수 신 : 장 관(통기)   사본: 경기원, 재무부, 농림수산부, 상공부

발 신 : 주 제네바 대사

제 목 : UR 법제화 작업

대: WGV-0128

이성주 참사관은 1.27 GATT 사무국 LINDEN고문을 면담, 대호사항및 기타 관련 사항에대해 GATT 사무국의 견해를 문의한바, 동 결과를 아래 보고함.

1. UR 의정서와 MTO 협정상의 수락시한의 차이에 따른 의정서에 대한 별도의 수락 서기탁문제

O 양문서의 수락시한이 상이하게 된것은 당초 의정서 7항 당시에는 MTO 협정이 구체화되지 않음으로써 동경 ROUND등 과거의 MTN협상 전례를 감안 작성되었기 때문임.

O UR 협상 결과의 대부분 (일부 결정 사항등제외)이 첨부될 MTO 협정이 합의된 이상, 협상 참가국은 MTO 협정 수락서만 기탁하면되며 의정서 7항에 예정된 바와같이 별도의 수락서 기탁은 불요함.

(법제화 작업 과정에서 동 7항은 재조정될것임. 동일한 이유로 서비스 기본협정 29조등 여타협정의 최종규정도 조정 대상임)

O 당초 의정서 7항 규정은 93.1.1.동 의정서 발효를 목표로 하되 동 시한을 맞추지 못하는 국가에 대해 6개월간의 여유 (6개월 경과후에는 가입 협상을거쳐야 함. 이는 7항 B 에서 93.1.1.이후 93.6.30까지의 기간중에 감축을 개시하는 국가는 전체감축율의 2/5를 감축토록 규정하고 93.6.30-94.12.31.까지 기간에 대한 언급이 없다는 사실에 비추어 명백)만을 부여하기 위한 의도였으나, 동 규정은 이제 무의미하게 되었음.

O 수락서 기탁 대상이 MTO 하나로 단일화 됨으로써 의정서 7항이 예정했던 93.6.30 까지의 수락시한 제한은 소멸될것이며 협상 참가국은 MTO 협정 14조 규정에 따라 92.11.부터 동 협정 발효후 2년까지 수락서 기탁이 가능함

2. 93.1.1.이후 MTO 협정 수락시 MTO 관련 제협정상의 의무부담 적용 방식

통상국   2차보

PAGE 1   92.01.29   08:10 WG

외신 1과 통제관

0030

0 MTO 협정 14조 2항에 따라 93.1.1.이후 협정발효후 2년까지의 기간동안 수락서를 기탁하는 국가의 경우 93.1.1.발효한 것과 같은 (AS IF)제반 의무를 부담하게됨

0 이는 기본적으로 MTO 협정 수락을 고의로 지연함으로써 UR 협상 결과에 따른 관련 의무이행을 회피 또는 지연함을 방지하기 위한 규정임.

0 관세의 경우 수락시점에 적용되는 INSTALLMENT를 바로 적용하면 되므로 비교적 간단함.

0 비관세의 경우 구체적 MODALITIES 는 자신이 알기로 아지 결정된바 없으나 향후 양자협상과정에서 구체화될 것으로 봄 (양허대상 모든비관세 조치의 해제 또는 완화 년도를 양허표에게 기하는 것도 한가지 방법이 될수 있음)

0 농산물 분야 최소시장 접근 은 7년간의 PRO-RATA를 적용하면 될것으로 봄.

3. 향후 법체화 그룹작업 일정

0 GATT 사무국은 내부적으로 결정, 2.5 회의에 제시할 작업 일정은 아래와 같음.

- 2차 회의(2.5-7) 작업대상 예시목록, MTO 협정검토
- 3차회의(2.17-21) 단일 분쟁해결 절차 검토 —— 어
- 4차회의 (3.9-13) MTO 협정과 기타 협정등과의 관계 및 CROSS-CUTTING 잇슈
- 5차회의(3.23-27) 개별 협정 검토

4. UR 협상 종결 및 발효절차   9 3. 1. 1 ?

0 모든 사항이 순조롭게 진행된다는 전제하에 부활절 이전 최종의정서 채택회의 (실무급가능성이 높음) 및 92년말 이전의 MTO 협정 및UR 협상 결과의 발효시기 결정을 위한 각료회의를 거쳐 93.11. 발효를 목표로 하고 있음. ?

(최종의정서 상으로는 최종 의정서 채택회의, MTO 협정의 국제적 이행 관련 회의 및 UR협상 발효시기 결정회의 3가지 회의가 예정되어, 다소 모호한 면이 있으나, 자신의 판단으로 마지막 2가지 회의는 한데묶어 각료급 회의로 개최될 가능성이 높다고 봄)

0 부활절 이전 회의 및 년말경의 각료회의에서 채택될 문서는 편제가 달라질 뿐 MTO협정에 첨부되지 않는 일부 결정사항등을 제외하고는 거의 동일한 내용이 될것임.

0 브라질 (3년), 일본(18개월), 스위스 (국민투표)등 일부국가에 국내 절차상의 문제가 있으나 93.1.1.발효가능 여부는 기본적으로 미국의 국내절차에 달려있음.

미국이 년내 국내절차 완료시 일본의 지연이 다소문제가 될수있겠으나 (브라질, 스위스등은 발효를 지연시킬 만큼의 경제력 결여), 일본 정부의 사전양해등의 편법도

PAGE 2

0031

고려 가능하다고 봄.끝
　(대사 박수길-국장)

발 신 전 보

분류번호	보존기간

번   호 : WGV-0194   920201 1430   종별 :

수   신 : 주   제네바   대사. 총영사//

발   신 : 장 관 (통 기)

제   목 : UR 법제화 작업

대 : GVW-0198

1. UR 법제화 작업과 관련 본부는 최종의정서 초안 Text간의 일관성 및 법적 합치성을
   검토 중인바, fact상의 오류에 관한 list 및 통합 분쟁해결 절차 단일 text 시안등
   사무국 작성 작업문서가 배포 되는대로 송부바람.

2. 번호 UR 법제화 작업 그룹의 작업 일정과 본부 인력사정을 감안, 제3차 회의시
   (2.17-21) 본부 직원이 귀지 출장 예정이며, 제4차 및 제5차 회의의 경우
   필요시 본부 직원이 참여토록할 예정임을 참고바람.   끝.

(통상국장 김 용 규)

		보 안 통 제	

앙 고 재	92 년 2 월 1 일	통상 기획 과	기안자 성 명 임영웅	과 장	신기방	국 장 전결	차 관	장 관		외신과통제

0033

외 무 부

종 별 :

번 호 : GVW-0263

일 시 : 92 0203 1700

수 신 : 장관(봉기)

발 신 : 주제네바대사

제 목 : UR 법제화 작업

대: WGV-0198

표제 작업관련 제 2차 회의소집 에어그램사실적 오류에 관한 리스트 및 법제화 그룹 과제에 관한 예시리스트를 우선 별첨 송부함.

첨부: 상기 FAX 1부(GVW(F)-0073)

(차석대사 김삼훈-국장)

통상국

92.02.04   06:20 ED

외신 1과 통제관

0034

주 제 네 바 대 표 부

번 호 : GVW(F) - 0093   년월일 : 20203   시간 : 1800

수 신 : 장   관 (특기)

발 신 : 주 제네바대사

제 목 :

GVW - 263 관련

총 28 매(표지포함)

보 안	
봉 재	

외신과	
봉 재	

배부처	장관실	차관실	一차보	二차보	기획실	감사관	총영사관	아주국	미주국	구주국	중아국	국기국	경제국	통상국	문협국	영교국	총무과	감사관	공보관	의연원	처외대	수대실	안기부	국가차관	경기	상공부
														6												

0035

<u>Legal Drafting Group</u>   31 January 1992

ILLUSTRATIVE LIST OF POINTS FOR POSSIBLE CONSIDERATION IN THE LEGAL DRAFTING GROUP

<u>Informal Note by the Secretariat</u>

The following list, requested by the Legal Drafting Group at its first meeting on 23 January 1992, is based on points identified by the Secretariat as well as points made by delegations at that meeting. It remains open to delegations to take up other points not mentioned in the text. A suggested schedule for the Group's work is at Annex 3.

The secretariat is circulating separately initial and informal lists of corrections to the English, French and Spanish texts of MTN.TNC/W/FA for the purpose of the Legal Drafting Group. The lists are in principle concerned only with the correction of clear errors and omissions.

A. <u>Review of the Agreement establishing the Multilateral Trade Organization</u> (Annex IV of MTN.TNC/W/FA)

   (See self-contained note at Annex 1.)

B. <u>Relationship between MTO Agreement and other agreed texts</u>

   (See self-contained note at Annex 2.)

C. <u>Integration of dispute settlement texts</u>[1]

   -   review of draft integrated text to be circulated by the secretariat.

D. <u>Other points common to a number of texts ("cross-cutting issues")</u>

   Examination to determine whether, in addition to adaptation required by relationship of texts to MTO provisions, there is need for texts to be aligned, altered or clarified as regards:

   1. <u>Legal form</u> of each text.

---

[1]<u>Understanding on Rules and Procedures Governing the Settlement of Disputes under Articles XXII and XXIII of the General Agreement on Tariffs and Trade</u> (Section S of MTN.TNC/W/FA), <u>Elements of an Integrated Dispute Settlement System</u> and <u>Integrated Dispute Settlement System: Suspension of Concessions</u> (Section T of MTN.TNC/W/FA)

0036

- 2 -

2. Institutional provisions

   (a) Is there a need to harmonize terminology used to describe
        the activities of various bodies?

   (b) Relationships with other international organizations.

3. Final clauses (See list in Annex 2)

4. Descriptions, terminology and treatment of legal concepts, in
    particular:

   (a) Consistency between provisions of different texts (including
        the General Agreement) as well as precedence of rights and
        obligations under one MTO annex over rights and obligations
        under another MTO annex.

   (b) Other points raised by delegations:

   - Provisions on exceptions and derogations.

   - Treatment of obligations of parties with respect to measures
      of sub-national governments.

   - Treatment of obligations of parties with respect to
      transparency (publication, notification, and multilateral
      surveillance).

   - Treatment of obligations of parties with respect to
      protection of confidential information and/or privacy.

E. Review of individual agreements

   - confirm in each case that conclusions under B and D above are
      reflected in the text concerned

   - verify cross-references in the agreement

   - note, for review from the point of view of their legal conformity
      and internal consistency, the schedules of concessions or other
      material that will be added to the text as result of Track 1 or 2
      negotiations

   - confirm that the text is complete

F. Final Act (Section A of MTN.TNC/W/FA)

   - are there any points relating to this text which require
      clarification in the light of the preceeding work of the Group?

0037

- 3 -

Annex 1: Points for Possible Consideration
Regarding the Draft MTO Agreement

Article II:1

Would the meaning not be clearer if:

- in the second sentence, "shall have all members as parties" were replaced by "are binding on all members"?

- and in the third sentence "may have limited membership" were replaced by "shall be binding only on those members that have accepted them"?

Article II:2

Would the text be improved by amendment to read "Any member which has not acceded to any agreement ..... is encouraged to accept such agreement"?

Article II, Footnote

(also footnotes to Articles XI and XIV)
In the light of the results of the Uruguay Round, does the relationship between the MTO Agreement and existing rights of contracting parties under the Protocol of Provisional Application and accession protocols need to be clarified?

Article III:6

Does this paragraph have implications for Part B of the FOGS text (section Y of MTN.TNC/W/FA), which was drafted in the context only of the GATT?

Article V:5

Should this paragraph explicitly provide that the Goods Council will carry out the present functions of the CONTRACTING PARTIES and the GATT Council, except insofar as these will be exercised by the Ministerial Conference and the General Council?

Article V:6 and V:7

Should these paragraphs explicitly provide, for the Services Council and TRIPs Council, that these bodies should carry out the functions attributed to the Councils envisaged by Article XXV of the Services agreement and Article 68 of the TRIPs agreement, except insofar as these will be exercised by the Ministerial Conference and the General Council?

Article VI

It is presumed that this will not affect any arrangements for cooperation with intergovernmental bodies and agencies that are provided for in the annexed agreements.

Article VI:4

Should there also be provision for the Director-General and the MTO Secretariat to service the GATT of 30 October 1947?

0038

- 4 -

Article IX:3	Is there any inconsistency between Article IX.3 and the waiver provisions in the Multilateral Trade Agreements in Annex 1 of the MTO agreement? If so, should the application of IX:3 be subordinated to the additional requirements or procedures of the annexed agreements? What is the status of the draft understanding on the interpretation of Article XXV of the GATT (Section V of MTN.TNC/W/FA)?
Article X:2	Is the meaning of "each member" in the final line in fact "each such member"?
Article X:3	Is there a need for precision to indicate that when amendments relate to institutional matters, any party not accepting the amendment would have to withdraw from the agreement?
Article XI	What meaning is to be given to "acceptance on a definitive basis"?
Article XI, footnote	See footnote to Article II.
Article XII:1	Would it be more logical to delete the phrase "which accepts .... Annexes 1, 2 and 3", and substitute a new second sentence: "Such terms shall include acceptance of this Agreement, including the Multilateral Trade Agreements set out in Annexes 1, 2 and 3"?
Article XII:2	Should "General Council" be replaced by "MTO"? Is a provision similar to the second sentence of Article XIV:2 needed to specify when the agreement enters into force for parties which accede under Article XII?
Article XIII:1	Does this paragraph mean that non-application cannot be invoked between original members, even as regards Annexes 1:B and 1:C?
Article XIII:2	To clarify the text, would it be desirable to redraft this paragraph to read "Paragraph 1 shall apply to the Multilateral Trade Agreements listed in Annex 1A only to the extent that non-application clauses in the predecessor agreements were applied between members at the time of entry into force of this agreement"?
Article XVI.1	Does the expression "customary practice of the General Agreement on Tariffs and Trade, including voting practices" require clarification?

0039

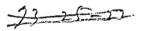

- 5 -

Article XVI.2   It may be necessary to consider the relationship of the provisions of this paragraph to the corresponding provisions of the agreements in Annexes 1 and 4.

Article XVI.2, footnote See footnote to Article II.

Article XVI.4   It may be necessary to consider the relationship of the provisions of this paragraph to the corresponding provisions of annexed agreements.

Article XVI   Should Article XVI also include a denunciation clause covering Tokyo Round agreements that are replaced by agreements included in Annex 1A and Annex 4, since these new agreements would be legally distinct from their predecessor agreements?

Annex 1A   Can language similar to that used in protocols of accession be included to ensure that the original GATT text and its associated legal instruments are applied as rectified, amended or otherwise modified up to the date of acceptance of the MTO?

Note: In addition to the above points, a number of technical corrections to the MTO text are indicated in the informal list of corrections circulated by the secretariat on 31 January.

0040

- 6 -

Annex 2: Points on relationship between MTO Agreement and other agreed texts

(i)   Which of the texts listed MTN.TNC/W/FA:

    (a)   should be annexed to the MTO?

    (b)   can be adopted by decisions of the Ministers, separate from the MTO Agreement?

    (c)   represent guidelines for negotiations that need not appear either in the MTO Annexes or as separate Ministerial decisions?

(ii) Institutional provisions

Should the provisions on the establishment and functions of bodies in the annexed Agreements be aligned with the provisions of Article V of the MTO Agreement? (See also the points on Article V in Annex 1.)

Would it be helpful to have a provision in the MTO which says that references in the Agreements in its Annex 1 to "contracting parties", "PARTIES", "signatories", etc. should be taken as meaning MTO members, or should the Agreements themselves be aligned with the MTO? Similarly, how should references to the MTO Secretariat and the GATT Secretariat be handled?

(iii) Dispute Settlement

Pro memoria: the relationship of any specific dispute settlement procedures in individual texts with the integrated dispute settlement procedures of the MTO will need to be examined.

(iv) Final provisions (Acceptance, participation, territorial application, reservations, entry into force, duration, national legislation, review, amendment, withdrawal, non-application between particular parties, secretariat, deposit, treaty registration.)
What final provisions do the Agreements in Annexes 1,2, and 3 to the MTO need?
How are any inconsistencies between the final provisions of the MTO and the final provisions in other agreements to be dealt with?
Do the provisions in the MTO on amendment require changes in the amendment provisions in any of the annexed agreements?

0041

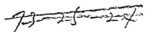

- 7 -

Annex 3: Timetable and working procedures

An appropriate timetable and procedures should be established to permit the Group's work to be completed within the time-frame set for completion of the Uruguay Round as a whole, on the basis of intensive and extended sessions which should be kept within the Legal Drafting Group itself. These should include working arrangements to ensure full conformity of the English, French and Spanish texts.

The following tentative schedule of meetings and of points to be taken up at each meeting is suggested for consideration by the Group:

Second meeting (5-7 February 1992):   Discussion of illustrative list
                                        Review of MTO Agreement

Third meeting [17-21 February 1992]:   Review of relationship between MTO
                                        and other texts

Fourth meeting [9-13 March 1992]:   Review of draft unified text on
                                        dispute settlement
                                        Discussion of cross-cutting issues

Fifth meeting [23-27 March 1992]:   Review of individual texts

0042

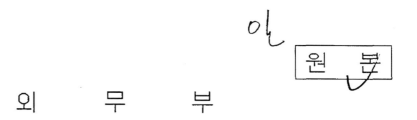

외 무 부

종 별 :

번 호 : GVW-0293   일 시 : 92 0206 1100

수 신 : 장 관(봉기, 경기원, 재무부, 농림수산부, 상공부, 특허청)

발 신 : 주 제네바 대사대리

제 목 : UR 법제화 그룹 2차회의(1)

    연: GVW-0168

    1. 표제그룹 2차 회의가 2.5 MATHUR 전 갓트사무차장 주재로 개최되며, 법제화 그룹 과제리스트와 MTO 협정에 관해 논의하였는바, 요지아래 보고함.

    (이참사관, 신서기관 참석)

    가. 법제화 그룹 과제에 관한 예시리스트 및 향후협상일정

    (1) 미국은 현재 법제화 그룹 과제에 관한 예시리스트와 관련 시장접근, 서비스, 양자 협상(TRACK1,2)의 결과를 UR 협상문서에 포함시키는 작업도 본 그룹에서 다루어야 할 사항임을 언급하고, 인도, 모로코가 서비스 협정문안에 양허표 양식의 누락되어 있음을 지적하고 보완 필요성을 언급한외에는 사무국 예시 리스트에 별다른 이견없었음.

    (2) 스웨덴은 개별 협정에 규정된 유사한 용어의일관성 확보작업을 언급하면서 용이하게 하기위해 사무국이 일목요연한 도표(MATRIX)를작성하여 줄것을 요청함.

    (3) 기타: 일부 국가로부터 본 그룹회의 기록을 보다상세히 작성, 배포해 달라는것을 요청, CROSS-CUTTING ISSUES 에 관한 논의 기간을 확대조정할 필요성에 관해 언급, 무역과환경작업반 (3.10-11 개최예정)과 중복되는 4차회의 일정 조정에 관한 요청등이 있었음.

    나. MTO 협정논의

    (1) EC 는 MTO 협정이 UR 협상 참여자들의 협상에 의해 이루어진 문안(NEGOTIATED TEXT)이라고하면서 금후 실질문제에 변경을 가하지 않는범위에서 타협정과의 일관성을 유지하는 방향에서 논의에 참여할 것을 언급한 반면, 미국은 의장의 주석(ANNOTATION)에 명시된 바와같이 추가적인 보완이 필요하다고 언급(PPA 관련주석을 예시)하여 대조적인 입장을 보였음.

통상국   2차보   청와대   안기부   경기원   재무부   농수부   상공부
특허정

PAGE 1   92.02.06   20:43 FN

                                            외신 1과 통제관

                                              0043

(2) PPA 관련 2조 각주 규정에 관해 미국은 규범제정 그룹에서 PPA 와 PA 에 규정된조부조항 폐지 여부에 대한 결정이 없었음을 지적하고 MTO 가 설립된 이후에도 조부조항은 유효하다고 주장하였음(스위스 동조). 이에 대해 EC,싱가폴, 호주등은 MTO협정 11조문안(ACCEPTANCE ON A DEFINITIVE HASES) 및 MTO협정의 ANNEX (MTO 범위)1 A 에 PPA 는제외된다는 규정을 인용, MTO 협정시 발효가되면 PPA 나 조부조항은 무효 가 된다는 입장을 표명하였고, 아르헨티나는 동건은 성격상 TRACK 4에서 논의되어야 할 사항이라고 언급함.

(3) 2조 3항 ' LEGALLY DISTINET,.,..' 문안 관련사무국은 동항이 MTO 협정을 수락하지 않는기존 GATT 체약 당사국의 경우 기존 갓트가 적용된다는 점을 의미한다고 언급한바, 당분간(최소한 MTO 협정의 수락마감 시한) 또는그이상의 양체제 공존에따른 법적문제 및신.구 갓트의 구분문제와 연관되어 ANNEX 1A 로첨부될 재협정의 첨부 형태 및 방식등에 관한참가국의 문의가 있었는바, MATHUR 의장은사무국 작성 예시리 스트 5 PAGE ANNEX 1A 에 제시되어 있는 방식으로 할수 밖에 없지않느냐는 반응을 보였음.(UR 협상결과 및GATT 발족이후의 각종 선언 결정, 양해 등을모두 수용한 CLEAN TEXT 를 작성, 첨부하는 것은 현실적으로 불가능하다는 입장)

2. 2.6 회의에서는 MTO 협정을 계속 논의할예정이며, 2.17-21 간 열릴 예정이었던 3차 회의는 이사회 일정(2.13 개최)과 관련 2.19-21 간 개최키로 하였는바, 연호로건의한 본부 대표파견을 재건의함. 2.18 °.

3. 통합 분쟁 해결에 관한 TEXT 는 3차 회의시배포될 예정임. 끝
(차석대사 김삼훈-국장)

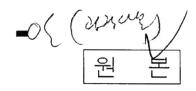

외 무 부

종 별 :

번 호 : GVW-0307   일 시 : 92 0207 1630

수 신 : 장 관(봉기,경기원,재무부,농림수산부,상공부,특허청)(

발 신 : 주 제네바 대사대리

제 목 : UR 법제화 그룹 2차회의(2)

연: GVW-293

1. 연호 표제회의가 2.6 속개되어 MTO 협정 4조에서 12조까지 논의하였는바, 구체적인 결론없이 각국이 협정문안의 문제점을 열거하는 방식으로 진행되었음.

회의 결과는 아래 보고함. (이참사관,신서기관참석)

가. 4조(타국제기구와의 관계)

스위스가 해당국제기구를 3조 6항과 같이 IMF, IBRD등으로 명기할 필요성을 언급한데 대해 EC는 3조 6항은 실질문제에 대한 규정이고 4조1항은 절차적 규정이므로 현문안을 수정할 필요가 없다고 지적함.

나. 5조(MTO 구조)

O 스웨덴이 각료회의를 누가 개최하며 개최 결정절차, 각료회의 의사규칙관련 언급이 누락되어 있음을 지적하였으며 일부 국가가 동조함.

이에대해 EC는 누락사항을 최종의정서에 규정하거나 UR 협상결과 이행회의에서 1차 각료회의 시기를 결정하고, 2차 회의부터는 각료회의 의사 규칙에 정해지는 바에 개최되는 방안도 있을 것이라고 함. 인도는 최종의정서 보다 이행회의에서 결정하는 것이 합리적이라는 의견을 제시함.

O 홍콩은 분쟁해결 기구 (DSB) 및 TPRM 의 기능에 관해서도 현 5,6,7항과 같이 상세히할 필요성이 있다는 의견을 제시함 (멕시코,인도동조)

O 카나다, 뉴질랜드등이 3항 관련 추후 새로운 기관의 신설 필요성이 있을 가능성에 대해 기관 개폐에 대한 신축성이 필요하다고 발언한데 대해 미국은 기관 개폐에 대한 신축성을 부여할경우 10조 (개정)와의 상충문제가 발생할 수 있다는 점을 언급하고 3항에 언급된 각기관을 UR 협상 결과에 의해 설치키로 합의된 기관으로 항구성을 부여 해야 한다고 함.

통상국   2차보   경기원   재무부   농수부   상공부   특허정

PAGE 1   92.02.08   08:22 WG

O 미국,카나다, 싱가폴등 다수국가가 각기관간 위계관계, 기능.역할 분담등이 현 협정상불 분명한점이 많다고 지적하고 이에대한 명료화 작업 필요성을 언급함. 특히 미국은 각료회의와 일반이사회 관계와 관련 각료회의중 일반이사회 개최 가능성 여부 및 일반 이사회가각료 회의에서 수임을 받아야 되는지, 아니면 자체적인 권한이 있는지의 여부가 불분명하다고 언급

O 위계문제와 관련 EC는 현 TEXT가 TOP-DOWNORDER 로 명백히 규정하고 있다고 하면서 각료회의와 각료회의 중간에 개최되는 일반이사회 밑에 보조기관으로 3개 분야별 이사회가있고, 분쟁해결기구 (DSB), TPRM은 보조기관이 아니고 일반 이사회각 동격의 지위를 누린다고 함.

이에 대해 멕시코, 인도등이 DSB, TPRM 이 고유기능을 가지고 있음을 인정하나, 일반이사회와 동격이 되어야 하느지 의문을 표시함.

O 탄자니아는 분야별 이사회의 년 8회 개최 규정의 경직성에 우려를 표명하였으나 의장은 동 규정은 실질문제로 TRACK 3 에서 다룰수 없다고 언급함.

O 일부 대표로 부터 3항, 4항을 통합하는 의견 제시도 있었음.

O 분야별 이사회의 권한과 관련된 사무국에서 리스트당의 의견과 관련 싱가폴,인도등은 분야별 이사회가 해당분야에 대해 전권을 갖는 역할을 하고 일반 이사회는 광범위 한정책결정이나 각분야에 공통되는 사항을 취급해야 할것이라는 의견을 표명

O MATHUR 의장은 현 갓트에 총회개최에 관한 특별 규정이 없고 의사 규칙에따라 운영되어 왔음을 지적하고 일반이사회는 각료회의 사이에 개최되는 것으로 이해해야 할것이라고 언급함.

　　다. 6조(사무국)

O 스위스가 MTO 사무국이 신갓트와 기존 갓트를 동시에 관리할 경우에 생기는 재정분담 문제등을 지적함.

　　라. 7조(예산 및 분담금)

O 미국이 일반이사회에서의 예산승인 결정방법 (예2/3 다수결), 분담금 체납국가에 대한 제재규정설치 (일반이사회에 일임 곤란), 예산위원회의 위원국 선출방법 (일반이 사회에서 선출)등 현문안의 상세화를 주장한데 대해 EC는 반대 (EC 는 MTO협정문안 교섭당시 가급적 간단한 TEXT 가 되어야 한다는 일반적 합의가 있었다는점 및 12.20 문서 MTO 관련주석 (ANNOTATION)는 타협정과의 관계에 대해서만 추가작업이

PAGE 2

필요하다는 것으로 이해해야된다 하면서 미국의 제안 실질내용의 변경을 의미한다고 반론)

　O 의장은 예산 승인 결정 과정과 관련 특별한 규정이 없으면 9조 1항이 적용되는 것으로 이해한다고 언급

　마. 8조(MTO 지위)

　O 카나다가 본부 협정에 (HEADQUATER AGREEMENT)에대한 규정 추가 필요성을 언급한바, 사무국은 별도규정이 없어도 본부 협정 체결이 가능하다고 본다는 의견을 제시

　바. 9조(회원국 공동 행동)

　O 미국이 의사 결정 방식 관련 3항은 정족수규정이 있는 반면 1항에는 없다는 문제점 및 2항 관련 각료회의, 일반 이사회의 MTO 협정자체에 대한 해석권에 대한 규정이 누락된 반면, MTO 협정에 첨부될 하부 협정에 대한 해석권을 보유하는 것으로 되어있음을 지적하고, 하부결정에 대한 해석권을 현문안대로 각료회의, 일반 이사회에 부여해야 할것인지 아니면 분야별 이사회에 부여해야 할지 여부에 관해 자체입장을 정하지 못했다는 점을 언급함. (인도,멕시코도 유사한 의견을 개진함)

　O 싱가폴은 여타 협정에서의 웨이버 규정과 3항의 웨이버 규정과의 일관성 문제를 검토하고 차이가 클 경우 해결 방안을 논의해야 할 것이라고 하면서 이를 위해 사무국이 대조표를 작성하여 줄것을 요청하였고 인도, 스웨덴, 멕시코가 이에동조함. (멕시코는 가급적 모든 웨이버 규정의 단일화를 희망함)

　사. 10조(개정 및 수정)

　O 미국은 현 갓트 30조 1항과 비교하면서 기존 갓트규정이 개정내용을 수락하는 국가에 대해서만 발표하는 것으로 규정함으로써 FREE-RIDER 를 방지하는데 미흡했다는점 및 현문안에는 기존 GATT 상의 수락 정족수에 대한 차등 (전회원국국 2/3)이 사려졌다고 지적하고 이에대해 좌입장을 검토중이라고 언급함. 미국은 4항및 5항의 CONSENSUS 방식이 개정절차를 BLOCK할 가능성에 우려를 표명하고 3항 관련 미수락국 처리문제에 관한 각료회의 결정방식의 구체화명시 필요성을 언급함. 2항관련 사무국의견 (예시 리스트)에 대해 호주만이 사무국 의견대로 수락한 국가만에 대해 효력을 갖는다고 발언을 한 반면 EC, 카나다는 제도분야 협상과정을 설명하면서 ALL MEMBER 를 의미한다는 입장을 표시함. (사무국도 ALL MEMBER에 대해 적용되도록 하자는것이 협상참여자 의의도 였다고 설명)

O 호주, 알젠틴, 싱가폴등은 이를 EACH MEMBER 를 이해했다고 하면서 ALL MEMBER를 의매할 경우기존 갓트 규정과 상충되는 문제점을 심각히 다루어야 할 사항이라는 의견을 개진함. 이에대해 MATHUR 의장은 MTO 협정과 여타협정 상충시 MTO 협정이 우서한다 는 16조 3항을 상기시킴.

O 카나다는 <u>각협정의 개정권</u>이 각료회의에 부여되어야 하는지 아니면 분야별 이사회에 부여되어야 하는지 아직 결정하지 못했다고 하면서 향후 새로운 협정이 체결될 경우 이를 MTO 내로 도입하는 방식이 누락되었음을 지적함. (인도도 동일 입장표명)

아. 11조(원 가입국)

O 미국은 DEFINITIVE BASIS 의 의미가 조부조항과 직접적인 관련이 없고 다만 갓트를 잠정적이아니고 확정적 (항구적)으로 적용한다는 의미로 해석한다는 입장을 표시한 반면 EC는 ANNEX 1A에도 PPA 제외가 분명히 언급되어 있다고하면서 이는 분명히 PPA 상의 조부조항을 철폐하기 위한 의미라고 주장한바, <u>사무국은 EC 입장이 타탕하는 의견을 제시</u>

자. 12조(가입)

O 중국은 관세영역의 가입과관련 갓트 33조의 'GOVN'T ACTIONG ON BEHALF OF'가 삭제된 점을 지적하고 갓트와의 일관성을 유지하는 차원에서 상기 문구를 포함시킬 것을 제안하였으나 미국, EC는 제도분야 협상시 동건을 충분히 토의한 다음 동 문구를 삭제키로 한것이라고 하면서 중국 제안을 반대함.

2. 사무국은 무역과 환경 작업반 회의와 중복되어 있는 4차 회의기간을 당초 3.9-13 대신 3.2-6로 앞당기는 방안을 검토중인 것으로 보임.

현재 회의진행 상황으로 보아 협정문안을 확정하기에는 추가적인 작업이 필요할 것으로 보이며, 따라서 사무국이 제시한 작업 일정이 준수될런지는 현재로서는 불부명한 상황임.끝

(차석대사 김삼훈-국장)

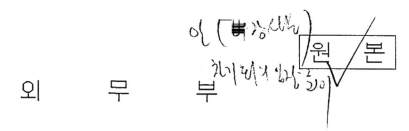

외　무　부

종　별 :

번　호 : GVW-0315　　　　　　　　　　일　시 : 92 0207 1930

수　신 : 장 관(봉기,경기원,재무부,농수산부,상공부)

발　신 : 주 제네바 대사대리

제　목 : UR 법제화 제2차회의(3)

연: GVW-0307

1. 2.7 속개된 표제회의는 MTO 협정문잔여조항 (13조-16조) 검토를 마치고 금차회의를 종료한바 동결과 아래 보고함.(이성주 참사관참석)

　가. 제 13조(협정 불적용)

0 우선 현문안 2항에 따르면 현재 불적용 규정이 발동되는 국가 상호간 이외에는 1항이 예정하고있는 써비스협정, TRIPS 협정 불적용이 불가능하다는 모순이 지적된바, EC 는 2항의 취지가 ANNEX 1A관련 MTO 에로의 전환시점에서 현 GATT 회원국간 발동되고 있는 기존의 불적용 케이스 이상으로 불필요하게 새로운 케이스가 확대되는 것을 방지하기위한 것이라고 설명하고, 2항의 'ANNEX 1'은 'ANNEX 1A'의 착오였다고 해명 (사무국도 사무국 착오임을 확인)

0 미국은 2항이 ANNEX 1A 협정에만 적용된다 하더라도, 동항 표현이 'HAS BEEN INVOKED' 로 되어있는 것과 관련 과거 발동하였다가 해제된 경우도 포함되는지의 여부가 불명확한점 및 UR협상결과 형성될 새로운 협정 (예: 농산물,선적전검사, 원산지규정, 섬유등이 불적용대상에 포함되지 않는다는 문제점을 지적

0 상기에 대해 EC 는 ANNEX 1A 의 불적용은 MTO 발효 또는 해당국의 가입시점까지 실제로 불적용의 발동되는 경우에 한한다고 답변,

(인도,싱가폴도 동일 의견)하고, 농산물 협정등 새로운 UR 협상 결과도 당연히 2항의 대상으로 포함된다고 발언 (스웨덴은 ANNEX 관련 혼선을 막기위해 사무국이 ANNEX 포함 대상협정의 LIST 작성을 요청)

0 싱가폴은 불적용은 ANNEX 1A, IB, 1C 별로 전체적으로 발동 (1A 협정의 일부에 대한 선별발동 불가)해야 하는 것으로 이해한다 하면서, 특히 ANNEX 1A 협정 관련 현재 동경라운드 특정 CODE 에 대해서만 불적용을 발동하는 국가의 경우 동불적용

통상국　　2차보　　경기원　　재무부　　농수부　　상공부

대상을 ANNEX 1A 협정 전체로 확대해야 할것이라고 언급

(사무국도 같은 견해 표명)

O PAKISTAN 은 서비스협정 불적용 조항 (30조 1항)을 언급하면서, 이는 서비스협상 그룹에서 협상에 의해 합의된 내용인바, 동 조항이 MTO협정상의 불적용 조항과 상치할 경우 MTO16조 3항에 따라 실효되는 결과를 가져온다고 하면서 여사한 규정간 상충문제에 대해 면밀한 검토가 필요하다는 입장 개진

나. 제14조(수락, 발효, 기탁)

O 미국이 2항 AS IF 표현 (소급적용)관련 동구체적 적용방식을 문의하고, 사무국이 GVW-0128로 기보고한 내용으로 답변한바, 미국은 이점을 보다 분명히 하기위한 문안 작성을 요구

다. 제 15조(탈퇴)

O EC 가 MTO 체제하에서는 MTO 회원국은 모든 부속협정의 당사국의 되므로 개별협정상의 탈퇴규정은 의미가 없어진다고 하면서 이에대한 조정 필요성을 언급한바, 미국, 카나다가 동조

O 미국은 탈퇴시 미납분담금 청산의무 규정신설필요성 언급.

라. 제 16조(최종 규정)

O 홍콩이 TRIP 협정, TBT CODE 등을 예시, 일부개별 협정에 유보허용 조항이 있다고 언급하고 동문제 해결 방안 검토를 위해 사무국이 대조표를 작성해 줄것을 요청

O 동경라운드 폐기조항 신설 필요성 (예시 LIST 상사무국 의견)에 대해 홍콩, 스웨덴, 미국등이 지지 (단 ANNEX 4 협정은 폐기대상에서 제외주장)

O 카나다는 1항과 관련 갓트의 기존 관행을 따른다는 기본 취지는 합당하나, 앞으로 MTO 가 어떠한 방향으로 발전될지 정확히 예측키는 어려운 상황에서 'SHALL RESPECT' 의 표현은 지나치게 강하므로 표현의 완화 또는 투표 절차, 패널등의 결정사항등 내용별로 세분화하여 규정할 필요성도 있다는 의견제시 (미국도 동조, 미국은 특히 9조상 1국 1투표권 규정과 동규정간 INTERNAL CONSISTENCY 도 결여되 있음을 지적)

마. 향후 작업 계획등

O MATHUR 의장은 차기회의 계획과 관련 아래사항을 언급

- 차기회의에서는 MTO 와 여타 협정과의 관계를 검토할 예정

- 이를 위해 발효, 유보, 협정불적용, 탈퇴, 개정규정에 대한 대조표 및 각협정의

명칭을 포함한 MTO 협정 첨부 대상 협정에 대한 LIST 를 사무국이 준비할 예정이라고 언급

- IDSS 문안은 차기회의에서의 논의대상은 아니나 차기회의시까지 배포 예정

- 서비스 양허표 누락을 포함 MTN.TNC/W/FA 에 대한 착오 시정작업 추진

- 법제화 그룹 회의록은 주요 쟁점을 중심으로 작성 (개개의 발언 기록 불가)하되, 동쟁점은 (1)추가검토를 요하는 사항 (2) 실질문제에 해당되는사항 (3) 금번 토의 결과에 따라 사무국 차원의조정 (참가국 입장 불기속 전제) 사항등으로 분류될수 있을 것임.

- 차기 3차 회의는 2.19-21 간, 4차 회의는 3.3-6 간 개최

2.금차 회의 결과에 대한 당관의 평가

가. 대부분의 국가가 현문안의 문제점만 지적해 나가는 방식으로 회의가 진행, 구체적인 대안모색 노력은 없었으므로, 거의 대부분의 잇슈에 대해 차후 재론이 불가피 할것으로 전망

나. MTO 협정의 사실상의 초안작성국인 EC와 카나다는 상기 각국의 문제점 지적에 대해 가급적이면 현 문안에 대한 수정 또는 변경을 최소화하려는 태도를 보인 반면, 미국의 토의에 깊이 개입하지는 않으면서도 상기 EC 의 태도에 대해 불만 표시

다. 전체적으로 MTO 협정은 12.20 시한에 쫓기어 성급하게 작성되었다는 점이 금번 회의과정에서 재차 확인되고, 상당수의 잇슈가 기술적 작업대상인지 실질적 내용과 관련되는 사항인지의 경계도 불분명하여 당초 예상보다 훨씬 어려운 작업이 될 것으로 예상

라. 금차 회의에서 재기된 주요 문제점등 포함 TEXT 전반에 대한 면밀한 검토를 통해 차기회의에 대비한 구체적 아국입장 정립 및 차기회의에 본부 대표 파견이 필요할 것으로 판단.끝

(차석대사 김삼훈-국장)

외 무 부

종 별 :

번 호 : GVW-0354　　　　　　　　　　일 시 : 92 0213 1930

수 신 : 장 관(통기)

발 신 : 주 제네바 대사대리

제 목 : UR/법제화 그룹

　　갓트 사무국은 별첨 전문을 통해 제3차 표제회의가 2.19-21간 개최됨을 통보하여
왔는바, 이를 별첨 송부함.

　　첨부: 상기 전문(GATT/AIR/3291).(GVW(F)-0103)

　　(차석대사 김삼훈-국장)

통상국

PAGE 1　　　　　　　　　　　　　　　　　　　　　　92.02.14　　08:59 WG

주 제 네 바 대 표 부

번 호 : GVW(F) - 6/03   년월일 : 2.07/3   시간 : 1/ 30

수 신 : 장   관(통기)

발 신 : 주 제내바대사

제 목 : GVW-0354

총 2 매(표지포함)

보 안 통 제	

외신관 능 세	

7/03-2-1   0053

GATT/AIR/3291   12 FEBRUARY 1992

SUBJECT: URUGUAY ROUND: LEGAL DRAFTING GROUP

1.   THE THIRD MEETING OF THE LEGAL DRAFTING GROUP WILL BE HELD ON
WEDNESDAY, 19 FEBRUARY 1992 AT 10 A.M. IN THE CENTRE WILLIAM RAPPARD. THE
MEETING MAY CONTINUE ON 20 AND 21 FEBRUARY.

2.   THE CHAIRMAN PROPOSES THAT THE MEETING TAKE UP TWO MATTERS:

        (I)   REVIEW OF RELATIONSHIP BETWEEN MTO AND OTHER TEXTS IN
               MTN.TNC/W/FA: (AN ILLUSTRATIVE LIST OF POINTS FOR POSSIBLE
               CONSIDERATION IN THE LEGAL DRAFTING GROUP: NOTE BY THE
               SECRETARIAT OF 31 JANUARY 1992);

        (II)   FURTHER REVIEW OF THE AGREEMENT ESTABLISHING THE MULTILATERAL
               TRADE ORGANIZATION (ANNEX IV OF MTN.TNC/W/FA): (NOTE BY THE
               SECRETARIAT: TO BE CIRCULATED);

3.   THE GROUP WILL HAVE THE FOLLOWING NEW DOCUMENTS BEFORE IT AT THE
MEETING:

        (I)   NOTE ON THE SECOND MEETING (MTN.TNC/LD/2);

        (II)   POINTS ARISING FROM THE DISCUSSION OF THE MTO TEXT: INFORMAL
               NOTE BY THE SECRETARIAT;

        (III) TENTATIVE LISTING BY THE SECRETARIAT OF THE INSTRUMENTS TO BE
               ATTACHED TO THE MTO ANNEXES;

        (IV)   A DRAFT INTEGRATED TEXT ON DISPUTE SETTLEMENT PREPARED BY THE
               SECRETARIAT;

        (V)   LEGAL FORM OF TEXTS IN MTN.TNC/W/FA: INFORMAL NOTE BY THE
               SECRETARIAT, DATED 6 FEBRUARY 1992 (CIRCULATED AT THE LAST
               MEETING);

        (VI)   FINAL PROVISIONS IN INSTRUMENTS COVERED BY THE DRAFT FINAL ACT;

        (VII) INSTITUTIONAL ISSUES IN INSTRUMENTS COVERED BY THE DRAFT FINAL
               ACT;

        (VIII) INITIAL LISTS OF EDITORIAL CORRECTIONS TO THE ENGLISH, FRENCH
               AND SPANISH TEXTS OF MTN.TNC/W/FA: ADDENDUM.

4.   GOVERNMENTS PARTICIPATING IN THE MULTILATERAL TRADE NEGOTIATIONS, AND
WISHING TO BE REPRESENTED AT THIS MEETING, ARE REQUESTED TO INFORM ME OF
THE NAMES OF THEIR REPRESENTATIVES AS SOON AS POSSIBLE.

                                                      A. DUNKEL

92-0159

                                                              0054

외   무   부

110-760 서울 종로구 세종로 77번지   /   (02)720-2188   /   (02)725-1737 (FAX)

문서번호 통기 20644-

시행일자 1992. 2.14.(   )

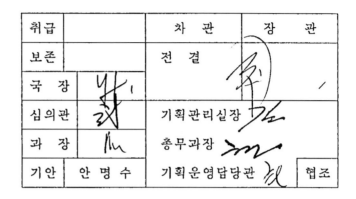

수신 내부결재

참조

제목   UR/법제화 그룹회의 참가 정부대표임명

　　　　스위스 제네바에서 개최되는 UR/법제화 그룹 제3차 회의 (92.2.19-21)에 참석할
정부대표를 "정부대표 및 특별사절의 임명과 권한에 관한 법률"에 의거, 아래와 같이
임명할 것을 건의합니다.

- 아   래 -

1. 회 의 명 : UR/법제화 그룹 제 3차 회의

2. 기간 및 장소 : 92.2.19-21, 스위스, 제네바

3. 정부대표 : 통상기구과 사무관 안명수

4. 출장기간 : 2.17-23 (6박7일)

5. 훈   령 : 별첩

6. 소요경비

　　가. 항공료 : $2,109

　　나. 체재비 : $66 X 6박 = $396

0055

다. 일식비 : ($20 + $42) X 7일 = $434

(총 액 : $2,939)

라. 지변항목 : 경제활동, 국외여비.

첨 부 : 훈 령.   끝.

외 무 부 장 관

0056

훈 령
===============

1. UR/법제화 그룹은 92.1.13 UR/무역협상위원회 (TNC)에서 결정된 mandate에 따라
   UR 협정 초안(Draft Final Act)의 내부적 일관성과 법적 합치성을 확보하는
   작업을 수행하도록 임무를 부여받았음.

2. 상기 UR/법제화 그룹에서의 작업이 중립적이며 기술적인 성격을 갖는 점을
   감안하여, 동그룹에서의 작업이 UR 협상 참가국의 권리·의무의 균형에 변경을
   초래하지 않도록 하는 범위 내에서 진행되도록 유의하면서 회의에 임할것.

3. 금번 제 3차 UR/법제화 그룹회의에서는 MTO 협정과 제반 다자간 무역협정 text와의
   관계가 주요의제로 논의될 예정임. MTO 설립 협정이 제반 다자간 무역협정에 대한
   umbrella의 성격을 갖게 되므로 발효, 유보, 협정부적용, 탈퇴, 개정 등에 관련된
   조항이 상충되지 않도록 조정하고, 기타 용어상의 통일을 기하는 방향으로 회의가
   진행되도록 기여할 것.

4. 금번 제 3차 회의에서는 특정 쟁점에 대한 결론 도출보다는 MTO 설립협정과 제반
   다자간 무역 협정과의 관계에 관한 사무국 문서를 기초로 현 UR 협정 초안상의
   문제점을 지적 해나가는 방향으로 논의가 진행될 것으로 예상되는바, 제기되는
   쟁점에 대한 각 참가국의 동향을 면밀히 파악함으로써 향후 UR/법제화 그룹회의에
   대한 대책을 수립할 것.   끝.

0057

발 신 전 보

분류번호 | 보존기간

번 호 : WGV-0268   920215 1041   CJ   종별 :

수 신 : 주   제네바   대사. 총영사/

발 신 : 장 관 (통 기)

제 목 : UR/법제화 그룹 제3차 회의

1. 92.2.19-21간 귀지 개최 표제회의에 통상기구과 안명수 사무관이 2.17-22간 귀지
    출장 예정인바, 귀관 관계관과 함께 참석토록 조치바람 (본부대표 2.17(월) 21:45
    SR-729편 귀지 도착. Mon Repos 호텔 예약바람)

2. 훈 령

    ~~가. UR/법제화 그룹은 92.1.13 UR/무역협상위원회 (TNC)에서 결정된 mandate에~~
    ~~따라 UR 협정 초안의 내부적 일관성과 법적 합치성을 확보하는 작업을~~
    ~~수행하도록 임무를 부여받았음.~~

    가. ~~설립~~ UR/법제화 그룹에서의 작업이 중립적이며 기술적인 성격을 갖는 점을
        감안하여, 동그룹에서의 작업이 UR 협상 참가국의 권리.의무의 균형에 변경을
        초래하지 않도록 하는 범위 내에서 진행되도록 유의하면서 회의에 임할것.

    나. 금번 제 3차 UR/법제화 그룹회의에서는 MTO 협정과 제반 다자간 무역협정
        text와의 관계가 주요의제로 논의될 예정임.

    다. MTO 설립 협정이 제반 다자간 무역협정에 대한 umbrella의 성격을 갖게되므로
        발효, 유보, 협정부적용, 탈퇴, 개정 등에 관련된 조항이 상충되지 않도록
        조정하고, 기타 용어상의 통일을 기하는 방향으로 회의가 진행되도록 기여하고,
        구체적인 쟁점에 대하여는 본부대표 지참 자료 및 회의 분위기를 감안하여
        적의 대처함.

보 안 통 제

앙 고 재	92년 월 일	통상기구과	기안자 성명 안명수	과 장	심의관	국 장 전결	차 관	장 관	외신과통제

다. 금번 제 3차 회의에서는 특정 쟁점에 대한 결론 도출보다는 MTO 설립협정과
제반 다자간 무역 협정과의 관계에 관한 사무국 문서를 기초로 현 UR 협정
초안상의 문제점을 지적 해나가는 방향으로 논의가 진행될 것으로 예상되는바,
제기되는 쟁점에 대한 각 참가국의 동향을 면밀히 파악함으로써 향후 UR/법제화
그룹회의에 대한 대책을 수립함.   끝.

(통상국장 김 용 규)

외 무 부

종 별 :

번 호 : GVW-0398   일 시 : 92 0219 1930

수 신 : 장 관(통기,경기원,재무부,농림수산부,상공부,특허청)

발 신 : 주 제네바 대사

제 목 : UR 법제화 그룹회의 3차회의(1)

표제회의가 2.19 MATHUR 의장주재로 개최되어 MTO협정과 여타 협정과의 관계를 검토하였는바, 요지 아래 보고함.(이참사관, 안사무관 참석)

1. MTO 협정 ANNEX 1A 수록대상 TEXT

가. 제반 UR TEXT중 어느것을 MTO 설립협정 ANNEX 1A 에 포함시킬 것인지 여부와 관련 갓트 사무국이 비공식 문서를 배포함. (FAX 편 송부)

나. 인도는 금융서비스 약속에 관한 UNDERSTANDING은 UR 협상 종결만을 위한 가이드라인에 불과하므로 최종의정서에서 제외되어야 한다고 언급 (멕시코 동조). 이에대해 일본은 서비스협상이 계속적인 과정이라고 지적하고 제외에 반대입장을 표명

다. 콜롬비아는 사무국 문서에 가이드라인으로서의 성격을 갖는 농산물 협정 PART B 중 특정 ASPECT 가 MTO 협정 ANNEX 1A 에 포함되도록 되어 있는것과 관련 동 ASPECT 를 보다 구체화할 필요성을 지적함. (우루과이, 미국동조)

라. 이씨는 사무국 작성문서에 대체적으로 동의한다고 전제한후 동문서 PAGE 1,4번째 PARA (STAND-ALONEAGREEMENTS)와 관련 MTO 설립 협정 ANNEX상의 UR 협정이 MTO 설립협정의 불가분의 일부를 구성하는데에는 더이상 논란의 여지가 없다고 언급함으로써 사무국 문서에 불만을 표시함. (이와 관련 홍콩은 ANNEX 4상의 협정이 불가분의 일부를 구성하는지 여부는 추가적인 검토가 필요하다고 지적)

마. 카나다와 미국은 각료회의가 MTO 설립협정 ANNEX 에 포함되지 않은 TEXT 를 채택 (각료회의 결정)하는 것과 관련, MTO협정 발효 이전에 각료회의 형식으로 결정을 내릴수 있는지의 법적 문제점 및 UR 협상결과의 일부가 MTO 협정 발효 이전에 이행될수도 있다는 것을 문제점으로 지적함. 이에 대해 갓트사무국 ROSSLER 법률국장은 각료회의가 결정을 내릴때 발효일자를 MTO협정 발효일자에 일치시킴으로써 동문제점을 해결 할수 있다고 답변함. 일본, 인도도 동건은 큰문제가 되짐 않는다는

통상국   경기원   재무부   농수부   상공부   특허청

의견을 피력함.

바. 파키스탄은 GATT ('93)이 MTO 설립협정 ANNEX1A 에 포함됨으로써 실질적으로 GATT('47)이 GATT ('47)에서 규정하고 있는 개정절차에 따르지않고 개정되는 결과를 초래한다고 지적하고 이에대한 사무국의 해명을 요청함. ROSSLER법률국장은 MTO 설립협정 발효로 GATT('47)이 GATT ('93)으로 대체되는 것이며, GATT ('47)은 존속하여 MTO 에 가입하지 않는 체약국간에 계속 적용된다고 답변함.

사. 일본은 갓트 17조, BOP, 24조, 25조, 28조에 관한 UNDERSTANDING 은 MTO 설립협정 ANNEX 1A 에 포함하기 보다는 각료의 결정대상으로 하는 것이 바람직하다고 언급함.

아. 스웨덴은 MTO 설립협정 ANNEX 1A 에 수록될 GATT 의 ASSOCIATED LEGAL INSTRUMENTS 를 구체적으로 명시할 필요성이 있음을 지적함. 이에대해 ROESSLER 법률국장은 WAIVER, ENBLEINGCLAUSE, PPA 등이 포함된다고 해석하나 동문제는 법제화 그룹과는 별도의 작업이라고 언급함.

자. 인도, 스웨덴은 MTO 설립협정 ANNEX 에 포함한 제반 TEXT간의 상호관계에 대해 사무국측의 해명을 요청한바, ROSSLER 법률국장은 이는 복잡한 문제로서 특별법 우선의 원칙이 원용될수 있을 것이라고 언급함.

차. 파키스탄, 인도는 한시성 협정 (예:섬유협정등)와 항구적 성격의 협정간의 구별 필요성을 언급하고, 한시성 협정의 경우 각료회의 결정형식이 바람직하다고 한반면 미국 및 사무국은 한시성 및 항구성이 기준이 되는 것은 타당치않다는 의견이 었음.

2. 서비스 양허표 양식

사무국이 2차 법제화 그룹회의시 누락이 지적된 서비스협상 양허표 양식 (FAX 송부)을 금번 회의시 배포한 것과 관련, 일본이 동 양허표 양식은 SVC 협상그룹에서의 논의를 거쳐 작성되어야 할것이라고 언급하였으며 (스웨덴동조), 이에 대해 이씨, 파키스탄은 사무국이 양허표양식을 배포한 것은 2차 회의시 합의에 따른것이라는 점을 지적함.끝

(대사 박수길-국장)

외 무 부

종 별 :

번 호 : GVW-0416

일 시 : 92 0221 1940

수 신 : 장관(봉기,경기원,재무부,농림수산부,상공부,특허청)

발 신 : 주제네바대사

제 목 : UR 법제화 그룹 3차회의

(2)연: GVW-0398

표제회의가 2.20 속개되어 MTO 협정과 여타 TEXT 와의 관계를 검토한후 2.21.종료된바, 요지 하기 보고함.

1. MTO 협정 ANNEX 에 포함될 TEXTS 의 범위

0 금융서비스 양허 UNDERSTANDING과 관련 연호 개도국과 선진국간의 입장대립이반복되자 ROESSLER 법률국장은 동 UNDERSTANDING 이 향후 양허협상시 양허의 범위를정하는데 있어서 REFERENCE 역할을 하는등 법적인 기능을 갖는다고 언급.

또한 MATHUR 의장은 서비스담당 부서로 부터 동 UNDERSTANDING 이 미래에도 RELEVANCE 를 갖는다는 자문을 근거로 사무국이 배경문서를 작성했으며, 동 문제를 TRACK4 에 회부하는것은 시간적 제약요건을 감안할때 바람직하지 않다고 언급.

0 이씨는 사무국 배경문서에 각료의 결정대상으로 분류한 TEXT들중 일부는 UR 협상과 직접관련이 없는 절차적인 성격을 가지므로(예:LDC 관련 MEASURE) 동 TEXT 들도 추가로 구별할 필요성이 있다고 발언

0 아국은 사무국 배경문서 내용에 일반적으로 동의하며, UR 협상 TEXT 들중 일부를 각료의 결정형식으로 채택하는데 별 문제점이 없으며,특정 TEXT 를 MTO 협정 ANNEX 에 포함시킬것인지 혹은 각료의 결정대상으로 할것인지는TEXT 의 성격에 따라 결정할 문제라고 지적함,또한 향후 개정의 필요성을 감안할때 MTO설립 협정 ANNEX 에 포함시킬 TEXT 의 수를 제한하는 것이 바람직할 것이며, 기존 갓트조문을 보다 명확히하고 있는 갓트 조문관련 UNDERSTANDING 들은 각료의 결정대상으로 하여도 무방할 것이라고 발언함.(갓트 조문관련 UNDERSTANDING 처리문제와 관련 일본이 아측입장에 동조한 반면 미국은 소극적 입장표명)

통상국   2차보   경기원   재무부   농수부   상공부   특허정

92.02.22   08:04 DQ

외신 1과 통제관

0062

O 카나다는 IMPLEMENTING CONFERENCE 에서 각료들이 최종의정서 발효시기를 결정하는 것과 관련 갓트 체약국단은 서비스 협정 발효문제를 결정할 권한이 없다고 언급. 이에대해 MATHUR 의장은 동각료회의는 체약국단 회의가 아니라 UR 협상참가국 각료회의 라고 답변

2. 제도 조항(INSTITUTIONAL PROVISIONS)

O 미국은 1) 기존 TEXT 들에 포함된 위원회설치에 관한 규정에 변경을 가하지 않는것이 바람직하며, 2) 각 TEXT 에서 사용하고 있는 회원국 지칭용어(PARTY, MEMBER, SIGNATORY 등)에 일관성이 결여된 것과 관련 각 TEXT 를 검토하여 조정해야 할것이라고 언급(카나다,브라질,싱가폴 동조)

O 태국은 MTO 협정 5조 5.6.7항에 분야별 이사회가 관련 협정을 'OVERSEE'하도록 규정된것과관련, 동 용어의 의미가 불분명하다는 점지적(싱가폴, 인도동조)

3. 최종조항(FINAL PROVISIONS)

가. 탈퇴

O 이씨는 TEXT 들간의 일관성 확보를 위해 탈퇴에 관한 조항은 MTO 협정 15조 만을 존치시키고 여타 TEXT 상의 탈퇴 관련 조항은 TBT 협정만을 제외하고는 모두 철폐해야 하며,가입관련 조항도 MTO 협정 12조만을 존치시키고 갓트 포함 여타 MTO 협정ANNEX 1A 상의 모든 TEXT 에 포함된 가입관련 조항이 철폐되어야한다고 언급(카나다동조)

나. 가입

O 미국은 MTO 협정의 가입관련 조항만을 존치시킬 경우, 특히 관세영역의 가입을 규정하고있는 갓트 26조 5항 C 폐기의 법적 효과에대해 사무국이 배경문서를 작성해 줄것을 요청(싱가폴, 홍콩 동조)

O LINDEN 사무총장 보좌관은 갓트 26조 5항 C폐기문제와 관련, MTO 협정의 가입조항이 모든 여타 TEXT 에 포함된 가입규정을 대체토록 하는 것이 기본취지라고 답변.

O 미국은 서비스협정의 가입조항(28조 1항)에 규정된 양허표 유지의무는 가입자체와는 직접 관련이 없는 조건에 불과하므로 동조건이 삭제되는 것은 아니라 언급

다. 유보

O 유보조항과 관련 홍콩은 개별 TEXT 에 포함된 유보조항은 가급적 존치시키는 것이 바람직하다고 언급

PAGE 2

0063

O 이씨는 유보 불가를 규정한 MTO 협정 16조 2항 말미에 '부속협정에 달리 규정되어 있지 않는한'이라는 단서를 추가할것을 제의한바 아국포함 대다수 참가국이 동의함.

라. 국내 입법

O MTO 설립협정 16조 4항(부속협정 이행을 위해 변경이 필요한 국내법을 동협정에 일치시키기 위해 노력)과 관련 다수 참가국들은 동조항이 UR협상 결과로서 참가국들이 부담하게 될 의무를 약화시킬 것이므로 동조항을 보다 엄격하게 할 필요성이 있다고 지적

O 미국은 동 조항이 UR 협상결과의 국내적 이행에 영향을 미치지 않을 것이라고 언급

마. 개정

O 일본은 개별 TEXT 에 포함된 개정관련 규정이 존치되어야 한다고 발언

O 인도는 개정에 관한 공시 결정을 일반이사회가 행하더라도 실질적인 개정협상은 관련이사회(상품,서비스,지적재산권 이사회)에서 관장해야 할 것이라고 언급

4. 향후 작업계획

MATHUR 의장은 차기회의는 3.3 부터 개최하여 통합분쟁해결 TEXT와 CROSS-CUTTING ISSUE 를 검토하되, 2.25(화)10:00 (ROOM E) 부터 필요시 2.28까지 비공식 회의를 개최하여 MTO 와 여타 TEXT와의 관계 및 MTO 협정문안을 추가 검토키로함. 끝

(대사 박수길-국장)

외 무 부

종 별 :

번 호 : GVW-0452

일 시 : 92 0227 1920

수 신 : 장관(통기, 경기원)

발 신 : 주제네바대사

제 목 : UR/법제화그룹 비공식회의(1)

1. 표제회의가 2.25-26 MATHUR 의장 주재로 개최되어 MTO 협정조문에 대해 사무국에서 배포한 비공식 문서(2.18자)를 중심으로 논의가 있었는바, 주요쟁점 조문에 대한 논의 요지 아래보고함.

가. 2조(MTO 범위)

0 MTO 협정의 ANNEX 4 에 규정된 동경라운드 일부 협약과 MTO 협정과의 관계 설정 문제와관련 홍콩, 브라질은 사무국안을 지지하면서 ANNEX 4 에 규정된 협약은 MTO협정의 필수부분(INTEGRAL PART)이 될수 없으며 다만 MTO가 동협약과 관련된 사항에대해 제도적인 기반을 제공할 수 있을뿐이라고 언급하였음.

0 이에대해 EC, 미국, 뉴질랜드는 ANNEX 4 에 규정된 협약도 MTO 협정의 INTEGRAL PART 이며다만 MTO 회원자격과 관련 회원국이 반드시 가입해야 하는 협정이 아닐뿐이라고 반박함.

나. 9조(회원국 공동행동)

0 2항 관련 사무국안이 각료회의, 일반이사회의 MTO 협정 및 개별 협정에 대한 해석권을 보유한다고 규정되어 있는것과 관련 미국,인도는 분쟁해결 절차와 관련된 해석권과 개별협정에 대한 해석권은 전문성이 있는 분쟁해결 기구와 분야별 이사회가갖는것이 효율적이며 각료회의, 일반 이사회는 공통문제(CROSS-CUTTING ISSUES)를 다루는것이 적절하다고 언급함.

0 3항의 웨이버 부여 조항과 관련 TRIPS협정에는 웨이버 조항이 포함되어 있지 않는바,웨이버 조항의 TRIPS 분야 적용은 실질문제에 대한 논의가 되므로 동건은 추후TRIPS 협상그룹 의장에 문의하기로 함.

다. 10조(개정 및 수정)

0 2항 관련 회원국의 2/3 수락시 개정내용이 모든 회원국에 발표한다는 사무국안에

통상국   2차보   경기원

대해 일본은 관련 개별협정에 달리 규정하지 않는한 수락한 국가에만 발효하는 것으로 변경할 것을 제안함

  0 미국은 현행 갓트 관례를 유지하는 것을지지한다고 하면서 사무국안에 유보를표시하고 MTO의 기존 갓트 관례 존중 조항이 16조 1항에 규정되어 있으나, 이를 인용하기에는 너무 애매하다고 언급함.

  0 사무국의 ROESSLER 법률국장은 1965년 이후 갓트30조의 개정절차를 통해 갓트규정이 변경된 적이 없었으며 별도의 협정, 결정,양해등(동경라운드 협정, ENABLINGCLAUSE)으로 신축성있게 갓트 규정이 개정되어 왔다고언급함.

  2. 5조(MTO 구성)과 관련 비공식회의 논의결과를 기초로 사무국에서 작성한 문안과 사무국 기구 도표를 별첨 송부하며 2.19-21간 회의에서 논의된 MTO과 타협정간의관계를 정리한 사무국 NON-PAPER(NO.342, 2.25자)를 금파편 송부함.

  첨부: MTO 5조 문안(2.26자).

  (GVW(F)-0135).끝

  (대사 박수길-국장)

주 제 네 바 대 표 부

제네(경) 20644-**210**   1992. 2. 28

수신 : 장   관

참조 : 통상국장

제목 : UR법제화 그룹

연 : GVW - 452

표제회의 관련 사무국에서 배포한 비공식 문서를 별첨 송부합니다.

첨부 : 1.   NO. 342(2.25자)

2.   NO. 365(2.28자) .

3.   갓트 관련 법률문서 List .   끝.

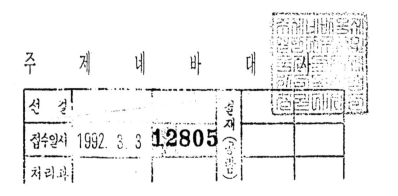

0067

외 무 부

종 별 :

번 호 : GVW-0479

일 시 : 92 0228 2100

수 신 : 장 관(봉기,경기원)

발 신 : 주 제네바 대사

제 목 : UR 법제화 그룹 비공식 회의(2)

연: GVW-0452

1. 표제회의가 2.27-28(오전) MATHUR 의장 주재로 속개되어 MTO 협정안과 MTO 협정에 부속될 협정에 대한 논의가 있었는바, 요지 아래 보고함.

　가. 5조(MTO 구조)

O 2.26 배포된 사무국안 및 구조도표와 관련 홍콩은 구조도표에 상응하게 사무국안 1항을 수정한 별첨안을 제시하였음.

O 사무국안 2항 첫째문장과 관련 사무국은 IBRD헌장의 관련 규정을 원용하였다고하면서 MTO의 권한 근원이 각료회의라는 것을 MTO협정에 명시적으로 규정하는 것이추후 혼란의 소지를 방지할 수 있을 것이라고 언급함. 이에대해 EC,일본은 동규정 표현이 너무 강하다고 하면서 협정안 5조가 TOP-TOWN ORDER 로 권한 관계가 규정되어있음 을 감안, 현행 5조 1항을 그대로 유지하는 것을 지지한다고 함.

O 카나다, EC는 사무국안 3항에 일반 이사회의 권한에서 추후 다자무역 협상 추진 과 협상결과의 이행권한을 삭제한 것은 원래 협정의 내용을 넘어선 것이라고 언급함.

　나. 13조(협정 부적용)

O 사무국안의 3항 관련 EC는 사무국안을 지지한다고 언급한 반면,브라질,홍콩,멕시코,우루과이는 동조항은 CROSS NONAPPLICATION 을 의미하는 것으로 이는 91.12.MTO협정안에 대한 합의 결과를 넘어선 것이며, UR협상 결과의 SINGLE UNDERTAKING 정신에 따라협정 부적용은 제한적으로 적용해야 한다는 점을 고려할때 12.20 협정안의 2항(ANNEX 1를 ANNEXA1 로 수정)을 선호한다고 언급함.

　다. 16조(최종 조항)

O 1항(갓트 관행존중 조항) 관련 카나다는 별첨안을 제안하면서 이는 기존 갓트관례와 갓트규정 해석에 관한 계속성을 유지하고 9조(개정)와 관련 MTO 의

통상국 　경기원

92.03.01　00:04 FN

외신 1과 통제관

0068

투표관행등 갯트관례 존중 규정을 보다 명확히 하기 위한 것이라고 설명함. 이에대해 미국, EC, 태국은 MTO 는갯트의 계속성 유지와 함께 MTO 의 발전에 따른 신축성도 부여하여야 하는데 카나다 제안은 전자만을 강조한 것이라고 지적함. 홍콩은 사무국안대로 패널결정등 갯트 결정사항의 계속성 유지문제와 투표관행등 절차문제를 분리하는 것을선호한다고 하면서 사무국안을 지지함.

0 3항(MTO 협정의 UR 협정에 대한 우선조항)관련, EC는 3항을 삭제할 것을 제안하였고 카나다는 MTO 협정과 타협정간의 일관성 유지측면과 MTO 협정의 MTO 에대한 기본 헌법적인 규정으로서 타협정 보다 우선한다는 측면에서 3항을 유지하자고 함(인도동조)

0 4항(국내법의 MTO 협정 합치규정) 관련 카나다는 'WHERE CHANGES -- AGREEMENTS ANNEXED HERE TO'부분을 삭제하자고 제의하자 미국은 동건 논의는 실질문제이므로 TRACK 3 에서 다룰 사항이 아니라고 언급하였으며 홍콩, 인도는 동조항은 협상을봉해타협된 문안으로 국내법의 합치 의무를 강화시킬수 없을 바에는 현행대로 유지하는것이 바람직 하다고 함

라. 일본은 11조(가입),14조(수락,발효,등록) 관련 수정안을 회람하였는바, 별첨 팩시 송부함.

(handwritten) 앞에 check (BOP앞으로)

2. 2.19-21 제 3차 회의에서의 MTO 협정에 부속될 법률문제 관련 논의결과를 정리한 사무국 비공식문서와 갯트 관련 법률문서 LIST 가 배포되었는바, 금파편 송부함.

3. 의장은 예정대로 제 4차회의를 3.3-6간 개최되어 통합분쟁해결 절차에 관한 SINGLETEXT 와 공통문제(CROSS-CUTTING ISSUES)를 논의할 예정이며 3.16 주간에 비공식 회의를 개최하여 CROSS-CUTTING ISSUES 와 MTO협정 문안에 대해 추가 논의할 계획이라 함.

첨부: 1. MTO 협정 5조 관련 홍콩제안
   2. MTO 협정 16조관련 카나다 제안
   3. MTO 협정 11조, 14조 관련 일본제안
   (GVW(F)-0141).끝
   (대사 박수길-국장)

주 제 네 바 대 표 부

04

번 호 : GVW(F) - 0141   년월일 :2022.8   시간 : 21:00

수 신 : 장   관 (통기, 경기원)

발 신 : 주 제네바 대사

제 목 : UR 법제화 2급 비공식 회의(2)

총 7 매(표지포함)

보 안 통 제	

외신관 통 제	

배부처	장관실	차관실	일차보	이차보	기획실	의정실	분석관	의전장	아주국	미주국	구주국	중아국	국기국	경제국	통상국	문협국	영교국	총무과	감사관	공보관	연구원	청와대	총리실	안기부	공보처	경기인	상공부
														0											1	

0070

<u>Proposal by Hong Kong</u>

<u>Article V</u>

1.   The MTO shall have a Ministerial Conference under which there shall be a General Council, a Dispute Settlement Body and a Trade policy Review Body. Under the General Council, there shall be a Council for Goods, a Council for Services, a Council for TRIPs (hereinafter referred to as the "Special Councils"), a Committee on Budget, Finance and Administration, a Committee on Trade and Development, a Balance of Payments Committee and other subsidiary bodies established by the General Council it deems appropriate. Each of these bodies shall be open to representatives of all the members. There shall also be a secretariat.

2.   All powers conferred by this Agreement and the Multilateral Trade Agreements shall be vested in the Ministerial Conference. The powers conferred by the Plurilateral Trade Agreements in Annex 4 shall be vested in the competent bodies established in those Agreements. The Ministerial Conference shall meet at least once every two years.

3.   The Ministerial Conference shall also have the power to launch further multilateral trade negotiations as appropriate, and decide on the implementation of results negotiated among and adopted by members of the MTO.

FA1/fa-hkg
27 February 1992

0071

Article XVI:1

Proposed redraft by Canada:

"The MTO shall be guided by the practice, experience, and other interpretative materials of the General Agreement on Tariffs and Trade (1947) and its associated legal instruments, including the Tokyo Round Agreements and Arrangements, in carrying out its functions and tasks, so as to promote continuity of interpretation and practice between the GATT (1947) and the MTO. Insofar as practicable, decisions of the MTO shall be taken by consensus, following the practice of the GATT (1947)."

FA/fa-can

0072

28 February 1992

Proposals by Japan

Article IIIbis (former Article XI)
Membership

1.   Contracting parties to the General Agreement on Tariffs and Trade of
30 October 1947, and the European Communities, which accept this Agreement
and the Multilateral Trade Agreements in accordance with Article XIV, shall
become original Members of the MTO.

2.   Membership is open to all other States and separate customs
territories possessing full autonomy in the conduct of their external
commercial relations and of the matters provided for in this Agreement and
the Multilateral Trade Agreements. They shall become Members by accession
in accordance with Article XIVbis.

fa-jap

0073

- 2 -

Article XIV
Acceptance and entry into force

1. This Agreement shall be open for acceptance, by signature or otherwise, as from 1 November 1992 until two years after the date of its entry into force pursuant to paragraph 2 below, unless otherwise decided by the Implementing Conference or the subsequent meeting provided for in the Final Act Embodying the Results of the Uruguay Round of Multilateral Trade Negotiations, to Uruguay Round participants that qualify under paragraph 1 of Article IIIbis.

2. The date of entry into force of this Agreement shall be set by the Implementing Conference or the subsequent meeting referred to in paragraph 1 above.

3. This Agreement shall enter into force:

    (1) For the participants accepting this Agreement before or on the date set out in paragraph 2, on that date;

    (2) For the participants accepting this Agreement after the date set out in paragraph 2, on the thirtieth day following their acceptance.

4. The entry into force of the Multilateral Trade Agreements shall be governed by the paragraphs 1 to 3 above.

5. In the case of any concession or other obligations in the Multilateral Trade Agreements, which the participants shall implement according to a certain time schedule, including in the case of transitional provisions, such a time schedule shall be deemed to begin on the date set out in paragraph 2, irrespective of the date of entry into force of this Agreement for each participant, unless otherwise expressly provided in the Multilateral Trade Agreements.

fa-jap

0074

- 3 -

Article XIVbis (former Article XII)

Accession

1.   ...

2.   ...

fa-jap

0075

- 4 -

Article XIVter (former paragraph 3 of Article XIV)
Depository

1.   Prior to entry into force of this Agreement, the original texts of
this Agreement and Multilateral Trade Agreements shall be deposited with
the Director-General to the CONTRACTING PARTIES of the General Agreement on
Tariffs and Trade, in his capacity as depository of the Uruguay Round
Results. He shall promptly furnish certified true copies thereof and a
notification of each acceptance and accession pursuant to the provisions of
Articles XIV and XIVbis to each Uruguay Round participant.

2.   The original texts of this Agreement and the Multilateral Trade
Agreements shall, upon entry into force of this Agreement, be deposited
with the Director-General of the MTO, as well as any amendment thereto and,
if any, new agreements negotiated under the authority of the Ministerial
Conference conferred by paragraph 2 of Article V and any amendment thereto.

fa-jap

0076

외 무 부

종   별 :

번   호 : GVW-0500   일   시 : 92 0304 1600

수   신 : 장관(봉기,경기원) 사본:박수길대사

발   신 : 주 제네바 대사대리

제   목 : UR 법제화 그룹 제 4차 공식회의

표제 회의가 3.3(화) MATHUR 의장 주재로 개최된바, 동결과 아래 보고함. (이성주 참사관참석)

1. 회의 진행방식

0 회의 벽두 의장이 금차 회의 2개의제(분쟁해결 및 공통사항)에 대해 참가국의 GENERAL COMMENT 만 청취하고 분쟁해결에 관해서는 3.4-6 간 비공식회의 형식으로 실질토의를 해나가며, 공통사항에 대한 실질토의는 사무국 준비 및 참가국의 추가 검토를 위해 3.23 예정 제 5차 회의에서 취급하기로 제의함에 따라, 동 의제대로 합의됨.(비공식회의결과 청취를 위한 금주중 1회정도의 공식회의 소집 가능성을 열어둠)

0 또한 필요시 제 5차 회의에 앞서 3.16 시작 주간에 다시 한차례 비공식 협의를 갖고 MTO 협정 또는 분쟁해결 문제 토의를 계속할 가능성도 시사함.

2. 봉합 분쟁해결

0 사무국은 기 배포한 비공식 문서(332 및 332-A)에 추가하여 별첨 비공식문서 (387)을 추가로 배포함.

0 사무국은 332 와 관련 본 그룹의 토의를 요하는 사항은 BRACKET 또는 주석 형태로 표시되었음을 설명함.

0 일부국이 GENERAL COMMENT 형식으로 제기한 주요사항은 아래와 같음.

- 개별 협정상의 특별 규정에 대한 면밀한 검토 필요성(미국, 카나다, 인도)

- 66년도 절차에 관한 1.12 항 BRACKET 처리에대한 이의 제기(멕시코, 이집트)

- 20.5 항 및 28 페이지 '실질규정상의 상충' 조항이 BRACKET 처리된데 이의 제기(EC)

- 주석 A 가 보조금 문제만 언급한데 대한 의문제기 (인도)- GATT 22조,

통상국   2차보   국기국   경기원

23조에따른 분쟁해결 '표현이 MTOAGREEMENTS 에 따른 분쟁해결'이라는 표현으로 당초대로남아 있는 부분이 공존하고 있는점

- ANNEX 4 협정에 대한 봉합분쟁 해결 절차적용 여부에 대한 추가 검토 필요성(홍콩)

3. 공통사항(CROSS CUTTING ISSUES)

O MATHUR 의장은 92.1.31 배포 ILLUSTRATIVE LIST OFPOINTS (156) D 항의 각 ITEM 을 설명하면서 여타ITEM 은 대부분 MTO 협정 및 MTO 협정과 여타 협정간의 관계 토의시 상당부분 취급되었다고 하고, 특히 4항 A, B 및 실질규정상의 상충 여부에 대한 집중 토의가 필요하다고 언급한후, 이를 위해 사무국이 문제점을 파악(IDENTIFY, LIST 를 작성토록 요청할 계획이라고 설명함.

O 스웨덴만이 GENERAL STATEMENT 를 통해 상계관세 부과와 반덤핑간의 절차 봉일필요성을 언급함. 끝첨부: 1. 사무국 비공식 문서(332)

2. 사무국 비공식 문서(387)

3. 제 4차 회의 봉보 전문(AIR/3296)

(GVW(F)-153)

(차석대사 김삼훈-국장)

주 제 네 바 대 표 부

번 호 : GVW(F) - *0153*　　년월일 : *20304*　　시간 : *1600*

수 신 : 장　　관 (통기, 경기원)

발 신 : 주 제네바대사

제 목 : *GVW-0500 첨부*

총 *37* 매 (표지포함)

보 안 봉 제	

외신과 봉 제	

153-31-1

0079

GATT/AIR/3296   27 FEBRUARY 1992

SUBJECT: URUGUAY ROUND: LEGAL DRAFTING GROUP

1.   THE FOURTH MEETING OF THE LEGAL DRAFTING GROUP WILL BE HELD ON
TUESDAY, 3 MARCH 1992 AT 3 P.M. IN THE CENTRE WILLIAM RAPPARD.   THE MEETING
MAY CONTINUE ON 4, 5 AND 6 MARCH.

2.   THE CHAIRMAN PROPOSES THAT THE MEETING TAKE UP TWO MATTERS:

   (I)   INTEGRATED TEXT ON DISPUTE SETTLEMENT (DRAFT UNDERSTANDING ON
          RULES AND PROCEDURES GOVERNING THE SETTLEMENT OF DISPUTES:
          NOTE BY THE SECRETARIAT OF 21 FEBRUARY 1992);

   (II)   OTHER POINTS COMMON TO A NUMBER OF TEXTS IN MTN.TNC/W/FA
          ("CROSS-CUTTING ISSUES"). (AN ILLUSTRATIVE LIST OF POINTS FOR
          POSSIBLE CONSIDERATION IN THE LEGAL DRAFTING GROUP: NOTE BY
          THE SECRETARIAT OF 31 JANUARY 1992);

3.   SINCE THE THIRD MEETING, THE FOLLOWING NEW DOCUMENTS HAVE BEEN
CIRCULATED:

   (I)   NOTE ON THE THIRD MEETING (MTN.TNC/LD/3);

   (II)   POINTS ARISING FROM THE REVIEW OF RELATIONSHIPS BETWEEN THE
          AGREEMENT ESTABLISHING THE MTO AND OTHER AGREED TEXTS IN THE
          DRAFT FINAL ACT (MTN.TNC/W/FA): INFORMAL NOTE BY THE
          SECRETARIAT DATED 25 FEBRUARY 1992.

   (III) INSTITUTIONAL QUESTIONS RELEVANT TO THE DRAFTING OF THE
          MTO AGREEMENT: INFORMAL NOTE BY THE SECRETARIAT DATED
          26 FEBRUARY 1992.

   (IV)   NOTE ON DISCUSSION OF INSTRUMENTS TO BE ATTACHED TO THE MTO
          AGREEMENT: INFORMAL NOTE BY THE SECRETARIAT DATED 28 FEBRUARY
          1992.

4.   GOVERNMENTS PARTICIPATING IN THE MULTILATERAL TRADE NEGOTIATIONS, AND
WISHING TO BE REPRESENTED AT THIS MEETING, ARE REQUESTED TO INFORM ME OF
THE NAMES OF THEIR REPRESENTATIVES AS SOON AS POSSIBLE.

                                             A. DUNKEL

92-0247

387   3 March 1992

<u>DRAFT DECISION</u>

<u>Application and Review of the Understanding on Rules and Procedures
Governing the Settlement of Disputes
under the Multilateral Trade Organization</u>

The Ministers,

   <u>Agree</u> that existing rules and procedures of the General Agreement on
Tariffs and Trade (GATT) in the field of dispute settlement shall remain in
effect until the date of entry into force of the Understanding on Rules and
Procedures Governing the Settlement of Disputes under the Multilateral
Trade Organization. It is further agreed that the Understanding shall be
applied only in respect of new requests for consultations made on or after
the date of entry into force of said Understanding. With regard to
disputes for which the request for consultations was made before the date
of entry into force of said Understanding, it is agreed that GATT dispute
settlement rules and procedures in effect immediately prior to the date of
entry into force of said Understanding shall continue to apply unless the
parties to a dispute agree otherwise. In respect of outstanding disputes,
raised under the 1947 General Agreement on Tariffs and Trade, the rôle of
the GATT Council of Representatives shall be assumed by the Dispute
Settlement Body to the extent that the parties to the dispute are members
of the Dispute Settlement Body. If one or more of the parties to the
dispute are not members of the Dispute Settlement Body, the GATT Council of
Representatives shall remain in operation for the purpose of dealing with
such disputes only. In respect of outstanding disputes raised under the
1979 MTN Agreements and Arrangements, the rôle of the relevant Committees
or Councils shall continue for the purpose of dealing with outstanding
disputes:

   <u>Agree</u> that a full review of dispute settlement rules and procedures
under the Multilateral Trade Organization, as set out in said
Understanding, shall be completed within four years after its entry into
force, and a decision shall be taken on the occasion of the first meeting
at Ministerial level after the completion of the review, whether to
continue, modify or terminate such dispute settlement rules and procedures.

0081

332

DRAFT UNDERSTANDING ON RULES AND PROCEDURES
GOVERNING THE SETTLEMENT OF DISPUTES

The Draft Understanding on Rules and Procedures Governing the Settlement of Disputes under the Multilateral Trade Organization which encompasses Sections S and T of the Draft Final Act (MTN.TNC/W/FA) is reproduced hereunder. This is a preliminary text. As indicated in the text, this draft is subject to further amendments or corrections. The full text of Appendix 2 will be supplied later.

0082

753-37-G

332

UNDERSTANDING ON RULES AND PROCEDURES GOVERNING
THE SETTLEMENT OF DISPUTES

1. Coverage and Application

1.1 These rules and procedures shall apply to disputes brought
pursuant to the consultation and dispute settlement provisions of
the Multilateral Trade Organization (MTO) agreements listed in
Appendix 1 to this Understanding, hereinafter referred to as the
"covered agreements."

1.2 These rules and procedures shall apply subject to any
special or additional provisions on dispute settlement contained
in the covered agreements. Such special or additional procedures
are identified in Appendix 2 to this Understanding. To the
extent that there is a difference between the rules and
procedures of this Understanding and the special or additional
rules and procedures set forth in a covered agreement, the
special or additional rules and procedures in the covered
agreement shall prevail.[a]

2. Administration

2.1 The Dispute Settlement Body (DSB)[b] established pursuant to
the Agreement Establishing the MTO shall administer these rules
and procedures and, except as otherwise provided in a covered
agreement, the consultation and dispute settlement provisions of
the covered agreements.[c] Accordingly, the DSB shall have the
authority to establish panels, adopt panel and Appellate Body
reports, maintain surveillance of implementation of rulings and
recommendations, and authorize suspension of concessions and
other obligations under the covered agreements.[1]

---

[a] This needs to be reviewed in light of the Subsidies
agreement provisions.

[b] The name of this Body may be changed.

[c] This needs to be reviewed in light of the Subsidies
agreement provisions.

[1] [With respect to disputes arising under covered
agreements contained in Annex 4 to the MTO agreement, the term
"member" as used herein shall refer only to those members that
are parties to the relevant Annex 4 agreements. Where the DSB
administers the dispute settlement provisions of a covered
agreement contained in Annex 4, only those members that are
parties to that agreement may participate in decisions or actions
taken by the DSB with respect to that dispute.]

0083

- 2 -

2.2 The DSB shall inform the relevant MTO councils and committees of any developments in disputes related to provisions of the respective covered agreements.

2.3 The DSB shall meet as often as necessary to carry out its functions within the time-frames provided in this Understanding.

2.4 Where the rules and procedures of this Understanding provide for the DSB to take a decision, it shall do so by consensus.[2]

[If the above sections are included, the following portions drawn from section T would be deleted, since the Dispute Settlement Body will be established in the MTO Agreement, not this text, and since coverage and application are covered above:

[Dispute Settlement Body

1.   The Members of the Multilateral Trade Organization this Understanding agree that the rules and procedures of this Understanding shall apply to disputes brought under the Agreements listed in Annexes 1 and 4 of the MTO to this Understanding ("the covered Agreements"), subject to any special or additional provisions on dispute settlement contained in these covered Agreements.

2.   Members hereby establish a Dispute Settlement Body to exercise the authority of the General Council and the Councils and Committees of the covered Agreements regarding the implementation of the rules and procedures set out in this Understanding for disputes arising under the covered Agreements. It shall have the authority to establish panels, adopt panel and Appellate Body reports, maintain surveillance of implementation of rulings and recommendations, and authorize suspension of concessions and other obligations under the covered Agreements.

3.   Membership in the Dispute Settlement Body shall be open to all members of the MTO. Councils and Committees charged with the administration of the covered Agreements shall be fully informed of developments in disputes involving obligations under the Agreements that they administer.

4.   The Dispute Settlement Body shall meet as necessary to carry out its functions within the time-frame provided in this Understanding. The Dispute Settlement Body shall follow The procedures outlined in this Understanding apply to the resolution of disputes, except where special or

---

[2] The Dispute Settlement Body shall be deemed to have decided by consensus if no member of the Dispute Settlement Body formally objects to the decision.

0084

- 3 -

additional rules and procedures exist in a particular covered Agreement. Such special or additional procedures are set out in Appendix 2 to this Understanding. To the extent that there is a difference between the said rules and procedures of this Understanding and the other rules and procedures set forth in a covered Agreement, the those other rules and procedures of the covered Agreement shall prevail. In disputes involving provisions under more than one covered Agreement, if there is a conflict between special or additional rules and procedures of such Agreements under review, and where the parties to the dispute cannot agree on rules and procedures within twenty days of the establishment of the panel, the Chairman of the Dispute Settlement Body, in consultation with the parties to the dispute, shall determine the rules and procedures to be followed within ten days after a request by either member. The Chairman of the Dispute Settlement Body shall be guided by·the principle that special or additional rules and procedures should be used where possible, and the rules and procedures set out in this Understanding should be used to the extent necessary to avoid conflict.]

[The following provisions will require renumbering. For the present they retain the paragraph numbers in section S of the Draft Final Act for ease of reference.]

1. General Provisions

1.1 [The members of the MTO (hereinafter referred to as "members") affirm their adherence to the basic mechanism for the management of disputes heretofore applied by the General Agreement on Tariffs and Trade (GATT [1947]), as further elaborated and modified herein.][d]

1.2 The dispute settlement system is a central element in providing security and predictability to the multilateral trading system. Members recognize that it serves to preserve the rights and obligations of members under the covered agreements, and to clarify the existing provisions of those agreements in accordance with customary rules of interpretation of international law. Recommendations and rulings of the DSB cannot add to or diminish the rights and obligations provided in the covered agreements.

1.3 The prompt settlement of situations in which a member considers that any benefits accruing to it directly or indirectly under the covered agreements are being impaired by measures taken by another member is essential to the effective functioning of

---

[d] Consider deletion of this provision, and define "members" in the following paragraph.

0085

the MTO and the maintenance of a proper balance between the
rights and obligations of members.

1.4   Recommendations or rulings made by the DSB shall be aimed at
achieving a satisfactory settlement of the matter in accordance
with **this Understanding and under the covered agreements.**

1.5   All solutions to matters formally raised under **these
procedures with respect to any of the covered agreements,**
including arbitration awards, shall be consistent with **those
agreements** and shall not nullify or impair benefits accruing to
any **member** under **those agreements,** nor impede the attainment of
any objective of **those agreements.**

1.6 Mutually agreed solutions to matters formally raised under
the consultation and dispute settlement provisions of the covered
agreements shall be notified to the DSB **and the relevant councils
and committees,** where any member may raise any point relating
thereto.

1.7   Before bringing a case, **a member** shall exercise its judgment
as to whether action under **these procedures** would be fruitful.
The aim of the [MTO] [DSB] is to secure a positive solution to a
dispute. A solution mutually acceptable to the parties to a dispute and consistent with **the covered agreements** is clearly to be
preferred. In the absence of a mutually agreed solution, the
first objective of **the dispute settlement mechanism** is usually to
secure the withdrawal of the measures concerned if these are
found to be inconsistent with **the provisions of any of the
covered agreements.** The provision of compensation should be
resorted to only if the immediate withdrawal of the measure is
impracticable and as a temporary measure pending the withdrawal
of the measures which are inconsistent with **a covered agreement.**
The last resort which this Understanding provides to the **member**
invoking this procedure is the possibility of suspending the
application of concessions or other obligations **under the covered
agreements** on a discriminatory basis vis-à-vis the other **member,**
subject to authorization by the DSB of such measures.

1.8   In cases where there is a violation of the obligations assumed under **a covered agreement,** the action is considered <u>pri-
ma facie</u> to constitute a case of nullification or impairment.
This means that there is normally a presumption that a breach of
the rules has an adverse impact on other **parties to that covered
agreement,** and in such cases, it shall be up to the **member**
against whom the complaint has been brought to rebut the claim of
nullification or impairment.

1.9   The provisions of this Understanding are without prejudice
to the rights of members to seek authoritative interpretation of
provisions of **a covered agreement** through joint action under the
MTO agreement or a covered agreement.

- 5 -

1.10 It is understood that requests for conciliation and the use of the dispute settlement procedures should not be intended or considered as contentious acts and that, if disputes arise, all members will engage in these procedures in good faith in an effort to resolve the disputes. It is also understood that complaints and counter-complaints in regard to distinct matters should not be linked.

1.11 This Understanding shall be applied only with respect to new requests for consultations under the consultation provisions of the covered agreements made on or after the date of entry into force of this Understanding. With respect to disputes for which the request for consultations was made under the General Agreement on Tariffs and Trade dated 30 October 1947 or under any other predecessor agreement to the covered agreements before the date of entry into force of this Understanding, the relevant dispute settlement rules and procedures in effect immediately prior to the date of entry into force of this Understanding shall continue to apply.[e]

1.12 [Notwithstanding paragraph 1.12 above, if a complaint is brought by a developing contracting party, that contracting party may choose to apply, as an alternative to this Understanding, the provisions of the Decision of the CONTRACTING PARTIES of 5 April 1966 (BISD 14S/18), instead of the provisions of this Understanding. In that event, the same procedures shall apply that would have applied to cases brought pursuant to the 1966 Decision immediately prior to the date of entry into force of this Understanding, including the procedures contained in the Decision of the Council of 12 April 1989 (BISD 36S/61).][f]

2. Consultations

2.1 The members reaffirm their resolve to strengthen and improve the effectiveness of consultative procedures employed by members.

2.2 Each member undertakes to accord sympathetic consideration to and afford adequate opportunity for consultation regarding any representations made by another member concerning measures

---

[e] This provision will require transition provisions for the existing GATT Council.

[f] This provision, taken verbatim from Section S, must be modified before it can be included in an integrated text.

- 6 -

affecting the operation of the **covered agreements** taken within the territory of the former.[3]

2.3 If a **request for consultations** is made pursuant to a covered **agreement, the member** to which the request is made shall, unless otherwise mutually agreed, reply to the request within ten days after its receipt and shall enter into consultations in good faith within a period of no more than thirty days from the date of the request, with a view to reaching a mutually satisfactory solution. If the **member** does not respond within ten days, or does not enter into consultations within a period of no more than thirty days, or a period otherwise mutually agreed, from the date of the request, then the **member** that requested the holding of consultations may proceed directly to request the establishment of a panel.

2.4 In the course of consultations in accordance with the provisions of a covered agreement, before resorting to further action under this Understanding, members should attempt to obtain satisfactory adjustment of the matter.

2.5 Consultations shall be confidential, and without prejudice to the rights of either member in any further proceedings.

2.6 If the consultations fail to settle a dispute within sixty days after the request for consultations, the complaining party may request the establishment of a panel. The complaining party may request a panel during the sixty-day period if the **consulting** parties jointly consider that consultations have failed to settle the dispute.

2.7 **All such requests** for consultations shall be notified to the **DSB and the relevant councils and committees** by the member which requests consultations. Any request for consultations shall be submitted in writing and shall give the reasons for the request, including identification of the measures at issue and an indication of the legal basis for the complaint. [**Consider moving this paragraph up to follow 2.3.**]

2.8 In cases of urgency, including those which concern perishable goods, **members** shall enter into consultations within a period of no more than ten days from the date of the request. If the consultations have failed to settle the dispute within a

---

[3] Where the provisions of any other covered agreement concerning measures taken by regional or local governments or authorities within the territory of a member contain provisions different from the provisions of this paragraph, the provisions of such other **covered agreement** shall prevail.

0088

period of twenty days after the request, the complaining party may request the establishment of a panel.

2.9 In cases of urgency, including those which concern perishable goods, the parties to the dispute, panels and the appellate body shall make every effort to accelerate the proceedings to the greatest extent possible.

2.10 During consultations members should give special attention to the particular problems and interests of developing members.

2.11 Whenever a member other than the consulting members considers that it has a substantial trade interest in consultations being held pursuant to Article XXII:1 of the GATT [1993],[9] such member may notify the consulting members and the DSB, within ten days of the circulation of the request for consultations under said Article, of its desire to be joined in the consultations. Such member shall be joined in the consultations, provided that the member to which the request for consultations was addressed agrees that the claim of substantial interest is well-founded. In that event they shall so inform the DSB. If the request to be joined in the consultations is not accepted, the applicant member shall be free to request consultations under Article XXII:1 or XXIII:1 of the GATT [1993].

3. <u>Good Offices, Conciliation and Mediation</u>

3.1 Good offices, conciliation and mediation are procedures that are undertaken voluntarily if the parties to the dispute so agree.

3.2 Proceedings involving good offices, conciliation and mediation, and in particular positions taken by the parties to the dispute during these proceedings, shall be confidential, and without prejudice to the rights of either party in any further proceedings under these procedures.

3.3 Good offices, conciliation and mediation may be requested at any time by any party to a dispute. They may begin at any time and be terminated at any time. Once terminated, the complaining party can then proceed with a request for the establishment of a panel.

3.4 When good offices, conciliation or mediation are entered into within sixty days of a request for consultations, the complaining party must allow a period of sixty days from the date of the request for consultations before requesting the

---

[9] Review this in light of any corresponding provisions in the covered agreements.

- 8 -

establishment of a panel. The complaining party may request a panel during the sixty days if the parties to the dispute jointly consider that the good offices, conciliation or mediation process has failed to settle the dispute.

3.5 If the parties to a dispute agree, procedures for good offices, conciliation or mediation may continue while the panel process proceeds.

3.6 The Director-General may, acting in an _ex officio_ capacity, offer his or her good offices, conciliation or mediation with the view to assisting members to settle a dispute.

4. **Establishment of Panels**

4.1   If the complaining party so requests, a panel shall be established at the latest at the DSB meeting following that at which the request first appears as an item on the DSB's agenda, unless at that meeting the DSB decides by consensus not to establish a panel.

4.2 The request for a panel shall be made in writing. It shall indicate whether consultations were held, identify the specific measures at issue and provide a brief summary of the legal basis of the complaint sufficient to present the problem clearly. In case the applicant requests the establishment of a panel with other than standard terms of reference, the written request shall include the proposed text of special terms of reference.

5. **Terms of Reference of Panels**

5.1 Panels shall have the following terms of reference unless the parties to the dispute agree otherwise within twenty days from the establishment of the panel:

"To examine, in the light of the relevant provisions in [the covered agreement(s) cited by the parties to the dispute,] the matter referred to the DSB by [name of party] in document DS/   and to make such findings as will assist the DSB in making recommendations or in giving the rulings provided for in the agreement(s)."

---

⁴   If the complaining party so requests, a meeting of the Dispute Settlement Body shall be convened for this purpose within fifteen days of the request, provided that at least ten days' advance notice of the meeting is given.

/0090

- 9 -

5.2 Panels shall address the relevant provisions of any covered agreement cited by the parties to the dispute.

5.3 In establishing a panel, the DSB may authorize its Chairman to draw up the terms of reference of the panel in consultation with the parties to the dispute subject to the provisions of subparagraph 1 above. The terms of reference thus drawn up shall be circulated to all members. If other than standard terms of reference are agreed upon, any member may raise any point relating thereto in the DSB.

6. Composition of Panels

6.1 Panels shall be composed of well-qualified governmental and/or non-governmental individuals, including persons who have served on or presented a case to a panel, served as a representative of an MTO member or of a contracting party to the GATT [1947] or as a representative to a council or committee of any covered agreement or its predecessor agreement, or in the Secretariat, taught or published on international trade law or policy, or served as a senior trade policy official of a member.

6.2 Panel members should be selected with a view to ensuring the independence of the members, a sufficiently diverse background and a wide spectrum of experience.

6.3 Citizens of members whose governments[5] are parties to the dispute shall not serve on a panel concerned with that dispute, unless the parties to the dispute agree otherwise.

6.4 To assist in the selection of panelists, the secretariat shall maintain an indicative list of governmental and non-governmental individuals possessing the qualifications outlined in paragraph 1 above, from which panelists may be drawn as appropriate. That list shall replace the roster of non-governmental panelists that was established by the GATT CONTRACTING PARTIES on 30 December 1984, and other rosters and indicative lists established under any of the covered agreements, but shall include the names of persons on those rosters and indicative lists at the time of entry into force of this Understanding. Members may periodically suggest names of governmental and non-governmental individuals for inclusion on the indicative list, providing relevant information on their knowledge of international trade and of the sectors or subject matter of the covered agreements, and those names shall be added to the list upon approval by the DSB. For each of the panelists

---

[5] In the case customs unions or common markets are parties to a dispute, this provision applies to citizens of all member countries of the customs unions or common markets.

0.091,

- 10 -

on the list, the list shall indicate specific areas of experience or expertise of the individuals in the sectors or subject matter of the covered agreements.

6.5 Panels shall be composed of three panelists unless the parties to the dispute agree, within ten days from the establishment of the panel, to a panel composed of five panelists. Members shall be informed promptly of the composition of the Panel.

6.6 The Secretariat shall propose nominations for the panel to the parties to the dispute. The parties to the dispute shall not oppose nominations except for compelling reasons.

6.7 If there is no agreement on the panelists within twenty days from the establishment of a panel, at the request of either party, the Chairman of the DSB, in agreement with the Chairman of the relevant committee or council, shall form the panel by appointing the panelists whom he or she considers most appropriate in accordance with any relevant special or additional procedure of the covered agreement, after consulting with the parties to the dispute. The Chairman of the DSB shall inform the members of the composition of the panel thus formed no later than ten days from the date he or she receives such a request.

6.8 Members shall undertake, as a general rule, to permit their officials to serve as panelists.

6.9 Panelists shall serve in their individual capacities and not as government representatives, nor as representatives of any organization. Governments shall therefore not give them instructions nor seek to influence them as individuals with regard to matters before a panel.

6.10 When a dispute is between a developing member and a developed member the panel shall, if the developing member so requests, include at least one panelist from a developing member.

6.11 Where panelists are not drawn from Geneva, any expenses, including travel and subsistence allowance, shall be met from the MTO budget.

7. Procedures for Multiple Complainants

7.1 Where more than one member requests the establishment of a panel related to the same matter, a single panel may be established to examine these complaints taking into account the rights of all members concerned. A single panel should be established to examine such complaints whenever feasible.

.0092

- 11 -

7.2 The single panel will organize its examination and present its findings to the DSB so that the rights which the parties to the dispute would have enjoyed had separate panels examined the complaints are in no way impaired. If one of the parties to the dispute so requests, the panel will submit separate reports on the dispute concerned. The written submissions by each of the complainants will be made available to the other complainants, and each complainant will have the right to be present when one of the other complainants presents its view to the panel.

7.3 If more than one panel is established to examine the complaints related to the same matter, to the greatest extent possible the same persons shall serve as panelists on each of the separate panels and the timetable for the panel process in such disputes shall be harmonized.

8. Third Parties

8.1 The interests of the parties to a dispute and those of other parties to the covered agreements cited by the parties to the dispute shall be fully taken into account during the panel process.

8.2 Any party to a covered agreement at issue in a dispute, having a substantial interest in a matter before a panel and having notified its interest to the DSB, (hereinafter referred to as a "third party") shall have an opportunity to be heard by the panel and to make written submissions to the panel. These submissions shall also be given to the parties to the dispute and shall be reflected in the panel report.

8.3 Such third parties shall receive submissions of the parties to the dispute for the first meeting of the panel.

8.4 If a third party considers a measure already the subject of a panel nullifies or impairs benefits accruing to it under any covered agreement, that member may have recourse to normal dispute settlement procedures under this Understanding. Such a dispute shall be referred to the original panel wherever possible.

9. Function of Panels

9.1 The function of panels is to assist the DSB in discharging its responsibilities under this Understanding and the covered agreements. Accordingly, a panel should make an objective assessment of the matter before it, including an objective assessment of the facts of the case and the applicability of and conformity with the covered agreements and make such other findings as will assist the DSB in making recommendations or in

0093

- 12 -

giving the rulings provided for in the covered agreements. In this connection, panels should consult regularly with the parties to the dispute and give them adequate opportunity to develop a mutually satisfactory solution.

10. Panel Procedures

10.1 Panels shall follow the Working Procedures appended hereto unless the panel decides otherwise after consulting the parties to the dispute.

10.2 Panel procedures should provide sufficient flexibility so as to ensure high-quality panel reports, while not unduly delaying the panel process.

10.3 After consulting the parties to the dispute, the panelists shall, as soon as practicable and whenever possible within one week after the composition and terms of reference of the panel have been agreed upon, fix the timetable for the panel process, taking into account the provisions of paragraph [2.9], if relevant.

10.4 In determining the timetable for the panel process, the panel shall provide sufficient time for the parties to the dispute to prepare their submissions.

10.5 Panels should set precise deadlines for written submissions by the parties and the parties should respect those deadlines.

10.6 Each party to the dispute shall deposit its written submissions with the Secretariat for immediate transmission to the panel and to the other party or parties to the dispute. The complaining party shall submit its first submission in advance of the responding party's first submission unless the panel decides, in fixing the timetable referred to in the subparagraph 3 above and after consultations with the parties to the dispute, that the parties should submit their first submissions simultaneously. When there are sequential arrangements for the deposit of first submissions, the panel shall establish a firm time period for receipt of the responding party's submission. Any subsequent written submissions shall be submitted simultaneously.

10.7 The opinions expressed by the individual panelists on the matters shall be anonymous.

10.8 Where the parties to the dispute have failed to develop a mutually satisfactory solution, the panel shall submit its findings in a written form. In such cases, the report of a panel shall set out the findings of fact, the applicability of relevant provisions and the basic rationale behind any findings and recommendations that it makes. Where a settlement of the matter among

0094

the parties to the dispute has been found, the report of the panel shall be confined to a brief description of the case and to reporting that a solution has been reached.

10.9 In order to make the procedures more efficient, the period in which the panel shall conduct its examination, from the time the composition and terms of reference of the panel have been agreed upon to the time when the final report is provided to the parties to the dispute, shall, as a general rule, not exceed six months. In cases of urgency, including those relating to perishable goods, the panel shall aim to provide its report to the parties to the dispute within three months.

10.10 When the panel considers that it cannot provide its report within six months, or within three months in cases of urgency, it shall inform the DSB in writing of the reasons for the delay together with an estimate of the period within which it will submit its report. In no case should the period from the establishment of the panel to the submission of the report to the members exceed nine months.

10.11 In the context of consultations involving a measure taken by a developing member, the parties may agree to extend the periods established in paragraphs [2.6] and [2.8]. If, after the relevant period has elapsed, the consulting parties cannot agree that the consultations have concluded, the Chairman of the DSB shall decide, after consultation with the parties, whether to extend the relevant period and, if so, for how long. In addition, in examining a complaint against a developing member, the panel shall accord sufficient time for the developing member to prepare and present its argumentation. The provisions of paragraphs [18.1] and [19.4] are not affected by any action pursuant to this paragraph.

10.12 Where one or more of the parties is a developing member, the panel's report shall explicitly indicate the form in which account has been taken of relevant provisions on differential and more-favourable treatment for developing members that form part of the covered agreements which have been raised by the developing member in the course of the dispute settlement procedures.

10.13 The panel may suspend its work at any time at the request of the complaining party for a period not to exceed twelve months. In the event of such a suspension, the time frames set out in paragraphs [10.9], [10.10], [18.1] and [19.4] shall be extended by the amount of time that the work was suspended. If the work of the panel has been suspended for more than twelve months, the authority for establishment of the panel shall lapse.

- 14 -

11. Right to Seek Information

11.1 Each panel shall have the right to seek information and technical advice from any individual or body which it deems appropriate. However, before a panel seeks such information or advice from any individual or body within the jurisdiction of a member it shall inform the government of that member. Any party should respond promptly and fully to any request by a panel for such information as the panel considers necessary and appropriate. Confidential information which is provided shall not be revealed without formal authorization from the party providing the information.

11.2 Panels may seek information from any relevant source and may consult experts to obtain their opinion on certain aspects of the matter.

12. Confidentiality

12.1 Written memoranda submitted to the panel or the Appellate Body shall be considered confidential, but shall be made available to the parties to the dispute.[h]

12.2 Panel deliberations shall be secret.

12.3 The reports of panels shall be drafted in the absence of the parties in the light of the information and the statements made.

13. Interim Review Stage

13.1 Following the consideration of rebuttal submissions and oral arguments, the panel shall submit the descriptive (factual and argument) sections of its draft report to the parties. Within a period of time set by the panel, the parties shall submit their comments in writing.

13.2 Following the deadline for receipt of comments from the parties, the panel shall issue an interim report to the parties, including both the descriptive sections and the panel's findings and conclusions. Within a period of time set by the panel, a party may submit a written request for the panel to review precise aspects of the interim report prior to circulation of the final report to the members. At the request of a party, the panel shall hold a further meeting with the parties on the issues

---

[h] This provision should refer to both the panel and Appellate Body and be moved to follow paragraph 16.

identified in the written comments. If no comments are received from any party within the comment period, the interim report shall be considered the final panel report and circulated promptly to the members.

13.3 The findings of the final panel report shall include a discussion of the arguments made at the interim review stage. The interim review stage shall be conducted within the time period set out in paragraph [10.9].

14. Adoption of Panel Reports

14.1 In order to provide sufficient time for the members of the DSB to consider panel reports, the reports shall not be considered for adoption by the DSB until twenty days after they have been issued to the members.

14.2 Members having objections to panel reports shall give written reasons to explain their objections for circulation at least ten days prior to the DSB meeting at which the panel report will be considered.

14.3 The parties to a dispute shall have the right to participate fully in the consideration of the panel report by the DSB, and their views shall be fully recorded.

14.4 Within sixty days of the issuance of a panel report to the members, the report shall be adopted at a DSB meeting[6] unless one of the parties formally notifies the DSB of its decision to appeal or the DSB decides by consensus not to adopt the report. If a party has notified its intention to appeal, the report by the panel shall not be considered for adoption by the DSB until after completion of the appeal. This adoption procedure is without prejudice to the right of members to express their views on a panel report.

15. Appellate Review

Standing Appellate Body

15.1 A standing Appellate Body shall be established by the DSB. The Appellate Body shall hear appeals from panel cases. It shall

---

[6] If a meeting of the DSB is not scheduled within this period at a time that enables the requirement of paragraphs [14.1] and [14.4] to be met, a meeting of the DSB shall be held for this purpose.

0097

- 16 -

be composed of seven persons, three of whom shall serve on any
one case. Members of the pool shall serve in rotation.'

15.2 **The DSB shall appoint persons to serve on the Appellate
Body for a four-year term, and each person** may be reappointed
once. However, the terms of three of the seven persons appointed
immediately after the entry into force of this Understanding
shall expire at the end of two years, to be determined by lot.
Vacancies shall be filled as they arise. A person appointed to
replace a person whose term of office has not expired shall hold
office for the remainder of his or her predecessor's term.

15.3 **The Appellate Body shall be comprised of** persons of
recognized authority, with demonstrated expertise in law,
international trade and the **subject matter of the covered
agreements** generally. They shall be unaffiliated with any
government. The Appellate Body membership shall be broadly
representative of membership in the MTO. All persons serving on
the Appellate Body shall be available at all times and on short
notice, and shall stay abreast of **dispute settlement** activities
and other relevant activities of the MTO. They shall not
participate in the consideration of any disputes that would
create a direct or indirect conflict of interest.

15.4 Only parties to the dispute, not third parties, may appeal
a panel decision. Third parties which have notified the DSB of a
substantial interest in the matter pursuant to paragraph [8.2]
may make written submissions to, and be given an opportunity to
be heard by, the Appellate Body.

15.5 As a general rule, the proceedings shall not exceed sixty
days from the date a party formally notifies its intent to appeal
to the date the Appellate Body issues its decision. In fixing
its timetable the Appellate Body shall take into account the
provisions of paragraph [2.9], if revelant. When the appellate
body considers that it cannot provide its report within sixty
days, it shall inform the DSB in writing of the reasons for the
delay together with an estimate of the period within which it
will submit its report. In no case shall the proceedings exceed
ninety days.

15.6 An appeal shall be limited to issues of law covered in the
panel report and legal interpretation developed by the panel.

15.7 The Appellate Body shall be provided with appropriate
administrative and legal support as it requires.

' This subparagraph may need further clarification.

0098

- 17 -

15.8 Where persons serving on the Appellate Body are not drawn from Geneva, any expenses, including travel and subsistence allowance, shall be met from the MTO budget.

Procedures for Appellate Review

15.9 Working procedures shall be drawn up by the Appellate Body in consultation with the Chairman of the DSB and the Director-General, and communicated to the members for their information.

15.10 The proceedings of the Appellate Body shall be confidential.

15.11 Opinions expressed in the Appellate Body report by individual persons serving on the Appellate Body shall be anonymous.

15.12 The Appellate Body shall address each of the issues raised in accordance with paragraph [15.6] during the appellate proceeding.

15.13 The Appellate Body may uphold, modify or reverse the legal findings and conclusions of the panel.

Adoption of Appellate Reports

15.14 An appellate report shall be adopted by the DSB and unconditionally accepted by the parties to the dispute unless the DSB decides by consensus not to adopt the appellate report within thirty days following its issuance to the members.[7] This adoption procedure is without prejudice to the right of members to express their views on an appellate report.

16. Ex Parte Communications

16.1 No ex parte communications are permitted between the panel or Appellate Body and the parties to the dispute concerning matters under consideration by the panel or Appellate Body.

[Insert here paragraph 12.1, covering both panels and the Appellate Body.]

17. Panel and Appellate Body Recommendations

17.1 Where a panel or the Appellate Body concludes that a measure is inconsistent with a covered agreement, it shall

---

[7] If a meeting of the DSB is not scheduled during this period, such a meeting of the DSB shall be held for this purpose.

0099

recommend that the member concerned[8] bring the measure into conformity with that Agreement[9]. In addition to its recommendations, the panel or Appellate Body may suggest ways in which the member concerned could implement the recommendations.

17.2 In accordance with paragraph [1.2] above, in their findings and recommendations, the panel and Appellate Body cannot add to or diminish the rights and obligations provided in the covered agreements.

18. Time-Frame for DSB Decisions

18.1 Unless otherwise agreed to by the parties to the dispute, the period from the establishment of the Panel by the DSB until the DSB considers the panel or appellate report for adoption shall not as a general rule exceed nine months where the report is not appealed or twelve months where the report is appealed. Where either the panel or the Appellate Body has acted, pursuant to paragraph [10.10] or [15.5], to extend the time of providing its report, the additional time taken shall be added to the above periods.

19. Surveillance of Implementation of Recommendations and Rulings

19.1 Prompt compliance with recommendations or rulings of the - DSB is essential in order to ensure effective resolution of disputes to the benefit of all members.

19.2 Particular attention should be paid to matters affecting the interests of developing members with respect to measures which have been subject to dispute settlement.

19.3 At a DSB meeting held within thirty days[10] of the adoption of the panel or Appellate Body report, the member concerned shall inform the DSB of its intentions in respect of implementation of the recommendations and rulings of the DSB. If it is

---

[8] The "member concerned" is the party to the dispute to which the panel or Appellate Body recommendations are directed.

[9] With respect to recommendations in cases not involving a violation of the GATT [1993] [and any other covered agreement], see Section [24].

[10] If a meeting of the DSB is not otherwise scheduled during this period, such a meeting of the DSB shall be held during this period for this purpose.

impracticable to comply immediately with the recommendations and rulings, the member concerned shall have a reasonable period of time in which to do so. The reasonable period of time shall be:

(a) the period of time proposed by the member concerned, provided that such period is approved by the DSB; or, in the absence of such approval,

(b) a period of time mutually agreed by the parties to the dispute within forty-five days following adoption of the recommendations and rulings; or, in the absence of such agreement,

(c) a period of time determined through binding arbitration within ninety days following adoption of the recommendations and rulings[11]. In such arbitration, a guideline for the arbitrator[12] should be that the reasonable period of time to implement panel or Appellate Body recommendations should not exceed fifteen months from the adoption of a panel or Appellate Body report. However, that time may be shorter or longer, depending upon the particular circumstances.

19.4 Except where the panel or the Appellate Body has extended, pursuant to paragraph [10.10 or 15.5], the time of providing its report, the period from the date of establishment of the panel by the DSB until the determination of the reasonable period of time shall not exceed fifteen months unless the parties to the dispute agree otherwise. Where either the panel or the Appellate Body has acted to extend the time of providing its report, the additional time taken shall be added to the fifteen-month period; provided that unless the parties to the dispute agree that there are exceptional circumstances, the total time shall not exceed eighteen months.

19.5 Where there is disagreement as to the existence or consistency with covered agreements of measures taken to comply with the recommendations and rulings such dispute shall be decided through recourse to these dispute settlement procedures, involving resort to the original panel wherever possible. The panel shall issue its decision within ninety days of referral of the matter to it. When the panel considers that it cannot provide its report within this time frame, it shall inform the DSB in writing

---

[11] If the parties cannot agree on an arbitrator within ten days after referring the matter to arbitration, the arbitrator shall be appointed by the Chairman of the Dispute Settlement Body within ten days, after consulting the parties.

[12] The expression "arbitrator" shall be interpreted as referring either to an individual or a group.

- 20 -

of the reasons for the delay together with an estimate of the
period within which it will submit its report.

19.6 The DSB shall keep under surveillance the implementation of
adopted recommendations or rulings. The issue of implementation
of the recommendations or rulings may be raised at the DSB by any
member at any time following their adoption. Unless the DSB
decides otherwise, the issue of implementation of the
recommendations or rulings shall be on the agenda of the DSB
meeting after six months following the establishment of the
reasonable period of time pursuant to paragraph [19.3] and shall
remain on the DSB's agenda until the issue is resolved. At least
ten days prior to each such DSB meeting, the party concerned
shall provide the DSB with a status report in writing of its
progress in the implementation of the recommendations or rulings.

19.7 If the matter is one which has been raised by a developing
member the DSB shall consider what further action it might take
which would be appropriate to the circumstances.

19.8 If the case is one brought by a developing member, in
considering what appropriate action might be taken the DSB shall
take into account not only the trade coverage of measures
complained of, but also their impact on the economy of developing
members concerned.

20. Compensation and the Suspension of Concessions

20.1 Compensation and the suspension of concessions or other
obligations are temporary measures available in the event that
the recommendations and rulings are not implemented within a
reasonable period of time. However, neither compensation nor the
suspension of concessions or other obligations is preferred to
full implementation of a recommendation to bring a measure into
conformity with the covered agreements. Compensation is
voluntary and, if granted, shall be consistent with the covered
agreements.

20.2 If the member concerned fails to bring the measure found to
be inconsistent with a covered agreement into compliance there-
with or otherwise comply with the recommendations and rulings
within the reasonable period of time, such member shall, if so
requested, and no later than the expiry of the reasonable period
of time, enter into negotiations with any party to the dispute,
with a view to developing mutually acceptable compensation. If no
satisfactory compensation has been agreed within twenty days
after the expiry of the reasonable period of time, any
complaining party may request authorization from the DSB to
suspend the application to the party concerned of concessions or
other obligations under the covered agreements.

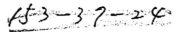

0102

외 무 부

종 별 :

번 호 : GVW-0519 　　　　　　　일 시 : 92 0306 1800

수 신 : 장 관(통기, 경기원, 재무부, 농수산부, 상공부)사본:박수길대사

발 신 : 주 제네바대사대리

제 목 : UR 법제화 그룹 비공식회의

　　연: GVW-0500

　　1. 3.4-5 양일 MATHUR 의장 주재로 열린 표제비공식 회의에서는 DUNKEL 최종협상안상의 STEXT와 T TEXT를 종합하여 사무국이 준비한 단일TEXT (332) 및 연호 387 을 검토한바, 동 결과 아래 보고함.

　　가. 개별 협정상의 특별 분쟁해결 규정(1.1, 2.1 및 주석 A, C 및 APPENDIX 2)

　　- 주석 A, C 에 언급된 보조금 협정 포함 모든 개별협정의 분쟁해결 관련 규정에대한 참가국 및 사무국의 면밀한 검토후 3.23 이후 적절한 시기에 재검토

　　- APPENDIX 2 관련 세이프가드 협정 27항이 특별규정인지의 여부를 놓고 미국, EC(삭제주장) 및 싱가폴, 홍콩이 상반된 견해 표명

　　- 일본, 미국, 홍콩이 항공 서비스 부속서 5항의 포함 필요성 언급

　　나. ANNEX 4 협정(주석 1)

　　- ANNEX 4 협정이 통합분쟁 해결절차의 적용 대상인지의 여부에 관해 선진국(적용대상)및 개도국이 상반된 입장(개도국은 ANNEX 4협정은 SINGLE UNDERTAKING 대상이 아니며, 특히 정부조달 협정은 UR 밖에서 논의되고 있음을 언급)

　　- LINDEN 고문도 ANNEX 협정이 통합절차의 적용을 받을것인가의 여부는 해당 협정 기구가 결정할 문제임을 인정함.(단, 주석 1은 협정기구가 DSB 의 관할을 인정할 것이라는 전제로 작성된 것이라고 해명)

　　다. 경과규정(1, 11 항 및 사무국 문서 387)

　　- 경과규정을 본문에 포함할 것인지, 또는 각료회의 결정형식으로 할것인지의 여부와 관련사무국은 동 내용의 한시성에 비추어 각료회의 결정 형식을 선호

　　- 각료 선언문안(387)의 4 번째 문장관련 미국은 MTO 협정 발효전에 패널 보고서가 채택된 분쟁의 이행에 대한 감시(SURVEILLANCE) 기능의 유지 필요성을 언급하면서,

---

통상국　　경기원　　재무부　　농수부　　상공부

따라서 DSB 로 하여금 GATT 이사회 권한을 수행케 하는 사무국 문안내용보다는 이사회에 대한 경과규정을 두는 것이 좋다는 입장

　　라. 66 년 절차(1.12 항)

　　- 동 조항이 동경라운드 협정 및 서비스, TRIPS협정에 적용되는가의 여부와 관련선.개도국의 입장 대립

　　- 개도국도 서비스, TRIPS 협정에의 적용은 강하게 주장하지 않았음.

　　- 동규정의 당초 제안국인 멕시코는 동 절차에 의해 처리된 분쟁의 경우에도 패널 보고서가 채택된 이후에는 통합절차에 적용시키자는 제의를 하였으나, 균형을 잃은제안이라고 선진국이 강하게 반대

　　마. 제 3국 권리(8.2 항)

　　- GATT 에서 비교적 명확히 정립된 'SUBSTANTIALINTERESTS'의 개념이 서비스, TRIPS 의 경우에는 어떻게 적용될 것인지의 문제가 제기된 바, 해당 협상 관계자와 협의후 재검토키로 함.

　　바. 교차 보복 승인(SECTION 20)

　　- 파키스탄이 20.4 항(A) 관련 승소국이 해당분야에서의 보복을 우선 모색했는지의 여부검증 필요성을 주장한 바, 미국은 이는 T3 권한밖의 사항이라고 강력 반발

　　- 20.2 항, 20.4 항 통합등 일부 조문 재배열 필요성이 지적됨.

　　- 25.5 항 존치여부와 관련 대부분 국가가 현 DUNKEL문안에 특정분야에 대한 보복을 금지하는 규정이 없으므로 삭제해야 한다는 의견인데 반해, EC 는 현재의 DUNKEL문안이 최종문안이 아니며 장래 필요성에 대비해서도 동조항을 유지해야 한다는 입장을 강하게 주장

　　- 20.7 항의 마지막 문장관련 인도가 동 문장의 모호성(적절한 절차를 따르지 않았다고 중재기구가 판정할 경우에도 DSB 가 보복을 자동 승인하게 되는 문제)을 지적하고, 이에 따른 수정 필요성을 제의한데 대해 미국이 강하게 반대(T3 권한밖의 사항)

　　사. NON-VIOLATION 분쟁(SECTION 24)

　　- TRIPS, 써비스 협정에의 적용여부를 두고 각국이 다양한 견해 표명

　　0 미국, 스위스: 양협정에 적용 가능

　　0 카나다, 인도, 일본: TRIPS 협정에는 적용불가

　　0 EC : 써비스 협정에는 적용 가능, TRIPS협정 적용 가능성 여부에 대해서는 입장

유보

　아. 실질규정의 상충(28 페이지)

　- EC 는 동 조항의 괄호 제거, 14항 앞으로 이전 및 주석 삭제를 주장

　- 미국은 동조항이 분쟁해결 절차의 BLOCKAGE수단으로 악용될 가능성이 있으므로상충되는 조항이 있는 여부 확인 및 있는 경우 동 해결책을 모색하는 것이 법제화 그룹의 임무라는 입장.

　2. 향후 계획

　가. 3.16 주간 비공식 회의를 재개, MTO 문제에 관한 2차 논의를 가진후 시간이있으며 분쟁해결 문제도 일부 재논의

　나. 3.16 회의 이전 사무국이 가급적 332 에 대한REVISED TEXT 를 준비

　다. 3.23 주간에는 공봉사항을 논의하며, 분쟁해결 2차 논의도 가급적 3월말 까지 완료할수 있도록 노력. 끝

　첨부: 표제회의 검토자료(사무국 배포) 4매

　(GVW(F)-162)

　(차석대사 김삼훈-국장)

주 제 네 바 대 표 부

번 호 : GVW(F) - 0162　　년월일 : 20306　　시간 : 1800
수 신 : 장　　관 (동기, 경기원, 재무, 농수산, 상공부)
발 신 : 주 제네바대사　　　　　　　사본 : 박수길 대사
제 목 : GVW-0511

총　5　매 (표지포함)

보 안 봉 제	

외 신 관 봉 제	

#62 5부

0106

2 March 1992

Dispute Settlement Understanding

Provisions to be reviewed

Section 1: Coverage and Application

Paragraph 1.1 - Paragraph 2.1:

These two points relate to the principle that special and
additional provisions in covered agreements prevail. [The reason for
the particular reference to the Subsidies Agreement will have to be
clarified.]

Footnote to Section 2.1:

The need for the footnote depends on the extent to which the
Annex 4 agreements will use the Integrated System.

Provisions in [ ] in pages 2 and 3:

If the first part of the Section is accepted, the
provision in [ ] can be deleted.

General Provisions

Paragraph 1.1:

The provision seems unnecessary and can be deleted. In such case, the
word 'Members' in the third line of paragraph 1.2 should be replaced
by "Members of the MTO" (hereinafter referred to as 'members').

Paragraph 1.11:

This paragraph deals with the same subject as the proposed Ministerial
Decision on transitional measures. If the paragraph is to be kept,
the text should be amended as in the Decision.

Paragraph 1.12:

This paragraph should be modified to reflect the intentions in respect
of the scope of the paragraph i.e. whether it should apply only to
GATT disputes or to disputes under other Annex 1A agreements.

Consultations

Paragraph 2.11:

There is no obvious reason why members with a substantial interest
could not be joined in all consultations under the Integrated System.

0107

Confidentiality

Paragraph 12.1:-

It seems reasonable to move this provision to follow paragraph 16.
[This would seem also to apply to paragraphs 12.2 and 12.3.]

Appellate Review

Footnote to paragraph 15.1:

The detailed procedural provisions could be left to be established by
the Appellate Body.

Compensation and the Suspension of Concessions

Footnote to paragraph 20.4(f):

MTN.GNS/W/120 is for the time being the relevant document.

Paragraph 20.5:

The paragraph should be retained. There are such prohibited areas.

Complaints under Article XXIII: 1(b) and 1(c) of GATT

These sections (at least 1(b)) would seem to be applicable to Services
(where there are non-violation rules corresponding to XXIII:1(b)) and
TRIPS (which refers to Articles XXII and XXIII of GATT, including
non-violation rules).

Conflicts of Substantive Provisions

The existence of such conflicts will be examined in the Legal Drafting
Group.

0108

Cross-cutting issues ("Other points common to a number of texts")

(Points made by the Chairman in the meeting of the
Legal Drafting Group on 3 March 1992)

The category of "cross-cutting issues" appears to overlap with the
Group's earlier examination of the relationship between the MTO Agreement
and other agreed texts. Some relevant questions are listed in Part D of
the Illustrative List of Points for Possible Consideration in the Legal
Drafting Group of 31 January (numbered 156). Several of the listed points
have already been touched on, and perhaps even largely exhausted, in the
course of the Group's previous discussion. The cross-cutting issues listed
in Section D are:

[The bracketed numbers are those of relevant informal compilations by
the Secretariat.]

1.   Legal form of each text. Is there anything to be added to the earlier
      discussion of the tentative listing of texts to be attached to the
      MTO? [316]

2.   Institutional provisions. Did the MTO discussion bring out all
      cross-cutting issues on terminology? Are there any problems with the
      specific provisions in some agreements on relations with other
      international organizations? [229]

3.   Final clauses. This point was discussed in detail in relation to the
      MTO. Are there other issues? [228]

4(a) Point 4(a) concerns questions of consistency between provisions of
      different texts, as well as of precedence of rights and obligations
      between texts in Annex 1A. These matters seem likely to make up the
      core of the cross-cutting issues that may require the Group's
      attention. The secretariat for its part will be attempting to
      identify cross-cutting issues of this type and the results will, if
      sufficiently substantial, be made available to the Group. It would be
      most helpful if delegations could inform the secretariat of any points
      which they have noted.   ,

4(b) Other points suggested by delegations:

      -    Exceptions and derogations. While derogations have already been
           discussed in the light of the MTO provisions, there may be some
           issues with respect to exceptions. To what extent do GATT
           Articles XX and XXI relate to individual texts in MTN.TNC/W/FA?
           The Secretariat could produce a compilation of references in
           these texts.

      -    Sub-national governments. Do differences in provisions in this
           area raise any problems, particularly with those in the Agreement
           on the Interpretation of Article XXIV? A similar compilation
           could be produced by the Secretariat.

                                                              ./.

- 2 -

- **Transparency provisions.** Is there any need to harmonize such provisions?
  The FOGS agreement on notifications, a central notifications registry, and a working party to review notification provisions might need to be amended and/or extended to take account of new agreements in MTN.TNC/W/FA.

- **Confidential information** Is there any need to harmonize such provisions?

This list is not intended to be exhaustive, or to define the issues requiring examination.

0110

외　무　부

원　본

종　별 :

번　호 : GVW-0596　　　　　　　　　　일　시 : 92 0318 1000

수　신 : 장 관(통기,경기원,재무부,농수산부,상공부,특허청)

발　신 : 주 제네바 대사대리

제　목 : UR/법제화 그룹 비공식 회의

연: GVW-0519(1)GVW(F)-187(2)

1. MTO 협정안 검토를 위한 표제회의가 3.16 부터 개최되어 그간의 논의를 반영하여 사무국이 작성한 연호 수정안(DOCUMENT 462, REVISED TEXT)을 91.12.20 자 초안과 비교, 검토하는 방식으로 논의가 진행되었는바, 3.17 까지 논의 요지를 아래보고함.(이하 인용된 부분은 수정안을 지칭함.)(이참사관, 신서기관 참석)

가. 전문

0 회원국(첫째항)

- 미국이 'THE PARTIES TO THIS AGREEMENT' 를 'THE CONTRACTING PARTIES TO THEGATT OF 1947 AND E.C' 로 대체할 것을 제의하였으나, 카나다등이 회원국에 대한 지칭은 일반적인 용어를 사용할 것을 주장하여 미국이 자국의 제안을 철회함.

0 목적(둘째항)

- EC 가 '완전 고용에의 기여'(CONTRIBUTING TO FULL EMPLOYMENT)는 당초의 '완전고용 달성'(ENSURING FULL EMPLOYMENT)의 취지에 어긋나므로 동항은 당초안으로 복귀할 것을 주장

0 타협정과의 관계(2P 첫째항)

- 동항에서 두번 사용된 GATT 의 개념이 애매하다는 지적이 있었는바(미국)

- 미국은 첫째 GATT 는 GATT '47 을, 두번째 GATT 는 GATT '93 으로 이해한데 반해

- 홍콩은 모두 GATT '47 을 의미한다고 발언함.

- 사무국은 동항에서 사용된 GATT 의 개념은 특정 GATT 를 지칭하지 않고 일반적인 개념으로 사용되었다고 언급하고, 문안에 대한 사무국의 추가 검토후 금명간 재논의할 것을 제의함.

통상국　　2차보　　경기원　　재무부　　농수부　　상공부　　특허청

PAGE 1　　　　　　　　　　　　　　　　　　　　92.03.19　　08:08 DS

외신 1과 통제관

0111

나. 제 2조 (범위)

0 초안의 주석(잠정 가입의정서: PPA)

- 미국이 PPA 에 대한 결론이 나지 않았으므로 초안의 주석이 유지되어야 한다고주장한데 대해

- EC 는 인도등은 잠정 가입의정서는 MTO부속서에 포함되지 않을 것이므로 주석을 없앤 수정안을 지지함.

2. 2,3 항(ANNEX 4 협정의 지위)

- EC 와 뉴질랜드는 ANNEX 4 도 ANNEX 1,2,3와 함께 MTO 협정의 INTEGRAL PART 이며,ANNEX 4와 ANNEX 1,2,3 의 차이는 단지 ANNEX 4가 타부속 협정에 비해 가입국이제한되어 있다는 점임을 주장하면서, 당초안을 지지함.

- 미국, 카나다, 일본, 싱가폴, 홍콩등은 ANNEX 4는 MTO 의 INTEGRAL PART 가 아니라고 규정한 동수정안을 지지함.(미국은 ANNEX 4 협정을 수락하지 아니한 MTO 회원국에 대해서는 권리,의무관계가 없다는 제 3항 마지막 문장의 필요성을 지적함)

0 4항(ANNEX 4 비가입국)

- 홍콩, 인도는 동항의 'SHALL CONSIDER' 가 동 비가입국에 대해 가입의 의무를의미하는 인상이 있으므로 초안으로 복귀할 것을 주장한데 대해

- 사무국은 'SHALL CONSIDER' 는 가입 의무를 의미하지 않는다고 해석함.

다. 제 3조(기능)

0 1항(MTA 및 TPA 와의 관계)

- 미국, 카나다가 1항의 MTA 앞에 THIS AGREEMENT(MTO협정)를 추가 할것을 제의한데 대해

- 싱가폴은 MTA 와 PTA 의 2중 구조 및 이에대한 MTO 기능의 차이를 규정한 동 수정안을 지지함.

0 2항(향후 다자봉상 협상 추진)

- 미국 및 스웨덴(북구)이 THE FRAMEWORK 를 A FRAMEWORK 로 수정할 것을 제의한데 대해

- EC 는 향후 다자 봉상협상을 MTO 아닌 타기관(예: IMF) 이 추진한다는 것은 곤란하므로 'THE' 로 하되 향후 협상에 대해서는 FRAMEWORK보다는 FORUM 을 제공하는것이므로 수정안 2항보다는 당초안 2,3 항을 지지함.

0 3항(통합 분쟁해결 체제)

PAGE 2

- EC 는 초안에 규정된 분쟁해결 절차의 적용범위(실질문제)를 삭제한 것은 TRACK3의 권한 밖이므로 초안으로의 복귀를 주장한데 대해
- 홍콩, 싱가폴등은 동 규정의 ANNEX 4 의 지위와 관련성을 주장하면서 수정안을지지함.
0 6항(타기구와의 협력)
- 미국은 수정안의 '국제 경제정책 일관성에의 기여'(CONTRIBUTE BY COOPERATING)개념은 그 방법이 구체화되기 어려운 개념임에 비추어 당초안에로의 복귀(COOPERATE)를 제의한대 대해
- 태국은 수정안을 지지하면서, 구체방안은 갓트기능(FOG) 그룹에서 논의될 성질의 것이라고 언급함.
라. 제 5조(구조)
0 미국은 동 수정안이 MTO 기구들간의 HIERARCHY를 명확하게 설정하지 못하였으며, 또한 향후 다자 교섭의 추진권한이 어느기구에 있는지 불분명하다고 지적하면서, 이를 보완한 수정안을 제출함.(별첨 1)
0 캐나다도 동 수정안이 상하관계 설정에 실패한점을 지적하면서, 미국이 지적한향후 다자협상 추진문제는 제 3조에 규정되어 있음에 비추어 일반이사회(GC) 와 분쟁해결 기구(DSB)및 특별이사회(SC) 간의 관계가 보다 명확화될 필요성만을 감안한 수정안을 제출함.(별첨2)
마. 제 6조(사무국)
0 4항(사무국 직원의 활동)
- 캐나다는 수정안이 사무국지원의 활동 제한기준을 당초안 제 3항의 MIGHT REFLECT ON '에서' ADVERSELY REFLECT ON' 으로 축소한 것은 중대한 변화임을 지적함.
- 이에 대해 사무국은 'MIGHT REFLECT ON '기준은 너무 광범위하여 현실성이 부족하다고 답변함.
0 2,3 항
- 일본은 동항의 일반이사회(GC) 를 각료회의(MINISTERIAL CONFERENCE) 로 수정할 것을 제의함.
- 사무국은 이에 동의하면서, 다만 MC 가 개최되지 않은 기간을 GC 가 MC 를 대체하는 것으로 수정한 것을 권고함.

PAGE 3

0113

바. 제 7조(예산 및 분담금)

- 미국은 연간 예산안은 GC 에 의해서 승인되어야 함을 명시하기 위해서 제 2항의 마지막문장(THE GENERAL COUNCIL..)을 제 3항으로 하고 동문장의 REGULATIONS 뒤에상기 취지로 ' AND ANNUAL BUDGET ESTIMATE'를 추가할 것을 제의함.(제3항이 4항이됨)

사. 제 8조(지위)

0 2,3항(특권면제의 대상)

- 사무국은 OFFICERS 은 이사회의장, DG 등 간부만을 포함하는 개념인바, 기타 사무국 직원은제 2항에 의해서 COVER 되므로 3항에서는 OFFICERS 용어를 사용함이 적절 하다함.

- 태국은 제 3항중 회원국 대표는 타 국제협정에 의해서 규율되고 있으므로 삭제할 것을 제의하면서, 제 2항 및 3항을 깨함으로 하되 특권 및 면제를 본부 소재국 이외의 회원국에서 부여하는 경우에는 '구체적이거나 특정한 갓트 관련 임무'를 수행하는 경우로 한정할 것을 제의함.

아. 제 9조(MC 및 GC 의 결정)

0 1항(투표권)

- 미국은 1국 1 투표권과 관련, EC 가 개개 회원국의 투표권에 추가하여 EC 자체의 투표권을 갖지 않는다는 점을 명확히 규정할 필요성을 제기함.

- 뉴질랜드, 일본, 카나다, 태국등이 제 11조(EC를 회원국 취급)와 관련하여 이에 동조한 반면, EC 는 이중 투표권을 향유할 의도가 전혀없으나, EC 만을 적시하는데는 반대한다는 입장을 표명함.

- 한편, 사무국은 이중 투표권 관련 오존층에 관한 국제 협약상의 유사규정(이중투표권 금지)을 예시하면서 동 규정의 예에 따르는 것도 방안이 될수 있을 것이라고하였으나, EC 는 이에도 반대함.

0 2항(협정해석 정족수)

- 홍콩, EC, 일본, 인도등이 협정해석은 CONSENSUS 에 의해서 이루어져야 한다는점을 명확히 규정해야 하며, 제 1항(다수결 결정)의규정에 비추어서도 동항에 CONSENSUS 를 명문화시킬것을 제의함.

- 이에 대해 카나다등은 협정해석을 콘센서스로 한다고 못박을 경우 콘센서스 부재시 2/3 다수결결정이 가능한 현행 관례(체약국단공동행동)를 변경하게 되므로

PAGE 4

곤란하다함.

　ㅇ 2항(협정 해석기관)

　- EC, 인도등은 협정해석권이 일차적으로 해당 SC 에 있으므로 동조항의 MC 해석권을 SC의 권고에 기초해서 극히 제한적으로 사용되어야 할것을 주장한데 대해

　- 미국, 카나다는 MC 의 권한상(제 5조) 독자적인 해석권 부여를 주장함.

　2. 금 3.16 주간에는 MTO 문제를 계속 논의하고, 3.23 주간에는 공식회의를 개최하여 공봉문제를 논의한뒤 바로 비공식회의를 열어 4월말까지 개별 TEXT 검토를 진행할 예정이며, 중간에 3.30 주간에 분쟁해결 및 MTO 협정안 논의를 계속할 예정임.
끝

　(차석대사 김삼훈-국장)

　첨부: 1. 미국제출안(5조)

　2. 카나다 제출안(5조)

　3. 협상일정(GVW(F)-191)

주 제 네 바 대 표 부

번 호 : GVW(F)-0/위   년월일 : 20위 /8   시간 : /2 ∞

수 신 : 장   관 (통기,경기원,재무부,농림수산부,상공부,특허청)

발 신 : 주 제네바대사

제 목 : UR 협상 관계 기사 송부

총 8 매 (표지포함)

보 안	
통 제	

외신판	
통 제	

배부처	장관실	차관실	一차보	二차보	의정실	분석단	아주국	미주국	구주국	중아국	국기국	장경국실	통상국실	외기민	첫외대	단기부	공보처	경기원	상공부	재무부	농수부	동자부	환경처	파기처림	특허청
			/										0				/	/	/	/					/

USA - PROPOSED RE-DRAFT   B-1

Article IV
Organs of the MTO

1.   There are established as the principle organs of the MTO:

(a)   the Ministerial Conference;

(b)   the General Council;

     (i)   the Dispute Settlement Body;

     (ii)   the Trade Policy Review Body;

     (iii)   the Committee on Trade and Development;

     (iv)   the Committee on Balance-of-Payments
            Restrictions;

     (v)   the Committee on Budget, Finance and
            Administration;

(c)   the Council on Trade in Goods, the Council on Trade in
        Services and the Council on Trade-Related Aspects of
        Intellectual Property Rights; and,

(d)   the bodies provided for under the Multilateral Trade
        Agreements.

0117

2.   Except as otherwise specified in this Agreement, the
functions of the MTO specified herein shall be carried out by
the Ministerial Conference. The Ministerial Conference shall
keep under review, supervise and further the operation of this
Agreement and the Multilateral Trade Agreements, and shall keep
under review the Plurilateral Trade Agreements. Except as
specifically provided for in the Multilateral Trade Agreements,
it shall launch and conclude multilateral trade negotiations
and decide on the implementation of their results. The
Ministerial Conference shall be composed of representatives of
all of the Members. The Ministerial Conference shall meet at
least once every two years.

3.   In the intervals between meetings of the Ministerial
Council, its functions shall be conducted by the General
Council, except that the authority to launch further
multilateral trade negotiations or decide on the legal form or
on the entry into force of the results of such negotiations
shall be reserved to the Ministerial Conference. The General
Council shall also decide on all issues referred to it under
this Agreement or by the Ministerial Conference; it shall
establish and approve the rules of procedure for the Committee
on Budget, Finance and Administration, the Committee on Trade
and Development and the Committee on Balance-of-Payments
Restrictions; and it shall establish its own rules of
procedure. The General Council shall be composed of
epresentatives of all of the Members and shall meet as
ppropriate.

0118

4.   The General Council shall convene from time to time as
the Dispute Settlement Body, to discharge the responsibilities
of the Dispute Settlement Body as provided in the Understanding
on Rules and Procedures Governing the Settlement of Disputes
provided for in Annex 2. The Dispute Settlement Body shall
promulgate such rules of procedure as it deems necessary for
the fulfillment of those responsibilities.

5.   The General Council shall also convene from time to time
as the Trade Policy Review Body, to exercise the powers of the
General Council with respect to the responsibilities described
in Annex 3 and shall promulgate such rules of procedure as it
deems necessary for the fulfillment of those responsibilities.

6.   The Committee on Trade and Development, the Committee on
Balance-of-Payments Restrictions and the Committee on Budget,
Finance and Administration shall carry out the functions
assigned to them by this Agreement, by the Multilateral Trade
Agreements and any additional functions assigned to them by the
General Council. Membership in these committees shall be open
to representatives of all interested Members and shall be set
every two years at the meetings of the Ministerial Conference.

0119

7.   The Council on Trade in Goods shall oversee the
functioning of the Multilateral Trade Agreements in Annex 1A.
The Council on Trade in Services shall oversee the functioning
of the Multilateral Trade Agreement in Annex 1B. The Council
on Trade-Related Aspects of Intellectual Property Rights shall
oversee the functioning of the Multilateral Trade Agreement in
Annex 1C. Each of the above Councils shall establish its own
rules of procedure subject to the approval of the General
Council. Membership in the above Councils shall be open to
representatives of all interested Members and shall be set
annually by the General Council. The above Councils shall meet
as necessary to carry out their functions.

8.   The bodies provided for under the Plurilateral Trade
Agreements shall operate within the institutional framework of
the MTO. As appropriate, they shall launch and conclude
plurilateral trade negotiations in their respective spheres and
decide on the implementation of the results of such
negotiations.

9.   Each of the bodies referred to in paragraphs 1 and 7
bove shall establish the relevant subsidiary bodies provided
or in the Multilateral Trade Agreements or the Plurilateral
ade Agreements and unless, in relation to a particular
ɔsidiary body relating to a Multilateral Trade Agreement, the
nisterial Conference or General Council decides otherwise,
establish other subsidiary bodies.

0120

MTO AGREEMENT

Redraft Articles V as follows:

Article V

Structure of the MTO

1. There shall be a Ministerial Conference open to representatives of all the members, which shall meet at least once every two years. The Ministerial Conference shall exercise the functions of the MTO, and may launch multilateral trade negotiations and implement the results of such negotiations.

2. There shall be a General Council open to representatives of all the members, which shall meet regularly or as appropriate. In the time between Ministerial Conferences, the General Council shall exercise the powers of the Ministerial Conference.

3. The General Council shall establish a Council for Goods, a Council for Services and a Council for TRIPs. These bodies shall be open to representatives of all members. The General Council also shall establish a Committee on Trade and Development, a Committee on Balance-of-Payment Restrictions, a Committee on Budget, Finance and Administration, and it may establish other subsidiary bodies, as appropriate. The General Council shall establish its own rules of procedure and shall approve the rules of procedure of its subsidiary bodies.

4. Subject to the guidance of the General Council, the Council for Goods shall oversee the functioning of Annex 1A, the Council for Services shall oversee the functioning of Annex 1B, and the Council for TRIPs shall oversee the functioning of Annex 1C. These bodies shall carry out the functions assigned to them by their respective agreements and the General Council. With the approval of the General Council, these bodies may establish committees or other subsidiary bodies and shall approve their rules of procedure.

5. In exercising its functions under Annex 2, the Dispute Settlement Body shall act on behalf of the General Council.

6. In exercising its functions under Annex 3, the Trade Policy Review Body shall act on behalf of the General Council.

0121

Tentative Timetable for Consideration by the Legal Drafting Group
of Individual Texts in the Draft Final Act

The attached list should be regarded as no more than a first
indication of how individual texts might be taken up. A firm timetable can
only be established when some experience has been gained of the time
required for review of individual texts.

The timetable assumes that the MTO and Dispute Settlement texts will
be discussed in the week of 30 March, and that informal discussion of these
and other texts will continue thereafter with a view to finalizing the
texts. It also assumes that the Group does not meet in the week before
Easter.

ldg92-25

0122

Date	Texts to be reviewed (references are to sections of MTN.TNC/W/FA)
25 March	P (Article II:1(b) of GATT) Q (Article XVII) U (Article XXIV) V (Article XXV) W (Article XXVIII) R (Balance of Payments) Article XXXV (having regard to MTO provisoins on non-application)
26 March	M (Safeguards)
27 March	
6 April	D (Rules of Origin) E (Preshipment Inspection) Customs Valuation Agreement H (Import Licensing)
7 April	G (Technical Barriers to Trade) L (Sanitary and Phytosanitary Measures) N (TRIMS)
8 April	F (Anti-Dumping) I (Subsidies and Countervailing Duties)
9 April	O (Textiles and Clothing) Y (FOGS, including TPRM (Annex 3 to MTO))
10 April	B (Least-Developed Countries) C (Uruguay Round Protocol) GATT 1993
21 April	Annex II (Services)
22 April	Annex III (TRIPs)
23 April	L (Agriculture) A (Final Act) Signatures MTO Annex 4 texts
24 April	All remaining separate texts for Ministers.

ldg92-25

외 무 부

종 별 :

번 호 : GVW-0631   일 시 : 92 0323 1100

수 신 : 장관(봉기,경기원,재무부,농수산부,상공부,특허청)

발 신 : 주 제네바 대사

제 목 : UR/법제화 그룹 비공식 회의(MTO,2)

　　　연: GVW(F)-0187(1)

　　　　GVW-0596(2)

　　　　GVW-0519(3)

　　　연호, 사무국 MTO 협정안에 대한 3.18-19 간 표제회의 논의 요지를 아래 보고함.(
이참사관, 신서기관 참석)

　　　1. 제 9조 3항(웨이버)

　　　- 개별 협정에 웨이버 조항이 있는 경우는 해당 SC 가 웨이버 결정권을 갖되, 유사
조항이 없는 경우 (예: TRIPS 협정안) 또는 수개협정에 관련된 사항인 경우에는 MC 에
웨이버 부여권이 있다는 사무국 수정안에 대해 홍콩, 인도, 카나다, 방글라데시는
찬성함.

　　　- 미국, 일본은 동 사무국 수정안이 TRIPS 협정안에 웨이버 조항을 두지 않은 당초
협상의도에 어긋난다는 문제점을 지적

　　　- EC 는 사무국 수정안의 2중 구조에 반대하면서 웨이버에 관한 일원적 권한을 MC
에 부여하고자 하는 12.20 초안을 지지

　　　2. 제 10조(개정 및 수정)

　　　O 1항(의결 정족수)- 투표국 2/3 이상인 동시에 회원국 과반수인 찬성투표에 의한
개정안 의결 규정에 대해

　　　- EC, 일본, 홍콩, 인도는 협정 개정은 협정해석과도 관계가 있으므로 콘센서스를
주장한 반면

　　　- 카나다, 미국은 사무국안을 지지함.

　　　O 제 2항(수정안 발효)

　　　- 수정안 효력 발생 관련 미국, 뉴질랜드,카나다는 동조 제 1항 규정에 비추어 MFN

통상국　　경기원　　재무부　　농수부　　상공부　　특허정　　오사인

PAGE 1   92.03.24   05:20 DS

　　　　　　　　　　　　　　　　　　　　　　　외신 1과 통제관

　　　　　　　　　　　　　　　　　　　　　　　　0124

원칙등 갓트의 기본 요소 수정안 미수락국에 대한 효력발생 여부는 콘센서스로 결정해야 함을 지적

 - 스위스는 동 조항 3번째 문장관련, 절차적 사항은 무방하나 제도 관련 사항은중요한 사항이므로 동의하는 국가에 대해서만 효력이 발생할 것을 주장

 0 제 5항(ANNEX 4 확대 또는 축소)

 - EC, 카나다, 미국은 동 조항 신설 필요성 찬성,홍콩, 인도는 반대

3. 제 11조 (원회원국)

(동조항은 별첨 1의 미국 수정안을 중심으로 논의)

 0 미국 수정안 제출 배경

 - 12.20 초안 및 사무국 수정안은 원회원국의 양허표 제출 의무를 명확하게 규정하지 못했음.

 0 양허표 제출 의무

 - 인도, 방글라데쉬는 현 갓트 체제에서 양허표를 제출하지 않는 개도국이 상당수 있음을 지적(사무국은 20여개국 이라함)하면서 미국 수정안 반대

 - 미국, 카나다는 GATT '93 은 성질상 별개의 협정이며, 푼타 선언상의 개도국우대 원칙이 개도국의 의무 면제를 의미하지 않음을 지적하면서 양허표 제출은 의무화 되어야 한다고주장

 0 양허표 제출 범위

 - 미국, EC, 카나다는 SINGLE-UNDERTAKING 원칙에따라 농산물 및 서비스 양허표제출이 포함되어야 한다고 주장

 - 인도, 방글라데쉬는 서비스 협정 제 28조가 완전 합의된 것이 아니라 하면서,이에 반대입장 표명

4. 제 12조(ACCESSION)

 - 제 2항 관련, 미국이 정족수를 현 갓트 규정과 같이 전체 회원국의 2/3 로 할것을 주장한데 대해 인도가 반대

5. 제 13조 (협정 부적용)

 0 제 2항(ANNEX 1 A 협정 부적용) 관련, 일본,EC 는 동항의 취지인 GATT '47 의부적용 범위가 현재 이상으로 확대되는 것을 방지한다는 점에 대해 사무국 수정안이 분명치 않다고 지적하면서 GATT '47 회원국에 대해서는 MTO협정 발효 당시에 실제로 부적용되고 있는 국가간에만 ANNEX 1 A 상의 부적용이 가능하다는 점을 분명히 하

PAGE 2

0125

수정문안을 제의하여 다수국이 이에 동조

　　ㅇ 제 3항(부적용 통보 의무)

　　- 두번째 문장 역통보의 구체적 내용에 대한 다수국의 의문 제기에 대해

　　- 사무국은 일방이 협정 부적용 통보시 자동적으로 상호 부적용 효과를 가져오는 것은 사실이지만, 동규정은 타방이 교차 부적용(예: 1B 협정부적용을 통보받은 국가가 상대국에 대해 IC협정 부적용 희망)의 경우를 상정한 것이라고 설명

　　- 상기 사무국 설명에 다수국이 교차 불적용에 의한동 조항 이용 확대를 바람직하지 않다면서 삭제 주장

　　- 스위스, 카나다는 서비스 협정의 불적용 규정과 유사한 규정의 도입(부적용 사유 제출, WP 구성심사등) 필요성 주장, (하기 제 5항과도 관련)

　　ㅇ 제 5항(운용 점검)- 미국은 동 조항이 무의미하다고 하면서 삭제주장

　　- 사무국은 동 조항은 현 GATT 35 조 2항 내용을 그대로 수용한 것이며, 1961 년 일본의 요청을 동조항이 발동된 사례가 있다고 설명

　　- 일본, 인도, EC 등이 동 조항 유지를 지지하고, 카나다는 구체 CASE 를 심사할수 있도록 오히려 강화하자는 입장 표명하였으나 다수국이 이에 반대

　　ㅇ 본 13조의 필요성 관련 미국(협정 부적용 관련조항은 각 협정에 일임)과 EC(MTO 협정에서 일괄 규정하고 각 협정상의 별도 부적용 조항은 삭제)의 입장이 대립

　　6. 제 14조(수락, 발금, 기탁)

　　ㅇ 제 3항 기타 대상 협정 관련 미국, EC 는ANNEX 4 도 MTO 협정의 INTEGRAL PART이므로기탁 대상이라는 점을 분명히 하고자 밑에서 3째줄 AGREEMENT 뒤에 TOGETHER WITH ITS ANNEXES 를추가할것을 제의하였으나, 일본등은 이에 반대(사무국도 반대입장에 동조)

　　7. 제 5조(MTO 구조)

　　(연호 (2) 동 제5조에 대한 논의를 반영, 미국, 카나다가 합동 제의한 수정안(별첨 2)을 논의하였음.

　　가. 제 1항(MC)

　　ㅇ 향후 다자협상 개시 권한

　　- 카나다는 협상의 성질에 따라 MC, GC 또는 SC가 협상 개시를 결정할수 있을 것이라 설명함.

　　ㅇ 협상 수행(CONDUCT)

- 카나다는 MTO 의 일반적인 권한(제2조)을 명확히 하기 위해 MC 의 CONDUCT 권한을 규정하였다고 설명한데 대해

- 인도는 CONDUCT 단어 삭제를, EC 는 CONDUCT 단어를 CONCLUDE 로 수정할 것을제의

0 협상결과 이행(IMPLEMENT, 마지막 문장)

- 일본은 동 문장은 제2조에 비추어 불필요하므로 삭제할 것을

- EC 는 협상 결과 이행권을 GC 또는 SC에 위임할수 있도록 할 것을 주장

나. 제 5항 및 6항(COMMITTEE 및 SC 구성국)

- 동기구의 구성국을 GC 에서 결정한다

(제 5항 마지막 문장, 제 6항 마지막 두번째 문장의 SHALL BE DETERMINED BY THE GC) 는 규정은 회원국의 참여를 제한하게 되며, 현 갓트관행을 승계한다는 취지에도 어긋나므로 이를 삭제할 것을 홍콩, 인도, 태국등이 주장.

다. 제 6항(SC 설치 권한)

- 미, 카나다는 제안 설명에서 GC 와 SC 간의 상하구조를 명확히 하기 위해 GC에 의한 SC의 설치 규정(첫째 문장)을 두었다고 설명한데 대해

- 인도는 SC 는 해당 협정에 근거하여 설치되는 것이라는 점을 강조(브라질,카나다 동조)

라. 제 7항의 PTA 보조기관에 대해 MC 또는GC 에 대한 보고절차를 추가할 것을 일본, 호주가 제의

마. 의장은 상기 5조(MTO 구조)의 중요성에 비추어 내주에 개별 협정문을 심의하기 전에 5조에 대해서는 최소한 기본적인 합의를 도출해야 하므로 금번 논의를 반영하여 미.카가 새로운 공동제안을 제출해 이를 기초로 3.20일 다시 논의키로 함.끝

첨부: GVW(F)-200

(대사 박수길-국장)

주제네바대표부

변 호 : GVW(F) - 0200   년월일 :20323   시간 : 110

수 신 : 장   관 (통기,경기원,재무부,농림수산부,상공부,특허청)

발 신 : 주 제네바대사

제 목 : UR 협상 동녁 초부

총 4 매(표지포함)

보 안	
봉 재	

외신관	
봉 재	‥‥

0128

1992-03-23 16:40   KOREAN MISSION GENEVA   2 022 791 0525   P.05

134   우루과이라운드 법제화 그룹 회의

Article XI

Original Membership

Contracting parties to the General Agreement on Tariffs and Trade - 1947 as of the date of entry into force of this Agreement and the European Communities which accept this Agreement and all of the Multilateral Trade Agreements and which, by the date of entry into force of this Agreement, have submitted the schedules of concessions and specific commitments provided for respectively in the General Agreement on Tariffs and Trade - 1993 and the General Agreement on Trade in Services in Annex 1B, shall be eligible to become original members of the MTO.

0129

18 March 1992

USA/Canada Proposed Re-Draft

ARTICLE IV

Structure of the MTO

1. There shall be a Ministerial Conference composed of representatives of all the Members, which shall meet at least once every two years. Except as otherwise specified in this Agreement, the functions of the MTO shall be carried out by the Ministerial Conference. Except as otherwise provided in the Multilateral Trade Agreements, it shall launch and conduct multilateral trade negotiations. It also shall have the authority to implement the results of multilateral trade negotiations.

2. There shall be a General Council composed of representatives of all the Members, which shall meet as appropriate. In the intervals between meetings of the Ministerial Conference, its functions shall be conducted by the General Council, except that the authority to implement the results of multilateral trade negotiations shall be reserved to the Ministerial Conference. The General Council also shall decide on all issues referred to it under this Agreement or by the Ministerial Conference. The General Council shall promulgate its own rules of procedure and the rules of procedure for the Committee on Budget, Finance and Administration, the Committee on Trade and Development and the Committee on Balance-of-Payments Restrictions.

3. The General Council shall convene from time to time as the Dispute Settlement Body to discharge the responsibilities of the Dispute Settlement Body as provided in the Understanding on Rules and Procedures Governing the Settlement of Disputes provided for in Annex 2. The Dispute Settlement Body shall promulgate such rules of procedure as it deems necessary for the fulfillment of those responsibilities.

4. The General Council shall also convene from time to time as the Trade Policy Review Body to exercise the powers of the General Council with respect to the responsibilities described in Annex 3 and shall promulgate such rules of procedure as it deems necessary for the fulfillment of those responsibilities.

5. The Ministerial Conference shall establish the Committee on Trade and Development, the Committee on Balance-of-Payments Restrictions and the Committee on Budget, Finance and Administration which shall carry out the functions assigned to them by this Agreement, by the Multilateral Trade Agreements and any additional functions assigned to them by the General Council. Membership in these committees shall be open to representatives of

0130

all interested Members and shall be determined by the General Council.

6.   The General Council shall establish a Council for Trade in Goods, a Council for Trade in Services and a Council for Trade-Related Aspects of Intellectual Property Rights.   Subject to the guidance of the General Council, the Council for Trade in Goods shall oversee the functioning of Annex 1A, the Council for Trade in Services shall oversee the functioning of Annex 1B, and the Council for Trade-Related Aspects of Intellectual Property Rights shall oversee the functioning of Annex 1C.   These Councils shall carry out the functions assigned to them by their respective agreements and by the General Council.   Membership in these Councils shall be open to representatives of all Members and shall be determined by the General Council.   These Councils shall meet as necessary to carry out their functions.

7.   The bodies provided for under the Plurilateral Trade Agreements shall carry out the functions assigned to them under those Agreements and shall operate within the institutional framework of the MTO.   As appropriate, they shall launch and conclude plurilateral trade negotiations in their respective spheres and decide on the implementation of the results of such negotiations.

8.   The Council for Trade in Goods shall establish the subsidiary bodies provided for in Annex 1A; the Council for Trade in Services shall establish the subsidiary bodies provided for in Annex 1B and the Ministerial Decision on Institutional Arrangements; and the Council for Trade-Related Aspects of Intellectual Property Rights shall establish the subsidiary bodies provided for in Annex 1C. With the approval of the General Council, these Councils may establish other subsidiary bodies or consolidate existing ones.

0131

외 무 부

종   별 :

번   호 : GVW-0642   일   시 : 92 0323 1950

수   신 : 장관(봉기,경기원,재무부,농림수산부,상공부,특허청)

발   신 : 주 제네바 대사

제   목 : UR/법제화그룹 비공식회의(MTO,3)

연 : GVW(F)-0187 (1), GVW-631 (2) GVW-596(3)

연호, 사무국 MTO 협정안에 대한 3.20 표제회의논의 요지를 아래 보고함(신서기관 참석)

1. 제 5조(구조)

(연호 (2) 논의에 기초하여 미.카나다가 재차 제출한 별첨 1수정안에 대한 논의가 진행됨)

0 제1항

- 둘째 문장 전반부 'EXCEP- THIS AGREEMENT'는 당초 취지이상으로 MC 의 권한을 제한한다는 EC, 일본, 스위스, 홍콩등 다수국의 주장에 의해 삭제키로 함.

- 둘째 문장중 ' HAVE THE POWERS NECESSARY TO' 도 MC 의 권한을 제한하게 되므로 삭제하자는 주장이 있었음(인도, 스웨덴, 일본)

0 제3,4항(DSB MCU TRRB 지위)

- EC 는 의장 선임문제등과 관련해서 GC와 DSB 및 TPRB 를 별개의 기구로 규정할것을 주장한데 대해 미국은 DSB 및 TPRB 를 GC와 별개기구로 규정하면 GC 의 보조기관으로 해석될 가능성이 있다하여 이에 반대

0 제5항(위원회)

- 동 항의 마지막 문장중 INTERESTED 단어는 구성국을 제한하므로 ALL 로 교체키로 함.

0 제7항(PTA)

- 호주는 PTA 기구의 GC 에 대한 보고규정을 명문화하자고 재차 강조(우루과이,홍콩동조)하였으나, 카나다는 동문제는 PTA개별규정에 따를 것을 주장

0 제8항(SC 기구)

통상국   경기원   재무부   농수부   상공부   특허청

PAGE 1   92.03.24   09:23 FB

외신 1과 통제관

0132

- 인도가 첫째 문장 후반부 CONSOLIDATE EXISTING ONESAS APPROPRIATE 는 기존의기구를 통합하는 권한을 SC 에 주게되므로 삭제를 주장한데 대해

- 카나다는 각협정간의 기능 중복에 따른 기구의 중복설치를 방지키 위해 동구절이 필요하다고 주장

0 SC 와 위원회의 지위관계

- 실질문제를 취급하는 SC 가 CTD,BOP,행정예산위보다 상위기관이므로 제5항(위원회)과 제6항(SC)의 위치를 바꾸자는 인도주장을 반영, 제 5항 이하는 재배열하기로함.

2. 제 16조(기타사항)

0 제 1항(GATT 와 MTO 의 연속성)

- 3째줄의 'GUIDED BY THE PRINCIPLES, PRATICES ---'관련, PRINCIPLES 은 MTO 가 GATT 결정에 기속될 가능성이 있으므로 삭제를 주장하는 미국에대해, EC 는 12.20초 안의 'RESPECT THE---' 를 고집하여 카나다의 타협안' GUIDED BY THEDECISIONS, PROCEDURES AND CUSTOMARY PRACTICES 를'채택키로 함.

- 부표관행 관련 이의 연속성을 명문화한 12.20초안을 고집한 EC와 이의 불연속성을 명문화하자는 미국의 입장 대립이 있었으나, 동조항은 일반적인 연속성 확보에 관 한 조항이므로 동조항에서는 부표권 문제를 다루지 않기로함.(카나다 제외)

0 제 3항(갓트 사무국과 MTO 사무국관계)

- 동항은 잠정적인 성격이 강하므로 FA 에서 규정하자는 미측에 대해 일본, EC,홍콩등의 주장으로 동항의 첫째 문장은 제14조(ACCEPTANCE)의 2년 경과 기간에 비추어존치하되 둘째 문장은 삭제하거나 다른곳에서규정하도록 함.

0 12.20 초안 3항(상충규정의 효력)

- 미국,카나다등이 동조항의 부활 필요성을 강력주장한데 대해 일부 국가는 최초의 MC 이전에 규정간의 상충문제를 해소해야 된다는 의견을제시함.

0 제 4항(국내법의 일치 문제)- EC 는 동조항에 찬성하면서 사무국 주석의 마지막 문장에 대한 이의를 제기했으며

- 싱가폴은 동조항의 삭제를

- 홍콩,인도,스웨덴은 규정의 강화 또는 유지를

- 미국은 동조항에 대한 어떠한 변경도반대한다는 입장을 개진함.

0 제 5항(유보)

- 미국은 둘째 문장의 FOREGOING 은 삭제할것을 주장하면서 별첨 2의 수정안을

제시하면서, PPA(또는 PA) 1항(B)의 GRANDFATHER CLAUSE에 의한 유보는 계속되어야 함을 주장

　　3. 부속서(첨부문서)

　　0 부속서 1(MTA)

　　- 부속서 1A 는 예시목록이라는 사무국 설명에대해, 다수국가가 이에 동의함.

　　- 1(D) 에 UR 협상결과가 추가되어야할것이라는 EC 지적에 대해 사무국은 동사항은1(C) 에서 포함하고 있음을 설명함.

　　- 한편, 1(E) 가 BRACKET 으로 되어 있는데대한 카나다의 설명요구에 대해 사무국측은 미국의PPA 1(B)에 대한 우려는 유보조항으로 해결할수있지 않겠느냐는 생각이라고 답변함.

　　0 부속서 4(PTA)

　　- 홍콩은 부속서 4의 TITLE 을 TEXT TO BEINCLUDED 에서 TITLE OF TEXTS TO BE INCLUDED 로수정할 것을 제의

　　4. 내주에는 3.23-24 간 공식회의를 개최하여 공통문제를 협의한뒤, 3.25.부터는 연호(3)일정대로 INDIVIDUAL TEXT 를 논의할 예정임.끝

　　첨부:(GVW(F)-0203)(대사 박수길-국장)

주 제 네 바 대 표 부

번 호 : GVW(F) - 02-03   년월일 : 20323   시간 : 1950

수 신 : 장   관 (롱기, 경기원, 재무부, 농림수산부, 상공부, 특허청)

발 신 : 주 제네바대사

제 목 : UR 협상

총 4 매 (표지포함)

<table>
<tr><td>보 안
통 제</td><td></td></tr>
</table>

<table>
<tr><td>외신관
통 제</td><td></td></tr>
</table>

<table>
<tr><td>백
부
처</td><td>장관실</td><td>차관실</td><td>차관보</td><td>외경국</td><td>분석관</td><td>아주국</td><td>미주국</td><td>구주국</td><td>중아국</td><td>특지득</td><td>정부사</td><td>통상국</td><td>외교국</td><td>청와대</td><td>안기부</td><td>농수부</td><td>경기원</td><td>상공부</td><td>재무부</td><td>통상국</td><td>한은행처</td><td>특허청</td><td>특기청</td></tr>
<tr><td></td><td>/</td><td>/</td><td></td><td>/</td><td>/</td><td></td><td></td><td></td><td></td><td>0</td><td></td><td></td><td></td><td></td><td>/</td><td>/</td><td>/</td><td>/</td><td>/</td><td>/</td><td></td><td>/</td><td></td></tr>
</table>

20 March 1992

Proposed Re-Draft

ARTICLE IV

Structure of the MTO

1. There shall be a Ministerial Conference composed of representatives of all the Members, which shall meet at least once every two years. Except as otherwise specified in this Agreement, the Ministerial Conference shall have the powers necessary to carry out the functions of the MTO. Except as otherwise provided in the Multilateral Trade Agreements, it shall launch multilateral trade negotiations. It also shall have the authority to decide on the implementation of the results of multilateral trade negotiations. The Ministerial Conference may establish subsidiary bodies or consolidate existing ones as appropriate.

2. There shall be a General Council composed of representatives of all the Members, which shall meet as appropriate. In the intervals between meetings of the Ministerial Conference, its functions shall be conducted by the General Council. The General Council also shall decide on all issues referred to it under this Agreement or by the Ministerial Conference. The General Council shall promulgate its rules of procedure and the rules of procedure for the committees provided for in paragraph 5.

3. The General Council shall convene as appropriate as the Dispute Settlement Body to discharge the responsibilities of the Dispute Settlement Body provided in the Understanding on Rules and Procedures Governing the Settlement of Disputes provided for in Annex 2. The Dispute Settlement Body shall promulgate such rules of procedure as it deems necessary for the fulfillment of those responsibilities.

4. The General Council shall convene as appropriate as the Trade Policy Review Body to exercise the powers of the General Council provided for in Annex 3 and shall promulgate such rules of procedure as it deems necessary for the fulfillment of those responsibilities.

5. The Ministerial Conference shall establish the Committee on Trade and Development, the Committee on Balance-of-Payments Restrictions and the Committee on Budget, Finance and Administration which shall carry out the functions assigned to them by this Agreement, by the Multilateral Trade Agreements and any additional functions assigned to them by the General Council. Membership in these committees shall be open to representatives of interested Members.

0136

6. There shall be a Council for Trade in Goods, a Council for Trade in Services and a Council for Trade-Related Aspects of Intellectual Property Rights, which shall operate under the general guidance of the General Council. The Council for Trade in Goods shall oversee the functioning of Multilateral Trade Agreements in Annex 1A, the Council for Trade in Services shall oversee the functioning of the Multilateral Trade Agreement in Annex 1B, and the Council for Trade-Related Aspects of Intellectual Property Rights shall oversee the functioning of Multilateral Trade Agreement in Annex 1C. These Councils shall carry out the functions assigned to them by their respective agreements and by the General Council. They shall promulgate their respective rules of procedure subject to the approval of the General Council. Membership in these Councils shall be open to representatives of all Members. These Councils shall meet as necessary to carry out their functions.

7. The bodies provided for under the Plurilateral Trade Agreements shall carry out the functions assigned to them under those Agreements and shall operate within the institutional framework of the MTO.

8. The Council for Trade in Goods, the Council for Trade in Services and the Council for Trade-Related Aspects of Intellectual Property Rights shall establish subsidiary bodies as required in the Multilateral Trade Agreements in Annex 1, by Ministers or by the Ministerial Conference, and may establish other bodies or consolidate existing ones as appropriate. These bodies shall promulgate their respective rules of procedure subject to the approval of their respective Councils.

0137

#2

"Reservations" Language

(a) No reservations may be made in respect of any provisions of this Agreement.

(b) Reservations in respect of any of the provisions of the General Agreement on Tariffs and Trade - 1993 or any other of the Multilateral Trade Agreements may only be made in accordance with the provisions set out in those agreements.

(c) Reservations in respect of a provision of a Plurilateral Trade Agreement shall be covered by the provisions of that Agreement.

(d) Notwithstanding the provisions of paragraph (b) above, Original Members of the MTO may enter reservations in respect of the provisions of the General Agreement on Tariffs and Trade - 1993 concerning specified mandatory existing legislation which, as of the date of entry into force of this Agreement, was subject to coverage under paragraph 1(b) of the Protocol of Provisional Application of the General Agreement on Tariffs and Trade - 1947 and under equivalent provisions of the Protocols of Accession.

0138

203-4-4

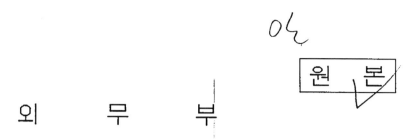

외　무　부

종　별 :

번　호 : GVW-0650　　　　　　　　일　시 : 92 0324 1820

수　신 : 장 관(봉기,경기원,재무부,농수부,상공부,특허청)

발　신 : 주 제네바 대사

제　목 : UR/법제화 그룹 제 5차 공식회의(공봉문제,1)

1. 3.23 표제회의가 개최되어 공봉문제 의 범위,추진방향 및 사무국 문서(522. 별첨 1)에 대한 일반 토의가 있었는바, 결과 아래 보고함.

　　가. 공봉문제의 범위

　　0 CANADA 등 일부국이 상기 사무국 문서에 포함된 사항외에 LEGAL FORM 제도 관련 사항, FINALCLAUSES 등 사무국 문서 402 에 포함된 여타 사항의 취급 필요성을 제기하였으나 의장은 동문제들에 대한 검토를 배제하지는 않았으나 여타 사항 논의시 상당 검토가 이루어 졌음을 상기시킴(EC도 같은 입장)

　　0 미국은 TRACK 3 에서 협정들간 실질 내용이 상충하는 경우 이를 조화시켜야 한다고 언급한뒤 검토대상 사항을 다수 예시하면서 이를 조만간(가능하면 3.24) 문서로 제출하겠다고 제의함.

　　0 싱가폴, 인도, 일본등은 실질 내용에 대한 변경(협상의 REOPENING)은 TRACK 3 의 권한 밖이라고 지적하고, 조화를 위한 조화에도 반대한다는 입장을 표명(카나다도 신중한 입장표명)

　　나. 작업 방식

　　0 미국이 TASK FORCE 설치를 제의(EC 지지)한데 대해 의장은 앞으로의 작업 진행을 보아가면서 결정키로 함.

　　2. 사무국 문서 522 에 대한 논의

　　가. A 1 (용어)

　　0 다수 국가가 용어문제가 검토대상임은 인정하면서도 개별 협정의 특수성에 비추어 신중히 검토해야 할 사항임을 지적함.

　　나. A 2(개별 협정상의 체약국단)

　　0 다수국가가 개별협정상의 체약국단(CONTRACTINGPARTIES)의 용어를 해당 특별

통상국　2차보　　　　　　　　　　　　경기원　　재무부　　농수부　　상공부

특허청

PAGE 1　　　　　　　　　　　　　　　　92.03.25　　05:03 FN

이사회(SC) 로 바꾸자는 사무국안에 대해 각협정상의 CP 는경우에 따라 MC 또는 GC 를 의미하는 경우도 있다는 문제점을 제기함.

　다. B (보조금 협정과 TRIMS 협정상의의무면제 기간)

　0 미국은 사무국이 지적한 문제점(양규정의상충)을 인정한데 대해 카나다, EC 는양협정은 각각 다른 사항을 규정하고 있으므로 상충되지 않는다는 입장

　라. D(LLDC 에 대한 정의)

　0 미국은 LLDC 에 대한 정의는 각국이 독자적으로 결정할 사항이라는 입장 표명

　0 오지리, 나이제리아, 탄자니아는 LLDC 의 정의는 UN 의 정의에 따라야 한다는사무국 의견 지지입장 피력

　마. C 항(PSI 와 CV)

　0 사무국의 추가검토가 필요하다는 의장의 설명에따라, 논의 대상에서 제외

　3. 3.24 에는 개별협정(P.Q.U.V.W.R.M)의 사무국 수정안(자구수정) 배포 및 설명에 이어, 공통문제 범위에 대한 미국제안을 논의 예정임. 끝

　첨부: 사무국 문서 522 (GVW(F)-207)

　(대사 박수길-국장)

PAGE 2

0140

주 제 네 바 대 표 부

번 호 : GVW(F) - 0207   년월일 : 20324   시간 : 1820

수 신 : 장 관 (동기,경기원,재무부,농림수산부,상공부,특허청)

발 신 : 주 제 네 바 대 사

제 목 : UR 협상

총 5 매(표지포함)

보 안	
통 제	

외신관	
통 제	

0141

Cross-Cutting Issues

Informal Note by the Secretariat

Following the discussion in the Legal Drafting Group at its fourth meeting, the secretariat has identified, for examination by the Group, the four specific cross-cutting issues discussed in this note. Selection of these issues is not meant to suggest that there are no others: further issues may be raised by members of the Group.

It is recognized that the task of the Group is not to renegotiate the substance of individual texts in the Final Act, nor to attempt to harmonize their provisions. Hence, in relation to the cross-cutting issues noted in section D.4 of the Illustrative List of Points, the approach adopted by the secretariat has been not to raise issues merely because they have been treated differently in different parts of the Final Act. For example, although certain concepts, such as "industry", injury" and "like products", have not been treated identically in the texts on anti-dumping and countervailing measures, these have not been seen as requiring the Group's attention in this context. The issues identified as requiring attention, in a situation in which the individual texts are no longer stand-alone agreements, are those where two or more provisions of the Final Act texts regulate the same measure or set of measures, but do so differently, in a manner which could set up conflicting obligations, or lead to uncertainty in determining the nature of the obligations and the parties to which the obligations apply.

A.   Terminology to be used in the MTO Agreement and its Annexes

Since texts which were negotiated as stand-alone agreements will now be attached to the MTO and will be enforced by an integrated dispute settlement system, it may be advisable to carry out a rectification in some respects of the terminology used therein.

1.   With respect to references to the governments or States participating in the agreements:

The MTO refers to "Members". References within the texts in the Annexes to "parties", "Parties" (Services), "PARTIES" (TRIPs), "participants" and "signatories" should be rectified to "Members of the MTO" or "Members". This rectification would clarify the underlying legal situation that the obligations described in each text are created not by virtue of acceptance or accession to that text, but by virtue of the membership of each government in the MTO and the inclusion of that text in the MTO Annexes.

2.   With respect to references to members acting jointly:

The MTO refers to the "Ministerial Conference", the "General Council" and various other bodies. The MTO annexes refer to the "CONTRACTING PARTIES" (GATT), the "PARTIES" (Services), the "Council" (TRIPS), or the "Committee" (most of the agreements). The latest (12 March 1992) draft of the MTO prepared by the Secretariat provides that the

functions of the CONTRACTING PARTIES under the GATT 1993 shall be
carried out by the Council on Trade in Goods, and the functions of the
PARTIES under the General Agreement on Trade in Services shall be
carried out by the Council on Trade in Services. Alternatively, the
references to the CONTRACTING PARTIES and the PARTIES, respectively,
could simply be rectified to correspond to the appropriate MTO body.

B. <u>Transition periods: conflicting timetables in the Subsidies and TRIMs texts</u>

Article 28 of the Agreement on Subsidies provides that

"Subsidy programmes that have been established within the territory of
any signatory before the date on which such a signatory signed this
Agreement and which are inconsistent with the provisions of this
Agreement shall be:...brought into conformity with the provisions of
this Agreement within 3 years of the date of entry into force of this
Agreement for such signatory and until then shall not be subject to
Part II of this Agreement."

Article 5.2 of the TRIMS text provides that

"2. Each contracting party shall eliminate all TRIMs which are
notified under paragraph 1 above within two years of the date of entry
into force of this Decision in the case of a developed contracting
party, within five years in the case of a developing contracting
party, and within seven years in the case of a least-developed
contracting party."

Developing countries may receive an extension of this deadline under
Article 5.3. Article 5 of the TRIMS text in effect provides a limited-time
waiver for any local-content subsidy program notified under the TRIMs
text.

<u>If a measure falls under both provisions, which of the relevant
deadlines should apply?</u>

C. <u>Coverage of the Agreements on Preshipment Inspection and on Customs Valuation</u>

A question arises whether there is any conflict between the provisions
of the Preshipment Inspection agreement, notably those relating to price
verification, and the obligations of parties under the Agreement on Customs
Valuation, since both agreements would be part of the MTO package, and
therefore applicable to all GATT members.

0143

341dg92

Preshipment inspection, as defined in Article 1 of the PSI agreement covers a variety of activities, of which price verification is only one. Price verification itself is carried out for a variety of purposes, of which customs valuation might be one.

The PSI agreement is, in effect, a provision on special and differential treatment, recognizing the right of governments of developing countries only ("user contracting parties") to resort to the services of PSI entities and defining the conditions under which such activities are to be carried out. However, these activities will need to be carried out consistently with the obligations of governments under the Agreement on Customs Valuation.

Footnote 1 to Article 2.20 of the PSI agreement specifically states that, with respect to customs valuation, the obligations of contracting parties resorting to the services of preshipment inspection entities shall be those which they have accepted in the General Agreement and related instruments [i.e. the Valuation Code].

Would it be helpful to revise Footnote 1 to Article 2.20 in order to make explicit the obligation to respect the requirements of the Valuation Agreement?

Is there any other way of dealing with the problem?

D.   Designation of least-developed countries in MTN.TNC/W/FA

Nine[1] texts in MTN.TNC/W/FA include special provisions for least-developed countries. Two of these texts offer definitions.

Text R (Measures in favour of least-developed countries) refers in paragraph 1 to:

"... the least-developed countries recognized as such by the United Nations, and for so long as they remain in that category...".

Article 27.2 of Text I (Subsidies) exempts developing countries from the prohibition in Article 3 of the same text on the use of subsidies contingent on export performance. Under Article 27.2(a), this exemption is unconditional for those developing countries listed in Annex VII to the Agreement. Annex VII(a) lists by name the least-developed countries that are contracting parties to the GATT. It also notes, by name, the least-developed countries that apply the GATT on a de facto basis.

The list of countries that are recognized by the United Nations as least-developed is regularly revised and appears to be generally accepted as authoritative. The listing in section (a) of Annex VII to the Subsidies Agreement would appear likely to become out of date, and in any case refers to contracting parties rather than MTO members.

---

[1] In Sections B, G, L, N, O, R, S, GATS and TRIPS.

341dg92

0144

- 4 -

1. <u>Can the Group agree that if a definition of least-developed countries is required for texts in MTN.TNC/W/FA, it should be in terms similar to those used in text B?</u>

2. <u>As regards the Subsidies text, can the Group agree that a less-specific definition, similar to that in text B, might appropriately be substituted for that in section (a) of Annex VII?</u> (If so, it would need to be decided whether the exemption should be restricted to less-developed Members of the MTO, bearing in mind that the MTO text does not appear to provide a basis for <u>de facto</u> application to non-Members).

341dg92

외 무 부

종   별 :

번   호 : GVW-0657   일   시 : 92 0325 1000

수   신 : 장 관(통기,경기원,재무부,농수부,상공부,특허청)

발   신 : 주 제네바 대사

제   목 : UR/법제화 그룹 제5차 공식회의(공통문제 2)

　　3.24 표제회의에서는 개별 협정에 대한 사무국수정안(별첨 1)와 미국제안 (별첨 2)에 대한 일반토의가 있었는바, 요지 아래 보고함.

　　1. 사무국 수정안(INFORMAL NOTE 537)

　　0 동 NOTE 내용에 대해 EC 등 상당수 국가가 예비적 의견임을 전제로 대체적 동의를 표명한 반면, 카나다는 용어에 대한 검토는 신중한 접근이 필요하다고 지적함.

　　한편, 인도와 일본은 사무국의 제안에 대체적으로 동의하면서도, 세이프 가드 협정 관련 사항(2P마지막 문장)과 웨이버 및 협정 부적용(3P둘째 물장) 문제는 개별 협상 그룹의 의도가 존중되어야 함을 언급함.

　　2. 미국제안 (1146 J)

　　0 공통문제를 3개의 작업범주 (HARMONIZATION,용어의 일치, 실질 내용의 상충)로분류하고 검토대상을 광범위하게 예시하면서 HARMONIZATION 에 대해서는 소규모 작업반을 구성해서 추진하자는 미국제안에 대해 대다수 국가들이 T3 의 MANDATE 를들어 이의를 제기하여 동 제안은 일반 토의자료로서는 받아들여지지 아니함.(단, 향후검토 과정에서 사실상 상당한 참고자료로 활용될 것으로 보임.)

　　0 동 미국제안에 대한 주요 논의 내용은 아래와 같음.

　　- 동 제안의 제 1항 HARMONIZATION 관련다수국들이 HARMONIZATION 을 위한 HARMONIZATION은 UR 일정에 비추어 무의미하며, 실질문제에 대한 HARMONIZATION 은 T3 권한 밖의 사항이라하여 이에 대해서는 신중한 접근이 필요함을 지적

　　II 항의 용어의 일치, 특히 B 의 의미가 다른데도 같은 용어가 사용된 경우에 대해서도 각협상 그룹의 협상 배경이 존중되어야 하며, 만일 의미의 혼돈 또는 상충의 가능성이 있다면 이는 향후 구체적인 PANEL 과 같은 구체적인 해석기관에 맡겨져야 할 사항임을 다수국이 지적함.

통상국	경기원	재무부	농수부	상공부	특허청	

PAGE 1   92.03.26   05:25 DS

- 제 III 항 실질 내용의 상충과 관련 어떤사항들이 서로 상충하는 가에 대해서는 T3 가 파악하는 것이 유용하다고 대체적인 의견의 일치를 보면서도, 상충되는조항을 조화시키는 사항은 T3권한 밖이라는데 의견의 일치가 있었음.

- 소규모 TASK FORCE 구성 제의에 대해서도 상당수국가가 반대함.

0 아국도 미국제안에 대해 상기 취지의 이의를 제기하였는바, HARMONIZATION 을위한 HARMONIZATION 은 그 작업 필요성에 비해 시간이 너무 많이 걸리는 작업이므로 UR 협상 시한에 비추어 바람직하지 않으며, 또한 T3 MANDATE 에 비추어 각 협상 그룹의 협상 배경이 존중되어야 함을 지적하면서, 실질 내용에 관한 상충 여부 파악의 유용성은 인정하지만 T4 가동문제와 관련해서 조심스럽게 다루어야 할 사항임을 언급함. 소규모 작업반 구성에 대해서는 복수의 작업반 구성은 협상인력등감안 바람직하지 않으므로, 작업반 구성이 필요하다면 단일의 작업반만을 구성하여 단계적으로 개별 TEXT 를 검토 하여 나가자고 제의함.

3. 의장 종합 및 향후 작업 방향

0 의장은 회의결과를 아래와 같이 종합하고,참가국의 동의를 구한바, 특별히 이의를 제기한 국가는 없었음. (1) 동일용어가 협정에 따라 다른 의미로 사용되었다 하더라도 당초 협상의도를 존중해야 한다는 것이 다수의견인 것으로 이해됨.(2) 실질적인 조화작업이 필요한지 여부 결정기준은 이러한 차이가 향후 협정 이행과 관련의무의 상충을 가져오거나 혼란을 야기할 것인가의 여부가 될 것으로 봄. (3) 상기 조화작업의 내용도 기술적 사항에 속하는 사항과 권리.의무의 변경을 야기할 사항으로 구분될수 있다고 봄. (4)앞으로 예정대로 비공식회의를 통해 협정별 검토작업을해나가되, 동과정에서 상기 (2) (3)문제를 검토해 나갈수 있을 것임.

4. 건의사항

0 향후 T3 또는 T4 의 작업과 관련, 상기미측 제안 문서에 제시된 사항들에 대한검토 및 아국입장 정립이 필요한 것으로 사료되는바, 검토회시 바람.

첨부: 1. 사무국 수정안(DOC 537)

2. 미국 제안(1146 J)

(GVW(F)-210)

(대사 박수길-국장)

PAGE 2

0147

주 제 네 바 대 표 부

번 호 : GVW(F) - 0210   년월일 : 20325   시간 : 1000

수 신 : 장   관 (총기, 경기원, 재무부, 농림수산부, 상공부, 특허청)

발 신 : 주 제네바대사   !

제 목 :

GVW - 657전문

총 36 매 (표지포함)

보 안	
통 제	

외신판	
통 제	

0148

24 March 1992

REVIEW OF INDIVIDUAL TEXTS IN THE DRAFT FINAL ACT

Informal Note by the Secretariat

The present working paper has been prepared to assist the Legal Drafting Group in its consideration of a first group of individual texts in the Draft Final Act (MTN.TNC/W/FA) as suggested under item E of the Illustrative List of Points (Document 156 of 31 January 1992).

The purpose of the present note is to suggest how the texts in the Draft Final Act could be rectified to reflect (i) the discussion in the Legal Drafting Group at its meeting of 23 March 1992 concerning the terminology to be used in the MTO Agreement and its Annexes; (ii) the terms of the Draft Agreement Establishing the MTO; (iii) the Draft Understanding on Rules and Procedures Governing the Settlement of Disputes; (iv) the list of errors and omissions for corrections in the text of the Draft Final Act (Document 155 of 31 January 1992).

The rectifications in the attached texts[1] are made taking into account the following points. These points are non-exhaustive and the rectifications would be reviewed if the approach followed in this note is not supported in the discussion in the Legal Drafting Group.

Terminology

The terminology used in the individual texts has been rectified where appropriate:

- With respect to governments or States participating in the decisions for the interpretation of GATT Articles or in the Agreement on Safeguards, references within the texts to "contracting parties" have been rectified to "Members".

- With respect to references to "the General Agreement on Tariffs and Trade" and "the General Agreement" in the individual texts, it is suggested to use "GATT 1993" for GATT, dated 1993 in Annex 1A of the MTO and "GATT 1947" for GATT, dated 30 October 1947, to ensure consistency with Article II:5 of the MTO Agreement.

- The references to "developing contracting parties", "developing countries" or "less-developed contracting parties" are replaced by the term "developing Members" and the references to "least-developed countries" or "least-developed contracting parties" by "least-developed Members".

---

[1] Suggested rectifications have been marked by overstriking the words to be replaced, and the suggested replacements are in bold and underlined.

FA:

0149

Provisions relating to the settlement of disputes

There appears to be a need to update the text of a number of provisions in the individual texts to take account of the draft text of the Understanding on Rules and Procedures Governing the Settlement of Disputes.

Relationship of the provisions of the MTO to the covered texts

The provisions on waivers and non-application to be included respectively in Articles IX and XIII of the MTO Agreement are still under discussion. It is suggested that the discussion on the treatment of the text of the Understandings on the Interpretation of Articles XXV and XXXV of the GATT be taken up after a decision is taken in the context of the MTO.

Additional Technical Corrections

Understanding on the Interpretation of Article XXIV: In paragraph 4, line 6, the reference to the "1990 Decision on Article XXVIII" should be replaced by "the Understanding on the Interpretation of Article XXVIII of the General Agreement on Tariffs and Trade".

Agreement on Safeguards: In paragraph 20, line 7, it is suggested to replace "for" by "after".

The attached texts are suggested revisions of the following sections of the Draft Final Act, to be reviewed during the Group's meetings in the week of 23 March.

P   Understanding on the Interpretation of Article II:1(b) of the General Agreement on Tariffs and Trade

Q   Understanding on the Interpretation of Article XVII of the General Agreement on Tariffs and Trade

R   Balance-of-Payments Provisions of the General Agreement on Tariffs and Trade

T   Understanding on the Interpretation of Article XXIV of the General Agreement on Tariffs and Trade

V   Understanding on the Interpretation of Article XXV of the General Agreement on Tariffs and Trade

X   Understanding on the Interpretation of Article XXXV of the General Agreement on Tariffs and Trade

W   Understanding on the Interpretation of Article XXVIII of the General Agreement on Tariffs and Trade

M   Agreement on Safeguards

FA: 0150

F. UNDERSTANDING ON THE INTERPRETATION OF ARTICLE II:1(b) OF THE GENERAL AGREEMENT ON TARIFFS AND TRADE 1993

1.   It is agreed that in order to ensure transparency of the legal rights and obligations deriving from Article II:1(b), the nature and level of any 'other duties or charges' levied on bound tariff items, as referred to in that provision, shall be recorded in the Schedules of tariff concessions against the tariff item to which they apply. It is understood that such recording does not change the legal character of 'other duties or charges'.

2.   The date as of which 'other duties or charges' are bound, for the purposes of Article II, shall be the date of the Uruguay Round Protocol to the General Agreement on Tariffs and Trade 1993. 'Other duties or charges' shall therefore be recorded in the Schedules of concessions at the levels applying on this date. At each subsequent renegotiation of a concession or negotiation of a new concession the applicable date for the tariff item in question shall become the date of the incorporation of the new concession in the Schedules of concessions. However, the date of the instrument by which a concession on any particular item was first incorporated into the General Agreement GATT 1947 shall also continue to be recorded in column 6 of the Loose-Leaf Schedules.

3.   'Other duties or charges' shall be recorded in respect of all tariff bindings.

4.   Where a tariff item has previously been the subject of a concession, the level of 'other duties or charges' recorded in the Schedules of concessions shall not be higher than the level obtaining at the time of the first incorporation of the concession in the Schedules. It will be open to any contracting-party Member to challenge the existence of an 'other duty or charge', on the ground that no such 'other duty or charge' existed at the time of the original binding of the item in question, as well as the consistency of the recorded level of any 'other duty or charge' with the previously bound level, for a period of three years after the deposit with the WTO Secretariat of the Schedule in question.

5.   It is agreed that the recording of 'other duties or charges' in the Schedules of concessions is without prejudice to their consistency with rights and obligations under the General Agreement GATT 1993 other than those affected by paragraph 4 above. All contracting-parties Members retain the right to challenge, at any time, the consistency of any 'other duty or charge' with such obligations.

6.   For the purposes of this decision Understanding, the procedures provisions of Articles XXII and XXIII of the GATT 1993 and the normal-GATT procedures-of-consultation-and-dispute-settlement Understanding on Rules and Procedures Governing the Settlement of Disputes will apply.

---

*The-legal-form-of-this-decision-will-be-decided-at-a-later-stage.

FA:

7.   It is agreed that "other duties or charges" omitted from a Schedule at the time of its deposit with the MTO Secretariat shall not subsequently be added to it and that any "other duty or charge" recorded at a level lower than that prevailing on the applicable date shall not be restored to that level unless such additions or changes are made within six months of the deposit of the Schedule.

8.   The decision in paragraph 2 above regarding the date applicable to each concession for the purposes of Article II:1(b) supersedes the decision regarding the applicable date taken by the GATT 1947 Council on 26 March 1980 (BISD 27S/22).

0152

9. UNDERSTANDING ON THE INTERPRETATION OF ARTICLE XVII OF THE GENERAL AGREEMENT ON TARIFFS AND TRADE 1993

Noting that Article XVII provides for obligations on ~~contracting parties~~ Members in respect of the activities of the state trading enterprises referred to in Article XVII:1, which are required to be consistent with the general principles of non-discriminatory treatment prescribed in the ~~General Agreement~~ GATT 1993 for governmental measures affecting imports or exports by private traders;

Noting further that ~~contracting parties~~ Members are subject to their GATT obligations in respect of those governmental measures affecting state trading enterprises;

Recognizing that this ~~decision~~ Understanding is without prejudice to the substantive disciplines prescribed in Article XVII;

1. It is agreed that in order to ensure the transparency of the activities of state trading enterprises, such enterprises shall be notified to the ~~CONTRACTING-PARTIES~~ Council on Trade in Goods, for review by the working party to be set up under paragraph 5 below, in accordance with the following working definition:

> "Governmental and non-governmental enterprises, including marketing boards, which have been granted exclusive or special rights or privileges, including statutory or constitutional powers, in the exercise of which they influence through their purchases or sales the level or direction of imports or exports."

This notification requirement does not apply to imports of products for immediate or ultimate consumption in governmental use or in use by an enterprise as specified above and not otherwise for resale or use in the production of goods for sale.

2. It is agreed that each ~~contracting-party~~ Member shall conduct a review of its policy with regard to the submission of notifications on state trading enterprises to the ~~CONTRACTING-PARTIES~~ Council on Trade in Goods, taking account of the provisions of this ~~decision~~ Understanding. In carrying out such a review, each ~~contracting-party~~ Member should have regard to the need to ensure the maximum transparency possible in its notifications so as to permit a clear appreciation of the manner of operation of the enterprises notified and the effect of their operations on international trade.

3. Notifications shall be made in accordance with the 1960 questionnaire on state trading (BISD, 9S/184), it being understood that ~~contracting parties~~ Members shall notify the enterprises referred to in paragraph 1 above whether or not imports or exports have in fact taken place.

4. Any ~~contracting-party~~ Member which has reason to believe that another ~~contracting-party~~ Member has not adequately met its notification obligation may raise the matter with the ~~contracting-party~~ Member concerned. If the

FA:

0153

210-36-7

- 7 -

matter is not satisfactorily resolved it may make a counter-notification to the ~~CONTRACTING-PARTIES~~ Council on Trade in Goods, for consideration by the working party set up under paragraph 5 below, simultaneously informing the ~~contracting-party~~ Member concerned.

5. A working party shall be set up, on behalf of the ~~CONTRACTING-PARTIES~~ Council on Trade in Goods, to review notifications and counter-notifications. In the light of this review and without prejudice to Article XVII:4(c), the ~~CONTRACTING-PARTIES~~ Council on Trade in Goods may make recommendations with regard to the adequacy of notifications and the need for further information. The working party shall also review, in the light of the notifications received, the adequacy of the 1960 questionnaire on state trading and the coverage of state trading enterprises notified under paragraph 1 above. It shall also develop an illustrative list showing the kinds of relationships between governments and enterprises, and the kinds of activities, engaged in by these enterprises, which may be relevant for the purposes of Article XVII. It is understood that the ~~GATT~~ MTO Secretariat will provide a general background paper for the working party on the operations of state trading enterprises as they relate to international trade. Membership of the working party shall be open to all ~~contracting-parties~~ Members indicating their wish to serve on it. It shall meet within a year of the entry into force of this Understanding and thereafter at least once a year. It shall report annually to the ~~CONTRACTING-PARTIES~~ Council on Trade in Goods.

0154

R. <u>UNDERSTANDING ON THE BALANCE-OF-PAYMENTS PROVISIONS OF THE GENERAL</u>
<u>AGREEMENT ON TARIFFS AND TRADE 1993</u>

The <u>CONTRACTING-PARTIES (Correction Document 155)</u>
<u>Members</u>

<u>Recognizing</u> the provisions of Articles XII, XVIII:B of the ~~General~~
~~Agreement~~ <u>GATT 1993</u> and of the 1979 Declaration on Trade Measures taken for
Balance-of-Payments Purposes (hereafter referred to as the
"1979 Declaration") and in order to clarify such provisions.[1]

<u>Decide</u> as follows:

<u>Application of Measures</u>

1. ~~Contracting-parties~~ <u>Members</u> confirm their commitment to publicly
announce, as soon as possible, time-schedules for the removal of
restrictive import measures taken for balance-of-payments purposes. It is
understood that such time-schedules may be modified as appropriate to take
into account changes in the balance-of-payments situation. Wherever a
time-schedule is not publicly announced, justification shall be provided as
to the reasons therefor.

2. ~~Contracting-parties~~ <u>Members</u> confirm their commitment to give
preference to those measures which have the least disruptive effect on
trade. Such measures (hereafter referred to as "price-based measures")
shall be understood to include import surcharges, import deposit
requirements or other equivalent trade measures with an impact on the price
of imported goods. It is understood that, notwithstanding the provisions
of Article II, price-based measures taken for balance-of-payments purposes
may be applied in excess of the duties inscribed in the schedule of a
~~contracting-party~~ <u>Member</u>. Furthermore, the amount by which the price-based
measure exceeds the bound duty shall be clearly and separately indicated
under the notification procedures of this ~~Decision~~ <u>Understanding</u>.

3. ~~Contracting-parties~~ <u>Members</u> shall seek to avoid the imposition of new
quantitative restrictions for balance-of-payments purposes unless, because
of a critical balance-of-payments situation, price-based measures cannot
arrest a sharp deterioration in the external payments position. In those
cases in which a ~~contracting-party~~ <u>Member</u> applies quantitative
restrictions, justification shall be provided as to the reasons why
price-based measures are not an adequate instrument to deal with the

---

[1] Nothing in this ~~Decision~~ <u>Understanding</u> is intended to modify the
rights and obligations of ~~contracting-parties~~ <u>Members</u> under Articles XII or
XVIII:B of the ~~General Agreement~~ <u>GATT 1993</u>. The dispute settlement
provisions of the ~~General Agreement~~ <u>GATT 1993 and the Understanding on</u>
<u>Rules and Procedures Governing the Settlement of Disputes</u> may be invoked
with respect to any matters arising from the application of restrictive
import measures taken for balance-of-payments reasons.

FA:

0155

balance-of-payments situation. A contracting-party Member maintaining quantitative restrictions shall indicate in successive consultations the progress made in significantly reducing the incidence and restrictive effect of such measures. It is understood that not more than one type of restrictive import measure taken for balance-of-payments reasons may be applied on the same product.

4. Contracting-parties Members confirm that restrictive import measures taken for balance-of-payments reasons may only be applied to control the general level of imports and may not exceed what is necessary to address the balance-of-payments situation. In order to minimise any incidental protective effects, restrictions shall be administered in a transparent manner. The authorities of the importing contracting-party Member shall provide adequate justification as to the criteria used to determine which products are subject to restriction. As provided in Articles XII:3 and XVIII:B:10, parties Members may, in the case of certain essential products, exclude or limit the application of surcharges applied across the board or other measures applied for balance-of-payments reasons. The term essential products shall be understood to mean products which meet basic consumption needs or which contribute to the contracting-party's Member's effort to improve its balance-of-payments situation, such as capital goods or inputs needed for production. In the administration of quantitative restrictions, discretionary licensing shall be used only when unavoidable and be progressively phased out. Appropriate justification shall be provided as to the criteria used to determine allowable import quantities or values.

Procedures for Balance-of-Payments consultations

5. The GATT Committee on Balance-of-Payments Restrictions (hereafter referred to as 'Committee') shall carry out consultations in order to review all restrictive import measures taken for balance-of-payments purposes. The membership of the Committee is open to all contracting parties Members indicating their wish to serve in it. The Committee shall follow the procedures for consultations on balance-of-payments restrictions approved by the GATT 1947 Council on 28 April 1970 and set out in BISD, Eighteenth Supplement, pages 48-53 (hereafter referred to as "Full consultation Procedures"), subject to the provisions set out below.

6. A contracting-party Member applying new restrictions or raising the general level of its existing restrictions by a substantial intensification of the measures shall enter into consultations with the Committee within four months of the adoption of such measures. The contracting-party Member adopting such measures may request that a consultation be held under Article XII:4(a) or Article XVIII:12(a) as appropriate. If no such request has been made, the Chairman of the Committee shall invite the contracting party Member to hold such consultation. Factors that may be examined in the consultation would include, inter alia, the introduction of new types of restrictive measures for balance-of-payments purposes, or an increase in the level or product coverage of restrictions.

7. All restrictions applied for balance-of-payments purposes shall be subject to periodic review in the Committee under paragraph 4(b) of

FA:

0156

- 10 -

Article XII or under paragraph 12(b) of Article XVIII, subject to the possibility of altering the periodicity of consultations in agreement with the consulting ~~contracting-party~~ Member or pursuant to any specific review procedure that may be recommended by the General Council.

8.   Consultations may be held under simplified procedures in the case of least-developed ~~contracting-parties~~ Members or in the case of ~~less-developed-contracting-parties~~ developing Members which are pursuing liberalisation efforts in conformity with the schedule presented to the Committee in previous consultations. Simplified consultations may also be held when the Trade Policy Review of a ~~less-developed-contracting-party~~ developing Member is scheduled for the same calendar year as the date fixed for the consultations. In such cases the decision as to whether a full consultation should be held will be made on the basis of the factors enumerated in paragraph 8 of the 1979 Declaration. Except in the case of least-developed ~~contracting-parties~~ Members, no more than two successive consultations may be held under simplified procedures.

Notification and Documentation

9.   A ~~contracting-party~~ Member shall notify to the ~~CONTRACTING-PARTIES~~ General Council the introduction of or any changes in the application of restrictive import measures taken for balance-of-payments purposes as well as any modifications in time schedules for the removal of such measures as announced under paragraph 1. Significant changes shall be notified to the ~~CONTRACTING-PARTIES~~ General Council prior to or not later than 30 days after their announcement. A consolidated notification, including all changes in laws, regulations, policy statements or public notices, shall be made available to the ~~GATT~~ MTO Secretariat on a yearly basis for examination by ~~contracting-parties~~ Members. Notifications shall include full information, as far as possible, at the tariff line level, on the type of measures applied, the criteria used for their administration, product coverage and trade flows affected.

10.   At the request of any ~~contracting-party~~ Member, notifications may be reviewed by the Committee. Such reviews would be limited to the clarification of specific issues raised by a notification or examination of whether a consultation under Article XII:4(a) or Article XVIII:12(a) is required. ~~Contracting-parties~~ Members which have reasons to believe that a restrictive import measure applied by another ~~contracting-party~~ Member was taken for balance-of-payments reasons may bring the matter to the attention of the Committee. The Chairman of the Committee shall request information on the measure and make it available to all ~~contracting-parties~~ Members. Without prejudice to the right of any member of the Committee to seek appropriate clarifications in the course of consultations, questions may be submitted in advance for consideration by the consulting ~~contracting-party~~ Member.

11.   The consulting ~~contracting-party~~ Member shall prepare a Basic Document for the consultations which, in addition to any other information considered to be relevant, should include: (a) an overview of the balance-of-payments situations and prospects, including a consideration of

FA:

0157

- 11 -

the internal and external factors having a bearing on the
balance-of-payments situation and the domestic policy measures taken in
order to restore equilibrium on a sound and lasting basis; (b) a full
description of the restrictions applied for balance-of-payments reasons,
their legal basis and steps taken to reduce incidental protective effects;
(c) measures taken since the last consultation to liberalise import
restrictions, in the light of the conclusions of the Committee; (d) plan
for the elimination and progressive relaxation of remaining restrictions.
References may be made, when relevant, to the information provided in other
GATT notifications or reports. Under Simplified Consultations, the
consulting ~~contracting-party~~ Member shall submit a written statement
containing essential information on the elements covered by the Basic
Document.

12.   The ~~GATT~~ MTO Secretariat shall, with a view to facilitating the
consultations in the Committee, prepare a factual background paper dealing
with the different aspects of the plan for consultations. In the case of
less developed ~~contracting-parties~~ Members, the Secretariat document will
include relevant background and analytical material on the incidence of the
external trading environment on the balance-of-payments situation and
prospects of the consulting ~~country~~ Member. The technical assistance
services of the ~~GATT~~ MTO Secretariat shall, at the request of a less
developed ~~contracting-party~~ Member, assist in preparing the documentation
for the consultations.

Conclusions of Balance-of-Payments consultations

13.   The Committee shall report on its consultations to the General
Council. In the case of full consultations, the report should indicate the
Committee's conclusions on the different elements of the plan for
consultations, as well as the facts and reasons on which they are based.
The Committee shall endeavour to include in its conclusions proposals for
recommendations aimed at promoting the implementation of Articles XII,
XVIII:B, the 1979 Declaration and this ~~Decision~~ Understanding. In those
cases in which a time-schedule has been presented for the removal of
restrictive measures taken for balance-of-payments reasons, the General
Council may recommend that, in adhering to such a time-schedule, a
~~contracting-party~~ Member shall be deemed to be in compliance with its
GATT 1993 obligations. Whenever the General Council has made specific
recommendations, the rights and obligations of ~~contracting-parties~~ Members
shall be assessed in the light of such recommendations. In the absence of
specific proposals for ~~Council~~ recommendations of the General Council, the
Committee's conclusions should record the different views expressed in the
Committee. In the case of simplified consultations, the report shall
include a summary of the main elements discussed in the Committee and a
decision on whether Full Consultations are required.

FA:

0158

U. UNDERSTANDING ON THE INTERPRETATION OF ARTICLE XXIV OF THE GENERAL AGREEMENT ON TARIFFS AND TRADE 1993

PREAMBLE

The ~~CONTRACTING-PARTIES~~ Members

Having regard to the provisions of Article XXIV of the GATT 1993;

. Recognizing that customs unions and free trade areas have greatly increased in number and importance since the establishment of the GATT 1947 and today cover a significant proportion of world trade;

Recognizing the contribution to the expansion of world trade that may be made by closer integration between the economies of the parties to such agreements;

Recognizing also that such contribution is increased if the elimination between the constituent territories of duties and other restrictive regulations of commerce extends to all trade, and diminished if any major sector of trade is excluded;

Reaffirming that the purpose of such agreements should be to facilitate trade between the constituent territories and not to raise barriers to the trade of other ~~contracting-parties~~ Members with such territories; and that in their formation or enlargement the parties to them should to the greatest possible extent avoid creating adverse effects on the trade of other ~~contracting-parties~~ Members;

Convinced also of the need to reinforce the effectiveness of the role of the ~~CONTRACTING-PARTIES~~ Council on Trade in Goods in reviewing agreements notified under Article XXIV, by clarifying the criteria and procedures for the assessment of new or enlarged agreements, and improving the transparency of all Article XXIV agreements;

Recognizing the need for a common understanding of the obligations of ~~contracting-parties~~ Members under Article XXIV:12;

Agree as follows:

1.   Customs unions, free trade areas, and interim agreements leading to the formation of a customs union or free trade area, to be consistent with Article XXIV, must satisfy the provisions of its paragraphs 5, 6, 7 and 8 inter alia.

Article XXIV:5

2.   The evaluation under Article XXIV:5(a) of the general incidence of the duties and other regulations of commerce applicable before and after the formation of a customs union shall in respect of duties and charges be based upon an overall assessment of weighted average tariff rates and of customs duties collected. This assessment shall be based on import statistics for a previous representative period to be supplied by the customs union, on a tariff line basis and in values and quantities, broken down by GATT country of origin. The ~~GATT~~ MTO Secretariat shall compute the weighted average tariff rates and customs duties collected in accordance with the methodology used in the assessment of tariff offers in the Uruguay Round. For this purpose, the duties and charges to be taken into consideration shall be the applied rates of duty. It is recognised that for the purpose of the overall assessment of the incidence of other regulations of commerce for which quantification and aggregation are difficult, the examination of individual measures, regulations, products covered and trade flows affected may be required.

3.   The "reasonable length of time" referred to in Article XXIV:5(c) should exceed ten years only in exceptional cases. In cases where ~~contracting-parties~~ Members believe that ten years would be insufficient they shall provide a full explanation to the ~~CONTRACTING-PARTIES~~ Council on Trade in Goods of the need for a longer period.

Article XXIV:6

4.   Paragraph 6 of Article XXIV establishes the procedure to be followed when a ~~contracting-party~~ Member forming a customs union proposes to increase a bound rate of duty. In this regard it is reaffirmed that the procedure set forth in Article XXVIII, as elaborated in the guidelines adopted by the GATT 1947 CONTRACTING PARTIES on 10 November 1980 (27S/26) and in the Understanding on the Interpretation of Article XXVIII of the General Agreement on Tariffs and Trade 1993, must be commenced before tariff concessions are modified or withdrawn upon the formation of a customs union or an interim agreement leading to the formation of a customs union.

5.   It is agreed that these negotiations will be entered into in good faith with a view to achieving mutually satisfactory compensatory adjustment. In such negotiations, as required by Article XXIV:6, due account shall be taken of reductions of duties on the same tariff line made by other constituents of the customs union upon its formation. Should such reductions not be sufficient to provide the necessary compensatory adjustment, the customs union would offer compensation, which may take the form of reductions of duties on other tariff lines. Such an offer shall be taken into consideration by the ~~contracting-parties~~ Members having negotiating rights in the binding being modified or withdrawn. Should the compensatory adjustment remain unacceptable, negotiations should be continued. Where, despite such efforts, agreement in negotiations on compensatory adjustment under Article XXVIII cannot be reached within a reasonable period from the initiation of negotiations, the customs union

FA:

0160

shall, nevertheless, be free to modify or withdraw the concessions; affected contracting-parties Members shall then be free to withdraw substantially equivalent concessions in accordance with Article XXVIII.

6.   The General-Agreement GATT 1993 imposes no obligation on contracting parties Members benefiting from a reduction of duties consequent upon the formation of a customs union, or an interim agreement leading to the formation of a customs union, to provide compensatory adjustment to its members.

<u>Review of Customs Unions and Free Trade Areas</u>

7.   All notifications made under Article XXIV:7(a) shall be examined by a working party in the light of the relevant provisions of the General Agreement GATT 1993 and of paragraph 1 of this Decision Understanding. The working party shall submit a report to the CONTRACTING-PARTIES Council on Trade in Goods on its findings in this regard. The CONTRACTING-PARTIES Council on Trade in Goods may make such recommendations to contracting parties Members as they deem appropriate.

8.   In regard to interim agreements, the working party may in its report make appropriate recommendations on the proposed timeframe and on measures required to complete the formation of the customs union or free trade area. It may if necessary provide for further review of the agreement.

9.   Substantial changes in the plan and schedule included in an interim agreement shall be notified, and shall be examined by the CONTRACTING PARTIES Council on Trade in Goods if so requested.

10. Should an interim agreement notified under Article XXIV:7(a) not include a plan and schedule, contrary to Article XXIV:5(c), the working party shall in its report recommend such a plan and schedule. The parties shall not maintain or put into force, as the case may be, such agreement if they are not prepared to modify it in accordance with these recommendations. Provision shall be made for subsequent review of the implementation of the recommendations.

11. Customs unions and members of free trade areas shall report periodically to the CONTRACTING-PARTIES Council on Trade in Goods, as envisaged by the GATT 1947 CONTRACTING PARTIES in their instruction to the GATT 1947 Council concerning reports on regional agreements (BISD 18S/38), on the operation of the relevant agreement. Any significant changes and/or developments in the agreements should be reported as they occur.

<u>Dispute Settlement</u>

12. The dispute settlement provisions of the General-Agreement GATT 1993 and the Understanding on Rules and Procedures Governing the Settlement of Disputes may be invoked with respect to any matters arising from the application of those provisions of Article XXIV relating to customs unions, free trade areas or interim agreements leading to the formation of a customs union or free trade area.

FA:

0161

Article XXIV:12

13.   Each ~~contracting-party~~ <u>Member</u> is fully responsible under the ~~General Agreement~~ <u>GATT 1993</u> for the observance of all provisions of the ~~General Agreement~~ <u>GATT 1993</u>, and shall take such reasonable measures as may be available to it to ensure such observance by regional and local governments and authorities within its territory.

14.   The dispute settlement provisions of the ~~General Agreement~~ <u>GATT 1993 and the Understanding on Rules and Procedures Governing the Settlement of Disputes</u> may be invoked in respect of measures affecting its observance taken by regional or local governments or authorities within the territory of a ~~contracting-party~~ <u>Member</u>. When the ~~CONTRACTING-PARTIES~~ <u>Council on Trade in Goods</u> ~~have~~ <u>has</u> ruled that a provision of the ~~General Agreement~~ <u>GATT 1993</u> has not been observed, the responsible ~~contracting-party~~ <u>Member</u> shall take such reasonable measures as may be available to it to ensure its observance. The provisions relating to compensation and suspension of concessions or other obligations apply in cases where it has not been possible to secure such observance.

15.   Each ~~contracting-party~~ <u>Member</u> undertakes to accord sympathetic consideration to and afford adequate opportunity for consultation regarding any representations made by another ~~contracting-party~~ <u>Member</u> concerning measures affecting the operation of the ~~General Agreement~~ <u>GATT 1993</u> taken within the territory of the former.

FA:

0162

V. UNDERSTANDING ON THE INTERPRETATION OF ARTICLE XXV OF THE GENERAL AGREEMENT ON TARIFFS AND TRADE

1. It is agreed that a request for a waiver or for an extension of an existing waiver shall describe the measures which the contracting party proposes to take, the specific policy objectives which the contracting party seeks to pursue and the reasons which prevent the contracting party from achieving its policy objectives by measures consistent with its obligations under the General Agreement.

2. A decision by the CONTRACTING PARTIES granting a waiver shall state the exceptional circumstances justifying the decision, the terms and conditions governing the application of the waiver, and the date on which the waiver shall terminate.

3. Any waiver granted for a period of more than one year shall be reviewed by the CONTRACTING PARTIES not later than one year after it was granted, and thereafter annually until the waiver terminates. In each review, the CONTRACTING PARTIES shall examine whether the exceptional circumstances justifying the waiver still exist and whether the terms and conditions attached to the waiver have been met. The CONTRACTING PARTIES, on the basis of the annual review, may extend, modify or terminate the waiver.

4. Any waiver in effect on the date of this Decision shall terminate, unless extended in accordance with the procedures above, on the date of its expiry or [ ] year[s] from the date of this Decision, whichever is earlier.

5. Any contracting party considering that a benefit accruing to it under the General Agreement is being nullified or impaired as a result of

    (a) the failure of the contracting party to whom a waiver was granted to observe the terms or conditions of the waiver, or

    (b) the application of a measure consistent with the terms and conditions of the waiver

may invoke the provisions of Article XXIII.

FA:

X. UNDERSTANDING ON THE INTERPRETATION OF ARTICLE XXXV OF THE GENERAL AGREEMENT ON TARIFFS AND TRADE

PREAMBLE

The CONTRACTING PARTIES

Having regard to the linked provisions of paragraph 1 of Article XXXV of the General Agreement on Tariffs and Trade;

Noting that by invoking Article XXXV a contracting party on the one hand, or a government acceding to the General Agreement on the other, declines to apply the General Agreement, or alternatively Article II of that Agreement, to the other party;

Desiring to ensure that tariff negotiations between contracting parties and a government acceding to the General Agreement are not inhibited by unwillingness to accept an obligation to apply the General Agreement as a consequence of entry into such negotiations;

Agree as follows:

A contracting party and a government acceding to the General Agreement on Tariffs and Trade may engage in negotiations relating to the establishment of a GATT schedule of concessions by the acceding government without prejudice to the right of either to invoke Article XXXV in respect of the other.

FA:

0164

W. UNDERSTANDING ON THE INTERPRETATION OF ARTICLE XXVIII OF THE GENERAL AGREEMENT ON TARIFFS AND TRADE 1993

1. For the purposes of modification or withdrawal of a concession, the ~~contracting-party~~ Member which has the highest ratio of exports affected by the concession (i.e., exports of the product to the market of the ~~country~~ Member modifying or withdrawing the concession) to its total exports shall be deemed to have a principal supplying interest if it does not already have an initial negotiating right or a principal supplying interest as provided for in Article XXVIII:1. It is however agreed that this paragraph will be reviewed five years from the date of this ~~decision~~ Understanding by the ~~Committee on Tariff Concessions~~ Council on Trade in Goods with a view to deciding whether this criterion has worked satisfactorily in securing a redistribution of negotiating rights in favour of small and medium-sized exporting ~~contracting-parties~~ Members. If this is not the case consideration will be given to possible improvements, including, in the light of the availability of adequate data, the adoption of a criterion based on the ratio of exports affected by the concession to exports to all markets of the product in question.

2. Where a ~~contracting-party~~ Member considers that it has a principal supplying interest in terms of paragraph 1 above, it should communicate its claim in writing, with supporting evidence, to the ~~contracting-party~~ Member proposing to modify or withdraw a concession, and at the same time inform the MTO Secretariat. Paragraph 4 of the "Procedures for Negotiations under Article XXVIII" (BISD 27S/26) shall apply in these cases.

3. In the determination of ~~contracting-parties~~ Members with a principal supplying interest (whether as provided for in paragraph 1 above or in Article XXVIII:1) or substantial interest, it is agreed that only trade in the affected product which has taken place on an MFN basis shall be taken into consideration. However, trade in the affected product which has taken place under non-contractual preferences shall also be taken into account if the trade in question has ceased to benefit from such preferential treatment, thus becoming MFN trade, at the time of the renegotiation or will do so by its conclusion.

4. When a tariff concession is modified or withdrawn on a new product (i.e., a product for which three years' trade statistics are not available) the ~~country~~ Member possessing initial negotiating rights on the tariff line where the product is or was formerly classified shall be deemed to have an initial negotiating right in the concession in question. The determination of principal supplying and substantial interests and the calculation of compensation shall inter alia take into account production capacity and investment in the affected product in the exporting ~~country~~ Member and estimates of export growth, as well as forecasts of demand for the product in the importing ~~country~~ Member. For the purposes of this paragraph "new product" is understood to include a tariff item created by means of a breakout from an existing tariff line.

FA:

0165

5.   Where a contracting-party Member considers that it has a principal supplying or a substantial interest in terms of paragraph 4 above, it should communicate its claim in writing, with supporting evidence, to the contracting-party Member proposing to modify or withdraw a concession, and at the same time inform the MTO Secretariat. Paragraph 4 of the "Procedures for Negotiations under Article XXVIII" (BISD 27S/26) shall apply in these cases.

6.   When an unlimited tariff concession is replaced by a tariff rate quota, the amount of compensation provided should exceed the amount of the trade actually affected by the modification of the concession. The basis for the calculation of compensation should be the amount by which future trade prospects exceed the level of the quota. It is understood that the calculation of future trade prospects should be based on the greater of:

   (i)   the average annual trade in the most recent representative three year period, increased by the average annual growth rate of imports in that same period, or by ten per cent, whichever is the greater; or

   (ii) trade in the most recent year increased by ten per cent.

In no case shall the liability for compensation exceed that which would be entailed by complete withdrawal of the concession.

7.   Any contracting-party Member having a principal supplying interest, whether as provided for in paragraph 1 above or in Article XXVIII:1, in a concession which is modified or withdrawn shall be accorded an initial negotiating right in the compensatory concessions, unless another form of compensation is agreed by the contracting-parties Members concerned.

FA:

0166

- 20 -

M. AGREEMENT ON SAFEGUARDS

PREAMBLE

The ~~CONTRACTING-PARTIES~~ Members:

~~Having~~ in mind the overall objective of the ~~contracting-parties~~ Members to improve and strengthen the international trading system based on the ~~General-Agreement-on-Tariffs-and-Trade~~ GATT 1993;

~~Recognizing~~ the need to clarify and reinforce the disciplines of the ~~General-Agreement~~ GATT 1993, and specifically those of its Article XIX (Emergency Action on Imports of Particular Products), to re-establish multilateral control over safeguards and eliminate measures that escape such control;

~~Recognizing~~ the importance of structural adjustment and the need to enhance rather than limit competition in international markets; and

~~Recognizing~~ further that, for these purposes, a comprehensive agreement, applicable to all ~~contracting-parties~~ Members and based on the basic principles of the ~~General-Agreement~~ GATT 1993, is called for;

Hereby agree as follows:

I

GENERAL

1. This Agreement establishes rules for the application of safeguard measures which shall be understood to mean those measures provided for in Article XIX of the ~~General-Agreement~~ GATT 1993.

II

CONDITIONS

2. A ~~contracting-party~~ Member[1] may apply a safeguard measure to a product only if the importing ~~contracting-party~~ Member has determined, pursuant to

---

[1] A customs union may apply a safeguard measure as a single unit or on behalf of a member state. When a customs union applies a safeguard measure as a single unit, all the requirements for the determination of serious injury or threat thereof under this Agreement shall be based on the conditions existing in the customs union as a whole. When a safeguard measure is applied on behalf of a member state, all the requirements for the determination of serious injury or threat thereof shall be based on the conditions existing in that member state and the measure shall be limited to that member state. Nothing in this Agreement prejudges the interpretation of the relationship between Article XIX and Article XXIV:8 of the ~~General-Agreement~~ GATT 1993.

FA:

0167

the provisions set out below, that such product is being imported into its territory in such increased quantities, absolute or relative to domestic production, and under such conditions as to cause or threaten to cause serious injury to the domestic industry that produces like or directly competitive products.

3.   (a)   A contracting-party Member may apply a safeguard measure only following an investigation by the competent authorities of the importing contracting-party Member pursuant to procedures previously established and made public in consonance with Article X of the General Agreement GATT 1993. This investigation shall include reasonable public notice to all interested parties and public hearings or other appropriate means in which importers, exporters and other interested parties could present evidence and their views, including the opportunity to respond to the presentations of other parties and to submit their views, inter alia, as to whether or not the application of a safeguard measure would be in the public interest. The competent authorities shall publish a report setting forth their findings and reasoned conclusions reached on all pertinent issues of fact and law.

       (b)   Any information which is by nature confidential or which is provided on a confidential basis shall, upon cause being shown, be treated as such by the competent authorities. Such information shall not be disclosed without permission of the party submitting it. Parties providing confidential information may be requested to furnish non-confidential summaries thereof or, if such parties indicate that such information cannot be summarized, the reasons why a summary cannot be provided. However, if the competent authorities find that a request for confidentiality is not warranted and if the party concerned is either unwilling to make the information public or to authorize its disclosure in generalized or summary form, the authorities would be free to disregard such information unless it can be demonstrated to their satisfaction from appropriate sources that the information is correct.

4.   In critical circumstances where delay would cause damage which it would be difficult to repair, a provisional safeguard measure may be taken pursuant to a preliminary determination that there is clear evidence that increased imports have caused or are threatening to cause serious injury. The duration of the provisional measure shall not exceed 200 days, during which period the pertinent requirements of this Section and Section VII shall be met. Such measures should take the form of tariff increases to be promptly refunded if the subsequent investigation referred to in paragraph 7 below does not determine that increased imports have caused or threatened to cause serious injury to a domestic industry. The duration of any such provisional measure shall count towards the initial period and any extension referred to in paragraphs 10, 11 and 12 below.

5.   Safeguard measures shall be applied to a product being imported irrespective of its source.

FA:

0168

- 22 -

6.   For the purposes of this Agreement:

    (a)   serious injury shall be understood to mean a significant overall impairment in the position of a domestic industry;

    (b)   in determining injury, a domestic industry shall be understood to mean the producers as a whole of the like or directly competitive products operating within the territory of a ~~contracting-party~~, Member, or those whose collective output of the like or directly competitive products constitutes a major proportion of the total domestic production of those products;   and

    (c)   threat of serious injury shall be understood to mean serious injury that is clearly imminent, in accordance with the provisions of paragraph 7 below. A determination of the existence of a threat of serious injury shall be based on facts and not merely on allegation, conjecture or remote possibility.

7.   (a)   In the investigation to determine whether increased imports have caused or are threatening to cause serious injury to a domestic industry under the terms of this Agreement, the competent authorities shall evaluate all relevant factors of an objective and quantifiable nature having a bearing on the situation of that industry, in particular, the rate and amount of the increase in imports of the product concerned in absolute and relative terms, the share of the domestic market taken by increased imports, changes in the level of sales, production, productivity, capacity utilization, profits and losses, and employment.

    (b)   The determination referred to in sub-paragraph 7(a) shall not be made unless this investigation demonstrates, on the basis of objective evidence, the existence of the causal link between increased imports of the product concerned and serious injury or threat thereof. When factors other than increased imports are causing injury to the domestic industry at the same time, such injury shall not be attributed to increased imports.

    (c)   The competent authorities shall publish promptly, in accordance with the provisions of paragraph 3 above, a detailed analysis of the case under investigation as well as a demonstration of the relevance of the factors examined.

8.   Safeguard measures shall be applied only to the extent as may be necessary to prevent or remedy serious injury and to facilitate adjustment. If a quantitative restriction is used, such a measure shall not reduce the quantity of imports below the level of a recent period which shall be the average of imports in the last three representative years for which statistics are available, unless clear justification is given that a different level is necessary to prevent or remedy serious injury. ~~Contracting-parties~~ Members should choose measures most suitable for the achievement of these objectives.

FA:

0169

9. (a) In cases in which a quota is allocated among supplying countries, the ~~contracting-party~~ Member applying the restrictions may seek agreement with respect to the allocation of shares in the quota with all other ~~contracting-parties~~ Members having a substantial interest in supplying the product concerned. In cases in which this method is not reasonably practicable, the ~~contracting-party~~ Member concerned shall allot to ~~contracting-parties~~ Members having a substantial interest in supplying the product shares based upon the proportions, supplied by such ~~contracting-parties~~ Members during a previous representative period, of the total quantity or value of imports of the product, due account being taken of any special factors which may have affected or may be affecting the trade in the product.

    (b) A ~~contracting-party~~ Member may depart from the provisions in (a) above provided that consultations under paragraph 27 are conducted under the auspices of the ~~Safeguards~~ Committee on Safeguards established in paragraph 36 of this Agreement and that clear demonstration is provided to the Committee that (i) imports from certain ~~contracting-parties~~ Members have increased in disproportionate percentage in relation to the total increase of imports of the product concerned in the representative period, (ii) the reasons for the departure from the provisions in (a) above are justified, and (iii) the conditions of such departure are equitable to all suppliers of the product concerned. The duration of any such measure shall not be extended beyond the initial period under paragraph 10 below. The departure referred to above shall not be permitted in the case of threat of serious injury.

10. Safeguard measures shall be applied only for a period of time as may be necessary to prevent or remedy serious injury and to facilitate adjustment. It shall not exceed four years, unless this is extended under paragraph 11 below.

11. The period mentioned in paragraph 10 above may be extended provided that the competent authorities of the importing ~~contracting-party~~ Member have determined, in conformity with the procedures set out in this Section, that: the safeguard measure continues to be necessary to prevent or remedy serious injury; that there is evidence that the industry is adjusting; and that the pertinent provisions of Sections III and VII below are observed.

12. The total period of a safeguard measure including the period of application of any provisional measure, the period of initial application, and any extension thereof shall not exceed eight years.

13. In order to facilitate adjustment, if the expected duration of a safeguard measure as notified under the provisions of paragraph 25 is over one year, it shall be progressively liberalized at regular intervals during the period of application. If the duration of the measure exceeds three

FA:

0170

years, the contracting-party Member applying such a measure shall review the situation not later than the mid-term of the measure and, if appropriate, withdraw it or increase the pace of liberalization. A measure extended under paragraph 11 above shall not be more restrictive than it was at the end of the initial period, and should continue to be liberalized.

14. No safeguard measure shall be applied again to the import of a product which has been subject to such a measure, taken after the date of entry into force of this Agreement, for a period of time equal to that during which such measure had been previously applied, provided that the period of non-application is at least two years.

15. Notwithstanding the provisions of paragraph 14 above, a safeguard measure with a duration of 180 days or less may be applied again to the import of a product if:

   (a) at least one year has elapsed since the date of introduction of a safeguard measure on the import of that product; and

   (b) such a safeguard measure has not been applied on the same product more than twice in the five-year period immediately preceding the date of introduction of the measure.

III

LEVEL OF CONCESSIONS AND OTHER OBLIGATIONS

16. A contracting-party Member proposing to apply a safeguard measure or seeking an extension shall endeavour to maintain a substantially equivalent level of concessions and other obligations to that existing between it and the exporting contracting-parties Members which would be affected by such a measure under the General-Agreement GATT 1993, in accordance with the provisions of paragraph 27 below. To achieve this objective, the contracting-parties Members concerned may agree on any adequate means of trade compensation for the adverse effects of the measure on their trade.

17. If no agreement is reached within 30 days in the consultations under paragraph 27 below, then the affected exporting contracting-parties Members are free, not later than 90 days after the measure is applied, to suspend, upon the expiration of 30 days from the day on which written notice of such suspension is received by the CONTRACTING-PARTIES General Council/Council on Trade in Goods, the application of substantially equivalent concessions or other obligations under the General-Agreement GATT 1993, to the trade of the contracting-party Member applying the safeguard measure, the suspension of which the CONTRACTING-PARTIES General Council/Council on Trade in Goods do does not disapprove.

18. The right of suspension referred to in paragraph 17 above shall not be exercised for the first three years that a safeguard measure is in effect.

FA:

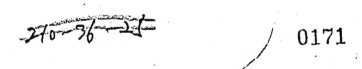

provided that the safeguard measure has been taken a result of an absolute increase in imports and that such a measure conforms to the provisions of this Agreement."

IV

DEVELOPING COUNTRIES MEMBERS

19. Safeguard measures shall not be applied against a product originating in a developing contracting-party Member as long as its share of imports of the product concerned does not exceed 3 per cent, provided that, developing contracting-parties Members with less than 3 per cent import share collectively account for not more than 9 per cent of total imports of the product concerned.[1]

20. A developing contracting-party Member shall have the right to extend the period of application of a safeguard measure for a period of up to two years beyond the maximum period provided for in paragraph 12 above. Notwithstanding the provisions of paragraph 14 above, a developing contracting-party Member shall have the right to apply a safeguard measure again to the import of a product which has been subject to such a measure, taken after the date of entry into force of this Agreement, for after a period of time equal to half that during which such a measure has been previously applied, provided that the period of non-application is at least two years.

V

EXISTING ARTICLE XIX MEASURES

21. Contracting-parties Members shall terminate all existing safeguard measures taken pursuant to Article XIX of the General-Agreement GATT 1993 not later than eight years after the date on which they were first applied or five years after the date of entry into force of this Agreement, whichever comes later.

VI

PROHIBITION AND ELIMINATION OF CERTAIN MEASURES

22. (a) A contracting-party Member shall not take or seek any emergency action on imports of particular products as set forth in Article XIX unless such action conforms with the provisions of Article XIX of the General Agreement applied in accordance with this Agreement.

---

[1] A contracting-party Member shall immediately notify such a decision to the CONTRACTING-PARTIES Committee on Safeguards.

FA:

~~210-36-26~~

(b) Furthermore, a contracting-party Member shall not seek, take or maintain any voluntary export restraints, orderly marketing arrangements or any other similar measures on the export or the import side.[1,2] These include actions taken by a single contracting-party Member as well as actions under agreements, arrangements and understandings entered into by two or more contracting-parties Members. Any such measure in effect at the time of entry into force of this Agreement shall be brought into conformity with this provision or phased out, in accordance with paragraph 23 below.

(c) Measures sought, taken or maintained by a contracting-party Member pursuant to other provisions of the General Agreement GATT 1993, or protocols and agreements or arrangements concluded within the framework of the General Agreement GATT 1993 are not included in the scope of this Agreement.

23. The phasing out of existing measures referred to in paragraph 22 above shall be carried out according to timetables to be presented to the Safeguards Committee on Safeguards by the contracting-parties Members concerned not later than 180 days after the date of entry into force of this Agreement. These timetables shall provide for all measures referred to in paragraph 22 above to be phased out or brought into conformity with this Agreement within a period not exceeding four years after the date of entry into force of this Agreement, subject to not more than one specific measure per importing contracting-party Member[3], the duration of which shall not extend beyond December 31, 1999. Any such exception must be mutually agreed between the parties Members directly concerned and notified to the Safeguards Committee on Safeguards for its review and acceptance within 90 days of the coming into force of this Agreement. The Annex to this Agreement indicates a measure which has been agreed as falling under this exception.

24. Contracting-parties Members shall not encourage nor support the adoption or maintenance by public and private enterprises of non-governmental measures equivalent to those referred to in paragraph 22 above.

---

[1] An import quota applied as a safeguard measure in conformity with the relevant provisions of the General Agreement GATT 1993 may, by mutual agreement, be administered by the exporting contracting-party Member.

[2] Examples of similar measures include export moderation, export-price or import-price monitoring systems, export or import surveillance, compulsory import cartels and discretionary export or import licensing schemes, any of which afford protection.

[3] The only such exception to which the European Community is entitled is indicated in the Annex to this Agreement.

FA:

0173

VII

NOTIFICATION AND CONSULTATION

25. A contracting-party Member shall immediately notify the
CONTRACTING-PARTIES Committee on Safeguards upon:

    (a) initiating an investigatory process relating to serious injury or
        threat thereof and the reasons for it;

    (b) making a finding of serious injury or threat thereof caused by
        increased imports; and

    (c) taking a decision to apply or extend a safeguard measure.

26. In making the notifications referred to in sub-paragraphs 25(b)
and (c) above, the contracting-party Member proposing to apply or extend a
safeguard measure shall provide the CONTRACTING-PARTIES Committee on
Safeguards with all pertinent information, which shall include evidence of
serious injury or threat thereof caused by increased imports, precise
description of the product involved and the proposed measure, proposed date
of introduction, expected duration and timetable for progressive
liberalization. In the case of an extension of a measure, evidence that
the industry concerned is adjusting shall also be provided. The
CONTRACTING-PARTIES General Council/Council on Trade in Goods or the
Safeguards Committee on Safeguards may request such additional information
as they may consider necessary from the contracting-party Member proposing
to apply or extend the measure.

27. A contracting-party Member proposing to apply or extend a safeguard
measure shall provide adequate opportunity for prior consultations with
those contracting-parties Members having a substantial interest as
exporters of the product concerned, with a view to, inter alia, reviewing
the information provided under paragraph 26 above, exchanging views on the
measure and reaching an understanding on ways to achieve the objective set
out in Paragraph 16 above.

28. A contracting-party Member shall make a notification before taking a
provisional safeguard measure referred to in paragraph 4 above.
Consultations shall be initiated immediately after the measure is taken.

29. The results of the consultations referred to in this Section, as well
as the results of mid-term reviews referred to in paragraph 13, any form of
compensation referred to in paragraph 16, and proposed suspensions of
concessions and other obligations referred to in paragraph 17, shall be
notified immediately to the CONTRACTING-PARTIES General Council/Council on
Trade in Goods by the contracting-parties Members concerned.

30. Contracting-parties Members shall notify promptly the
CONTRACTING-PARTIES Committee on Safeguards of their laws, regulations and
administrative procedures relating to safeguard measures as well as any
modifications made to them.

FA:

0174

31. Contracting-parties Members maintaining measures described in paragraphs 21 and 22 above which exist at the date on which this Agreement enters into force shall notify such measures to the CONTRACTING-PARTIES Committee on Safeguards, not later than 60 days after the entry into force of this Agreement.

32. Any contracting-party Member may notify the CONTRACTING-PARTIES Committee on Safeguards of all laws, regulations, administrative procedures and any measure or action dealt with in this Agreement that has not been notified by other contracting-parties Members that are required by this Agreement to make such notifications.

33. Any contracting-party Member may notify the CONTRACTING-PARTIES Committee on Safeguards of any non-governmental measures referred to in paragraph 24 above.

34. All notifications to the CONTRACTING-PARTIES General Council/Council on Trade in Goods referred to in this Agreement shall normally be made through the Safeguards Committee on Safeguards.

35. The provisions on notification in this Agreement shall not require any contracting-party Member to disclose confidential information which would impede law enforcement or otherwise be contrary to the public interest or would prejudice the legitimate commercial interests of particular enterprises, public or private.

VIII

SURVEILLANCE

36. There shall be a Safeguards Committee on Safeguards under the authority of the CONTRACTING-PARTIES General Council/Council on Trade in Goods, which shall be open to the participation of any contracting-party Member indicating its wish to serve on it. The Committee will have the following functions:

   (a) to monitor, and report annually to the CONTRACTING-PARTIES General Council/Council on Trade in Goods on, the general implementation of this Agreement and make recommendations towards its improvement;

   (b) to find, upon request of an affected contracting-party Member, whether or not the procedural requirements of this Agreement have been complied with in connection with a safeguard measure, and report its findings to the CONTRACTING-PARTIES General Council/ Council on Trade in Goods;

   (c) to assist contracting-parties Members, if they so request, in their consultations under the provisions of this Agreement;

FA:

0175

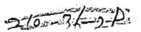

(d) to examine measures covered by paragraphs 21 and 22, monitor the phase-out of such measures and report as appropriate to the ~~CONTRACTING-PARTIES~~ General Council/Council on Trade in Goods;

(e) to review, at the request of the ~~contracting-party~~ Member taking a safeguard action, whether proposals to suspend concessions or other obligations are "substantially equivalent", and report as appropriate to the ~~CONTRACTING-PARTIES~~ General Council/Council on Trade in Goods;

(f) to receive and review all notifications provided for in this Agreement and report as appropriate to the ~~CONTRACTING-PARTIES~~ General Council/Council on Trade in Goods; and

(g) to perform any other function connected with this Agreement that the ~~CONTRACTING-PARTIES~~ General Council/Council on Trade in Goods may determine.

37. To assist the Committee in carrying out its surveillance function, the Secretariat shall prepare annually a factual report on the operation of the Agreement based on notifications and other reliable information available to it.

IX

DISPUTE SETTLEMENT

38. The provisions of Articles XXII and XXIII of the ~~General Agreement~~ GATT 1993, and the Understanding on Rules and Procedures Governing the Settlement of Disputes ~~under Articles XXII and XXIII of the General Agreement on Tariffs and Trade as adopted by the CONTRACTING-PARTIES~~ shall apply to consultations and the settlement of disputes arising under this instrument.

0176

ANNEX

EXCEPTION REFERRED TO IN PARAGRAPH 23

Parties concerned	Product	Termination
EC / Japan	Passenger cars, off road vehicles, light commercial vehicles, light trucks (up to 5 tonnes), and the same vehicles in wholly knocked-down form (CKD sets).	31 December, 1999.

0177

#2.

NON - PAPER
ISSUES OF A CROSS-CUTTING NATURE FOR POSSIBLE CONSIDERATION

I. HARMONIZATION

 A. Areas Where Harmonization is Desirable

o   We recognize that the task of the LDG is not to renegotiate
    the substance of the individual UR texts. However, in our
    view that does not mean that we should not attempt to
    harmonize some of the texts where we believe that is
    necessary. Proposals for such harmonization should be
    developed in smaller task forces that work in parallel with
    the LDG and report back to it when they have a proposal to
    make to the broader group.

o   There are several areas where such harmonization probably is
    desirable. A task force should look at each of these:

 --   Conformance of Antidumping and CVD provisions: Sweden
      was correct in noting in the LDG that there was
      agreement among negotiators that such an exercise would
      take place. If it is not to be done in the LDG, then
      some other arrangement must be made for it to be done.

 --   Treatment of Confidential Information: We believe that
      all confidential information submitted to MTO organs or
      to panels or the Appellate Body should be treated
      appropriately, i.e., not released without authorization
      from the person or authority providing such
      information. Accordingly, the confidentiality
      provisions in all texts should be examined with a view
      to harmonizing them where appropriate. Such provisions
      are found in Rules of Origin, PSI, TBT, S&P, Import
      Licensing, Subsidies, Antidumping, Safeguards, TRIPs,
      TRIMs, Services, Procurement, Customs Valuation, and
      Dispute Settlement. It would be appropriate for the
      Secretariat to prepare a compilation of all provisions
      on treatment of confidential material.

 --   Transparency provisions: We agree with the Secretariat
      suggestion in document 402 that the FOGS text, a
      central notifications registry, and a working party to
      review notification provisions might need to be
      amended. The LDG should request the Secretariat to
      prepare a compilation of all provisions on transparency
      in the various texts. A task force should also look at
      this.

0178

B. <u>Areas Where Harmonization Should be Considered</u>

o   Other cross-cutting issues that should be examined, to
     determine whether there is a need for harmonization, or for
     additional provisions, are as follows:

     --   Provisions related to <u>economic integration or customs
          unions/free-trade areas</u> (like GATT Article XXIV). A
          related question is whether the EC alone or the EC plus
          its member states will be parties, since that will
          determine whether the term "within the territory of the
          party" needs to be revised or harmonized across
          agreements;

     --   Provisions related to <u>sub-central governments</u> (like
          GATT Article XXIV:12) -- also related to the EC issue;

     --   The relationship of GATT <u>exceptions</u>, such as those in
          Articles XX and XXI, to Annex 1A agreements other than
          the GATT 1992.

o   Another issue that cuts across several agreements is the
     need for a <u>transition clause</u> -- not in the context of an
     amnesty or phase-in of obligations, but in terms of
     transition to an MTO agreement from a GATT agreement. For
     example, the dispute settlement text provides for those pre-
     existing cases that are in some stage of litigation at the
     time of entry into force of the MTO. Transition clauses are
     needed as well for pending cases covered by the Tokyo Round
     AD and CVD Codes. For example, the footnote to Article 19
     of the Antidumping Code recognizes the need for such a
     clause. It would be useful for the Secretariat to analyze
     all UR texts to determine where else such transition clauses
     might be necessary.

II.   CONSISTENCY OF TERMINOLOGY

   A. <u>Same Meaning (?) / Different Terminology (?)</u>

o   Examination of texts could suggest that certain terminology
     should be consistent throughout the texts, but it will
     require very careful analysis before rectifying the texts,
     since it would <u>not be</u> appropriate to merely replace all such
     terms globally. Such terminology includes:

     --   "less-developed country,"/"developing country "

     --   "domestic laws,"/"national laws";

     --   "business secrets,"/"business confidential
          information";

0179

-- "non-market economies,"/"economies in transition or transformation";

-- "territory,"/"customs territory,";

-- "authorities,"/"governments,"/"countries", etc. -- a global search should be done of all UR texts to determine what terms should be used.

B. Terminology usage that could create confusion

Although harmonization may be inappropriate for certain terminology, it will be important to have a negotiating history of certain terms where there is a commonality of terms across various agreements. A failure to specify different meanings for the same term (where negotiators intended a difference) could mean that the term takes on the same meaning with usage over time.

The following may not be an exhaustive list:

-- Rules of Origin/Subsidies: Refers to determinations of "domestic industry" and "like product" that are made in, inter alia, countervailing duty cases. Are they meant to have the same meaning?

-- TBT/Subsidies: common terms include "like product."

-- Services, TRIPs, TBT: all use the term "nationals." Are they meant to have the same meaning?

-- Safeguards/Subsidies: common terms include "like product," "domestic industry." In addition, common standards are used, such as injury factors and causation, with no cross-reference. Are these intended to have the same meaning?

-- AD/CVD: These two texts share many terms, e.g., "like product," domestic industry," "material injury," "interested parties," "related parties." As indicated, we believe the two texts should be conformed where appropriate.

-- Agriculture/Subsidies: The terms "subsidy" and "subsidization" are used in both texts, but only defined in the Subsidies Agreement. Should the Subsidies Agreement definitions be cross-referenced?

I. POTENTIAL SUBSTANTIVE CONFLICTS

In its note for the March 23-24 meeting, the Secretariat has identified only one of the potential conflicts between transition provisions (TRIMs/Subsidies). In addition, we see the following issues as potential conflicts and/or issues that could cause future confusion:

-- Safeguards/TRIMs: Is there a potential conflict between the transitional periods for eliminating TRIMs (Article 5) and for eliminating pre-existing Safeguards (Article 21)

Also, does para 2(c) of TRIMs Annex (regarding export prohibition) conflict with Article 23 of Safeguards Agreement, which would allow 4 years to eliminate a VRA?

-- TRIMs/Subsidies: Notification provisions in two texts may not be compatible.

-- Subsidies/Dispute Settlement: Need to clarify the relationship between the Subsidies remedy provisions and the dispute settlement text, including where the line is drawn between the DSB and the Subsidies Committee.

-- Customs Valuation/Dispute Settlement: Need to clarify the role of the Technical Committee and make time limits compatible.

-- TRIPs/Services: Is there adequate provision to facilitate the protection of ServiceMarks?

-- Safeguards/Subsidies: Can a safeguard measure imposed consistent with the Safeguards Agreement consist of a subsidy to a domestic industry and still be consistent with the Subsidies Agreement? Could it be actionable under the Subsidies Agreement?

-- MTO/Customs Valuation: Article 21.1 of the existing Valuation Code requires revision, since it allows developing countries to delay application of the Valuation Code for up to five years. Those developing countries already signatory to the Code should not get a renewed delay of five years upon joining the MTO.

-- Safeguards/Agriculture: Are these agreements to be read together to conclude that any agricultural VRA that is not tariffied must be phased out within the period specified in the Safeguards Agreement?

-- GATT Article XXVIII/Dispute Settlement: Para 6. of the GATT Article XXVIII understanding refers to a standard of calculating compensation that is specific to the replacement of a tariff by a tariff rate quota. It may be necessary to ensure that this standard applies only to Article XXVIII proceedings, since it was not meant to apply to the calculation of "equivalent" suspension of concessions or other obligations in the dispute settlement context.

-- Textiles/TRIPs: Are provisions for the treatment of trademarks compatible between these two texts?

-- FOGs/TBT: Are the notification processes in these two texts compatible?

-- Rules of Origin/AD/CVD: What are the implications for AD/CVD of the provisions in the Rules of Origin text for the treatment of inputs from or the completion of merchandise in third countries?

-- Rules of Origin/Government Procurement: Footnote 1 to Article 2(d) of Rules of Origin text needs clarification; does it effectively exclude government procurement?

-- TRIPs/GATT: Do Articles 51-60 of the TRIPs text need a footnote clarifying that they apply notwithstanding GATT Article III, since they were originally drafted with the expectation that they would be included in the Goods Annex?

-- Antidumping/Safeguards: Contrast Article 4.3 of Antidumping Agreement with footnote 1 to paragraph 2 of Safeguards Agreement. Is there a potential conflict here for customs unions?

0182

외 무 부

종 별 :

번 호 : GVW-0667

수 신 : 장 관(봉기)

발 신 : 주 제네바 대사

제 목 : UR/법제화 그룹

일 시 : 92 0325 2000

연: GVW-596, 631,642

1. 연호 MTO 협정 논의를 반영한 사무국수정안 (DOC 551)을 별첨 송부함.

2. 3.30 주간에 동수정안에 대한 심의가 있을 예정인바, 검토 의견 회시바람.

첨부: MTO 협정사무국 수정안(551).끝

(대사 박수길-국장)

통상국

PAGE 1

92.03.26   09:21 WG

외신 1과 통제관

0183

주 제 네 바 대 표 부

번 호 : GVR(F) - 0213　　　　년월일 : 20325　　시간 : 1P00

수 신 : 장　　관 (통기)

발 신 : 주 제네바대사

제 목 :

　　　　GVW-0628 회부

총 35 매 (표지포함)

보 안 통 제	

외신관 통 제	

<table>
<tr><td>배 보 치</td><td></td><td>장관실</td><td>차관실</td><td>1차보</td><td>2차보</td><td>의전장</td><td>기조실</td><td>감사관</td><td>안기부</td><td>정보
기획실</td><td>청와대</td><td>경제국</td><td>통상국</td><td>상정국</td><td>국기
구국</td><td>의연
국</td><td>재외
국민</td><td>영사
교민</td><td>중기
국</td><td>문화
국</td><td>정문
연구원</td><td>동구
일과</td><td>중소
진과</td><td>통상
협력</td><td>각기
처</td></tr>
<tr><td>치</td><td></td><td></td><td></td><td></td><td></td><td></td><td></td><td>0</td><td></td><td></td><td></td><td></td><td></td><td></td><td></td><td></td><td></td><td></td><td></td><td></td><td></td><td></td><td></td><td></td></tr>
</table>

0184

551   25 March 1992

DRAFT AGREEMENT ESTABLISHING THE MULTILATERAL TRADE ORGANIZATION

Informal note by the Secretariat

The attached further revision of the text of the MTO Agreement has been prepared by the Secretariat in the light of the discussion in the informal meetings of the Group during the week of 16 March 1992. The proposed text is printed alongside the text in the Draft Final Act. A number of drafting proposals by delegations that have not yet been discussed in the group are reproduced at the end of the text.

0185

25 March 1992

DRAFT AGREEMENT ESTABLISHING THE MULTILATERAL TRADE ORGANIZATION
SECOND REVISED TEXT

DRAFT FINAL ACT TEXT	REVISED TEXT (SECOND DRAFT)	REMARKS
AGREEMENT ESTABLISHING THE MULTILATERAL TRADE ORGANIZATION	AGREEMENT ESTABLISHING THE MULTILATERAL TRADE ORGANIZATION	
The Members,	The Parties to this Agreement,	
Recognizing that their relations in the field of trade and economic endeavour should be conducted with a view to raising standards of living, ensuring full employment and a large and steadily growing volume of real income and effective demand, developing the optimal use of the resources of the world at sustainable levels, and expanding the production and trade in goods and services,	Recognizing that their relations in the field of trade and economic endeavour should be conducted with a view to raising standards of living, ensuring full employment and a large and steadily growing volume of real income and effective demand, developing the optimal use of the resources of the world at sustainable levels, and expanding the production and trade in goods and services,	
Recognizing further that there is need for positive efforts designed to ensure that developing countries secure a share in the growth in international trade commensurate with the needs of their economic development,	Recognizing further that there is need for positive efforts designed to ensure that developing countries, and especially the least developed among them, secure a share in the growth in international trade commensurate with the needs of their economic development,	It was suggested that the question of the definition of the term "least-developed country" be addressed in the MTO Agreement or the Multilateral Trade Agreements.
Being desirous of contributing to these objectives by entering into reciprocal and mutually advantageous arrangements directed to the substantial reduction of tariffs and other barriers to trade and to the elimination of discriminatory treatment in international trade relations,	Being desirous of contributing to these objectives by entering into reciprocal and mutually advantageous arrangements directed to the substantial reduction of tariffs and other barriers to trade and to the elimination of discriminatory treatment in international trade relations,	

DRAFT FINAL ACT TEXT	REVISED TEXT (SECOND DRAFT)	REMARKS
Determined therefore, to preserve the basic principles and to further the objectives of the General Agreement on Tariffs and Trade and to develop an integrated, more viable and durable multilateral trading system encompassing the GATT as modified, all Agreements and Arrangements concluded under its auspices and the complete results of the Uruguay Round multilateral trade negotiations,	Resolved, therefore, to develop an integrated, more viable and durable multilateral trading system encompassing the General Agreement on Tariffs and Trade, the results of past trade liberalization efforts, and all of the results of the Uruguay Round of multilateral trade negotiations, Determined to preserve the basic principles and to further the objectives underlying this multilateral trading system,	
Agree as follows:	Agree as follows:	
Article I Establishment of the Organization The Multilateral Trade Organization (hereinafter referred to as "the MTO") is hereby established.	Article I Establishment of the Organization The Multilateral Trade Organization (hereinafter referred to as "the MTO") is hereby established.	

0187

DRAFT FINAL ACT TEXT	REVISED TEXT (SECOND DRAFT)	REMARKS
Article II **Scope of the MTO¹**	**Article II** **Scope of the MTO**	It has been proposed to retain the footnote in the Final Act text.
¹The provisions of the MTO Agreement are without prejudice to the substantive results of the Uruguay Round as it affects the existing rights of contracting parties under paragraph 1(b) of the Protocol of Provisional Application and under equivalent provisions of the Protocols of Accession.		
1. The Multilateral Trade Organization (MTO) shall provide the common institutional framework for the conduct of trade relations between the members of the MTO in matters related to the Agreements annexed hereto, which form an integral part of this Agreement. The Agreements and legal instruments set out in Annexes 1, 2 and 3 (hereinafter referred to as the Multilateral Trade Agreements) shall have all members as parties. Agreements and legal instruments (hereinafter referred to as the Plurilateral Trade Agreements) listed in Annex 4 may have limited membership.	1. The MTO shall provide the common institutional framework for the conduct of trade relations among its Members in matters related to the agreements and associated legal instruments included in the Annexes to this Agreement. 2. The agreements and associated legal instruments included in Annexes 1, 2 and 3 (hereinafter referred to as "Multilateral Trade Agreements") are integral parts of this Agreement, binding on all Members. 3. The agreements and associated legal instruments included in Annex 4 (hereinafter referred to as "Plurilateral Trade Agreements") are binding on those Members that have accepted them [and shall,] in the relations among those Members, be deemed to be integral parts of this Agreement.] The Plurilateral Trade Agreements do not create either obligations or rights for Members that have not accepted them.	The text in square brackets reflects the suggestion that the Plurilateral Trade Agreements be described as integral parts of this Agreement for those Members that are parties to these Agreements.
2. Any member which is not a signatory to any agreement in Annex 4 at the time of entry into force of this Agreement is encouraged to become a signatory to such agreement.	4. Any Member which is not party to the Plurilateral Trade Agreements shall consider whether it is feasible for it to accept them.	

0188

DRAFT FINAL ACT TEXT	REVISED TEXT (SECOND DRAFT)	REMARKS
3. The General Agreement on Tariffs and Trade, as it results from the Final Act of the Uruguay Round referred to above, is legally distinct from the Agreement known as the General Agreement on Tariffs and Trade, dated 30 October 1947.	5. The General Agreement on Tariffs and Trade in Annex 1A (hereinafter referred to as "GATT 1993") is legally distinct from the General Agreement on Tariffs and Trade, dated 30 October 1947, as subsequently rectified, amended or modified (hereinafter referred to as "GATT 1947").	The GATT 1993 is defined in Annex 1A as including protocols of accession, waivers etc. up to the entry into force of the MTO.
Article II Functions of the MTO 1. The MTO shall facilitate the administration and the operation of, and further the objectives of, this Agreement and the agreements annexed hereto, subject to the limitations specified in these agreements. 2. The MTO shall provide the framework for the implementation of the agreements annexed hereto, and any further agreements that may be negotiated and accepted under the auspices of this Agreement. 3. The MTO shall provide the forum for further negotiations among its members concerning their multilateral trade relations as may be decided by the Ministerial Conference. 4. The MTO shall administer an Integrated Dispute Settlement System as set out in Annex 2. These rules and procedures shall apply to all Multilateral Trade Agreements set out in Annex 1. The procedures shall also apply to the Plurilateral Trade Agreements listed in Annex 4 to the extent that the members which are parties to a dispute are signatories of such agreements.	**Article III** Functions of the MTO 1. The MTO shall facilitate the administration and operation, and further the objectives, of this Agreement and of the Multilateral Trade Agreements. The MTO shall also provide the framework for the administration and operation of the Plurilateral Trade Agreements. 2. The MTO shall provide a forum for negotiations concerning trade relations of its Members, including the negotiation of further trade agreements, and a framework for the implementation of the results of such negotiations. 4. The MTO shall administer the Understanding on Rules and Procedures Governing the Settlement of Disputes in Annex 2 to this Agreement. [Possible additional text on scope of application of the Understanding.]	The revised formulation of paragraphs 2 and 3 is intended to reflect the main elements that emerged from the discussion. It has been suggested that the question of a text in the MTO Agreement indicating the scope of application of the Understanding be discussed after the text of the Understanding has been finalized.

0189

DRAFT FINAL ACT TEXT	REVISED TEXT (SECOND DRAFT)	REMARKS
5. The MTO shall administer a Trade Policy Review Mechanism as set out in Annex 3.	5. The MTO shall administer the Trade Policy Review Mechanism provided for in Annex 3 to this Agreement.	
6. With a view to achieving greater coherence in global economic policy-making, the MTO shall cooperate, as appropriate, with the International Monetary Fund, the International Bank for Reconstruction and Development and affiliated agencies.	6. With a view to achieving greater coherence in global economic policy-making, the MTO shall cooperate, as appropriate, with the International Monetary Fund and with the International Bank for Reconstruction and Development and its affiliated agencies.	

DRAFT FINAL ACT TEXT	REVISED TEXT (SECOND DRAFT)	REMARKS
Article V **Structure of the MTO**	**Article IV** **Structure of the MTO**	As suggested, the order of Articles IV and V has been revised.
1. There shall be a Ministerial Conference open to representatives of all the members, which shall meet at least once every two years. The task of the Ministerial Conference shall be to review and supervise the operation of, and determine actions necessary to carry out the functions of, this Agreement and the agreements annexed hereto, to launch further multilateral trade negotiations as appropriate, and to decide on the implementation of results that may have been negotiated among and adopted by members of the MTO.	1. There shall be a Ministerial Conference composed of representatives of all the Members, which shall meet at least once every two years. The Ministerial Conference shall carry out the functions of the MTO.	The revised text was agreed in informal discussions subject to the reference in paragraphs 3 and 4 to the Chairman being accepted as sufficiently clarifying the relationship between the Dispute Settlement Body and the Trade Policy Review Body on the one hand and the General Council on the other.
2. There shall be a General Council open to representatives of all the members, which shall meet regularly, as appropriate. The task of the General Council shall be to carry out the functions of the MTO, including the supervision of the operation of this Agreement and the agreements annexed hereto, in the time between Ministerial Conferences, and decide on all issues conferred on it by this Agreement and by the Ministers.	2. There shall be a General Council composed of representatives of all the Members, which shall meet as appropriate. In the intervals between meetings of the Ministerial Conference, its functions shall be conducted by the General Council. The General Council shall also carry out the functions assigned to it by this Agreement. The General Council shall establish its rules of procedure and approve the rules of procedure for the Committees provided for in paragraph 7.	
3. The General Council shall establish a Dispute Settlement Body, a Trade Policy Review Mechanism, and subsidiary bodies, such as a Goods Council, a Services Council, a TRIPs Council, a Committee on Budget, Finance and Administration, a Committee on Trade and Development, and a Balance of Payments Committee. The General Council shall establish its own rules of procedure and shall approve the rules of procedure of its subsidiary bodies.	3. The General Council shall convene as appropriate as the Dispute Settlement Body to discharge the responsibilities of the Dispute Settlement Body provided for in the Understanding on Rules and Procedures Governing the Settlement of Disputes in Annex 2. The Dispute Settlement Body shall have its own chairman and shall establish such rules of procedure as it deems necessary for the fulfilment of those responsibilities.	
	4. The General Council shall convene as appropriate as the Trade Policy Review Body to discharge the responsibilities of the Trade Policy Review Body provided for in the Trade Policy Review Mechanism in Annex 3. The Trade Policy	

DRAFT FINAL ACT TEXT	REVISED TEXT (SECOND DRAFT)	REMARKS
4. There shall be a Council for Goods ("Goods Council") and a Council for Services ("Services Council"), and a Council for TRIPS ("TRIPs Council"), open to representatives of all members, which shall meet at least eight times per year.	Review Body shall have its own chairman and shall establish such rules of procedure as it deems necessary for the fulfilment of those responsibilities.	
5. The Goods Council shall oversee the functioning of the Agreements on Trade in Goods as set out in Annex 1A, as well as any other functions assigned to it by the General Council, except that the functions of dispute settlement shall be exercised by the Dispute Settlement Body. The Goods Council shall, as required, establish Committees to oversee the operation of the Agreements set out in Annexes 1A, or other subsidiary bodies, and shall approve their rules of procedure.	5. There shall be a Council for Trade in Goods, a Council for Trade in Services and a Council for Trade-Related Aspects of Intellectual Property Rights, which shall operate under the general guidance of the General Council. The Council for Trade in Goods shall oversee the functioning of the Multilateral Trade Agreements in Annex 1A, the Council for Trade in Services shall oversee the functioning of the Multilateral Trade Agreement in Annex 1B, and the Council for Trade-Related Aspects of Intellectual Property Rights shall oversee the functioning of the Multilateral Trade Agreement in Annex 1C. These Councils shall carry out the functions assigned to them by their respective agreements and by the General Council. They shall establish their respective rules of procedure subject to the approval of the General Council. Membership in these Councils shall be open to representatives of all Members. These Councils shall meet as necessary to carry out their functions.	
6. The Services Council shall oversee the functioning of Agreements on Trade in Services as set out in Annex 1B, as well as any other functions assigned to it by the General Council, except that the functions of dispute settlement shall be exercised by the Dispute Settlement Body. the Services Council shall, as required, establish Committees to oversee the operation of the Agreements set out in Annexes 1B, or other subsidiary bodies, and shall approve their rules of procedure.	6. The Council for Trade in Goods, the Council for Trade in Services and the Council for Trade-Related Aspects of Intellectual Property Rights shall establish subsidiary bodies as required. These subsidiary bodies shall establish their respective rules of procedure subject to the approval of their respective Councils.	
7. The TRIPs Council shall oversee the functioning of the Agreement on Trade-Related Aspects of Intellectual Property Rights, including Trade in connected Goods, as set out in Annex 1C, as well		

DRAFT FINAL ACT TEXT	REVISED TEXT (SECOND DRAFT)	REMARKS
as any other functions assigned to it by the General Council, except that the functions of dispute settlement shall be exercised by the Dispute Settlement Body. The TRIPs Council shall, as required, establish Committees to oversee the operation of the Agreements set out in Annex 1C, or other subsidiary bodies, and shall approve their rules of procedure.	7. The Ministerial Conference shall establish a Committee on Trade and Development, a Committee on Balance-of-Payments Restrictions and a Committee on Budget, Finance and Administration, which shall carry out the functions assigned to them by this Agreement and by the Multilateral Trade Agreements, and any additional functions assigned to them by the General Council. Membership in these Committees shall be open to representatives of all Members. 8. The bodies provided for under the Plurilateral Trade Agreements shall carry out the functions assigned to them under those Agreements and shall operate within the institutional framework of the MTO. These bodies shall keep the General Council informed of their activities on a regular basis.	

DRAFT FINAL ACT TEXT	REVISED TEXT (SECOND DRAFT)	REMARKS
Article IV Relations with other Organizations 1. The MTO shall make suitable arrangements with intergovernmental bodies and agencies which have related responsibilities to provide for effective cooperation.	**Article V** Relations with other Organizations 1. The General Council shall make appropriate arrangements for effective cooperation with other intergovernmental organizations that have responsibilities related to those of the MTO.	As suggested, the order of Articles IV and V has been reversed. A proposal to include in Article V:1 a provision calling for the avoidance of duplication of activities still needs to be discussed.
2. The MTO may make, as appropriate, suitable arrangements for consultation and cooperation with non-governmental organizations concerned with matters within the scope of the MTO.	2. The General Council may make appropriate arrangements for consultation and cooperation with non-governmental organizations concerned with matters related to those of the MTO.	
Article VI The Secretariat 1. The General Council shall appoint a Director-General as head of the Secretariat of the MTO. The powers, duties, conditions of service and terms of office of the Director-General shall conform to regulations approved by the General Council.	**Article VI** The Secretariat 1. There is established an MTO Secretariat headed by a Director-General. 2. The Ministerial Conference shall appoint the Director-General and adopt regulations setting out the powers, duties, conditions of service and terms of office of the Director-General.	
2. The Director-General shall appoint members of the staff, and shall fix their duties and conditions of service in accordance with regulations approved by the General Council.	3. The Director-General shall appoint the members of the staff of the Secretariat and determine their duties and conditions of service in accordance with regulations adopted by the Ministerial Conference.	

0194

DRAFT FINAL ACT TEXT	REVISED TEXT (SECOND DRAFT)	REMARKS
3. The responsibilities of the Director-General and of the members of the staff shall be exclusively international in character. In the discharge of their duties, they shall not seek or receive instructions from any government or from any other authority external to the Organization. They shall refrain from any action which might reflect on their positions as international officials. The Members shall respect the international character of the responsibilities of these persons and shall not seek to influence them in the discharge of their duties.	4. The responsibilities of the Director-General and the staff of the Secretariat shall be exclusively international in character. In the discharge of their duties, the Director-General and the staff of the Secretariat shall not seek or accept instructions from any government or any other authority external to the MTO. They shall refrain from any action which might adversely reflect on their position as international officials. The Members of the MTO shall respect the international character of the responsibilities of the Director-General and the staff of the Secretariat and shall not seek to influence them in the discharge of their duties.	
4. At the time of entry into force of the MTO, and until such time as the General Council shall have acted pursuant to paragraph 1, as far as practicable, the GATT Director-General and the ICITO/GATT Secretariat shall become the Director-General and Secretariat of the MTO.		In the revised text, this matter is dealt with in Article XVI:2.
Article VII **Budget and Contributions**	**Article VII** **Budget and Contributions**	
1. The Director-General shall present to the General Council the annual budget estimates and financial statement of the MTO. The General Council shall approve the accounts and the budget.	1. The Director-General shall present to the Committee on Budget, Finance and Administration the annual budget estimate and financial statement of the MTO. The Committee on Budget, Finance and Administration shall review the annual budget estimate and the financial statement presented by the Director-General and make recommendations thereon to the General Council. The annual budget estimates shall be subject to approval by the General Council.	

DRAFT FINAL ACT TEXT	REVISED TEXT (SECOND DRAFT)	REMARKS
2. The General Council shall apportion the expenditures of the Organization among the Members, in accordance with a scale of contributions to be fixed by the General Council, and each Member shall individually contribute promptly to the Organization its share of these expenditures.	2. The Committee on Budget, Finance and Administration shall propose to the General Council financial regulations which shall include provisions setting out:	A proposal according to which the financial regulations are to be based on considerations of budgetary efficiency still needs to be discussed.
	(a) the scale of contributions apportioning the expenses of the MTO among its Members; and	
3. The General Council shall decide on measures to be taken with regard to Members in arrears of their contributions.	(b) the measures to be taken in respect of Members in arrears.	
4. The Budget Committee shall elaborate the provisions of the MTO budget and MTO contributions for adoption by the General Council. The provisions shall be based, as far as practicable, on the provisions and practices for the GATT budget.	The financial regulations shall be based, as far as practicable, on the regulations and practices of the GATT 1947.	
	3. The General Council shall adopt the financial regulations and the annual budget estimates by a two-thirds majority comprising more than half of the Members of the MTO.	
	4. Each Member shall promptly contribute to the MTO its share in the expenses of the MTO in accordance with the financial regulations adopted by the General Council.	

0196

DRAFT FINAL ACT TEXT	REVISED TEXT (SECOND DRAFT)	REMARKS
Article VIII Status	**Article VIII** Status of the MTO	The revised text incorporates a joint proposal by several delegations.
1. The MTO shall have legal personality.	1. The MTO shall have legal personality and shall enjoy in the territory of each of its Members such legal capacity as may be necessary for the exercise of its functions.	
2. The MTO shall enjoy in the territory of each of the Members such legal capacity, privileges and immunities as may be necessary for the exercise of its functions.	2. The MTO shall enjoy in the territory of each of its Members such privileges and immunities as are necessary for the exercise of its functions.	
3. The representatives of the Members and the officials of the MTO shall enjoy such privileges and immunities as are necessary for the independent exercise of their functions in connection with the MTO.	3. The officials of the MTO and the representatives of the Members shall similarly enjoy such privileges and immunities as are necessary for the independent exercise of their functions in connection with the MTO.	
	4. The privileges and immunities to be accorded by a Member to the officials of the MTO and to the representatives of the Members shall be based on the provisions concerning privileges and immunities stipulated in the Convention on the Privileges and Immunities of the Specialized Agencies, approved by the General Assembly of the United Nations on 21 November 1947.	
	5. The MTO may conclude a headquarters agreement.	

0197

DRAFT FINAL ACT TEXT	REVISED TEXT (SECOND DRAFT)	REMARKS
		A proposal to insert after Article VIII two additional Articles on consultation, dispute settlement, notification and transparency is attached.
Article IX **Joint Action** 1. At meetings of the Ministerial Conference and the General Council, each Member of the MTO shall be entitled to one vote, and, except as otherwise provided for in this Agreement, decisions of the Ministerial Conference or the General Council shall be taken by a majority of votes cast.	**Article IX** **Decision-Making** 1. At the meetings of the Ministerial Conference and the General Council, each Member of the MTO shall have one vote. Except as otherwise provided for under this Agreement or the Multilateral Trade Agreements, decisions of the Ministerial Conference and the General Council shall be taken by a majority of the votes cast.	A proposal has been made to include in Article IX:1 (or XVI:1) a provision according to which the European Communities shall not exercise its right to vote if its Member States do so.
2. The Ministerial Conference or the General Council shall have the authority to interpret the provisions of the Agreements annexed hereto.	2. The Ministerial Conference may adopt [by consensus] [by a two-thirds majority comprising more than half of the Members] interpretations of this Agreement and of the Multilateral Trade Agreements.	The definition of the term consensus would need to be discussed if it were used in this Article. A proposal (attached) has been made that this authority be exclusive and that it be exercised on the basis of recommendations by the Special Council.
3. In exceptional circumstances not elsewhere provided for in this Agreement and the Multilateral Trade Agreements under Annex 1, the Ministerial Conference or the General Council may waive an obligation imposed on a member by this Agreement or a Multilateral Trade Agreement under Annex 1; Provided that any such decision shall be approved by a two-thirds majority of votes cast and that such majority shall comprise more than half the MTO members.	3. [In exceptional circumstances, the Ministerial Conference may waive an obligation imposed on a Member by this Agreement or a Multilateral Trade Agreement [which does not provide for the grant of waivers] [which provides for the grant of waivers]; Provided that any such decision shall be approved by a two-thirds majority comprising more than half of the Members of the MTO.]	This provision requires further discussion in the light of the various proposals made. The square brackets are meant to indicate the main proposals made.

0198

DRAFT FINAL ACT TEXT	REVISED TEXT (SECOND DRAFT)	REMARKS
	4. A decision by the Ministerial Conference or the General Council granting a waiver shall state the exceptional circumstances justifying the decision, the terms and conditions governing the application of the waiver, and the date on which the waiver shall terminate. Any waiver granted for a period of more than one year shall be reviewed by the Ministerial Conference or the General Council not later than one year after it was granted, and thereafter annually until the waiver terminates. In each review, the Ministerial Conference or General Council shall examine whether the exceptional circumstances justifying the waiver still exist and whether the terms and conditions attached to the waiver have been met. The Ministerial Conference or General Council, on the basis of the annual review, may extend, modify or terminate the waiver.	The essential parts of the Final Act text on waivers under Article XXV of the GATT have been included here. A proposal to include in paragraph 4 the provision in the Final Act text confirming the right to resort to Article XXIII of the GATT requires further discussion once it has been determined whether Article IX:3 of the MTO Agreement extends to waivers from obligations under the GATT.
	5. Decisions under a Plurilateral Trade Agreement, including any decisions on interpretations and waivers, shall be governed by the provisions of that Agreement.	

DRAFT FINAL ACT TEXT	REVISED TEXT (SECOND DRAFT)	REMARKS
Article X **Amendments and Modification** 1. Negotiations for amendments to this Agreement, or to any of Multilateral Trade Agreements in Annex 1, shall be concluded by the Ministerial Conference on the basis of consensus. 2. Any member accepting an amendment to this Agreement or any of the Multilateral Trade Agreements in Annex 1 shall deposit an instrument of acceptance with the Director-General of the MTO within such period as the Ministerial Conference may specify. Such amendments shall become effective for each member upon acceptance by —thirds of the members. 3. The Ministerial Conference may decide that any amendment made effective under this Article is of such a nature that any member which has not accepted it within a period specified by the Ministerial Conference shall be free to withdraw from this Agreement, or to remain a member with the consent of the Ministerial Conference.	**Article X** **Amendments** [1. Any Member of the MTO may submit to the Ministerial Conference a proposal to amend the provisions of this Agreement or the Multilateral Trade Agreements in Annex 1. The decision to submit an amendment of the provisions of this Agreement or the Multilateral Trade Agreements in Annex 1 to the Members of the MTO for acceptance shall be approved by consensus. 2. An amendment shall take effect for all Members upon acceptance by two-thirds of the Members. The Ministerial Conference may decide, upon the request of a Member which has not accepted an amendment, that the entry into effect of the amendment for that Member shall be suspended for a specified period of time. If the Ministerial Conference decides not to suspend the entry into effect of that amendment for that Member, the Member shall be free to withdraw from this Agreement as of the entry into effect of the amendment.]	The two main options presented with respect to these paragraphs reflect the view of many delegations that whether an amendment takes effect for all Members or only those Members that have accepted it would depend on whether the decision to submit an amendment for acceptance is taken by consensus or by a majority vote. However, for some delegations, an amendment should take effect only for those members which have accepted the amendment even if the decision to submit the amendment for acceptance is taken by consensus. Some delegations considered that, in the absence of a consensus requirement for the submission for acceptance, certain basic provisions of the Multilateral Trade Agreements should be amendable only by unanimity. The question of the definition of consensus would still need to be discussed.

0200

0201

DRAFT FINAL ACT TEXT	REVISED TEXT (SECOND DRAFT)	REMARKS
	[1. Any Member of the MTO may submit to the Ministerial Conference a proposal to amend the provisions of this Agreement or the Multilateral Trade Agreements in Annex 1. The decision to submit an amendment of the provisions of this Agreement or the Multilateral Trade Agreements in Annex 1 to the Members of the MTO for acceptance shall be approved by a two-thirds majority of its Members. 2. An amendment shall take effect for the Members that have accepted it upon acceptance by two thirds of the Members and thereafter for each other Member upon acceptance by it. The Ministerial Conference may decide by [consensus] [a two-thirds majority of the Members] that an amendment is of such a nature that any Member which has not accepted it within a specified period may remain a Member only with the consent of the Ministerial Conference.] 3. Any Member accepting an amendment to this Agreement or a Multilateral Trade Agreement in Annex 1 shall deposit an instrument of acceptance with the Director-General of the MTO within the period of acceptance specified by the Ministerial Conference.	
4. Amendments to the agreements in Annex 4 shall be made in accordance with the amending procedures in those agreements. Such amendments shall be notified to the General Council.		See paragraph 6 below for revised text.

DRAFT FINAL ACT TEXT	REVISED TEXT (SECOND DRAFT)	REMARKS
5. Modifications to the instruments set out in Annexes 2 and 3 shall be made by consensus in the Ministerial Conference or the General Council.	4. Any Member of the MTO may communicate to the Ministerial Conference a proposal to amend the Multilateral Trade Agreements included in Annexes 2 and 3. Such amendments shall take effect upon approval by the Ministerial Conference. The decision to approve the amendment shall be taken [by consensus] [by a two-thirds majority of the Members].	
	5. [The Ministerial Conference may decide to add an agreement to Annex 4, or delete an agreement from that Annex, [by consensus][by a two-thirds majority of the Members [comprising the Members that are party to the agreement]].	
	6. Amendments to a Plurilateral Trade Agreement shall be governed by the provisions of that Agreement.	
	7. An amendment to this Article shall take effect upon acceptance by all Members.	

0202

DRAFT FINAL ACT TEXT	REVISED TEXT (SECOND DRAFT)	REMARKS
Article XI[2] **Original Membership** [2]The provisions of the MTO Agreement are without prejudice to the substantive results of the Uruguay Round as it affects the existing rights of contracting parties under paragraph 1(b) of the Protocol of Provisional Application and under equivalent provisions of the Protocols of Accession. Contracting parties to the General Agreement on Tariffs and Trade and the European Communities which accept this Agreement and the Multilateral Trade Agreements, including acceptance on a definitive basis of the General Agreement on Tariffs and Trade, shall become original members of the MTO.	**Article XI** **Original Membership** The contracting parties to the GATT 1947 and the European Communities which accept this Agreement and the Multilateral Trade Agreements and [whose Schedules of Concessions and commitments are annexed to the GATT 1993 and] [whose Schedules of Specific Commitments are annexed to the General Agreement on Trade in Services in Annex 1B] shall become original Members of the MTO.	It has been proposed to retain the footnote in the Final Act text. The question of the definitive application of the GATT 1993 is covered in Section d. of Annex 1A. A proposal to restructure the Articles on membership, accession, acceptance and deposit is attached.
Article XII **Accession** 1. Any state or separate customs territory possessing full autonomy in the conduct of its external commercial relations and of other matters provided for in this Agreement, which accepts this Agreement and the Multilateral Trade Agreements set out in Annexes 1, 2 and 3, may accede on terms to be agreed between it and the General Council.	**Article XII** **Accession** 1. Any state or separate customs territory possessing full autonomy in the conduct of its external commercial relations and of the other matters provided for in this Agreement and the Multilateral Trade Agreements may accede to this Agreement, including the Multilateral Trade Agreements annexed thereto, on terms to be agreed between it and the MTO.	A proposal to mention specifically the need to establish schedules of concessions and specific commitments in this Article is attached.
2. Decisions on accession of new members shall be taken by the General Council and shall be approved by a two-thirds majority of votes cast and such majority shall comprise more than half the MTO members.	2. Decisions on accession shall be taken by the Ministerial Conference. The Ministerial Conference shall approve the agreement on the terms of accession by a two-thirds majority [comprising more than half] of the Members of the MTO.	

0203

DRAFT FINAL ACT TEXT	REVISED TEXT (SECOND DRAFT)	REMARKS
Article XIII **Non-application of the Agreement between Particular Members** 1.　The Multilateral Trade Agreements listed in Annex 1A, or the Multilateral Trade Agreements listed in Annex 1B or the Multilateral Trade Agreements listed in Annex 1C shall not apply as between any member and any other member if either of the members, at the time either becomes a member, does not consent to such application.　Such intention shall be notified to the General Council in advance of a decision being taken on membership.	**Article XIII** **Non-Application of Multilateral Trade Agreements between Particular Members** 1.　The Multilateral Trade Agreements in Annex 1A taken as a whole, or the Multilateral Trade Agreement in Annex 1B, or the Multilateral Trade Agreement in Annex 1C, or any combination thereof, shall not apply between any Member of the MTO and any other Member thereof, if either of the Members, at the time either becomes a Member, does not consent to such application.	The provisions of paragraphs 1, 2 and 3 require further discussion. See revised text of paragraphs 3 and 4 for the notification requirement.
2.　Paragraph 1 shall apply to the Multilateral Trade Agreements listed in Annex 1 only to the extent that non-application rights have been invoked between members in relation to such Agreements under the auspices of the General Agreement on Tariffs and Trade.	2.　Paragraph 1 shall apply in respect of the Multilateral Trade Agreements in Annex 1A between two Members which were contracting parties to the GATT 1947 at the time of entry into force of this Agreement only [if the GATT 1947 was not applied at that time between the two Members in accordance with Article XXXV of the GATT 1947.]	The formulation of the text in square brackets still needs to be discussed.

0204

DRAFT FINAL ACT TEXT	REVISED TEXT (SECOND DRAFT)	REMARKS
	3. Paragraph 1 shall apply between an original Member and another original Member only if the Member not consenting to the application so has notified [the CONTRACTING PARTIES to the GATT 1947 at their Special Session referred to in paragraph 3 of the Final Act Embodying the Results of the Uruguay Round of Multilateral Trade Negotiations.]	
	4. Paragraph 1 shall apply between a Member and another Member which acceded under Article XII only if the Member not consenting to the application has so notified the Ministerial Conference before the approval of the agreement on the terms of accession by the Ministerial Conference.	
5. The General Council may review the operation of this Article in particular cases at the request of any member and make appropriate recommendations.	5. The Ministerial Conference may review the operation of this Article in particular cases at the request of any Member and make appropriate recommendations.	

DRAFT FINAL ACT TEXT	REVISED TEXT (SECOND DRAFT)	REMARKS
	6. The non-application of a Plurilateral Trade Agreement between parties to that Agreement shall be governed by the provisions of that Agreement.	
Article XIV **Acceptance, Entry into Force and Deposit** 1. This Agreement shall be open for acceptance, by signature or otherwise, as from 1 November 1992, to Uruguay Round participants that qualify under Article XI. This Agreement shall enter into force on a date set by the Implementing Conference, the same date as the other Uruguay Round results become effective.	**Article XIV** **Acceptance, Entry into Force and Deposit** 1. This Agreement shall be open for acceptance, by signature or otherwise, by contracting parties to the GATT 1947 and the European Communities which are eligible to become original Members of the MTO in accordance with Article XI of this Agreement. Such acceptance shall apply to this Agreement and the Multilateral Trade Agreements annexed thereto. This Agreement and the Multilateral Trade Agreements annexed thereto shall enter into force on the date determined by Ministers in accordance with paragraph 3 of the Final Act Embodying the Results of the Uruguay Round of Multilateral Trade Negotiations and shall remain open for acceptance for a period of two years following that date unless the Ministers decide otherwise. An acceptance following the entry into force of this Agreement shall enter into force on the thirtieth day following the deposit of the instrument of acceptance.	

0206

DRAFT FINAL ACT TEXT	REVISED TEXT (SECOND DRAFT)	REMARKS
2. This Agreement shall remain open for acceptance by Uruguay Round participants that qualify under Article XI until a date two years from the date of the entry into force of this Agreement, unless otherwise decided by the implementing Conference. For these participants, it shall enter into force on the thirtieth day following the deposit of the instrument of ratification or acceptance. Participants accepting the MTO Agreement pursuant to this provision shall implement any concessions or other obligations, including any transitional provisions, established in the Multilateral Trade Agreements as if they had entered into force on the date of entry into force of the MTO.	2. A Member which accepts this Agreement after its entry into force shall implement those concessions and obligations in the Multilateral Trade Agreements that are to be implemented over a period of time starting with the entry into force of this Agreement as if it had accepted this Agreement on the date of its entry into force.	The revised text would not affect the transitional provisions of the individual Multilateral Trade Agreements.
3. Prior to entry into force of this Agreement, the text of this Agreement shall be deposited with the Director-General to the CONTRACTING PARTIES of the General Agreement on Tariffs and Trade, in his capacity as depositary of the Uruguay Round results. He shall promptly furnish a certified true copy thereof and a notification of each acceptance thereof to each signatory of the Agreement on the MTO. The Agreement shall, upon its entry into force, be deposited with the Director-General of the MTO, as well as any amendments thereto.	3. Until the entry into force of this Agreement the text of this Agreement and the Multilateral Trade Agreements shall be deposited with the Director General to the CONTRACTING PARTIES to the GATT 1947. The Director-General shall promptly furnish a certified true copy of this Agreement and the Multilateral Trade Agreements, and a notification of each acceptance thereof, to each signatory of this Agreement. This Agreement and the Multilateral Trade Agreements, and any amendments thereto, shall, upon the entry into force of this Agreement, be deposited with the Director General of the MTO.	

0207

DRAFT FINAL ACT TEXT	REVISED TEXT (SECOND DRAFT)	REMARKS
	4. The acceptance and entry into force of a Plurilateral Trade Agreement shall be governed by the provisions of that Agreement. Such Agreements shall be deposited with the Director General of the MTO.	
Article XV **Withdrawal** 1. Any Member of the MTO may withdraw from this Agreement. Any member, upon withdrawal from this Agreement, shall cease to be a party to the Multilateral Trade Agreements. Such withdrawal shall take effect upon the expiration of six months from the date on which written notice of withdrawal is received by the Director-General.	**Article XV** **Withdrawal** 1. Any Member may withdraw from this Agreement. Such withdrawal shall apply both to this Agreement and the Multilateral Trade Agreements and shall take effect upon the expiration of six months from the date on which written notice of withdrawal is received by the Director-General of the MTO.	
2. Withdrawal from the agreements in Annex 4 shall be governed by the provisions of those agreements.	2. Withdrawal from a Plurilateral Trade Agreement shall be governed by the provisions of that Agreement.	
Article XVI **Final Provisions** 1. The MTO shall respect the rules, decisions and customary practice of the General Agreement on Tariffs and Trade, including voting practices of the General Agreement and its associated legal instruments, including the Tokyo Round Agreements and Arrangements in carrying out its functions and tasks.	**Article XVI** **Miscellaneous Provisions** 1. Except as otherwise provided for under this Agreement or the Multilateral Trade Agreements, the MTO shall be guided by the rules, decisions and customary practices [including the voting practices,] followed by the CONTRACTING PARTIES of the GATT 1947 and the bodies established in the framework of the GATT 1947. The MTO shall continue the practice of decision-making by consensus followed under the GATT 1947.	

DRAFT FINAL ACT TEXT	REVISED TEXT (SECOND DRAFT)	REMARKS
	2. To the extent practicable, the Secretariat of the GATT 1947 shall become the Secretariat of the MTO, and the Director-General of the GATT 1947, until such time as the General Council has appointed a Director-General in accordance with Article VI:1 of this Agreement, shall serve as Director-General of the MTO.	Revised text corresponds to Article VI:4 of the Final Act text.
2. No reservations may be entered in respect of any provision in the Multilateral Trade Agreements in Annex 1. Reservations entered in respect of the Agreements in Annex 4 can only be made in accordance with the relevant provisions of those Agreements.¹ ¹The provisions of the MTO Agreement are without prejudice to the substantive results of the Uruguay Round as it affects the existing rights of contracting parties under paragraph 1(b) of the Protocol of Provisional Application and under equivalent provisions of the Protocols of Accession.		See paragraph 5 below for revised text on reservations.
3. In the event of a conflict between the provisions of this Agreement and the provisions of any of the Multilateral Trade Agreements in Annex 1, the provisions of this Agreement shall prevail.	3. [In the event of a conflict between the provisions of the Agreement and the provisions of any of the Multilateral Trade Agreements, the provisions of this Agreement shall prevail]	This provision may need to be reconsidered after the review of the texts of the Multilateral Trade Agreements has been finalized.
4. The Members shall endeavour to take all necessary steps, where changes to domestic laws will be required to implement the provisions of the agreements annexed hereto, to ensure the conformity of their laws with these Agreements.	4. The Members shall endeavour to take all necessary steps, where changes to domestic laws will be required to implement the provisions of the agreements annexed hereto, to ensure the conformity of their laws with these agreements.	Further discussions are necessary to determine whether the provision should be retained, deleted, reformulated or moved to the Final Act.

DRAFT FINAL ACT TEXT	REVISED TEXT (SECOND DRAFT)	REMARKS
	5. No reservations may be made in respect of any provisions of this Agreement. Reservations in respect of any of the provisions of the Multilateral Trade Agreements may only be made in accordance with the provisions set out in those Agreements. Reservations in respect of a provision of a Plurilateral Trade Agreement shall be governed by the provisions of that Agreement.	The revised text corresponds to paragraph 2 of the Final Act text. A proposal (attached) has been made to permit reservations to the GATT 1993 for measures covered by the existing legislation clause.
5. This Agreement shall be registered in accordance with the provisions of Article 102 of the Charter of the United Nations.	6. This Agreement shall be registered in accordance with the provisions of Article 102 of the Charter of the United Nations.	
Done at --- this -- day of --- one thousand nine hundred and ninety---, in a single copy, in the English, French and Spanish languages, each text being authentic.	Done at -- this -- day of -- one thousand nine hundred and ninety--, in a single copy, in the English, French and Spanish languages, each text being authentic.	
		A proposal to add a new Article XVII on transitional provisions is attached.

0210

DRAFT FINAL ACT TEXT	REVISED TEXT (SECOND DRAFT)	REMARKS
ANNEXES	ANNEXES (TO BE DRAFTED)	
<u>Annex 1</u> Annex 1A covers: - The General Agreement on Tariffs and Trade, as it results from the Final Act of the Uruguay Round, and its associated legal instruments, except the Protocol of Provisional Application;	<u>Annex 1</u> <u>Texts to be Included in Annex 1A*</u> • Texts of agreements with rectifications and adjustments to take into account their inclusion in the MTO Annex. 1. The General Agreement on Tariffs and Trade dated 1993, and associated legal instruments, which would include: a. The General Agreement on Tariffs and Trade dated 30 October 1947, as subsequently rectified, amended or otherwise modified (i.e., the text published as Volume IV of the BISD), without the provisions that are superseded by those in the MTO Agreement (i.e. entry into force, etc.). b. The Annexes to the above except Annex H, which deals with entry into force. c. Additional Annexes to the above Agreement incorporating the Final Act texts on Articles II:1(b), XVII, XXIV, XXV and XXVIII and on the balance-of-payment provisions. The text on Article XXXV would be annexed if not superseded by the MTO Agreement.	

DRAFT FINAL ACT TEXT	REVISED TEXT (SECOND DRAFT)	REMARKS
	d. A text declaring that, unless otherwise specified in the MTO Agreement or the Multilateral Trade Agreements, the General Agreement referred to in paragraph 1(a) above shall be applied as modified by the terms of legal instruments and decisions adopted by the CONTRACTING PARTIES until the entry into force of the MTO Agreement, which include, but are not limited to: - protocols and certifications relating to tariff concessions; - protocols of accession to the General Agreement, without their provisions on withdrawal; - waivers granted under Article XXV of the General Agreement and still in force; and - decisions of the CONTRACTING PARTIES on Differential and More Favourable Treatment, Reciprocity and Fuller Participation of Developing Countries, Trade Measures Taken for Balance-of-Payments Purposes, Safeguard Action for Development Purposes, Procedures under Article XXIII adopted in 1966, and paragraphs 2-4 and 24-25 of the Understanding Regarding Notification, Consultation, Dispute Settlement and Surveillance;	

DRAFT FINAL ACT TEXT	REVISED TEXT (SECOND DRAFT)	REMARKS
	The text would further declare that the above legal instruments shall not include the Protocol of Provisional Application of the GATT 1947 and the provisions in protocols of accession relating to provisional application or legislation existing on the date of the protocol;	
	[e. Text of a provision relating to measures under mandatory legislation presently justified under the existing legislation provision in the Protocol of Provisional Application or a protocol of accession;] and	A proposal according to which reservations to provisions of the GATT 1993 could be made in respect of measures covered by the existing legislation clause is attached.
	f. The Uruguay Round Protocol to the General Agreement on Tariffs and Trade 1993 (containing the Schedules of Concessions of the Original Members of the MTO).	
	2. Agreement on Safeguards	
	3. Agreement on Implementation of Article VI of the General Agreement on Tariffs and Trade 1993	
	4. Agreement on Subsidies and Countervailing Measures	
	5. Agreement on Trade-Related Aspects of Investment Measures	
- The Tokyo Round Agreements and Arrangements as they result from the Final Act of the Uruguay Round and their associated legal instruments, except those Agreements and Arrangements found in Annex 4; and		

0213

DRAFT FINAL ACT TEXT	REVISED TEXT (SECOND DRAFT)	REMARKS
	6. Agreement on Import Licensing Procedures 1993	
	7. Agreement on Implementation of Article VII of the General Agreement on Tariffs and Trade 1993	
	8. Agreement on Preshipment Inspection	
	9. Agreement on Rules of Origin	
	10. Agreement on Technical Barriers to Trade 1993	
	11. Agreement on Application of Sanitary and Phytosanitary Measures	
	12. Agreement on Agriculture (except for concessions to be included in the Uruguay Round Protocol)	
	13. Agreement on Textiles and Clothing	
	14. Agreement on Notification [from FOGS text]	
Annex 1B covers:	Texts to be included in Annex 1B	
the General Agreement on Trade in Services, and its associated legal instruments; and	General Agreement on Trade in Services and its associated legal instruments including Annexes	
Annex 1C covers:	Texts to be included in Annex 1C	
· the Agreement on Trade-Related Aspects of Intellectual Property Rights, including Trade in Counterfeit Goods (TRIPs).	Agreement on Trade-Related Aspects of Intellectual Property Rights, Including Trade in Counterfeit Goods	0214

DRAFT FINAL ACT TEXT	REVISED TEXT (SECOND DRAFT)	REMARKS
Annex 2	**Texts to be included in Annex 2**	
Annex 2 covers:	Understanding on Rules and Procedures Governing the Settlement of Disputes	
- the Integrated Dispute Settlement Understanding.		
Annex 3	**Texts to be included in Annex 3**	
Annex 3 covers:	Trade Policy Review Mechanism	
'The Trade Policy Review Mechanism.[1]		
[1] This annex will comprise the text of the TPRM provisions in Part I of the Decision of the CONTRACTING PARTIES of 12 April 1989 (L/6490), amended as necessary to take account of the need to extend the coverage of reviews to all subjects covered in the MTO Agreement.		
Note will also be taken of the consequential need to review the scope of the Outline Format for Country Reports in the Decision of the CONTRACTING PARTIES of 19 July 1989 (L/6552) and the Outline Format for Country Reports for Least-Developed Countries in the Decision of the Council of 16 May 1990 (L/6691).		
Annex 4	**Texts to be [included][listed] in Annex 4**	
Annex 4 covers:	Agreement on Trade in Civil Aircraft Agreement on Government Procurement International Dairy Arrangement Arrangement Regarding Bovine Meat	
- the Agreement on Trade in Civil Aircraft; - the Agreement on Government Procurement; - the International Dairy Arrangement; and - the Arrangement Regarding Bovine Meat.		

0215

1992-03-25 ' 21:48 KOREА ISSION GENEVA 2 022 791 0□ P.13

PROPOSALS NOT INCORPORATED INTO THE MTO DRAFT TEXT AND NOT YET DISCUSSED

Proposal for additional Articles to be inserted after Article VIII

Article A

Consultation and Dispute Settlement

1. Each member shall accord sympathetic consideration and shall afford adequate opportunity for consultation regarding such representations as may be made by another member with respect to any matter affecting the operation of this Agreement and its Annexes.

2. Where bilateral consultations under paragraph 1 have not led to a satisfactory solution, the matter may be submitted to multilateral consultation. The body in charge of such multilateral consultations shall be:

    (a) in the case of matters coming under the scope of any of the instruments listed in Annex 1 to this Agreement: the General Council;

    (b) in the case of matters coming under the scope of an agreement listed in Annex IV to this Agreement: the body established under the relevant agreement.

3. Without prejudice to the provisions of paragraph 2, where the bilateral consultations under paragraph 1 are not successful, the complaining party shall be free to refer the matter to the Dispute Settlement Body pursuant to the rules and procedures on dispute settlement as set out in Annex II to this Agreement.

Article B

Notification and Transparency

1. All notifications under any of the instruments listed in Annex 1 to this Agreement shall be addressed to the Director-General for circulation to the members. Notifications under an agreement listed in Annex IV to this Agreement shall follow the rules laid down in that agreement.

2. The Trade Review Mechanism (TPRM) established under Annex III to this Agreement shall be monitored by the General Council. All notifications with respect to the TPRM must be made to the Director-General.

Proposed revision of Article IX:2

The Ministerial Conference or the General Council shall have the exclusive authority to adopt interpretations of this Agreement and of the Multilateral Trade Agreements. They shall exercise this authority on the basis of recommendations submitted by the the Special Councils or the Dispute Settlement Body.

Such decisions shall be taken by a two thirds majority comprising more than half of the members.

Proposal to restructure Articles on Membership, Acceptance, Accession and Deposit

Article III bis (former Article XI) Membership

1. Contracting parties to the GATT 1947, and the European Communities, which accept this Agreement and the Multilateral Trade Agreements in accordance with Article XIV, and whose Schedules of Concessions and Commitments are annexed to the GATT 1993 and whose Schedules of Specific Commitments are annexed to the General Agreement on Trade in Services shall become original Members of the MTO.

P.14

SE 79 022 2

UN MISSION GENEVA K

21:49

1992-03-75

222 우루과이라운드 법제화 그룹 회의

0216

2. Membership is open to all other states and separate customs territories possessing full autonomy in the conduct of their external commercial relations and of the matters provided for in this Agreement and the Multilateral Trade Agreements. They shall become Members by accession in accordance with Article XIV bis.

Article XIV

Acceptance and entry into force

1. This Agreement shall be open for acceptance, by signature or otherwise, as from 1 November 1992 until two years after the date of its entry into force pursuant to paragraph 2 below, unless otherwise decided by the Implementing Conference or the subsequent meeting provided for in the Final Act Embodying the Results of the Uruguay Round of Multilateral Trade Negotiations, to Uruguay Round participants that qualify under paragraph 1 of Article IIIbis.

2. The date of entry into force of this Agreement shall be set by the Implementing Conference or the subsequent meeting referred to in paragraph 1 above.

3. This Agreement shall enter into force:

(1) For the participants accepting this Agreement before or on the date set out in paragraph 2, on that date;

(2) For the participants accepting this Agreement after the date set out in paragraph 2, on the thirtieth day following their acceptance.

4. The entry into force of the Multilateral Trade Agreements shall be governed by the paragraphs 1 to 3 above.

5. In the case of any concession or other obligations in the Multilateral Trade Agreements, which the participants shall implement according to a certain time schedule, including in the case of transitional provisions, such a time schedule shall be deemed to begin on the date set out in paragraph 2, irrespective of the date of entry into force of this Agreement for each participant, unless otherwise expressly provided in the Multilateral Trade Agreements.

Article XIVbis (former Article XII)

Accession

1. ...

2. ...

Article XIVter (former paragraph 3 of Article XIV)

Depository

1. Prior to entry into force of this Agreement, the original texts of this Agreement and Multilateral Trade Agreements shall be deposited with the Director-General to the CONTRACTING PARTIES of the General Agreement on the Tariffs and Trade, in his capacity as depository of the Uruguay Round Results. He shall promptly furnish certified true copies thereof and a notification of each acceptance and accession pursuant to the provisions of Articles XIV and XIVbis to each Uruguay Round participant.

2. The original texts of this Agreement and the Multilateral Trade Agreements shall, upon entry into force of this Agreement, be deposited with the Director-General of the WTO, as well as any amendment thereto and, if any, new agreements negotiated under the authority of the Ministerial Conference conferred by paragraph 2 of Article V and any amendment thereto.

Proposed revision of Article XII:1

Article XII

Accession

1. Any state or separate customs territory possessing full autonomy in the conduct of its external commercial relations and of the other matters provided for in this Agreement and the Multilateral Trade Agreements may become a member of the MTO by acceding to this Agreement and all of the Multilateral Trade Agreements annexed thereto, and submitting the schedules of concessions and specific commitments provided for respectively in the General Agreement on Tariffs and Trade - 1993 and the General Agreement on Trade in Services on terms to be agreed between it and the MTO.

Proposal for new Article XVII

Article XVII

Transitional Provisions

Any Member which is the contracting party to the General Agreement on Tariffs and Trade (1947) shall be committed not to withdraw its provisional application of the said Agreement during the period in which this Agreement remains open for acceptance in accordance with paragraph 1 of Article XIV.

Proposal on "reservations" language

(a) No reservations may be made in respect of any provisions of this Agreement.

(b) Reservations in respect of any of the provisions of the General Agreement on Tariffs and Trade - 1993 or any other of the Multilateral Trade Agreements may only be made in accordance with the provisions set out in those agreements.

(c) Reservations in respect of a provision of a Plurilateral Trade Agreement shall be covered by the provisions of that Agreement.

(d) Notwithstanding the provisions of paragraph (b) above, Original Members of the MTO may enter reservations in respect of the provisions of the General Agreement on Tariffs and Trade - 1993 concerning specified mandatory existing legislation which, as of the date of entry into force of this Agreement, was subject to coverage under paragraph 1(b) of the Protocol of Provisional Application of the General Agreement on Tariffs and Trade - 1947 and under equivalent provisions of the Protocols of Accession.

0218

外　務　部

종　별 :

번　호 : GVW-0687　　　　　　　　일　시 : 92 0326 2000

수　신 : 장관(통기,경기원,재무부,농림수산부,상공부,특허청)

발　신 : 주 제네바 대사

제　목 : UR/법제화 그룹 비공식회의(개별협정문,1)

연: GVW-0656

　3.25. 표제회의에서는 개별 TEXT 에 대한 연호사무국 수정안(537)에 대해 심의가있었는바, 요지 아래 보고함.(신서기관 참석)

　1. 2조 1항 기타부과금에 대한 양해(TEXT P)

　0 연호 사무국 문서 537의 INFORMAL NOTE 의 취지에따라 수정된 문안에 대해 다수국이 동의를 하면서, 2항 10줄의 'GATT 47'은 MTO 협정에비추어 'GATT'47 AS AMENDED' 로 이해함.

　0 EC 가 제2항 3쩨 문장과 4쩨문장이 상충되지 않느냐고 질문한데 대해 사무국은동항은 모두 관세양허에 관한 사항이므로 상충되지 않는다고 설명함.

　0 한편 태국이 제1항 4쩨줄의 SCHEDULES OF TARIFF CONCESSION 와 제2항 4쩨줄, 8줄의 SCHEDULES OF CONCESSIONS 의 용어 통일 필요성을 제기한데 대해 미국이 동용어의 해석 및 통일문제는 T 3 권한밖의 문제라 하여 이에 반대함.

　2. 17조 국영무역에 관한 양해(TEXT Q)

　0 사무국이 국영무역에 대한 통고문제는 실제적으로 상품무역 이사회(CTG)가 관장할것이므로 CP 를 CTG 로 수정했다고 설명한데대해 EC,인도,일본,태국등은 SC 의 개별협정 감독권(MTO 제 5조)을 근거로 이에 동의한 반면, 미국,카나다,스웨덴,홍콩등이 동 TEXT 상의 CP 는 MTO 협정 구조상 최고기관인 MC 에 해당한다 하여 사무국 수정안에 반대함.

　- 미국은 동용어 수정문제는 MTO 구조와 관련된 실질문제이므로 T3 권한 밖의 사항임을 주장

　0 제5항 국영무역 통보심의 관련, 사무국은 동사항은 갓트기능(TEXT Y) 심의때 함께 논의할 것을 제의하였는바, 미국,카나다는 동항의 독자성을 주장하며 TEXT Y

통상국　　2차보　　경기원　　재무부　　농수부　　상공부　　특허청

PAGE 1　　　　　　　　　　　　　　　　92.03.27　07:58 DQ

　　　　　　　　　　　　　　　　　　　외신 1과 통제관

0219

심의에 의해 동항의 취지가 변경되어서는 안될 것이라고 언급함.

    3. 12조, 18조 BOP 에 관한 양해(TEXT B)

    0 전문의 'MEMBERS' 및 'DECIDES AS FOLLOWS' 는 문맥상(1,2항의 CONFIRM) 삭제키로 합의함.

    0 제7항 및 9항의 GC 에 대해서는 BOP위원회는 MC 에 의해서 설치된다는 MTO협정규정에 비추어 사무국 수정안에 찬성하는 미국,EC,일본등의 다수국 의견과 동 TEXT는 BOP 위원회 절차 강화에 관한 사항이므로 SC로 해석된다는 인도 의견이 대립됨.

    4. 24조 관세동맹,자유무역지대에 관한 양해(TEXT U)

    0 전문 PARA 5 의 CTG 는 MC 로, 14항의 CTG 는 MTO 협정에 비추어 DSB 로 수정하기로함.

    0 제5항의 제28조에 대한 두번째 언급은 제4항상의 제28조에 대한 언급과 동일하게 해석되는 것으로 이해함.

    5. 25조 웨이버(TEXT V), 35조 협정 부적용(TEXT X)에 관한 양해

    0 MTO 협정의 관련 논의중이므로 토의 연기

    6. 28조 양허수정에 관한 양해(TEXT W)

    0 제 1항 CTC 의 CTG 변경 이유에 대해 사무국은 MTO 협정상 아직은 CTC 가 설립되지 않았기 때문이라 설명함.(다수국의 동의)

    0 제6항의 보상기준은 MTO 협정 전반에 적용되는 사항이 아니며 제 28조에만 적용되는 기준이라고 이해함.끝

    (대사 박수길-국장)

외 무 부

종 별 :

번 호 : GVW-0695　　　　　　　　　일 시 : 92 0327 1900

수 신 : 장 관(통기,경기원,재무부,농수산부,상공부,특허청)

발 신 : 주 제네바 대사

제 목 : UR/법제화 그룹 비공식 회의(개별문안,2)

　　연: GVW-687

　　1. 3.26 표제회의에서는 사무국 문서(537)상의 SG 협정문안에 대한 토의가 있었는 바, 요지 아래 보고함.

　　가. 제 4항(잠정조치)

　　0 동항 마지막 문장 전체 세이프가드 발동 기간에서 잠정 발동기간 차감관련 문안(COUNT TOWARDS)을 다.COUNTED AS A PART OF 로 명확화

　　나. 제 5항(SG 의 무차별 적용)

　　0 현 문안(IRRESPECTIVE OF ITS SOURCES)를 ON AN ERGAOMNES BASIS 로 대체하자는 홍콩의 강력한 희망표시가 있었으나 EC 의 반대로 받아들여지지 않음.

　　다. 제 6항(피해판정)

　　0 동항(B) 'IN DETERMINING INJURY' 뒤에 OR THETHREAT OF 를 미국의 제의로 추가하고, (B) 와(C) 의 순서를 변경함.

　　라. 제 9항(QUOTA MODULATION)

　　0 홍콩이 독립관세 영역인 자국의 갓트내 지위를 염두에 두고 동항 첫째줄 SUPPLYINGCOUNTRIES 를 SUPPLYING MEMBERS 로 수정할 것을 제의 하였으나 EC 등이 이는 현갓트 13조의표현을 차용한 것이며 동 규정하에서 EC,홍콩관련 아무런 문제점이 없었다 는 점 및 여사한 쿼타가 MTO 회원국과 MTO 비회원구 모두에게 적용될 경우 동 쿼타배정 관련, MTO회원국에게 협의권이 인정되어야 한다는 점에서 현문안을 지지함.

　　마. 제 17항(보상)

　　0 인도는 보상은 어디까지나 상품분야에 국한되어야 하므로 사무구 문서(537) 2PAGE 하단이 잘못된 것이라고 지적하고, 보상관련 사항은 상품이사회(CTG) 에서 다루어져야 함을 주장한 반면,미국, 카나다, 스웨덴은 GC 에서 다루어져야 한다는

통상국　　2차보　　경기원　　재무부　　농수부　　상공부　　특허청

PAGE 1　　　　　　　　　　　　　　　　　　92.03.28　　06:03 DS

　　　　　　　　　　　　　　　　　　　외신 1과 통제관

　　　　　　　　　　　　　　　　　　　　0221

입장표명
　바. 제 22항(회색 조치)

　O 동항(C) 회색조치로 분류되지 않는 '여타조항에 의한 조치' 관련, 동 여타조항이 ANNEX 1A협정상의 조항에만 국한되는지 또는 1B, 1C협정상의 조항도 포함되는지에 대해선.개도국간의 입장이 대립(카나다, 미국,노르웨이는 1B, 1C 포함 지지, 브라질, 아국,멕시코, 인도등은 1A 로 국한)

　사. 제 25항에서 35 항까지(통보, 협의 및 감시)

　O 통보, 협의, 감시 절차 관련 CP 를 CG 로 대체할 것인지, CTG 로 대체할 것인지, 또는 SAFEGUARDS COMMITTE 로 대체할 것인지의 여부는 MTO 의 전반적인 구조와 밀접한 관계가 있는 사항이므로 추후 재론키로함.

　2. 향후 법제화 그룹 일정은 별첨과 같이 3.30 주간에 분쟁해결 절차심의, 4.6-7 간 MTO 협정안 심의, 이어서 4.8 부터 개별문안 심의를 가질 예정임.

　첨부: 법제화 그룹 협상일정. 끝

　(GVW(F)-225)

　(대사 박수길-국장)

주 제 네 바 대 표 부

법 호 : GVW(F) - 0225   년월일 : 20327   시간 : 1800
수 신 : 장   관 (총기,경기원,재무부,농림수산부,상공부,특허청)
발 신 : 주 제네바대사
제 목 :

GVW-685 첨부

총   2   매 (표지포함)

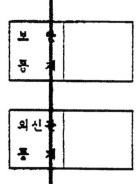

0223

· 25.3.92

<u>Tentative timetable for further work</u>
<u>in the Legal Drafting Group</u>

<u>Week of 30 March-3 April</u>

30 March (p.m.)   Introduction of revised MTO draft

30 March (p.m.)-2 April   Dispute Settlement text

<u>Week of 6-10 April</u>

6-7 April   MTO draft

8-10 April: Individual texts in MTN.TNC/W/FA:
                   O. Textiles and Clothing
                   D. Rules of Origin
                   E. Preshipment Inspection
                   J. Customs Valuation
                   N. TRIMS
                   G. Technical Barriers to Trade
                   L. Sanitary and Phytosanitary Measures
                   H. Import Licensing
                   F. Anti-Dumping
                   I.- Subsidies and Countervailing Duties
                   K. Government Procurement
                   Y. FOGS (including TPRM (Annex 3 to MTO)
                   V. Article XXV
                   X. Article XXXV

<u>Week of 21-24 April</u>: Individual texts in MTN.TNC/W/FA:
                   B. Least-Developed Countries
                   C. Uruguay Round Protocol
                   GATT 1993
                   Annex II (Services)
                   Annex III (TRIPS)
                   L. Agriculture
                   A. Final Act
                   Signatures
                   MTO Annex 4 texts
                   All remaining texts for Ministers

0224

발 신 전 보

분류번호	보존기간

번 호 : WGV-0481   920330 1302   종별 EG 긴급감

수 신 : 주   제네바   대사. 총영사

발 신 : 장 관 (통 기)

제 목 : UR/법제화 그룹 (분쟁해결 절차)

대 : GVW-0647

대호 분쟁해결 절차 관련 사무국 수정안 (Text 513)에 대한 검토의견을 별첨(Fax)
송부하니 표제회의시 참고바람.

첨 부(Fax) : 동 검토의견 1부.   끝.

(통상국장 김 용 규)

앙고재	92년 3월 28일 통괄과 안대경	기안자 성명	과 장 심의반	국 장 전결	차 관	장 관

보 안 통 제

외신과통제

0225

분쟁해결에 절차에 관한 사무국 수정안(Text)검토의견

문 항	쟁 점 및 검 토 의 견
1.1	<u>제2행. "MTO 설립 협정문"을 "to"이후에 삽입 여부등</u> 분쟁해결 규칙 및 절차에 관한 Understanding이 MTO 설립 협정 Annex 2에 수록되며, MTO 설립 협정문 제3조 4항에 MTO가 통합 분쟁해결 체제를 관장토록 명시되어 있으며, MTO 설립 협정문에 분쟁해결에 관한 실질 또는 절차 규정이 포함되어 있지 않기 때문에 1.1항 제2행에 "MTO 설립 협정문"을 삽입할 실익은 없을 것으로 보임.
1.2	1) <u>제3행. rules and 추가 여부</u> 용어상의 일관성 유지를 위해 추가가 바람직. 2) <u>제9행. 2개 이상의 협정과 관련된 분쟁에 있어서 각각의 협정에 포함된 특별규칙 및 절차 (spcial and additional rules and procedures)가 상호 상충할 경우 분쟁해결 기구 의장이 적용되어질 규칙 및 절차를 결정토록 할 것인지 여부</u> MTO 관장하의 협정중 다수가 분쟁해결에 관한 특별규칙 및 절차 규정을 포함하고 있기 때문에 협정별 특별규칙 및 절차 규정간의 상충 가능성이 예견됨. 단, 대부분의 특별규칙 및 절차가 패널 구성 이전 단계에서 적용되므로 별다른 문제가 없을 것이나, 패널 설치 이후 단계에서의 특별규칙 및 절차를 포함하고 있는 보조금 협정, 관세평가 협정 및 섬유협정(섬유협정의 경우 패널과 유사한 기능을 수행하는 TMB가 1차적인 분쟁해결 기능 수행)의 경우 문제가 되는바, 패널 설치가 결정된후 개별 협정상의 특별규칙 및 절차 적용 문제와 관련하여 분쟁 당사국간에 의견의 일치가 이루어지지 않는 경우 분쟁해결 기구 의장의 재정에 맡기도록 하는 것이 바람직.

0226

문 항	쟁 점 및 검 토 의 견
2.1	<u>각주. "MTO 설립 협정 Annex 4상의 협정 관련 분쟁의 경우, 소관위원회</u> <u>또는 이사회가 분쟁해결 규칙 및 절차에 관한 Understanding의 적용</u> <u>여부를 결정토록 한다 는 문구를 포함시킬 것인지 여부</u> MTO 설립 협정 Annex 4상의 협정 회원국들이 동시에 MTO 회원국이 될 것임을 전제로 하는 경우 상기 문구를 포함시킬 필요성은 없을 것으로 보이나, MTO Annex 4상의 협정 회원국중 일부가 Final Act 발효 이후에도 일정기간 동 Act를 수락치 못하는 과도기를 상정할 수 있으므로 이러한 국가들이 당사자인 분쟁의 경우 자신이 수락치 않은 분쟁해결 규칙 및 절차에 관한 Understanding이 자동적으로 적용된다는 것은 문제가 있으므로 상기 문구를 포함토록 하는 것이 적절함.
3.3	<u>제3행. this understanding and 를 the obligations 로 교체 여부</u> 교체하는 경우 협정상의 obligation을 강조함으로써 권리 측면을 소홀히 한다는 인상을 줄수 있으므로 원안대로 in accordance with this understanding and under the covered agreements가 바람직.

0227

문 항	쟁 점 및 검 토 의 견
3.6	제3행. MTO나 DSB 대신 dispute settlement mechanism으로 대체할 것인지 여부
	대체시 특별한 문제점은 없을 것이나 다소 막연한 인상을 주므로 dispute settlement mechanism of MTO가 바람직.
	제15행. this 를 the dispute settlement 로 교체 여부
	this 를 the dispute settlement로 교체하더라도 별다른 실질적인 차이는 없을 것이나 상기 3행에 dispute settlement mechanism을 추가할 경우에는 3.6항 의 전체적인 균형유지 측면에서 15행 에서도 this를 the dispute settlement로 교체하는 것이 바람직.
3.7	제1행. violation을 an infringement로 대체할 것인지 여부
	법률 용어로서 violation와 infringement가 동일한 의미이나, 3.7항이 분쟁해결에 관한 79년도 Understanding Annex 5항을 본뜬것으로서 동 Understanding Annex 5항이 infringement라는 용어를 사용하고 있는 점을 감안, an infringement로 대체함이 바람직.
	제5행. parties to 를 Members of로 대체할것인지 여부
	내부적 일관성을 위해 Member of 로 대체함이 바람직.
	제8행. claim of nullification or impairment를 charge로 대체할 것인지 여부
	상기 제1행에서와 동일한 이유로 대체가 바람직함.
3.10	3.10항 전체를 The entry into force and the application of this understanding shall be governed by a Ministerial decision adopted at the time of the MTO Implementing Congerence which contains transitional provisions.로 할것인지 여부.

0228

문 항	쟁 점 및 검 토 의 견
	각료급 이행회의(Implementing Conference)의 결정에 의해 분쟁해결 규칙 및 절차에 관한 understanding 을 포함한 모든 협정문이 발효하므로 3.10항에 동 understanding의 발효 시점과 각료급 이행회의 결정과의 관계를 규정할 필요성이 없을것으로 판단됨.
3.11	제2행. based on the GATT(1993)[or on any of the other agreemenents listed in Annex 1A to the Agreement Establishing the MTO]추가여부 MTO 설립 협정 발효이후 발생하는 분쟁의 경우를 상정한 것이므로 [ ]을 제거하여 추가하여도 무방. 제13행. GATT council of Represenatives로 할것인지 여부 기술적 수정에 해당되므로 문제점 없음. 제14행. once a panel report is adopted under the procedures established in this understanding the mechanism for the suspension of concessions established in paragraph 22.4 shall be applicable 추가여부 패널보고서 채택단계까지는 개도국 우대에 관한 1966년 결정을 적용하고, 보복단계에서는 자동적 보복 승인을 내용으로 하는 분쟁 해결 규칙 및 절차에 관한 understanding을 적용할수 있도록 허용할 것인지가 문제임. 과거의 예로 볼때 개도국들이 1966년 절차를 원용한 사례가 드물며 3.11항의 취지가 개도국 우대인 점을 감안할때 상기 문안추가에 대해 컨센서스가 이루어지는 경우 이에 반대치 않는 선에서 대처함이 바람직.
4.1	제2행. consultative를 the consultation 으로 대체 여부 consultative procedure와 consultaion procedure간에 뜻의 차이가 없으므로 대체 하여도 무방.

022()

문 항	쟁 점 및 검 토 의 견
4.11	<u>제4행 및 제15행 Article XX11 : 1 of the GATS Agreement or the corresponding provisions in other covered agreements 추가여부</u> 추가하여도 별다른 문제점 없음.
6.2	<u>제1행. the establishment of 추가여부</u> request for a panel의 의미를 보다 명확히한다는 면에서 추가가 바람직.
8.4	<u>제16행. In addition, the names of services experts proposed by the concil shall be incorporated in the indicative list upon approval by the DSB 추가여부</u> service 교역의 비중을 감안할때 추가하여도 별다른 문제점이 없음. <u>제19행 panelists를 individuals로 교체여부</u> list상의 panelist 후보는 panelist로 선정될때 까지는 개인에 불과 하므로 indevidual로 하여도 무방.
8.7	<u>제3행 패널 구성에 관한 분쟁당사국간 의견 불일치의 경우 패널구성의 주체를 MTO 사무총장으로 할것인지 여부</u> 현행 갓트 체제하에서 갓트사무총장에게 패널구성 권한이 있음에 비추어 별 문제점 없음.
8.7	<u>제4행. and 추가여부</u> 기술적 성격의 보완이므로 문제점 없음.

문 항	쟁 점 및 검 토 의 견
8.11	<u>제1행. 패널위원에 대한 경비지급 기준으로서 제네바 소재 여부를 명시할것인지 여부</u> 8.11항에 Geneva를 명시치 않고 if appropriate라는 일반적인 표현을 사용하는 것이 더 바람직.
10.2	<u>제 1, 2, 3행</u> 표현상의 문제로서 특별한 문제점 없음.
10.4	<u>제2행. report adopted by the DSB 추가여부</u> 패널이 설치되어 작업을 진행중인 동안 제3국이 동일한 사안으로 패널 설치를 요청할수 없도록하자는 취지로 해석됨. 제3국의 입장에서 볼때 협의과정에 참여할수 있는 가능성이 존재하며, 패널설치 결정시 이해 관계가 있는 제3국으로 참여의사를 표명함으로써 패널 과정에 참여할수 있음을 감안 할때, 수정안 대로 하는것이 바람직.
13.1	<u>제5행. government를 authorities로 대체여부</u> anthorities의 의미가 권한있는 당국으로서 정부를 포함하는 용어 이므로 별 문제점 없음.
14.2	<u>제 2, 3행. to the dispute 및 provided 추가여부</u> 뜻을 보다 명확히 한다는 점에서 추가가 바람직.
16.4	<u>제 2, 3행. to the dispute 및 provided 추가여부</u> parties의 뜻을 보다 명확히 한다는 점에서 추가가 바람직.

0231

문 항	쟁 점 및 검 토 의 견
17.1	<u>제4행. pool을 Appellate Body로 교체여부</u> 　　기술적인 수정으로서 별 문제점 없음 <u>제5행. such rotation shall be determined in the working procedures</u> <u>of the Appellate Body 추가여부</u> 　　rotation 방식을 상소기구의 절차규정에 정하도록 하는데 별 문제점 　　없음.
17.5	<u>제2행. to the dispute 추가여부</u> 　　party의 뜻을 보다 명확히 하는것이므로 별 문제점 없음.
17.8	8.11항과 동일
17.10	<u>제2행. "The reports of the Appellate Body shall be drafted.....and</u> <u>the statements made 추가여부</u> 　　14.2항과의 균형유지의 측면에서 볼때 별 문제점 없음.
17.11	<u>제2행. individual persons를 individuals로 대체여부</u> 　　별다른 문제점 없음.
18.1	<u>제1-3행의 표현을 There shall be no ex parte communications로</u> <u>수정할 것인지 여부</u> 　　동일한 의미이나 수정안대로 ex parte라는 법률용어 자체에 　　"일방 분쟁 당사자 만을 위한 (in the interests of one side only)" 　　라는 뜻이 내포되어 있으므로 수정안 대로 하여도 무방.

0232

문 항	쟁 점 및 검 토 의 견
21.6	<u>제10행. party를 Member로 교체여부</u> 내부적 일관성 확보를 위한 기술적 수정이므로 무방
22.2	<u>제4행. determined pursuant to paragraph 21.3 above 추가여부</u> 합리적이행기간을 규정하고 있는 21.3항을 refer함으로써 뜻을 보다 명확히 하는 것이므로 별 문제점 없음. <u>제11행. complaining party를 party having invoked the dispute</u> <u>settlement procedures로 대체여부</u> 동일한 의미 이므로 무방.
22.4	<u>(c) 5행. covered 추가여부</u> agreement 가 MTO 관할하의 협정이므로 covered 를 추가하여 agreement 의 뜻을 보다 명확히 한다는 점에서 추가하여도 무방. <u>(e) 5행 및 6행. also와 or를 삭제하고 6행에 and also 삽입여부</u> 교차보복 의사가 관련 이사회및 sectoral body에도 모두 통고되어야 하므로 수정안이 바람직. <u>(f) 서비스 및 TRIPs의 Sector 분류</u> 수정안대로 보다 구체화 시키는 것이 바람직. (g) 2.1항 각주와 동일
22.6	<u>13행. DSB 의장을 MTO 사무총장으로 대체여부</u> 현행 분쟁해결 절차에 의하면 갓트 사무총장이 arbitrator를 임명하므로 수정안대로 하여도 무방. <u>16행. pending the outcome을 during the course로 대체여부</u> 동일한 의미이므로 대체하여도 무방.

0233

문 항	쟁 점 및 검 토 의 견

22.7	제 2행 및 3행. suspended를 to be suspended로 교체여부
	
	  to be suspended가 보다 정확한 표현
	
	제5행. 중재자가 보복조치(안)이 해당 협정하에서 허용되는지 여부를
	
	결정할수있게 할것인지 여부
	
	  동 내용이 22.7항 첫번째 sentence인 "The arbitrator acting
	
	  pursuant to para 6 shall not examine the nature of the
	
	  concessions........"와 모순되므로 동 수정안 추가는 문제점이
	
	  있음.

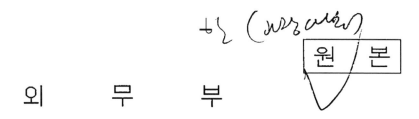

외 무 부

종   별 :

번   호 : GVW-0718　　　　　　　　　　　　일   시 : 92 0331 1900

수   신 : 장 관(통기,경기원,재무부,농수부,상공부,특허청)

발   신 : 주 제네바 대사

제   목 : UR/법제화 그룹(분쟁해결 절차,1)

　　　　대: WGV-0418

　　　　연: GVW-0647

　　MTO 통합 분쟁해결 절차에 관한 사무국 수정안(513)에 대한 3.30 논의 요지를 아래보고함. (이참사관, 신서기관 참석)

　　1. 1.1항(적용 범위)

　　0 MTO 협정문에 대한 분쟁이 통합분쟁해결 절차의 적용대상인지 여부(동항 주석)에 대해

　　- 미국은 MTO 협정문에 권리, 의무에 관한 실질규정이 없음을 논거로 적용대상이 아니라는 입장이며, 홍콩은 MTO 협정에 대한 분쟁은 MTO 협정 해석 조항(11조 2항)의 규율대상이며,부속협정이 모협정에 대한 분쟁을 규율할수는 없다는 이유로 미국입장에 동조함.

　　- EC, 카나다는 MTO 협정문이 실질규정을 포함하고 있으므로 적용대상이라는 입장인바, EC는 실질규정으로 16조 4항(국내법의 MTO 협정일치)을 카나다는 9조(웨이버)를 예로 듬. 아국,일본, 인도는 예비적 의견임을 전제로 EC,카나다 입장에 동조하면서, 웨이버 조항등 MTO관련 조항에 대한 합의가 도출된후 동문제를 재론할 것을 제의함.

　　0 상기관련, EC 가 분쟁해결 절차에 관한 양해 자체(예: 23조 일방조치)에 대한분쟁이 동절차의 적용대상이 되는가에 대해 의문을 제기한바

　　- 갓트 사무국은 고려 가능하다는 긍정적인 반응인데 비해

　　- 미국은 통합 분쟁 해결절차에 관한 양해의 모체인 T TEXT 의 ANNEX 2 에 동 양해 및TPRM 협정문이 포함되지 않았음을 들어 강력히 반대함.

　　- 인도는 상기 미국의 주장에 대해 S TEXT 가 ANNEX 2 를 언급만 하고 있을 뿐 동

통상국　　2차보　　경기원　　재무부　　농수부　　상공부　　특허청

내용까지 규정하고 있지 않음을 상기시키면서 미국의 주장에 반박함.

O 동 항 3째줄 THE LEGAL-ESTABLISHING 은 상이한 해석의 여지가 있으므로 이를삭제(332 에로복귀)하자는 미국의 제의에 대해

- 인도, 일본이 미국의 취지에 동의하면서 동문구를 각각 MULTILATERAL TRADE AGREEMENTS ANDPLURILATERAL TRADE AGREEMENTS ESTABLISHING, LEGALINITRUMENTS(또는 AGREEMENTS) LISTED IN APPENDIX I으로 수정할 것을 제의함.

2. 1.2항 (적용)

O 첫째 문장 및 둘째 문장의 분쟁해결 절차에 관한 규정 관련, 미국이 둘째 문장의 첫부분인 THE SPECIAL - PROCEDURES 를 생략하고 첫째문장의 ANY 를 SUCH AS (AS는 ARE 앞)바꿈으로서 APPENDIX II 특별 조항에 관한 EXHAUSTIVE LIST 로 바꾸어 이를 명확히 하자고 제의하여 카나다가 이에 동조한 반면

- EC 는 그럴경우 APPENDIX II 가 너무 길어져 실용적이지 못함을, 홍콩은 APPENDIX II 에포함되어 있는 정부조달 협정이 아직도 협상중이에 있음을 근거로 이에 반대함.

O 특별규정을 지칭하는 용어가 혼용되고(PROVISION,또는 RULE AND PROCEDURES) 있음을 지적하면서 이를 PROVISION 으로 통일하자는 미국의 제의에대해

- PROVISION 은 통상 실질에 관한 조항을 지칭한다는 인도의 COMMENT 가 있었으나 미국은 별첨 1의 수정안을 제출함.

O 주석 A 관련, 미국이 관세평가 협정을 예로들면서 동 1.2 항의 규정으로도 해결이 안되는 문제가 있을수 있다고 하면서 여사한 문제는 해당협정에서 재논의될 필요가 있음을 제기한데 대해, EC 도 보조금 협정을 예로 들면서 미측에 동의함.

한편 미국이 주석에 A 에 민간 항공협정이 빠져있다고 지적한데 대해 EC 는 해당협정을 일일이 다 지적할수는 없을 것이라는 입장을 표명

3. 2.1 항의 주석1(MTO 협정 부속서 4관련분쟁)

O 동 주석의 첫째, 둘째 물장은 내용상 제 2조1항의 본문으로 옮기자는 미국의 제의가 받아들여짐.

O 동 주석 마지막 문장의 필요여부에 대해서

- EC, 스위스는 부속서 4의 해당 협정 기구에서 통합 분쟁해결 절차 적용 여부를결정하게되면, 동 결정은 CONSENSUS 에 의하게 되는바,사실상 통합절차의 적용이 불가하므로 동문장의 삭제를 주장한 반면

- 홍콩은 MTO 협정 부속서 4의 정부 조달협정에대한 협상이 진행중임을 들어, 미국은 향후 MTO협정 부속서 4에 추가될 협정을 위해, 아국,일본등 MTO 협정을 비준하지 못한 부속서나 협정 가입국등을 위해 필요함을 지적함으로써

- 동문장을 괄호로 묶어 주석으로 남겨두기로 합의함.(단, 협정에 따라서는 기구와 발족 시기가 일정하지 않을 것임을 감안하여 INSTITUTIONAL BODY를 SIGNATORIES로 수정)

4. 2.4항(콘센서스에 의한 결정

0 동항은 민감한 사항이므로 재논의하지 말자는 미국의 제의가 받아들여짐.

5. 322 의 3.1항(GATT '47 절차와의 연속성)

0 호주, 뉴질랜드, 스위스가 MTO 협정 제 16조1항의 GATT '47 과 MTO 의 연속성확보의 추지를 살리기 위해 동항을 부활시키자는 입장인데 대해 미국, EC, 일본등은MTO상의 분쟁해결 절차를 갓트 '47 절차와 내용면에서 크게 다르며, 적용범위도 상이함을 내세워 수정안대로 삭제를 주장함.

6. 3. 3항 (권고 및 판정의목적)

0 미국은 권리, 의무의형평을 위해 OBLIGATION앞에 RIGHTS AND 추가 를 제의한데대해

0 홍콩, 인도등이 동항은 332 문안대로 THEOBLIGATIONS 이하를 THIS UNDERSTANDING AND UNDER THECOVERED AGREEMENT 로 수정할 것을 제의함.

- 이에 대해 미국이 THIS UNDERSTANDING 이 포함되는것은 당초 S TEXT 교섭시 GATT OBLIGATIONS' 로규정한 추지에 어긋난다고 주장한데 반해, 홍콩은 S TEXT 교섭 당시에는 T TEXT 및 봉합 분쟁절차를 상정하지 못한 상태이므로 사정이 다르다는 입장임.

0 동항은 제1조 1항 범위와도 연관이 있으므로 후자에 대한 합의가 도출된후 재논의 키로 함.

7. 3.8항(MTO 해석과의 관계)

0 JOINT ACTION 용어는 MTO 협정 논의시 더이상 사용치 않는 것으로 검토되고 있으므로 해당 용어가 결정되는대로 이에 따라 수정키로 함.

8. 3.10항(발효 및 적용시기)

0 미국이 도항은 3조 11항과 밀접한 연관이있으므로 추지에 따라 S TEXT 로 돌아갈것을 주장한데 대해

ㅇ 의장은 미국의 주장처럼 경과 규정 성격의 조항을 본문에 두는 것 보다는 사무국의 수정안을 받아들이는 것이 어떻겠느냐는 의견 제시를 하였으나

ㅇ 미국의 강경한 주장으로 S TEXT 로 돌아가기로 잠정합의함.

첨부: 미국수정안 (제 1조 2항)

(GVW(F)-235)

(대사 박수길-국장)

주 제 네 바 대 표 부

발 신 : GVE(F) - 235   년월일 : 2 0 3 3 1   시간 : 18 w

수 신 : 장   관 (동기, 경기원, 재무부, 농림수산부, 상공부, 특허청)

발 신 : 주 제녀바대사

제 목 :

Gvw - 918 관시

안공재	년 인 일	서기관	참사관	차석대사	대 사
		신			

보 안 동	검	신

외신 통	총 보	

총 2 매(표지포함)

0239

Proposed revision (U.S. proposal.)   92.3.30

1.2 The rules and procedures of this Understanding shall
     apply subject to such special or additional rules,
     procedures or provisions on dispute settlement
     contained in the covered agreements as are identified
     in Appendix 2 to this understanding. To the extent
     that there is a difference between the rules and
     procedures of this understanding and the special or
     additional rules, procedures or provisions set forth
     in appendix 2, the special or additional rules,
     procedures or provisions in Appendix 2 shall prevail.

0240

외　무　부

원　본

종　별 :

번　호 : GVW-0722　　　　　　　　　　　일　시 : 92 0331 2130

수　신 : 장관(통기,경기원,재무부,농수산부,상공부,특허청)

발　신 : 주 제네바 대사

제　목 : UR/법제화 그룹 비공식 회의(분쟁해결 절차, 2)

　　연: GVW-718

　　MTO 통합분쟁 해결 절차 (문서 513)에 대한 3.31 논의 요지를 아래 보고함.

　　(신서기관 참석)

　　1. 3.11 항(개도국 우대에 관한 1966 년 결정)

　　0 동항 첫째 문장의 MTO ANNEX 1A 관련, 개도국이 제소국인 경우 적용되는 1966년 갓트분쟁해결 절차가 ANNEX 1A 의 동경라운드협정에도 적용되는지 여부에 대해

　　- 미국, EC, 호주, 일본등 선진국은 '66 년 절차가 동경라운드 협정에도 적용된다는 결정은 어디에서도 찾아볼수 없으므로(동 문안에 대한 합의 부재) 갓트 '47 에만적용된다는 입장인데 대해

　　- 멕시코, 브라질, 칠레, 인도등은 '79 년 각료결정및 개별 동경협정이 갓트의관례를 존중한다라고 되어 있으므로 동경라운드 협정에도 적용된다는 입장임.

　　0 동항 마지막 문장 관련 66년 절차에 의한 패널 결정(상품분야)의 불이행시 통합분쟁해결 절차에 따라 서비스, TRIPS 분야에서의 보복을 할수 있는지 여부에 대해서도 상기와 같이 선진국은 교차 보복 불가를, 후진국은 교차 보복이 가능하다는 입장(미국이 개도국에 대하여 패널 구성절차 및 패널 결정 이행절차에 이중으로 특혜를주는 것은 곤란하다는 강경 입장으로 멕시코는 동문안에 대해 재고해 보겠다는 반응을 보임.)

　　2. 4.11항(제 3국의 협의권)

　　0 동항 첫째 문장에는 22조 1항에 의한 협의절차만 언급되어 있는데 반해, 동항마지막 문장에는 22조 1항 절차와 함께 23조 1항에의한 협의절차도 규정되어 있는 0 이유(EC 제기)에대해 사무국측은 제 3국이 참가할수 있는 협의절차를 22조 1항 절차인 때문이라고 설명함.(미국도 1958 년 결정을 들어 사무국에 동조)

| 통상국 | 2차보 | 경기원 | 재무부 | 농수부 | 상공부 | 특허청 | |

PAGE 1

92.04.01　　05:25 DW

외신 1과　통제관

0241

0 주석 G 에 예시된 해당 협정의 범위에 대해 사무국이 추가검토를 하기로함.

3. 8.3항(패널리스트 규정)

0 미국은 패널에 참가하는 제 3국의 인사도 패널리스트로 선출되어서는 곤란하다면서, 둘째줄 THE DISPUTE 뒤에 'OR THIRD PARTIES IN THE PANEL PROCESS '를 추가할것을 제의함.(사무국은 패널리스트 선정상의 어려움을 들어 난색 표명)

4. 8.4항 (패널리스트 명부)

0 현존 패널리스트 명부의 계속성 및 추후 체결될 협정의 패널리스트 명부의 포함을 위해 문안수정(11 P 2줄 REPLACE 를 INCLUDE 로 6줄 BUT SHALL INCLUDE 를 ANDSHALL RETAIN 으로)

0 마지막 두번째 문장의 GATS 전문가에대해서는 다수국이 특정협정만을 언급하는것은 곤란하다는 입장을 개진함.

5. 8.11항(패널리스트 경비)

0 IF APPROPRIATE 를 삭제하고, MTO 협정안의 구조를 감안하여 MTO BUDGET 뒤에APPROVED AND ADOPTED BY GENERAL COUNCIL BASED ON RECOMMENDATION OF BUDGET COMMITTEE 를 추가키로 함.

6. 10.2항(제 3국의 패널 참가 요건)

0 미국, EC, 카나다 등이 사무국 수정(2 째줄)안은 제3국의 패널 참고 요건인SUBSTANTIAL INTEREST를 제3국 자신이 결정할수 있도록 허용하고 있다는 이유를 들어이에 반대함.

- 이에 대해 태국은 4.11 항 협의에 참가할수 있는 제 3국의 요건으 들어 사무국수정안에 찬성함.

7. 10.4항

0 사무국 추가문안 (2째줄)은 당초 취지인 패널이 진행되는 동안에는 동일한 문제로 추가 패널설치를 요구할수 없다는 점이 적절하게 반영되어 있지 못하므로 REPORTADOPTED BY THE DSB 를 PROCEEDING 으로 수정함.

8. 11.1항(PANEL 의 TOR)

0 7째줄 사무국 추가문안과 관련, 미국,카나다등이 패널의 TOR 은 DSB 로 부터부여받은 것이므로 동 추가문안이 불필요하다는 입장에대해 홍콩은 동문안은 S TEXT상의 문안으로서 추가 검토가 필요하다는 입장임.

0 동항 취지에 따라 9줄 COVERED AGREEMENTS 앞에 RELEVANT 추가. 끝

(대사 박수길 -추장)

정 리 보 존 문 서 목 록

기록물종류	일반공문서철	등록번호	2020030053	등록일자	2020-03-09
분류번호	764.51	국가코드		보존기간	영구
명 칭	UR(우루과이라운드) / 법제화 그룹회의, 1992. 전2권				
생 산 과	통상기구과	생산년도	1992~1992	담당그룹	
권 차 명	V.2 4-12월				
내용목차					

0001

외 무 부

원 본

종   별 :

번   호 : GVW-0740   일   시 : 92 0402 1930

수   신 : 장관(봉기,경기원,재무부,농수산부,상공부,특허청)

발   신 : 주 제네바 대사

제   목 : UR/법제화 그룹 비공식회의(분쟁해결 절차,3)

대: WGV-0418

MTO 봉합분쟁해결절차(문서 513)에 대한 4.1논의 요지를 아래 보고함.

(신서기관 참석)

1. 13.1항(자료 요청)

0 패널이 정부뿐만 아니라 개인 또는 비정부기관에게도 자료를 요청할 수 있음에 비추어 마지막 줄의 MEMBER 를 PERSONS OR AUTHORITIES 로수정함

2. 18.2항(패널, 상소기관관과의 의사소통)

0 의사소통 주체의 명확성을 제고하기 위해 첫줄COMMUNICATIONS 뒤에 WITH PANELOR APPELLATE BODY를 추가

3. 22.2항(보상 및 보복 조치요건)

0 요건에 대한 명확성을 제고하기 위해 7줄의 ANY PARTY 뒤의 TO THE DISPUTE 를7줄의HAVING-PROCEDURES 로 수정

4. 22.3항(보복수준)

0 OBLIGATONS 뒤에 'AUTHORIZED BY THE DSB' 를 추가하자는 제의(홍콩, 인도)에대해 미국이 동문구는 S TEST 에 없는 것이라면서 반대함.

5. 22.4항(보복의 원칙 및 절차)0 (A) 항 3째줄,(B)항 4째줄, (C) 항2째줄 IN 을WITH RESPECT TO 로 수정

- 동 수정의 논거는 동(A),(B),(C) 항의 취지가 단순히 보복조치가 취해질수 있는 분야를 직시하는데 있는데 비해 IN 으로 표현하게 되면 각각의 분야에서 구제대상과 똑같은 성질의권리, 의무에 대한 보복을 해야된다는 의미로 해석될 여지가 있으므로 이를 방지하기 위한 것임

0 (C) 항 5줄 COVERED 에 대해서는 1.1항과의 일관성 및 명료성을 위해 필요하다는

통상국   2차보   경기원   재무부   농수부   상공부   특허청

PAGE 1   92.04.03   05:28 ED

외신 1과 통제관

0002

입장(아국,인도, 브라질등, 기본적으로 ANNEX 4협정은 COVERED AGREEMENT 가 아니라는 전제하)과 COVEREDAGREEMENT 의 표현은 ANNEX 4 협정문이통합분쟁 해결 절차의대상인 COVEREDAGREEMENT에 포함되는지 여부가 논란의 대상이 되고있는 점에 비추어부적절하며(미국), (G)항의'AGREEMENT'에 대한 설명에 비추어 오해의 여지가 있으므로 (카나다,EC) COVERED 를 추가할 필요가 없다는 입장이 대립

0 (F)항 서비스관련,협상그룹작업문서(MTN.GNS/W/120)의 내용에 기초한 동 문안은 협상그룹 작업문서의 가변적 성격에 비추어 적절하지 못하므로 아래와 같이 수정

   - SET OUT 을 IDENTIFIED 로 수정, MOST 및WHICH 이하삭제 하는 대신

   - 주석 13을 THE CURRENT DOCUMENT MTN.GNS/W/120INDENTIFIES 11 SUCH PRINCIPALSECTORS 로 수정

0 (G)항 6줄 AND 이하에 대해서는 EC는 TTEXT 에 없는 동문장을 추가하는 것은 T3권한밖이라는 입장인 반면, 카나다, 홍콩은 명료성을 제고하는 것이 필요하다는 입장임.

   - 한편 명료성을 위해 3째줄 AND 를 삭제하고그자리에 'TAKEN AS A WHOLE, AS WELL AS' 를 추가함.

   6. 22.5항(DSB 의 보복조치 승인제한)

0 현재의 MTO 관련 협정문안에 DSB 의보복조치 승인을 제한하는 규정이 없음에 비추어 동항을 삭제하자는 입장(미국,인도)과 정부조달협정이 현재 진행중인 점과 앞으로 체결될 협정등이 여사한 금지규정을 설정할 수도있다는 점을 감안하여 동항이필요하다는 입장(EC,홍콩,싱가폴)이 대립

   7. 22.6항(중재회부)

0 12째줄의 ORIGINAL PANEL 과 관련, 중재의 목적상 원래의 패널을 중재기관으로 하는 것은 문제가 있다는 EC의 지적에 대해 미국,일본등을 패널의 사실적 내용을 잘알고 있는 당초 패널 위원에게 중재업무를 맡기는 것이 중재의 실제취지에 부합된다는 입장임.

   (EC는 동문제에 대한 자국의 입장을고집하지는 않았음)

   8. 22.7항(중재의 임무)

0 중재임무의 기본전제에 관한 둘째문항에도 그취지상 주석 K 를 추가키로 함

0 마지막 문장중 사무국이 추가한 25P 의 AND UPON이하(중재절차 종료후 DSB 의보복조치승인)는T TEXT 상에 없는 문안이므로 삭제하자는 인도제의에 대해

0003

브라질,멕시코등이   동조한   반면,미국,카나다는   22.6항   마지막
문장(중재기간동안은보복 조치 불가)에 비추어 동문안이 필요하며, T TEXT는 급히
작성된 문안임을 주장하면서 강력반대함.끝

(대사 박수길-국장)

발 신 전 보

번 호 : WGV-O515   920403 1920 FO   종별 :

수 신 : 주 제네바   대사. 총영사

발 신 : 장 관 (통 기)

제 목 : UR/법제화 그룹 (MTO 설립 협정문)

대 : GVW-0667

1. 대호 MTO 설립 협정안에 관한 사무국 수정안 (Text 551)에 대한 검토의견을
   별첨(fax) 송부하니 표제회의시 참고바람.

2. 동 사무국 수정 Text중 Annex 1(e) 및 동 Text 마지막에 제시된 proposal on
   "reservations" language는 MTO원회원국의 경우 조부조항을 계속 원용할수 있도록
   하는 내용으로   되어 있는바, 이는 draft Final Act상의 MTO 설립 협정문
   Annex 1 A에 명시된 PPA 제외 조항과 동 협정문 16조 2항의 유보불가 조항과
   정면으로 배치되며 따라서 이는 성격상 track 4 협상에서 제기될 사항이라는 점을
   법제 그룹회의시 지적 바람.

3. 아울러 MTO 설립 협정 2조 3항 (Text 551의 경우 2조 5항) " GATT 93이 GATT 47과
   법적으로 상이하다"의 의미와 동 조항의 법적효과에 대한 갓트 사무국 (법률국)의
   의견을 파악.보고바람.

   첨 부(Fax) : 동 검토의견 1부.   끝.

(통상국장 김 용 규)

MTO 설립 협정문안 검토 의견 (Text 551)

WGVF-0129 920403 1921 FO

수정안	검토 의견
2조 MTO의 범위 4 항	원안과 수정안사이에 실질적인 차이가 없으므로 어느쪽이나 무방 (shall consider whether it is feasible for it to accept them라는 표현이 가입 의무를 지우는 것은 아님)
5 항	수정안에서 GATT 47을 as subsequently rectified, amended or modified로 보충 설명한 것은 Annex 1 A에 수록된 GATT 93가 GATT 47에 의거하여 성립된 법적문서 (associated legal instrument)를 포함한다는 점을 보다 명확히 하기 위한 것이므로 수정안대로 하여도 별다른 문제점이 없는 것으로 판단됨.
3조 MTO의 기능 1 항	<u>제2행 of this Agreement 추가 (text 462와 비교시)</u> MTO 설립 협정내에 사무국, 예산, 개정 회원국, 가입, 협정 부적용, 수락 및 발효, 철회등 절차 규정이 포함되어 있으므로 of this Agreement를 추가하는 것이 바람직함.

0006

수정안	검토 의견
2 항	<u>향후 다자간 협상 추진 및 동 협상 결과의 이행과 관련된 MTO 설립 협정문 초안 제2항 및 3항을 통합하고 forum과 framework앞의 the를 a로 대체</u> 수정안처럼 제3조 1항이 현재의 다자간 무역협상 관련 사항을 제2항이 향후 다자간 무역협상 관련 사항을 다루도록 재구성하는 것이 바람직함. forum과 framework앞에 the 혹은 a를 사용할 것인지의 문제는 다자간 무역협상이 MTO의 주관하에서만 이루어질 것이라는 점에서 the도 가능할 것이나 수정 text 551상의 2항이 미래의 상황을 규정하고 있으며, MTO 회원국들간의 무역협상이라 하더라도 MTO 밖에서 이루어질 가능성도 배제할 수 없을 것이므로 a forum, a framework이 보다 적절함.
4 항	분쟁해결 규칙 및 절차에 관한 Understanding의 적용범위 문제는 분쟁해결 text 토의 결과에 따라 결정될 문제이므로 추후 결정
5 항	법조문에 명시하다라는 뜻을 표현하는 데에는 set out 보다는 provide for나 stipulate가 더 적합
6 항	text 551~(MTO 설립 협정안과 동일)과 text 462의 내용은 실질적으로 동일하나 전자가 후자에 비해 MTO와 IMF, IBRD간의 협조를 보다 직접적으로 규정한다는데 있음. Draft Final Act중 FOG text 제10항에 "GATT should therefore pursue and develop its cooperation with the international organizations responsible for monetary and financial matters ..."라는 표현으로 갓트와 국제금융 기구간의 협력관계 추구 의무가 규정되어 있으므로 text 551대로 하여도 무방

0007

수정안	검토 의견
4조 MTO의 구조 3항 및 4항	Text 551 제3항과 4항에 따를 경우 GC가 DSB 혹은 TPRB로서 각각 분쟁해결과 TPRM 기능을 수행하게 되므로 별도로 DSB와 TPRB를 신설하거나 DSB 의장 및 TPRB 의장을 선출할 필요성이 없어짐. DSB와 TPRB를 별도로 신설할 것인지의 문제와 관련하여 본부로서는 flexible한 입장임 (UR 분쟁해결 협상그룹에서 아국은 분쟁해결 전담기구 신설에 반대한 바 있음). 단, DSB와 TPRB를 별도로 신설치 않는 방향으로 컨센서스가 이루어지는 경우 3항과 4항 마지막 SENTENCE중 DSB 의장과 TPRB 의장직 신설 부분이 삭제되어야 하며, 분쟁해결 규칙 및 절차에 관한 Understanding도 이에 따라 수정되어야 할 것임.
5 항	Text 551상의 5항은 MTO 설립 협정안 4항, 5항, 6항, 7항을 통합한 내용으로서, "분야별 이사회들이 일반이사회의 지도하에 운용된다" (operate under the general guidance of the General Council)는 내용을 추가함으로써 일반이사회와 분야별 이사회의 관계를 보다 명확히 한다는 점에서 바람직함.
7 항	MTO 설립 협정안은 무역개발위원회, 국제수지위원회 및 예산위원회의 설립 주체를 일반이사회로 규정하고 있으나 수정안은 설립 주체를 각료회의로 하고 있음. 상기 3개 위원회가 상설위원회이고, 일반이사회는 각료회의 비회기 기간중 각료회의 기능을 수행하게 되므로 일반이사회 대신 각료회의를 설립 주체로 하는 것도 무방함.

0008

수정안	검토 의견
8 항	MTO 설립 협정 Annex 4상의 협정도 MTO framework 내에서 운용되므로 자신들의 활동 실적을 정기적으로 일반이사회에 통보하는 것이 적절한 것으로 판단됨.
9조 의사 결정	
1 항	<u>이씨가 투표권을 행사할 수 있는지 여부</u> 이씨 회원국이 투표권을 행사하면서 이씨가 별도의 투표권을 행사하는 것은 형평에 어긋나므로 개별 회원국이 투표권을 행사하는 경우 이씨 자체는 투표권을 행사치 못하도록 명시하는 것이 바람직함.
2 항	<u>각료회의의 협정의 해석 관련 의사 결정을 컨센서스로 할 것인지 여부</u> 협정의 해석 문제는 모든 회원국의 권리·의무에 영향을 미치는 사항이므로 이와 관련된 각료회의의 의사 결정이 컨센서스에 의해 이루어지도록 명시하는 것이 바람직함.
3 항	Waiver는 특수한 상황에서 이루어지는 것이므로 MTO가 Waiver에 관한 일원적인 권한을 행사토록 규정한 MTO 설립 협정안대로 하는것이 바람직함.
10조 개정	—
1항 및 2항	MTO 설립 협정이나 MTO 설립 협정 Annex 1,2,3에 수록된 협정의 수정안 마련은 모든 회원국의 권리·의무에 직결되는 문제이므로 컨센서스에 의하여야 하며, 회원국 총수의 2/3 이상 수락시 발효토록 하는 option 1(15P의 1항 및 2항)이 바람직함.

0009

수정안	검토 의견
	(단, 갓트 30조 1항에 규정된대로 갓트 제1부의 수정은 모든 회원국이 수락하는 경우 발효토록해야 함).
4 항	분쟁해결 규칙 및 절차에 관한 Understanding 및 TPRM 협정의 수정안 마련도 컨센서스에 의하도록 하는것이 바람직하며 발효는 2/3 수락시로 하는것이 바람직함
11조 원회원국 자격	원회원국의 자격 요건으로 양허표 제출 의무 포함 여부와 관련, 선개도국간 입장 대립이 있을 수 있으므로 아국으로서는 컨센서스에 따르도록 함.
12조 가입	
2 항	신규 회원국 가입 의결 정족수와 관련, 현행 갓트 33조와 같이 전체 회원국 2/3로 하는것이 바람직함.
13조 협정 부적용	
2 항	MTO 회원국간 협정 부적용의 범위가 현행 갓트하에서의 부적용의 범위 이상으로 확대되는 것이 바람직하지 않으므로 MTO 협정 발효시 실제로 협정 부적용이 적용되고 있던 회원국간에만 Annex 1 A 협정의 부적용이 가능함을 명시하는 것이 바람직함.

0010

외 무 부

종 별 :

번 호 : GVW-0745   일 시 : 92 0403 1600

수 신 : 장관(봉기,경기원,재무부,농수산부,상공부,특허청)

발 신 : 주제네바대사

제 목 : UR/법제화 그룹 비공식회의(분쟁해결, 4)

연: GVW-0667

1. MTO 봉합분쟁 해결절차(문서 513)에 대한 4.2 논의 요지를 아래 보고함.

(신서기관 참석)

가. 25.4항(중재 결과 이행절차)

0 동항관련, 보조금.상계관세 협정문(ITEXT)의 제 8조 5항에 언급된 중재절차와동항과의 관계에 대한 심의 필요성이 제기되어 I TEXT 논의시 재론키로함.

나. 26항(NON-VIOLATION 분쟁)

0 26.1 및 26.2항 관련, NON-VIOLATION 분쟁에대한 갓트 23조 1(B) 및 제 23조 1(C) 절차가 갓트 '93 이외 기타 MTO 부속협정에 대해서도 적용되는지 여부는 동항의주석(27 P 및 28 P)대로 각협정에 대한 추가검토를 통해 결정할 사항이라는 점을확인함.

0 상기 추가 검토를 전제로하여 다수국이 예비적인 견해를 개진하였는바, 주요국입장은 아래와같음.

- 부속서 1(A) 에 대한 적용

. 23 1(B)의 적용에 대해서 특별히 이의를 제기한 국가는 없었으나 23 1(C) 는보조금협정및 반덤핑 협정에는 적용될 수 없다는 입장이 지배적이었음.

- 서비스 협정에 대한 적용

. 부정적인 입장: 서비스협정상의 관련 절차가 봉합분쟁해결 절차의 내용과 상이한 점이 많으므로 원 협상자의 취지에 따라 자동적인 적용은 곤란(태국,인도,브라질등)

. 적극적인 입장: 서비스 협정은 MTO 협정의 INTEGRAL PART 라는 점에서 다소상이한 규정이 있더라도 이는 해석 또는 수정을 통해 적용될 사항임.(미국, 카나다,EC등)

통상국   2차보   경기원   재무부   농수부   상공부   특허청

- TRIPS 협정에 대한 적용

. 부정적인 입장: 동협정에 NON-VIOLATION 절차가 없으므로 적용불가(카나다,태국,인도, 일본,브라질등)

. 적극적인 입장: MTO 협정과의 구조상 적용금지 규정이 없으므로 적용(미국,EC,뉴질랜드등)

다. 28항(실질 규정의 상충)

0 실질규정 간의 상충이 있는 경우 패널이 적용해야할 규정 및 절차에 대한 동항의 존치 필요여부에 대해

- 미국은 상충되는 실질규정은 MTO 협정발효 이전에 모두 수정해야 하며, 만일발효이후에 상충되는 규정에 대한 조화문제는 패널이나 상소기관등의 해석에 의해해결될수 있으므로 동향을 삭제하자는 입장인데 비해

- EC, 인도등은 상충규정의 존재를 대비해서 동조항이 필요하다는 입장인바, 논거는 상충규정에대한 해석은 패널이나 상소기관의 권한 사항이 아니고 DSB 권한 사항이라는 점임(EC 는 주석 M 을 원안대로 복귀시킬것을 요청)

- 동건은 당초의 주석대로 개별 협정문에 대한 검토를 완료한후 재논의키로 함.

5. 결정문안(마지막 페이지)

0 16줄 DSB 관련, 미국은 MTO 회원국과 GATT '47 회원국이 일치하지 않을 가능성이 있으므로 잠정적이나마 DSB 에게 갓트이사회의 권한을 대행케 하는 것은 문제가있음을 지적

- 일본은 상기 미국입장에 동조하면서 동 DRAFTDECISION 의 취지에 비추어 첫단둘째문장 이하를 3.10 항의 원안으로 대체하자는 일본의 제의가 있었으나 추후 재론키로함.

2. APPENDIX I 항의 특별절차에 해당하는 협정리스트에 대한 논의는 각협정 토의를 종료한후 이에 기초하여 사무국이 작성한 리스트를 중심으로 논의키로 함.

3. 4. 6주간에는 연호 MTO 설립 협정문 사무국 수정안(551) 논의에 이어 각협정문을 심의할 예정임.끝

(대사 박수길-국장)

외 무 부

종 별 :

번 호 : GVW-0769   일 시 : 92 0408 1000

수 신 : 장 관(봉기, 경기원, 재무부, 농림수산부, 상공부, 특허청)

발 신 : 주 제네바 대사

제 목 : UR/법제화 그룹 비공식 회의(MTO,1)

대: WGV-0515

1. MTO 설립협정안 제2차 수정안(TEXT 551)에 대한 논의는 MATHUR 의장의 제의로 매조항별심의 보다는 아래의 조항을 중점 논의하는 방식으로 진행키로함.- 제 2조 3항, 제 3조 2항, 제4조, 제8조, 제9조 1항2항 및 3항, 제 10조 1항 2항 4항 및 5항, 제 11조, 제12조, 제13조, 제 16조 1항 및 5항(MTO 구조에관한 제 4조는 다른 조항 논의후 심의키로함)

2. 동 수정안(TEXT 551)에 대한 4.6(월)논의에서는 각국이 종래의 입장을 고수하였는바, 요지 아래 보고함.

가. 2조 3항(ANNEX 4 협정의 지위)

0 ANNEX 협정(PTA) 이 동협정 당사국간에 MTO설립협정의 INTEGRAL PART 로서의 지위를 가지는가에 대하여 EC 및 카나다는 INTEGRAL PART라는 입장인 반면, 홍콩, 싱가폴, 일본등은 MTO 설립 협정안이 웨이버, 협정개정, 탈퇴문제등에 관해 PTA 를 각각의 협정에 따르도록 규정하고 있는점을 들어 INTEGRAL PART가 아니라는 입장임.

나. 2조 4항(ANNEX 4 협가입국 확대)

0 스웨덴이 동항의 가입 관련사항을 강화시키자는 제의를 한데 대해 EC, 카나다, 홍콩은 동조항의 의의는 단지 ANNEX 4 협정이 개방되어 있다는 점을 확인하는 것이므로 동조항을 삭제하여도 별문제가 없다는 입장임.

다. 3조 2항(향후 다자협상 추진 및 동결과 이행)

0 뉴질랜드, 미국, 일본은 협상결과 이행은 MTO체제내에서 이루어 질것이나(THE FRAME WORK)협상추진은 MTO 체제 밖에서도 추진 가능(AFORUM) 하다는 입장인 반면, 카나다, EC, 인도, 멕시코등은 협상추진, 이행 모두 MTO체제내에서 이루어져야 한다(THE) 는 입장임.

통상국   2차보   경기원   재무부   농수부   상공부   특허청

라. 제9조 1항(정책결정)

O EC 의 부표권에 관한 사항은 추후 토의키로함.

O 미국이 동항에서 MC 와 EC 의결 정족수 뿐만아니라 SC 및 기타위원회등 MTO전체 기관의 의결에 대해서도 규정하는 방향으로 동항을 수정할 것을 제의한대 대해

- 카나다, EC, 인도, 일본등 대다수국이 MC,GC 에대해서는 의결 정족수에 대한 규정이 필요하지만,SC 이하 각종 위원회등은 갓트의 관례인 CONSENSUS 가 적용되어야할 것이라며 이에 반대하여 미국의 자국제의를 철회

마. 제9조 2항(협정 해석 정족수 및 기관)

(동항은 31 PAGE EC 의 제안을 중심으로 논의함)

O SC 또는 DSB 의 권고에 기초하여 MC 또는 GC 가 해석권을 행사한다는 EC 의 제의에대해

- 인도, 스웨덴등이 동의한 반면, 카나다 및스위스는 SC 또는 DSB 의 건의가 없는경우에도 MC 또는 GC 가 독자적인 해석권을 행사할 수 있어야 한다는 입장임.

- 한편, 멕시코는 SC 및 DSB 의 건의내용과 관련, DSB 가 각협정의 실질문제에 대해서도 권고할 수 있는지 아니면 IDS 절차사항에 대해서만 건의할 수 있는지 여부를문의하면서 SC 와 DSB 의 권고영역을 구분할 필요성을 지적한데 대해, 일본은 권고주체 에 TPRB도 추가되어야 할 것이라는 의견을 제시하여 EC제안은 재논의하기로 함.

O 협정해석 채택정족수 관련, 아국, 홍콩, 미국,일본등 다수국이 콘센서스에 의한 채택입장을 표명하였으나, 상기 EC 제안의 재검토와 같은맥락에서 처리키로 함.

바. 제9조 3항(웨이버)

O EC,인도, 멕시코등은 MC 에 일원적인 웨이버 부여권을 부여하자는 입장인데 대해

- 미국, 카나다, 일본은 WAIVER 규정을 두고 있는 협정에 대해서만 MC의 웨이버부여권을 인정하자는 입장임.

(TPRIS 협정에 웨이버 규정이 없는 것은 MC의 웨이버 규정 적용을 상정한 것이라는 멕시코의 발언에 대해 미국은 TRIPS 협정에 안보를 이유로한 예외조항이 있는 점을 들어 멕시코 입장에 반대).끝

(대사 박수길-국장)

외 무 부

종 별 :

번 호 : GVW-0781　　　　　　　　　　　일　시 : 92 0409 1030

수 신 : 장 관(봉기,경기원,재무부,농수산부,상공부,특허청)

발 신 : 주 제네바 대사

제 목 : UR/법제화 그룹 비공식 회의(MTO,2)

　　대: GVW-0515

　　1. MTO 설립협정안 사무국 수정안(TEXT 551) 에 대한 4.7. 논의 요지 아래 보고함.

　　가. 제 10조 1항 및 2항(개정의결 정족수 및 효력)

　　0 아국, EC, 스웨덴, 브라질등은 협정의 단일성 유지를 위해서 제 1안(15 P, 컨센서스에 의한 수정안 채택)을 선호한 반면

　　0 미국, 카나다, 뉴질랜드, 호주등은 협정의 개정에 신축성을 부여한다는 논거로 제 2안(15 P,회원국 2/3에 의한 수정안 채택)을 선호함.

　　- 협정 개정안의 중요도(미수락국의 회원국 자격유지에 영향을 미치는)에 대한 결정에 대해서는 뉴질랜드는 회원국 2/3 에 의한 결정을, 인도는 컨선세스에 의한 결정을 선호함.

　　나. 제 10조 4항 (부속서 II 및 III 에 대한 수정)

　　0 미국은 12.20 초안으로의 복귀를 일본,뉴질랜드는 2/3 에 의한 수정을, 아국,스웨덴,홍콩, 멕시코등은 콘센서스에 의한 수정을 지지함.

　　다. 제 10조 5항(부속서 IV 협정의 추가 및 삭제)

　　0 부속서 IV 협정의 추가는 장려할 사항이 아니므로 동항은 삭제하는 것이 바람하다(인도)는 의견도 있었으나 대다수 국가가 동 조항의 필요성을 인정한바,

　　0 ANNEX 4 협정의 범위 변경에 대해 멕시코,싱가폴은 컨센서스에 의해, EC, 카나다,스웨덴, 일본등은 회원국 2/3 에 의해 결정할것을 선호함.

　　라. 제 10조 7항(제 10조의 개정 효력 발생 요건)

　　0 10조 제 1항 및 2항의 논의 결과에 따라 MFN등 MTO 기본원칙에 대한 개정시 발효는 동항의 적용(전체 회원국의 수락)대상으로할 수 있도록 하자는 제의가 있었음.

통상국　　2차보　　경기원　　재무부　　농수부　　상공부　　특허청

PAGE 1　　　　　　　　　　　　　　　　　　　　92.04.09　　23:36 DS

외신 1과 통제관

0015

마. 제 11조

O MTO 협정 발효후 경과기간 규정(14조 2항)에 비추어 첫줄 GATT 47 뒤에 ′ AS OF THE DATE OF ENTRY INTO FORCE′ 를 추가함.

O 파키스탄, 인도, 스리랑카는 수정안은 12.20 초안에 대한 실질사항의 변경이므로 이에 대한 논의는 T3 권한 밖이라는 입장인데 대해

- 미국, 카나다, 호주, 뉴질랜드등은 수정안을 지지함.

바. 제 12조 1항(가입주체)

O 관세 자치지역의 가입에 대해서는 현 GATT제도와 같이 주권국의 SPONSOR 가 필요하다는 취지를 추가하자는 파키스탄, 인도 제의에 대해 미국, EC, 카나다, 일본등이 이에 반대

사. 제 12조 2항(가입의결 정족수)

O 인도, 파키스탄, 카나다는 회원국의 과반수가 넘는 2/3 다수결에 의한 가입안을, 아국, 미국, 뉴질랜드, 홍콩은 회원국 2/3 에 의한 가입안을 지지

아. PTA 에 대한 가입절차 신설 여부

O 홍콩이 제 12조 3항을 신설하여 ′PTA 에의 가입은 해당협정에 따른다′ 는 규정을 두자는 제의에 대해 싱가폴이 동조한 반면, 호주, 스위스가 불필요하다는 입장(홍콩의 논거는 MTO 설립협정안에 PTA 에 대한 웨이버, 발효, 탈퇴에 관한 규정이 있다는 점임)

자. 제 13조 2항(GATT ′47 의 부적용 범위)

O 동 조항의 취지(MTO 협정 발효 당시의 GATT ′47 부적용 범위 확대 방지)를 보다 더 명확화 하기위한 문안 수정에 다수국이 동의(사무국은 12.20초안 2줄 ANNEX 1 은 ANNEX 1 A 의 착오임을 확인)

차. 제 13조 (부적용 통보)

O 동항 관련, 태국은 부적용 통보는 MTO 각료회의 뿐만 아니라 해당국에도 통보해야 한다는 의견을 제시

카. 제 16조 1항

O 미국은 GATT ′47 과 MTO 가 완전히 동일한 것이 아니므로 RULES 를 PROCEDURES로 수정할것을 제의한데 대해 카나다, 인도등이 동조함.

O 4줄의 투표관행에 관한 문구에 대해 미국, 일본, 인도등이 삭제할 것을 제의(동항 관련, 제 9조 1항의 EC 의 독자적인 투표권 문제가 제기되었으나, EC 의 강력한 반대로 논의가 진행되지 못하였음.)

PAGE 2

0016

한편, 동항 첫줄 및 둘째줄의 의미와, 첫째문장과 둘째문장과의 관계에 대한 의문이 제기되어(파키스탄), 이를 감안한 문안 수정필요성에 재 논의키로 함.

타. 제16조 3항(상충규정 존치여부), 제16조4항(국내법 일치)에 대해서는 각국이 합의점이 쉽게 도출되지 않는 회의 분위기를 감안, 논의를 생략하였음.

파. 첨부 A(P.31, 분쟁해결 및 봉고 절차에 관한 EC 제안)

0 동 조항의 필요성에 대해 인도가 동조한 반면, 미국, 카나다 등 상당수가 봉합분쟁 해결 절차 및 갓트 기능과 중복되는 점을 들어 불요하다는 입장임.

하. 첨부 F (유보에 대한 미국 제안)

0 동 제안이 PPA(PA)상의 조부조항의 원용을 가능케한다는 점에 대해 카나다, 일본, 멕시코, EC, 스웨던등이 강력 반대하였으며, 아국, 스위스, 홍콩등이 12.20 초안의 주석에 비추어 T3가 아닌 다른 차원에서 논의할 문제임을 지적함.

2. 회원국자격, 수락, 가입, 기탁에 관한 일본제안 C(P.31)에 대해서 논의하자는일본제의에 대해 뉴질랜드는 해당 규정에 비추어 논의 실익이 없음을 피력하였으며, 각국은 이에 대한 논의를 회피하였음. 한편, 제4조 3항 및 4항 관련 일반이사회가 필요에 따라 DSB 또는 TPRB 의자격으로 회합한다는 규정과 DSB 및 TPRB 에 각자의 의장을 둔다는 규정이 모순되지 않느냐는 아국 질문에 대해 의장은 MTO 협정상의구조(DSB 및 TPRB 의 필요성 및 이들에 대한 GC 와 동일한 지위부여)에 대한 타협안임을 설명함.

3. MATHUR 의장은 MTO 설립 협정 2차 수정안에 대한 금번 논의는 생산적이지 못하였다고 평가하였는바, 4.8 부터는 당초 일정대로 개별협정문에 대한 논의를 진행하고 그후로는 분쟁해결 절차, MTO 설립 협정안을 재논의할 전망이나 논의시기 및 방법등 구체적인 계획은 상금 미정임. 끝

(대사 박수길-국장)

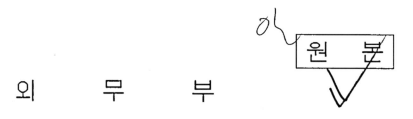

외 무 부

종 별 :

번 호 : GVW-0799

일 시 : 92 0410 1540

수 신 : 장 관(통기,경기원,재무부,상공부,특허청)

발 신 : 주 제네바 대사

제 목 : UR/법제화 그룹 비공식회의 (개별 협정문 1)

섬유협정 사무국 수정안(TEXT 611. 92.4.3)에 대한 4.8 표제회의에서 제기된 쟁점별 논의 요지를 아래 보고함.(강상무관, 신서 기관, 김상무관보 참석)1. 제 1조 6항(타협정과의 관계)

O 섬유 협정이 영향을 미칠수 있는 타협정의 범위와 관련, 논의가 있었는바,

O 동항 'GATT 1993' 이하를 'OTHER MTA AGREEMENTS INANNEX 1A TO MTO AGREEMENT'로 수정하자는 제의(인도)에 대해 TRIP 협정과의 관계 고려, GATT 1993 의 개념을 명확히 한후 다시 논의키로 함.

2. 제 2조 1항(협정 적용 대상국)

O 93.1.1 현재 GATT '47 회원국간의 규제에 동협정이 적용된다는 동항 마지막 문장에 대해 중국이 푼타 선언이후 UR 협상, 특히섬유협상에 적극 참여해 왔으며, 또한중국이 MFA 회원국임에 비추어 중국이 섬유협정에 가입할수 있도록 동 조항을 개정하여야 한다고 요청함.

O 에집트, 브라질, 코스타리카, 파키스탄, 인도등이 중국에 동조한 반면, 미국,카나다, EC 등은 협정 적용문제는 SINGLE-UNDERTAKING 원칙에 따라야 할것이라며 동문제 는 MTO 가입문제이므로 T3 에서 논의할 사항이 아니라는 입장을 개진함.

O 아국은 중국에 대한 동협정 적용방안은 적절히 강구되어야 할 사항이지만 T3 의 임무에 비추어 다른 차원에서 논의될 수 있을 것임을 지적함.

O 한편, 태국은 갓트 체약국중 MTO 협정 발효이후에 MTO 협정을 수락하는 국가에대한 섬유협정 적용 여부문제를 제기함.

3. 제 2조 4항(FORUM SHOPPING 관련)

O 갓트로 통합되지 않은 품목에 대해서는 갓트19조(일반 SG)에 의한 규제는 허용되지 않으며,동 협정 제 6조(잠정 SG)에 의한 규제만 가능하다는데 대해서는

통상국   2차보   경기원   재무부   상공부   특허청

92.04.11   04:09 FN

외신 1과 통제관

0018

아국을 비롯 거의 모든수입국, 수출국이 견해를 갑이하고, 이를 위해 제4항 두번째 문장을 수정하는 방법이 토의됨.

  0 그러나 멕시코가 비통합 품목에 대해 갓트 19조와 동협정 제 6조의 선택적 사용을 허용하자는 주장을 하여 최종결론은 유보함.

  0 미국은 비통합품목에 대해 갓트 19조를 적용하지 않는다는 전제하에 섬유협정 ANNEX 의 NOTE에 언급된 품목(비갓트 통합품목이나 잠정 SG가 적용될수 없는 품목)에 대해서는 갓트19조를 적용할수 있는 규정을 두어야 한다고 함.

  4. 제 2조 6항(섬유제품의 갓트 통합)

  0 통합의 의미와 관련 'INTEGRATION INTO GATT'93'이 적절한 표현이 아니라는 인식하에 'GATT '93 '을 수정하는 방안과 관련,

  - 홍콩, 인도는 'ANNEX 1A 상의 협정'으로,카나다는 'GATT '93의 세이프가드 협정'으로(보조금.반덤핑 협정등 제외) 수정할 것을 제의함.

  - 미국은 GATT '93 의 개념이 분명하지 않는데서 상기와 갑은 혼란이 왔음을 지적하고, 사무국이 GATT '93 에 대한 개념을 정리할 필요성을 제기함.

  5. 제 2조 14항 및 8조 12항(쿼타 수준의 조정기관)

  0 쿼타 수준을 조정하는 기관으로 미국, EC,카나다등 수입국은 CTG 를, 아국, 파키스탄,인도등 ITCB 국은 DSB 를 주장함.

  - 수입국은 8조 12항의 쿼타조정은 REVIEW 기능의 일환이므로 CTG 가 이를 관장하여야 한다는 주장

  - ITCB 국은 8조 12항의 쿼타 조정은 분쟁해결의 일환이므로 동 절차는 MTO 구조상 DSB 관할사항임을 주장.

  6. 제 2조 19항 및 20항(일반 세이프가드 조치)

  0 카나다는 동항의 용어를 세이프가드 협정상의 용어와 일치시키기 위한 문안 수정을 제의했는바, 이에 대해 가급적이면 당초 협상의도를 존중해서 문안수정을 자제하자는 다수국 의견이 개진되었는바,

  - 19항 두째줄 및 20항 6줄의 INITIATE 를 APPLY로 바꾸자는 카나다의 제의에 대해 이는 당초 협상결과를 변화시키는 실질내용의 변경이라는 아국, 홍콩등의 반대로카나다는 'SAFEGUARD MEASURE'를 'SAFEGUARD INVESTIGATION'으로 수정할 것을 다시제의함.

  - 20항 마지막 문장 관련, 카나다가 수출국이 양허나 다른 의무의 정지를

자제한다는 현 의장안 내용을 갓트 19조 3항(A) 및 세이프가드 협정 SECTION 3 상의 권리를 자제한다는 것으로 수정제의한데 대해 EC, 홍콩, 뉴질랜드등 다수국이 갓트 19조 3항(A) 는 보복조치의 자제만을 규정하고 있으나 세이프가드 협정 SECTION 3 에서는보상 및 보복의 자제를 규정하고 있어 카나다 수정안은 실질문제 변경이라는 점을지적함.(카나다 수정 제안 별첨)

7. PRODUCT COVERAGE 와 관련 520300(COTTON, CASDEDOR COMBED)는 농산물 COVERAGE 와 중복됨으로 이를 삭제하는데 잠정 합의함.(EC 는 농산물협상에 대한 기술적 검토후 최종 결정하겠다는 입장)

첨부: 1. 섬유협정문 수정안(관련 부분)

2. 카나다 수정안. 끝

(GVW(F)-252)

(대사 박수길-국장)

#2

8.4.92   28

Agreement on Textiles and Clothing

Proposal by (Canada)

2:19.   In any case, during the period of validity of this Agreement, in
        which a safeguard investigation is initiated by a party Member
        under Article XIX of the GATT 1993 in respect of a particular
        product within one year immediately following the integration of
        that product into GATT 1993 in accordance with the provisions of
        this Article, the provisions of Article XIX, as interpreted by
        the Agreement on Safeguards, shall apply, except as specifically
        provided in paragraph 20, below.

2:20.   Where a measure under paragraph 19 above is applied in the form
        of a non-tariff measure, the importing party Member concerned
        shall apply the measure in a manner as set forth in
        Article XIII 2(d) paragraph 2(d) of Article XIII of the GATT 1993
        at the request of any exporting party Member whose exports of
        such products were subject to restrictions under this Agreement
        at any time in the one-year period immediately prior to the
        initiation of the safeguard investigation. The concerned
        exporting party Member shall administer any such measure. The
        non-tariff measure shall not reduce the level of relevant exports
        below the level of a recent representative period, which shall
        normally be the average of exports from the concerned party
        Member in the last three representative years for which
        statistics are available. If the duration of such a measure is
        more than one year, it shall be progressively liberalised at
        regular intervals during the period of application. In such
        cases, paragraph 3(a) of Article XIX of the GATT 1993,
        interpreted by Section III of the Agreement on Safeguards, shall
        not apply.

0021

A:LDG92-37

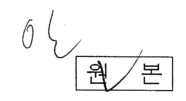

외 무 부

종 별 :

번 호 : GVW-0807　　　　　　　　　　일 시 : 92 0410 1800

수 신 : 장관(봉기, 경기원, 재무부, 상공부, 특허청)

발 신 : 주제네바대사

제 목 : UR/법제화 그룹, 비공식회의(개별협정문, 2)

　　4.9 개최된 개별협정문에 대한 표제회의 요지를 아래 보고함.(강상무관, 김재무관보, 신서기관, 김상무관보 참석)

　　1. 원산지 증명

　　가. 제 2조(행정 조치의 제한)

　　0 통합 원산지 규정이 마련되기까지 원산지 규정에 관련된 사항에 대해서는 일정행위가 요구되는 범위와 관련, 협정안의 행정결정에 법률과 규칙(REGULATION)을 추가하자는 일본의 재의에대해 동 제의가 본협정에서 합의된 내용을 수정하는 것이라는 EC 의 반대가 있었음.

　　나. 제 8조(분쟁해결 절차)

　　0 HS 제도가 마련된 이후 발생하는 동제도 해석에 대한 분쟁은 갓트 23조 절차에 앞서 CCC의 HS 위원회에 회부한다는 내용을 동조 제2항으로 신설하자는 EC의 제의에 대해

　　- 미국이 이에 동조한 반면, 카나다, 일본은 동 협정분쟁해결도 통합분쟁해결 절차의 차원에서 다루어질 사항이라는 점을 들어 반대하여

　　- 사무국에서 제 9조 4항에 조화제도에 관한 분쟁해결 절차에 관한 사항도 각료이사회(MC)에서 결정한다는 문안을 추가하자는 제의가 있었음.

　　2. 선적전 검사

　　가. 제2조 20항(가격증명)

　　0 동항의 수출국, 수입국 표현과 관련 COUNTRY의 용어를 MEMBER 로 바꾸자는 홍콩제의에 대해 사무국이 COUNTRY 의 개념에는 NON-MEMBER도 포함됨을 지적함.

　　3. 관세평가 협정문

　　가. 제 19조(협의)

통상국　　2차보　　경기원　　재무부　　상공부　　특허청

0 동 조항의 합의절차를 가능한 통합분쟁 해결절차와 일치시키기 위해 소규모 비공식규모를 통해 동조항 문안 작업을 다시 하기로 함.

나. 제 21조(개도국 우대)

0 개도국의 구체적인 범위에 대한 의문이 제기되었는바, 미국이 'NOT PARTY TO 1979 AGREEMENT ONARTICLE VII' 을 DEVELOPING MEMBER 뒤에 추가하자는 제의에 대해 사무국은 동취지를 주석으로 옮기자는 의견을 제시하였으나, 주석은 법적성격상 한시적일 수도 있으므로 동문구를 본문에 포함시킬 것을 미국, 카나다가 주장

4. TRIMS가. 제 4조(개도국 조항)

0 개도국이 TRIMS 규정을 이탈할수 있는 근거규정과 관련, 3줄 'RELATED PROVISION IN' 을 ITSASSOCIATED LEGAL INSTRUMENTS IN ANNEX 1A' 로 수정할것을 제의하면서동문구는 BOP 에 관한1979년 양해와 UR 양해를 의미한다고 언급한데 대해 미국, EC,카나다등이 문안을 구체화 시킬 필요성을 지적함.

나. 제 9조(검토)

0 MTO 발효후 5년이내 실시하는 검토와 필요한경우 협정문을 수정하는 권한과 관련, 검토권및 수정권한 모두 각료회의(MC)에 속한다는 카나다, 미국등의 입장과 수정권은 MC 권한이나 검토권은 상품협정 이사회(CTG) 권한이라는 개도국 및 EC 의 입장이 대립함.

5. 기타 공동사항

0 미국은 4.9 개별 협정문 논의시 사무국이 SINGLE-UNDERTAKING 원칙에 입각하여'동협정발효' 를 'MTO 발효'로 수정한 문구가 발견될때마다 원안대로 '동협정 발효'로 복귀할 것을 제의하였는바, 이에 대해 의장 및 대다수국이 무슨 의미가 있느냐는질문을 제기함.

- 동 제의는 협정해석의 오해를 없애기 위한것이라고 미국이 자국입장을 천명하고 있으나,SINGLE-UNDERTAKING 원칙에 비추어 볼때 저의가 분명치 않음(가능한 해석은첫째는 MTO 가발효안될 경우에 대비하여 개별협정의 독자적인 발효가능성을 확보하기 위한 것으로 볼수 있으며,둘째는 MTO 발효의 필요성 내지 실제 여부에 의문점을 시사함 으로써 동 협상그룹(T3) 및향후 협상에서 타국의 협조적인 자세를 유도하는 전략으로 볼수 있음.)끝

(대사 박수길-국장)

PAGE 2

0023

외 무 부

종 별 :

번 호 : GVW-0822   일 시 : 92 0413 1900

수 신 : 장관(통기,경기원,재무부,농림수산부,상공부,특허청)

발 신 : 주 제네바 대사

제 목 : UR/법제화그룹 비공식회의(개별협정문, 3)

1. 반덤핑 협정문 및 보조금.상계관세 협정문 사무국 수정안(TEXT 625)에 대한 4.10표제회의 내용 아래 보고함.

(강상무관, 김재무관보, 신서기관, 김상무관보 참석)

가. 공통사항

0 분쟁해결

- 양협정문의 분쟁해결 절차는 통합분쟁 해결절차(IDS) 를 상정하기 전에 협의된사항임에 비추어 당초 협상의도를 이탈하지않는 범위에서 관련조항 문안을 IDS 에일치하도록 다시 작성하여 논의키로 함.

0 최종조항(유보, 경과조치, 가입, 발효등)

- 양협정문 모두 협상그룹에서 최종조항을 논의하지 않았는바, 관련 규정은 MTO설립협정문이 확정된후 심의키로 함.

0 양협정문의 용어 일치

- 미국은 반덤핑 규정과 상계관세 규정간에는 용어가 통일되는 것이 바람직하다고 지적한뒤 사무국 수정안에 자국의 용어통일 제안을 첨가한 문서 사본을 각국에 회람한 바, 동제안은 4.22.주간에 심의키로 함.

나. 반덤핑 협정문

0 제 2조 4항 2(덤핑 마진 판정)

- 2.4.2 전단의 'NORMALLY' 의 표현과 관련 인도는 동표현으로 인해서 마지막문장에서 상정하고 있는 경우외에도 원칙(평균상정가격대 평균수출가격, 개별거래가격 비교) 적용을 하지 않는 예외가 있을수 있는지가 불분명함을 지적한바, EC 는'NORMALLY' 의 삭제는 실질내용의 변경이므로 T3 의 권한밖이라고함.

0 기타

통상국	2차보	경기원	재무부	농수부	상공부	특허청

- 조문에 대한 용어 및 표현의 수정이 수입국측 혹은 수출국측에서 제외되었으나,양측은 상대방측의 제안을 초안상의 뜻과는 다른의미가 있는 것으로 해석함으로써,대부분 거절함.(협상 참가국들은 가능한 T3 에서는 현협정문안에 어떠한 변경도 원치않고 있는것으로 보임)

다. 보조금.상계관세 협정문

0 제 5조(무역효과) 및 제 13조(금지)

- 미국은 보조금의 무역효과 한계를 규정한 제5조가 보조금 금지의 범위를 규정한제 3조의 취지에 위배되는 점이 있음을 지적하였으나 T3 권한밖임을 언급하여 토의가이루어지지 않았음.

0 제 7조 5항(위원회의 분쟁심의)

- 보조금 분쟁에 대해 보조금 상계관세위원회가 120일 이내로 심의를 마쳐야 한다는 동규정이 MTO 의 IDS 규정과 상치되는 것으로 확인되어 동조항의 IDS 에 대한특별 절차여부 문제가 제기됨.

0 제11조 7항(피해 조사 중단)

- 보조금이 DE MINIMIS 인 경우에는 즉각 피해조사가 중단되어야 한다는 규정과관련, 동보조금은 총체적으로 지급된 보조금에 해당하므로 동항 5,7,8째줄의 SUBSIDY를 SUBSIDIZATION 으로 수정해야한다는 미국의 제의에 대해 싱가폴이 동규정의 당초의도는 지급된 보조금을 각각 별개의 단위로 계산할 것을 상정한 것이므로 미국의수정안은 당초 협상의도를 변화시키는 제안이므로 받아들일수 없는 입장임을 피력

0 제 13조 2항(협의) 주석 2

- 동조항의 협의는 보상(4조 및 7조) 또는 분쟁해결(30조)의 기초가 되므로 주석2의 마지막줄은 PROVISIONS OF PARTS II AND III OR X OF THISAGREEMENT 로 수정키로함.

0 부속서 7(개도국 및 최빈개도국 정의)

- 협정문 12.20 초안의 부석서 7(A) 상의 최빈개도국 범위가 UN 총회에서 결정되는 최빈개도국의 범위와 상충될 가능성이 있음을 감안, 사무국이 동협정상의 최빈개도국의 범위는 UN 에서 최빈개도국으로 결정된 MTO회원국으로 한다고 수정한바, 동부속서 는 DEVELOPING MEMBER 개념에 대한 전반적인 검토후 재논의키로 함.

(동 문안 재논의 계획에 대해 일부 개도국이 동부속서는 타협의 산물이므로

PAGE 2

0025

수정대상이 아니라는 입장을 피력함)

   2. 다음회의는 별첨 일정에 따라 4.21. 주간에 개별협정문을 논의할 예정임.

   첨부: 미국제안 1부

   차기회의일정 1부

   (GVW(F)-257).끝

   (대사 박수길-국장)

주 제 네 바 대 표 부

번 호 : GVW(F) - 0257   년월일 : 2-04.13   시간 : 1500

수 신 : 장   관 (동기,경기원,재무부,농림수산부,상공부,특허청)

발 신 : 주 제네바대사

제 목 :

　　　　GVW-822 회복

총   매(표지포함)

┌─────┬─────────┐
│ 외신관 │   │
│ 통 제 │   │
└─────┴─────────┘

0027

Draft
10.4.92

<u>Tentative Timetable for Review of Texts
in the Legal Drafting Group</u>

22 April (p.m.)   G. Technical Barriers to Trade (Document 611)
- 24 April   L. Sanitary and Phytosanitary Measures
                       L. Agriculture
                       Y. FOGS, including TPRM (Annex 3 to MTO) (Document 627)
                       K. Government Procurement (text on Article IX:1(b))
                          (Document 626)

4 May - 8 May   Annex II (Services)
                       Annex III (TRIPs)
                       H. Import Licensing (Document 611)
                       V. Article XXV (Document 537)
                       X. Article XXXV (Document 537)
                       GATT 1993

11 May - 15 May   Other individual texts left outstanding and,
                       if time available, MTO Agreement and Dispute
                       Settlement Understanding

     The above meetings of the Group would be informal. A formal meeting
may be held some time over the period.

     No meetings of the Group are currently planned for the second half of
May.

     The document references in parenthesis are to draft rectified texts
already circulated by the Secretariat.

LDG92-40   0028

(31) #2

HARMONIZING CHANGES

10
—6 April 1992

Review of the Individual Texts
(Agreement on Implementation of Article VI of the
General Agreement on Tariffs and Trade
and Agreement on Subsidies and Countervailing Measures)

Informal Note by the Secretariat

INTRODUCTION

1. The present working paper has been prepared to assist the Group in its consideration of the following texts in the Draft Final Act (MTN.TNC/W/FA):-

   F. Agreement on Implementation of Article VI of the GATT;
   I. Agreement on Subsidies and Countervailing Measures.

2. Rectifications of a general nature have been made in accordance with the principles set out in paragraphs 1-5 of the secretariat note on the review of a previous set of texts (document 611).

3. The provisions in individual texts on dispute settlement will need to be examined in relation to those in the draft text of the Understanding on Rules and Procedures Governing the Settlement of Disputes in order that, inter alia, references in the Understanding to special or additional rules or procedures contained in the covered agreements can be finalized.

INDIVIDUAL TEXTS

4. The Agreement on Implementation of Article VI of the General Agreement on Tariffs and Trade

- Given that the Agreement on Implementation of Article VI of the GATT will be part of Annex 1A of the MTO, would the references to "Code" in the text be more appropriately replaced by the term "Agreement"?

- In the absence of a decision regarding the choice of MTO bodies which will undertake the function of "CONTRACTING PARTIES", it has been assumed that the term "Council for Trade in Goods" replaces "CONTRACTING PARTIES" in 4 of Article 15.

- With respect to final provisions, Article 19 (page 30) indicates that these provisions remain to be drafted. In considering the contents of such provisions, account will have to be taken of the fact that a number of issues dealt with in Article 16 of the existing Anti-Dumping Code, including acceptance and accession, entry into force, amendments, withdrawal, non-application, secretariat, deposit and registration, will be dealt with in the provisions of the Agreement establishing the MTO. It may, however, be appropriate to consider the inclusion in the anti-dumping text of the provisions appearing in Articles 16:1, 16:3, 16:6 and 16:7 of the existing Anti-Dumping Code. In addition, as suggested in the Draft Final Act (Page F.28 of document MTN.TNC/W/FA), at some stage consideration will have to be given to the possible inclusion of transition rules.

257-44-3

0029

- 2 -

5. The Agreement on Subsidies and Countervailing Measures

- Some final provisions remain to be drafted in Article 31. In considering the contents of such provisions, account will have to be taken of the fact that a number of issues dealt with in Article 19 of the existing Subsidies Code, including acceptance and accession, entry into force, amendments, withdrawal, non-application, secretariat, deposit and registration, will be dealt with in the provisions of the Agreement establishing the MTO. It may, however, be appropriate to consider the inclusion in this text of the provisions appearing in Articles 19:1, 19:3, 19:5, 19:6 and 19:10 of the existing Agreement. In addition, at some stage consideration may have to be given to the possible inclusion of transition rules for countervailing measures.

[NEXT PAGE IS 7]

0030

- 7 -

products are merely trans-shipped through the country of export, or such products are not produced in the country of export, or there is no comparable price for them in the country of export.

2.6 Throughout this Code Agreement the term "like product" ("produit similaire") shall be interpreted to mean a product which is identical, i.e., alike in all respects to the product under consideration, or in the absence of such a product, another product which although not alike in all respects, has characteristics closely resembling those of the product under consideration.

2.7 This Article is without prejudice to the second Supplementary Provision to paragraph 1 of Article VI in Annex I to the General-Agreement GATT 1993.

Article 3

Determination of Injury[1]

3.1 A determination of injury for purposes of Article VI of the General Agreement GATT 1993 shall be based on positive evidence and involve an objective examination of both (a) the volume of the dumped imports and the effect of the dumped imports on prices in the domestic market for like products, and (b) the consequent impact of these imports on domestic producers of such products.

3.2 With regard to the volume of the dumped imports the investigating authorities shall consider whether there has been a significant increase in dumped imports, either in absolute terms or relative to production or consumption in the importing country. With regard to the effect of the dumped imports on prices, the investigating authorities shall consider whether there has been a significant price undercutting by the dumped imports as compared with the price of a like product of the importing country, or whether the effect of such imports is otherwise to depress prices to a significant degree or prevent price increases, which otherwise would have occurred, to a significant degree. No one or several of these factors can necessarily give decisive guidance.

3.3 The examination of the impact of the dumped imports on the industry concerned shall include an evaluation of all relevant economic factors and indices having a bearing on the state of the industry, including actual and potential decline in sales, profits, output, market share, productivity, return on investments, utilization of capacity; factors affecting domestic prices; the magnitude of the margin of dumping; actual and potential

---

[1]Under this Code Agreement the term "injury" shall, unless otherwise specified, be taken to mean material injury to a domestic industry, threat of material injury to a domestic industry or material retardation of the establishment of such an industry and shall be interpreted in accordance with the provisions of this Article.

0031

- 8 -

negative effects on cash flow, inventories, employment, wages, growth, ability to raise capital or investments. This list is not exhaustive, nor can one or several of these factors necessarily give decisive guidance.

3.4 It must be demonstrated that the dumped imports are, through the effects of dumping, as set forth in paragraphs 2 and 3 of this Article, causing injury within the meaning of this Code Agreement. The demonstration of a causal relationship between the dumped imports and the injury to the domestic industry shall be based on an examination of all relevant evidence before the authorities. The authorities shall also examine any known factors other than the dumped imports which at the same time are injuring the industry, and the injuries caused by these other factors must not be attributed to the dumped imports. Factors which may be relevant in this respect include, inter alia, the volume and prices of imports not sold at dumping prices, contraction in demand or changes in the patterns of consumption, trade restrictive practices of and competition between the foreign and domestic producers, developments in technology and the export performance and productivity of the domestic industry.

3.5 The effect of the dumped imports shall be assessed in relation to the domestic production of the like product when available data permit the separate identification of that production on the basis of such criteria as the production process, producers' sales and profits. If such separate identification of that production is not possible, the effects of the dumped imports shall be assessed by the examination of the production of the narrowest group or range of products, which includes the like product, for which the necessary information can be provided.

3.6 A determination of a threat of material injury shall be based on facts and not merely on allegation, conjecture or remote possibility. The change in circumstances which would create a situation in which the dumping would cause injury must be clearly foreseen and imminent.[1] In making a determination regarding the existence of a threat of material injury, the authorities should consider, inter alia, such factors as:

    (i)   a significant rate of increase of dumped imports into the domestic market indicating the likelihood of substantially increased importations;

    (ii) sufficient freely disposable or an imminent, substantial increase in capacity of the exporter indicating the likelihood of substantially increased dumped exports to the importing country's market, taking into account the availability of other export markets to absorb any additional exports;

---

[1] One example, though not an exclusive one, is that there is convincing reason to believe that there will be, in the immediate future, substantially increased importations of the product at dumped prices.

0032

- 9 -

      (iii) whether imports are entering at prices that will have a
            significant depressing or suppressing effect on domestic prices,
            and would likely increase demand for further imports; and

      (iv) inventories of the product being investigated.

IMPORTS

No one of these factors by itself can necessarily give decisive guidance
but the totality of the factors considered must lead to the conclusion that
further dumped ~~imports~~ are imminent and that, unless protective action is
taken, material injury would occur.

(C-15.6)

3.7 With respect to cases where injury is threatened by dumped imports,
the application of anti-dumping measures shall be considered and decided
with special care.

(C-16.1)   *) EXCEPT AS*
                         PROVIDED IN
Article 4   *PARAGRAPH 2*
                         BELOW)
Definition of Industry

4.1 In determining injury the term 'domestic industry' shall be
interpreted as referring to the domestic producers as a whole of the like
products or to those of them whose collective output of the products
constitutes a major proportion of the total domestic production of those
products, except that

(C-16.1) *DOMESTIC*

      (i)   when producers are related[1] to the exporters or importers or are
            themselves importers of the allegedly dumped product, ~~the~~
            industry may be interpreted as referring to the rest of the
            producers;

      (ii) in exceptional circumstances the territory of a ~~Party~~ Member
            may, for the production in question, be divided into two or more
            competitive markets and the producers within each market may be
            regarded as a separate industry if (a) the producers within such
            market sell all or almost all of their production of the product
            in question in that market, and (b) the demand in that market is
            not to any substantial degree supplied by producers of the
            product in question located elsewhere in the territory.   In
            such circumstances, injury may be found to exist even where a

---

[1]For the purpose of this paragraph, producers shall be deemed to be
related to exporters or importers only if (a) one of them directly or
indirectly controls the other; or (b) both of them are directly or
indirectly controlled by a third person; or (c) together they directly or
indirectly control a third person, provided that there are grounds for
believing or suspecting that the effect of the relationship is such as to
cause the producer concerned to behave differently from non-related
producers. For the purpose of this paragraph, one shall be deemed to
control another when the former is legally or operationally in a position
to exercise restraint or direction over the latter.

0033

- 10 -

(C-16.2)

major portion of the total domestic industry is not injured, provided there is a concentration of dumped imports into such an isolated market and provided further that the dumped imports are causing injury to the producers of all or almost all of the production within such market.

4.2 When the industry has been interpreted as referring to the producers in a certain area, i.e., a market as defined in paragraph 1(ii), anti-dumping duties shall be levied* only on the products in question consigned for final consumption to that area. When the constitutional law of the importing country does not permit the levying of anti-dumping duties on such a basis, the importing ~~Party~~ Member may levy the anti-dumping duties without limitation only if (1) the exporters shall have been given an opportunity to cease exporting at dumped prices to the area concerned or otherwise give assurances pursuant to Article ~~7~~ 8 of this ~~Code~~ Agreement, and adequate assurances in this regard have not been promptly given, and (2) such duties cannot ~~be levied~~ ~~on~~ specific producers which supply the area in question.

(C-16.3) *ONLY ON PRODUCTS OF*

4.3 Where two or more countries have reached under the provisions of Article XXIV:8(a) of the ~~General Agreement~~ GATT 1993 such a level of integration that they have the characteristics of a single, unified market, the industry in the entire area of integration shall be taken to be the industry referred to in paragraph 1 above.

4.4 The provisions of paragraph 5 of Article 3 shall be applicable to this Article.

Article 5

Initiation and Subsequent Investigation

5.1 An investigation to determine the existence, degree and effect of any alleged dumping shall normally be initiated upon a written application by or on behalf of the domestic industry, as defined in Article 4:1.

5.2 An application under paragraph 1 shall include evidence of (a) dumping, (b) injury within the meaning of Article VI of the ~~General Agreement~~ GATT 1993 as interpreted by this ~~Code~~ Agreement and (c) a causal link between the ~~dumped imports~~ and the alleged injury. Simple assertion, unsubstantiated by relevant evidence, cannot be considered sufficient to meet the requirements of this paragraph. The application shall contain such information as is reasonably available to the applicant on the following:

  (i) identity of the applicant and a description of the volume and value of the domestic production of the like product by the applicant. Where a written application is made on behalf of the domestic industry, the application shall identify the

---

*As used in this ~~Code~~ Agreement 'levy' shall mean the definitive or final legal assessment or collection of a duty or tax.

0034

- 11 -

industry on behalf of which the application is made by a list of all known domestic producers of the like product (or associations of domestic producers of the like product) and, to the extent possible, a description of the volume and value of domestic production of the like product accounted for by such producers;

(ii) a complete description of the allegedly dumped product, the names of the country or countries of export or origin in question, the identity of each known exporter or foreign producer and a list of known persons importing the product in question;

(iii) information on prices at which the product in question is sold when destined for consumption in the domestic markets of the country or countries of origin or export (or, where appropriate, information on the prices at which the product is sold from the country or countries of origin or export to a third country or countries or on the constructed value of the product) and information on export prices or, where appropriate, on the prices at which the product is first resold to an independent buyer in the importing country;

(iv) information on the evolution of the volume of the allegedly dumped imports, the effect of these imports on prices of the like product in the domestic market and the consequent impact of the imports on the domestic industry concerned, as demonstrated by relevant factors and indices having a bearing on the state of the domestic industry, such as those listed in Article 3.2 and 3.3.

5.3 The authorities shall examine the accuracy and adequacy of the evidence provided in the application to determine whether there is sufficient evidence to justify the initiation of an investigation.

5.4 An investigation shall not be initiated pursuant to paragraph 1 unless the authorities have determined, on the basis of an examination of the degree of support for, or opposition to, the application expressed[1] by domestic producers of the like product, that the application has been made by or on behalf of the domestic industry, as defined in Article 4:1.

5.5 The authorities shall avoid, unless a decision has been made to initiate an investigation, any publicizing of the application for the initiation of an investigation. However, after receipt of a properly

---

[1]In the case of fragmented industries involving an exceptionally large number of producers, authorities may determine support and opposition by using statistically valid sampling techniques.

- 12 -

documented application and before proceeding to initiate an investigation, the authorities shall notify the government of the exporting country concerned.

5.6 Notwithstanding paragraph 1, if in special circumstances, the authorities concerned decide to initiate an investigation without having received a written application by or on behalf of a domestic industry for the initiation of such investigation, they shall proceed only if they have sufficient evidence of dumping, injury and a causal link, as described in paragraph 2, to justify the initiation of an investigation.

5.7 The evidence of both dumping and injury shall be considered simultaneously (a) in the decision whether or not to initiate an investigation, and (b) thereafter, during the course of the investigation, starting on a date not later than the earliest date on which in accordance with the provisions of this ~~Code~~ Agreement provisional measures may be applied.

5.8 An application under paragraph 1 shall be rejected and an investigation shall be terminated promptly as soon as the authorities concerned are satisfied that there is not sufficient evidence of either dumping or of injury to justify proceeding with the case. There shall be immediate termination in cases where the authorities determine that the margin of dumping is de minimis or that the volume of dumped imports, actual or potential, or the injury is negligible. The margin of dumping shall be considered to be de minimis if this margin is less than 2 per cent, expressed as a percentage of the normal value. The volume of dumped imports shall normally be regarded as negligible if the volume of dumped imports from a particular country is found to account for less than 1 per cent of the domestic market for the like product in the importing country unless countries which individually account for less than 1 per cent of the domestic market for the like product in the importing country collectively account for more than 2.5 per cent of that market.

5.9 An anti-dumping proceeding shall not hinder the procedures of customs clearance.

5.10 Investigations shall, except in special circumstances, be concluded within one year after their initiation, and in no case more than 18 months.

Article 6

Evidence

6.1 All interested parties in an anti-dumping investigation shall be given notice of the information which the authorities require and ample opportunity to present in writing all evidence which they consider relevant in respect of the investigation in question.

6.1.1 Exporters or foreign producers receiving questionnaires used in an anti-dumping investigation shall be given at least thirty days for

0036

- 13 -

reply.[1] Due consideration should be given to any request for an extension of the thirty day period and, upon cause shown, such an extension should be granted whenever practicable.

6.1.2 Subject to the requirement to protect confidential information, evidence presented in writing by one interested party shall be made available promptly to other interested parties participating in the investigation.

6.1.3 As soon as an investigation has been initiated, the authorities shall provide the full text of the written application received under Article 5:1 to the known exporters[2] and to the authorities of the exporting country and make it available, upon request, to other interested parties involved. Due regard shall be paid to the requirement for the protection of confidential information as provided for in paragraph 5.

6.2 Throughout the anti-dumping investigation all interested parties shall have a full opportunity for the defence of their interests. To this end, the authorities shall, on request, provide opportunities for all interested parties to meet those parties with adverse interests, so that opposing views may be presented and rebuttal arguments offered. Provision of such opportunities must take account of the need to preserve confidentiality and of the convenience to the parties. There shall be no obligation on any party to attend a meeting, and failure to do so shall not be prejudicial to that party's case. Interested parties shall also have the right, upon justification, to present other information orally.

6.3 Oral information provided under paragraph 2 shall be taken into account by the authorities only insofar as it is subsequently reproduced in writing and made available to other interested parties, as provided for in sub-paragraph 1.2.

6.4 The authorities shall whenever practicable provide timely opportunities for all interested parties to see all information that is relevant to the presentation of their cases, that is not confidential as defined in paragraph 5 and that is used by the authorities in an anti-dumping investigation, and to prepare presentations on the basis of this information.

---

[1] As a general rule, the time-limit for exporters shall be counted from the date of the receipt of the questionnaire, which for this purpose shall be deemed to have been received one week from the day on which it was sent to the respondent or transmitted to the appropriate diplomatic representative of the exporting country.

[2] It being understood that, where the number of exporters involved is particularly high, the full text of the request should instead be provided only to the authorities of the exporting country or to the relevant trade association.

0037

6.5 Any information which is by nature confidential, (for example, because its disclosure would be of significant competitive advantage to a competitor or because its disclosure would have a significantly adverse effect upon a person supplying the information or upon a person from whom he acquired the information) or which is provided on a confidential basis by parties to an investigation shall, upon good cause shown, be treated as such by the authorities. Such information shall not be disclosed without specific permission of the party submitting it.[1]

6.5.1 The authorities shall require interested parties providing confidential information to furnish non-confidential summaries thereof. These summaries shall be in sufficient detail to permit a reasonable understanding of the substance of the information submitted in confidence. In exceptional circumstances, such parties may indicate that such information is not susceptible of summary. In such exceptional circumstances, a statement of the reasons why summarization is not possible must be provided.

6.5.2 If the authorities find that a request for confidentiality is not warranted and if the supplier is either unwilling to make the information public or to authorize its disclosure in generalized or summary form, the authorities may ~~be free to~~ disregard such information unless it can be demonstrated to their satisfaction from appropriate sources that the information is correct.[2]

6.6 Except in circumstances provided for in paragraph 8, the authorities shall during the course of an investigation satisfy themselves as to the accuracy of the information supplied by interested parties upon which their findings are based.

6.7 In order to verify information provided or to obtain further details, the authorities may carry out investigations in other countries as required, provided they obtain the agreement of the firms concerned and provided they notify the representatives of the government of the country in question and unless the latter object to the investigation. The procedures described in Annex I shall apply to verifications carried out in exporting countries. The authorities shall, subject to the requirement to protect confidential information, make the results of any verifications available or provide disclosure thereof pursuant to paragraph 9, to the firms to which they pertain and may make such results available to the applicants.

6.8 In cases in which any interested party refuses access to, or otherwise does not provide, necessary information within a reasonable period or significantly impedes the investigation, preliminary and final

---

[1] ~~Parties~~ Members are aware that in the territory of certain ~~Parties~~ Members disclosure pursuant to a narrowly-drawn protective order may be required.

[2] ~~Parties~~ Members agree that requests for confidentiality should not be arbitrarily rejected.

[ADD FN
  IDENTICAL
   TO SCH FN 1; SEE PAGE 50]

- 15 -

determination, affirmative or negative, may be made on the basis of the facts available. The provisions of Annex II shall be observed in the application of this paragraph.

6.9 The authorities shall, before a final determination is made, inform all interested parties of the essential facts under consideration which form the basis for the decision whether to apply definitive measures. Such disclosure should take place in sufficient time for the parties to defend their interests.

6.10 The authorities shall, as a rule, determine an individual margin of dumping for each known exporter or producer concerned of the product under investigation. In cases where the number of exporters, producers, importers or types of products involved is so large as to make such a determination impracticable, the authorities may limit their examination either to a reasonable number of interested parties or products by using samples which are statistically valid on the basis of information available to the authorities at the time of the selection, or to the largest percentage of the volume of the exports from the country in question which can reasonably be investigated.

> 6.10.1 Any selection of exporters, producers, importers or types of products made under this paragraph shall preferably be chosen in consultation with, and with the consent of, the exporters, producers or importers concerned.

> 6.10.2 In cases where the authorities have limited their examination, as provided for in this paragraph, they shall nevertheless determine an individual margin of dumping for any exporter or producer not initially selected who submits the necessary information in time for that information to be considered during the course of the investigation, except where the number of exporters or producers is so large that individual examinations would be unduly burdensome to the authorities and prevent the timely completion of the investigation. Voluntary responses shall not be discouraged.

6.11 For the purposes of this ~~Code~~ Agreement, 'interested parties' shall include:

> (i) an exporter or foreign producer or the importer of a product subject to investigation, or a trade or business association a majority of the members of which are producers, exporters or importers of such product;

> (ii) the government of the exporting country; and

> (iii) a producer of the like product in the importing country or a trade and business association a majority of the members of which produce the like product in the importing country.

This list shall not preclude ~~Parties~~ Members from allowing domestic or foreign parties other than those mentioned above to be included as interested parties.

0039

I

- 16 -

6.12 The authorities shall provide opportunities for industrial users of the product under investigation, and for representative consumer organizations in cases where the product is commonly sold at the retail level, to provide information which is relevant to the investigation regarding dumping, injury and causality.

6.13 The authorities shall take due account of any difficulties experienced by interested parties, in particular small companies, in supplying information requested and provide any assistance practicable.

6.14 The procedures set out above are not intended to prevent the authorities of a ~~Party~~ Member from proceeding expeditiously with regard to initiating an investigation, reaching preliminary or final determinations, whether affirmative or negative, or from applying provisional or final measures, in accordance with relevant provisions of this ~~Code~~ Agreement.

Article 7

Provisional Measures

7.1 Provisional measures may be applied only if:

 (i) an investigation has been initiated in accordance with the provisions of Article 5, a public notice has been given to that effect and interested parties have been given adequate opportunities to submit information and make comments;

 (ii) a preliminary affirmative determination has been made of dumping and consequent injury to a domestic industry; and

 (iii) the authorities concerned judge such measures necessary to prevent injury being caused during the investigation.

7.2 Provisional measures may take the form of a provisional duty or, preferably, a security - by cash deposit or bond - equal to the amount of the anti-dumping duty provisionally estimated, being not greater than the provisionally estimated margin of dumping. Withholding of appraisement is an appropriate provisional measure, provided that the normal duty and the estimated amount of the anti-dumping duty be indicated and as long as the withholding of appraisement is subject to the same conditions as other provisional measures.

7.3 Provisional measures shall not be applied sooner than 60 days from the date of initiation of the investigation.

7.4 The application of provisional measures shall be limited to as short a period as possible, not exceeding four months or, on decision of the authorities concerned, upon request by exporters representing a significant percentage of the trade involved, to a period not exceeding six months. When authorities, in the course of an investigation, examine whether a duty lower than the margin of dumping would be sufficient to remove injury, these periods may be six and nine months, respectively.

0040

7.5 The relevant provisions of Article 9 shall be followed in the application of provisional measures.

Article 8

Price Undertakings

8.1 Proceedings may[1] be suspended or terminated without the imposition of provisional measures or anti-dumping duties upon receipt of satisfactory voluntary undertakings from any exporter to revise its prices or to cease exports to the area in question at dumped prices so that the authorities are satisfied that the injurious effect of the dumping is eliminated. Price increases under such undertakings shall not be higher than necessary to eliminate the margin of dumping. It is desirable that the price increases be less than the margin of dumping if such increases would be adequate to remove the injury to the domestic industry.

8.2 Price undertakings shall not be sought or accepted from exporters unless the authorities of the importing country have made a preliminary affirmative determination of dumping and injury caused by such dumping.

8.3 Undertakings offered need not be accepted if the authorities consider their acceptance impractical, for example, if the number of actual or potential exporters is too great, or for other reasons, including reasons of general policy. Should the case arise and where practicable, the authorities shall provide to the exporter the reasons which have led them to consider acceptance of an undertaking as inappropriate, and shall, to the extent possible, give the exporter an opportunity to make comments thereon.

8.4 If the undertakings are accepted, the investigation of dumping and injury shall nevertheless be completed if the exporter so desires or the authorities so decide. In such a case, if a negative determination of dumping or injury is made, the undertaking shall automatically lapse, except in cases where such a determination is due in large part to the existence of a price undertaking. In such cases the authorities may require that an undertaking be maintained for a reasonable period consistent with the provisions of this Code Agreement. In the event that an affirmative determination of dumping and injury is made, the undertaking shall continue consistent with its terms and the provisions of this Code Agreement.

_C-19.1(b)_

---

[1]The word "may" shall not be interpreted to allow the simultaneous continuation of proceedings with the implementation of price undertakings except as provided in paragraph 4.

0041

- 18 -

8.5 Price undertakings may be suggested by the authorities of the importing country, but no exporter shall be forced to enter into such an undertaking. The fact that exporters do not offer such undertakings, or do not accept an invitation to do so, shall in no way prejudice the consideration of the case. However, the authorities are free to determine that a threat of injury is more likely to be realized if the dumped imports continue.

8.6 Authorities of an importing country may require any exporter from whom undertakings have been accepted to provide periodically information relevant to the fulfilment of such undertakings, and to permit verification of pertinent data. In case of violation of undertakings, the authorities of the importing country may take, under this ~~Code~~ Agreement in conformity with its provisions, expeditious actions which may constitute immediate application of provisional measures using the best information available. In such cases definitive duties may be levied in accordance with this ~~Code~~ Agreement on goods entered for consumption not more than ninety days before the application of such provisional measures, except that any such retroactive assessment shall not apply to imports entered before the violation of the undertaking.

Article 9

Imposition and Collection of Anti-Dumping Duties

9.1 The decision whether or not to impose an anti-dumping duty in cases where all requirements for the imposition have been fulfilled and the decision whether the amount of the anti-dumping duty to be imposed shall be the full margin of dumping or less, are decisions to be made by the authorities of the importing country or customs territory. It is desirable that the imposition be permissive in all countries or customs territories ~~Parties~~ Members ~~to this Agreement~~, and that the duty be less than the margin, if such lesser duty would be adequate to remove the injury to the domestic industry.

9.2 When an anti-dumping duty is imposed in respect of any product, such anti-dumping duty shall be collected in the appropriate amounts in each case, on a non-discriminatory basis on imports of such product from all sources found to be dumped and causing injury, except as to imports from those sources, ~~from which price undertakings under the terms of this Code~~ ~~Agreement~~ have been accepted. The authorities shall name the supplier or suppliers of the product concerned. If, however, several suppliers from the same country are involved, and it is impracticable to name all these suppliers, the authorities may name the supplying country concerned. If several suppliers from more than one country are involved, the authorities may name either all the suppliers involved, or, if this is impracticable, all the supplying countries involved.

9.3 The amount of the anti-dumping duty shall not exceed the margin of dumping as established under Article 2.

0042

- 19 -

9.3.1 When the amount of the anti-dumping duty is assessed on a retrospective basis, the determination of the final liability for payment of anti-dumping duties shall take place as soon as possible, normally within 12 months, and in no case more than 18 months, after the date on which a request for a final assessment of the amount of anti-dumping duty has been made.[1]   Any refund shall be made promptly and normally in not more than 90 days following the determination of final liability made pursuant to this sub-paragraph. In any case, where a refund is not made within 90 days the authorities shall provide an explanation if so requested.

9.3.2 When the amount of the anti-dumping duty is assessed on a prospective basis, provision shall be made for a prompt refund, upon request, of any duty paid in excess of the margin of dumping. A refund of any such duty paid in excess of the actual margin of dumping shall normally take place within 12 months, and in no case more than 18 months, after the date on which a request for a refund, duly supported by evidence, has been made by an importer of the product subject to the anti-dumping duty. The refund authorized should normally be made within 90 days of the above-noted decision.

9.3.3 In determining whether and to what extent a reimbursement should be made when the export price is constructed in accordance with Article 2.3, authorities should take account of any change in normal value, any change of costs incurred between importation and resale, and any movement in the resale price which is duly reflected in subsequent selling prices, and should calculate the export price with no deduction for the amount of anti-dumping duties paid when conclusive evidence of the above is provided.

9.4 When the authorities have limited their examination in accordance with the second sentence of Article 6.10, any anti-dumping duty applied to imports from exporters or producers not included in the examination shall not exceed

    (a)   the weighted average margin of dumping established with respect to the selected exporters or producers or,

    (b)   where the liability for payment of anti-dumping duties is calculated on the basis of a prospective normal value, the difference between the weighted average normal value of the selected exporters or producers and the export prices of exporters or producers not individually examined,

provided that the authorities shall disregard for the purpose of this paragraph any zero and de minimis margins and margins established under the circumstances referred to in Article 6.8. The authorities shall apply

---

[1] It is understood that the observance of the time-limits mentioned in this sub-paragraph and in sub-paragraph 2 may not be possible where the product in question is subject to judicial review proceedings.

0043

- 20 -

individual duties or normal values to imports from any exporter or producer not included in the examination who has provided the necessary information during the course of the investigation, as provided for in Article 6.10.2

9.5 When exporters or producers in a country exports from which are subject to anti-dumping duties in an importing country who have not exported the product in question during the period of investigation can show that they are not related to any of the exporters or producers subject to anti-dumping duties in the exporting country, the authorities shall promptly carry out a review for the purpose of determining individual margins of dumping for any of these exporters or producers.   Such a review shall be initiated and carried out on an accelerated basis, compared to normal duty assessment and review proceedings in the importing country. No anti-dumping duties shall be levied on imports from such exporters or producers while the review is being carried out.   The authorities may, however, withhold appraisement and/or request guarantees to ensure that, should such a review result in a determination of dumping in respect of such producers or exporters, anti-dumping duties can be levied retroactively to the date of the initiation of the review.

Article 10

Retroactivity

10.1 Provisional measures and anti-dumping duties shall only be applied to products which enter for consumption after the time when the decision taken under Article 7:1 and Article 9:1, respectively, enters into force, subject to the exceptions set out in this Article.

10.2 Where a final determination of injury (but not of a threat thereof or of a material retardation of the establishment of an industry) is made or, in the case of a final determination of a threat of injury, when the effect of the dumped imports would, in the absence of the provisional measures, have led to a determination of injury, anti-dumping duties may be levied retroactively for the period for which provisional measures, if any, have been applied.   If the anti-dumping duty fixed in the final decision is higher than the provisional duty paid or payable, the difference shall not be collected.   If the duty fixed in the final decision is lower than the provisional duty paid or payable, or the amount estimated for the purpose of the security, the difference shall be reimbursed or the duty recalculated, as the case may be.

10.3 A definitive anti-dumping duty may be levied on products which were entered for consumption not more than 90 days prior to the date of application of provisional measures, when the authorities determine for the dumped product in question that:

  (i)   there is a history of dumping which caused injury or that the importer was, or should have been, aware that the exporter practices dumping and that such dumping would cause injury, and

0044

- 21 -

(ii) the injury is caused by massive dumped imports of a product in a relatively short time which in light of the timing and the volume of the dumped imports and other circumstances (such as a rapid build-up of inventories of the imported product) is likely to seriously undermine the remedial effect of the definitive anti-dumping duty to be applied, provided that the importers concerned have been given an opportunity to comment.

10.4 A definitive anti-dumping duty imposed when determinations of dumping and injury have been made following an investigation consistent with the relevant provisions of this ~~Code~~ **Agreement** may be levied on products which entered for consumption not more than 150 days prior to date of the application of provisional measures, if:

(i) the product subject to investigation is a like product to that in respect of which a definitive anti-dumping duty is in force in the importing country and is produced in or exported from a country not subject to that definitive anti-dumping duty;

(ii) an exporter or producer in the country subject to the existing definitive anti-dumping duty has a controlling interest in the party exporting the product subject to investigation from the third country;

(iii) exports of the product subject to investigation from the third country have increased significantly since the initiation of the investigation which resulted in the imposition of the existing definitive anti-dumping duty, and there is a corresponding decline of exports of the product from the country to which that duty applies by the exporter or producer which has a controlling interest in the party in the third country;

(iv) production in the third country of the product subject to investigation takes place in pre-existing facilities used to produce that product; and

(v) the authorities determine that imports of the product which take place under the conditions described in sub-paragraphs (ii)-(iv) seriously undermine the remedial effect of the existing definitive anti-dumping duty.

10.5 Notwithstanding sub-paragraphs (ii)-(v) of paragraph 4, a definitive anti-dumping duty imposed when determinations of dumping and injury have been made following an investigation consistent with the relevant provisions of this ~~Code~~ **Agreement** may also be levied retroactively on products which entered for consumption not more than 150 days prior to the date of application of provisional measures if the product referred to in sub-paragraph (i) of paragraph 4 is assembled or completed in the third country under conditions identical to those set forth in Article 12(ii)-(v) with regard to assembly or completion operations in an importing country.

0045

- 22 -

10.6 The authorities may, after initiating an investigation, take such measures as the withholding of appraisement or assessment as may be necessary to collect anti-dumping duties retroactively as provided for in paragraphs 3, 4 and 5, once they have sufficient evidence that the conditions set forth in those paragraphs are satisfied.

10.7 No duties shall be levied retroactively pursuant to paragraphs 3, 4 and 5 on products entered for consumption prior to the date of initiation of the investigation. In cases referred to in paragraph 4, no duties shall be levied retroactively pursuant to an investigation initiated more than 30 months after the initiation of the investigation which resulted in the imposition of the existing definitive anti-dumping duty referred to in sub-paragraph (i).

10.8 Except as provided in paragraph 1 above, where a determination of threat of injury or material retardation is made (but no injury has yet occurred) a definitive anti-dumping duty may be imposed only from the date of the determination of threat of injury or material retardation and any cash deposit made during the period of the application of provisional measures shall be refunded and any bonds released in an expeditious manner.

10.9 Where a final determination is negative, any cash deposit made during the period of the application of provisional measures shall be refunded and any bonds released in an expeditious manner.

Article 11

Duration and Review of Anti-Dumping Duties and Price Undertakings

11.1 An anti-dumping duty shall remain in force only as long as and to the extent necessary to counteract dumping which is causing injury.

11.2 The authorities shall review the need for the continued imposition of the duty, where warranted, on their own initiative or, provided that a reasonable period of time has elapsed since the imposition of the definitive anti-dumping duty, upon request by any interested party which submits positive information substantiating the need for a review.[1] Interested parties shall have the right to request the authorities to examine whether the continued imposition of the duty is necessary to offset dumping, whether recurrence of the injury would occur if the duty were removed or varied, or both. If, as a result of the review under this paragraph, the authorities determine that the anti-dumping duty is no longer warranted, it shall be terminated immediately.

---

[1]A determination of final liability for payment of anti-dumping duties as provided for in Article 9.3 does not by itself constitute a review within the meaning of this Article.

0046

- 23 -

11.3 Notwithstanding the provisions of paragraphs 1 and 2, any definitive anti-dumping duty shall be terminated on a date not later than five years from its imposition (or from the date of the most recent review under paragraph 2 if that review has covered both dumping and injury, or under this paragraph), unless the authorities determine, in a review initiated before that date on their own initiative or upon a duly substantiated request made by or on behalf of the domestic industry within a reasonable period of time prior to that date, that the continued imposition of the duty is necessary to prevent the continuation or recurrence of injury by dumped imports. The duty may remain in force pending the outcome of such a review.

11.4 The provisions of Article 6 regarding evidence and procedure shall apply to any review carried out under this Article. Any such review shall be carried out expeditiously and shall normally be concluded within twelve months of the date of initiation of the review.

11.5 The provisions of this Article shall _mutatis mutandis_ apply to price undertakings accepted under Article 8.

Article 12

Measures to Prevent Circumvention of Definitive Anti-Dumping Duties

12.1 The authorities may include within the scope of application of an existing definitive anti-dumping duty on an imported product those parts or components destined for assembly or completion in the importing country, if it has been established that:

    (i)   the product assembled or completed from such parts or components in the importing country is a like product to a product which is subject to the definitive anti-dumping duty;

    (ii)   the assembly or completion in the importing country of the product referred to in sub-paragraph (i) is carried out by a party which is related to or acting on behalf of[2] an exporter or producer whose exports of the like product to the importing country are subject to the definitive anti-dumping duty, referred to in sub-paragraph (i);

---

[1] When the amount of the anti-dumping duty is assessed on a retrospective basis, a finding in the most recent assessment proceeding under Article 9.3.1 that no duty is to be levied shall not by itself require the authorities to determine under this paragraph that the continued imposition of the anti-dumping duty is not necessary.

[2] Such as when there is a contractual arrangement with the exporter or producer in question (or with a party related to that exporter or producer) covering the sale of the assembled product in the importing country.

- 24 -

(iii) the parts or components have been sourced in the country subject
to the anti-dumping duty from the exporter or producer subject
to the definitive anti-dumping duty, suppliers in the exporting
country who have historically supplied the parts or components
to that exporter or producer, or a party in the exporting
country supplying parts or components on behalf of such an
exporter or producer;

(iv) the assembly or completion operations in the importing country
have started or expanded substantially and the imports of parts
or components for use in such operations have increased
substantially since the initiation of the investigation which
resulted in the imposition of the definitive anti-dumping duty;

(v) the total cost[1] of the parts or components referred to in
sub-paragraph (iii) is not less than 70 per cent of the total
cost of all parts or components used in the assembly or
completion operation of the like product[2], provided that in no
case shall the parts and components be included within the scope
of definitive measures if the value added by the assembly or
completion operation is greater than 25 per cent of the
ex-factory cost[3] of the like product assembled or completed in
the territory of the importing country.

(vi) there is evidence of dumping, as determined by a comparison
between the price of the product when assembled or completed in
the importing country, and the prior normal value of the like
product when subject to the original definitive anti-dumping
duty; and

(vii) there is evidence that the inclusion of these parts or
components within the scope of application of the definitive
anti-dumping duty is necessary to prevent or offset the
continuation or recurrence of injury to the domestic industry
producing a product like the product which is subject to the
definitive anti-dumping duty.

---

[1] The cost of a part or component is the arm's length acquisition price
of that part or component, or in the absence of such a price (including
when parts or components are fabricated internally by the party assembling
or completing the product in the importing country), the total material,
labour and factory overhead costs incurred in the fabrication of the part
or component.

[2] i.e., parts or components purchased in the importing country, parts
or components referred to in sub-paragraph (iii), other imported parts or
components (including parts or components imported from a third country)
and parts or components fabricated internally.

[3] i.e., cost of materials, labour and factory overheads.

0048

12.2 The authorities may impose provisional measures in accordance with Article 7:2 on parts or components imported for use in an assembly or completion operation only when they are satisfied that there is sufficient evidence that the criteria set out in sub-paragraphs (i)-(vi) are met. Any provisional duty imposed shall not exceed the definitive anti-dumping duty in force. The authorities may levy a definitive anti-dumping duty once all of the criteria in paragraph 1 are fully satisfied. The amount of the definitive anti-dumping duty shall not exceed the amount by which the normal value of the product subject to the existing definitive anti-dumping duty exceeds the comparable price of the like product when assembled or completed in the importing country.

12.3 The provisions of this ~~Code~~ Agreement concerning rights of interested parties and public notice shall apply mutatis mutandis to investigations carried out under this Article. The provisions of Articles 9 and 11 regarding refund and review shall apply to anti-dumping duties imposed, pursuant to this Article, on parts or components assembled or completed in the importing country.

Article 13

Public Notice and Explanation of Determinations

13.1 When the authorities are satisfied that there is sufficient evidence to justify the initiation of an anti-dumping investigation pursuant to Article 5, the ~~Party~~ Member or ~~Parties~~ Members the products of which are subject to such investigation and other interested parties known to the investigating authorities to have an interest therein shall be notified and a public notice shall be given.

13.1.1 A public notice of the initiation of an investigation shall contain or otherwise make available adequate information on the following:

(i) the name of the exporting country or countries and the product involved;

(ii) the date of initiation of the investigation;

(iii) the basis on which dumping is alleged in the application;

(iv) a summary of the factors which have led to the allegation of injury;

(v) the address to which representations by interested parties should be directed;

(vi) the time-limits allowed to interested parties for making their views known.

0049

C-22.4 DETERMINATION

- 26 -

13.2 Public notice shall be given of any preliminary or final determination, whether affirmative or negative, of any decision to accept an undertaking pursuant to Article 8, of the termination of such an undertaking, and of the revocation of a determination. Each such notice shall set forth or otherwise make available in sufficient detail the findings and conclusions reached on all issues of fact and law considered material by the investigating authorities and shall be forwarded to the ~~Party~~ Member or ~~Parties~~ Members the products of which are subject to such ~~finding~~ or undertaking and to other interested parties known to have an interest therein.

C-22.5

13.2.1 A public notice of the imposition of provisional measures shall set forth or otherwise make available sufficiently detailed explanations for the preliminary determinations on dumping and injury (insofar as there is no separate preliminary injury determination and a notice thereof) and shall refer to the matters of fact and law which have led to arguments being accepted or rejected; the notice shall, due regard being paid to the requirement for the protection of confidential information, contain in particular:

(i) the names of the suppliers, or when this is impracticable, the supplying countries involved;

C-22.5(ii)

(ii) a description of the product which is sufficient for customs purposes;

(iii) the margins of dumping established and a full explanation of the reasons for the methodology used in the establishment and comparison of the export price and the normal value under Article 2;

(iv) considerations relevant to the injury determination as set out in Article 3 (insofar as there is no separate notice concerning such injury determination);

C-22.6

(v) the main reasons leading to the determination.

THE ACCEPTANCE OF

13.2.2 A public notice of suspension or conclusion of an investigation in the case of an affirmative determination providing for the imposition of a definitive duty or a price undertaking shall contain or otherwise make available all relevant information on the matters of fact and law and reasons which have led to the imposition of final measures or the acceptance of a price undertaking, due regard being paid to the requirement for the protection of confidential information; it shall in particular contain the information described in sub-paragraph 13.2.1, as well as the reasons for the acceptance or rejection of relevant arguments or claims made by the exporters and importers, and the basis for any decision made under Article ~~6.9.2~~ 6.10.2.

13.2.3 A public notice of the termination or suspension of an investigation following the acceptance of an undertaking pursuant to

[NEXT PAGE IS 45]

0050

- 45 -

Article 9

Consultations and authorized remedies

9.1 If, in the course of implementation of a programme referred to in Article 8.2 above, notwithstanding the fact that the programme is consistent with the criteria laid down in Article 8.2, a signatory Member has reasons to believe that this programme has resulted in serious adverse effects to the domestic industry of that signatory Member, such as to cause damage which would be difficult to repair, such signatory Member may request consultations with the signatory Member granting the subsidy.

9.2 Upon request for consultations under paragraph 1 above, the signatory Member maintaining the subsidy programme in question shall enter into such consultations as quickly as possible. The purpose of the consultations shall be to clarify the facts of the situation and to arrive at a mutually acceptable solution.

9.3 If no mutually acceptable solution has been reached in consultations under paragraph 2 within 60 days of the request for such consultations, the requesting signatory Member may refer the matter to the Committee.

9.4 Where a matter is referred to the Committee, the Committee shall immediately review the facts involved and the evidence of the effects referred to in paragraph 1 above. If the Committee determines that such effects exist, it may recommend to the subsidizing signatory Member to modify this programme in such a way as to remove these effects. The Committee shall present its conclusions within 120 days from the date when the matter is referred to it under this provision. In the event the recommendation is not followed within 6 months, the Committee shall authorize the requesting signatory Member to take appropriate countermeasures commensurate with the nature and degree of the effects determined to exist.

0051

- 46 -

PART V: COUNTERVAILING MEASURES

Article 10

Application of Article VI of the ~~General Agreement~~ GATT 1993[1]

~~Signatories~~ Members shall take all necessary steps to ensure that the imposition of a countervailing duty[2] on any product of the territory of any ~~signatory~~ Member imported into the territory of another ~~signatory~~ Member is in accordance with the provisions of Article VI of the ~~General Agreement~~ GATT 1993 and the terms of this Agreement.

DOMESTIC INDUSTRY AS DEFINED IN ARTICLE 16.

Article 11

Initiation and subsequent investigation

APPLICA-TION

A-5.1

11.1 Countervailing duties may only be imposed pursuant to investigations initiated[3] and conducted in accordance with the provisions of this Agreement. An investigation to determine the existence, degree and effect of any alleged subsidy shall normally be initiated upon a written request by or on behalf of the ~~industry affected.~~ The ~~request~~ shall include sufficient evidence of the existence of (a) a subsidy and, if possible, its amount, (b) injury within the meaning of Article VI of the General

---

[1] The provisions of Parts II or III may be invoked in parallel with the provisions of Part V of this Agreement; however, with regard to the effects of a particular subsidy in the domestic market of the importing country, only one form of relief (either a countervailing duty, if other requirements of Part V are met, or a countermeasure under Articles 4 or 7 of this Agreement) shall be available. The provisions of Parts III and V may not be invoked regarding measures considered non-actionable in accordance with the provisions of Part IV of this Agreement. However, measures referred to in Article 8.1(a) above may be investigated in order to determine whether ~~or not~~ they are ~~generally available~~ specific within the meaning of Article 2 above.

[2] The term 'countervailing duty' shall be understood to mean a special duty levied for the purpose of off-setting any subsidy bestowed directly or indirectly upon the manufacture, production or export of any merchandise, as provided for in Article VI:3 of the ~~General Agreement~~ GATT 1993.

[3] The term 'initiated' as used hereinafter means procedural action by which a ~~signatory~~ Member formally commences an investigation as provided in paragraph 4 of this Article.

[4] ~~As defined in Article 16.~~

- 47 -

A WRITTEN APPLICATION BY OR ON BEHALF OF A DOMESTIC INDUSTRY FOR THE INITIATION OF SUCH INVESTIGATION,

Agreement GATT 1993 as interpreted by this Agreement[1], and (c) a causal link between the subsidized imports and the alleged injury. Before initiating an investigation, the authorities concerned shall satisfy themselves on the basis of positive evidence that the request is supported by the domestic industry. If in special circumstances the authorities concerned decide to initiate an investigation without having received ~~such a request~~, they shall proceed only if they have sufficient evidence on all points under (a) through (c) above *TO JUSTIFY INITIATION OF*

AN APPLICATION *AN INVESTIGATION.*

A-5.(

A-5.2

11.2 ~~A request~~ within the meaning of paragraph 1 shall in particular contain such evidence which can reasonably be expected to be available to the ~~complainant~~ on the following: (a) identity of the ~~complainant~~ and of the domestic industry on whose behalf the ~~complaint~~ is lodged, (b) evidence that the request is supported by the domestic industry, (c) evidence with regard to the existence, amount and nature of the subsidy in question, (d) volume and prices of the allegedly subsidized imports and their effect on the affected domestic industry, as demonstrated by developments in production, capacity utilization, sales, sales prices, stocks, consumption, market shares, profits or losses, and employment, and (e) evidence that any alleged material injury to a domestic industry is caused by subsidized imports, through the effects of subsidies, and not by other factors.

APPLICANT *APPLICATION* *APPLICANT*

11.3 Each ~~signatory~~ Member shall notify the Committee (a) which of its authorities are competent to initiate and conduct investigations referred to in this Article and (b) its domestic procedures governing the initiation and conduct of such investigations.

11.4 The competent authorities shall review the adequacy of the evidence provided in the request for the initiation of an investigation in light of any relevant and readily available information and determine whether the evidence is sufficient to justify the opening of an investigation.

THE EVIDENCE OF BOTH DUMPING AND INJURY

A-5.7

11.5 ~~Upon initiation of an investigation and thereafter, the evidence referred to in paragraph 1(a)-(e) above should be considered simultaneously. In any event the evidence of points (a) through (e)~~ shall be considered simultaneously (a) in the decision whether or not to initiate an investigation and (b) thereafter during the course of the investigation, starting on a date not later than the earliest date on which in accordance ~~with the provisions of this Agreement provisional measures~~ may be applied.

11.6 In cases where products are not imported directly from the country of origin but ~~are exported to the country of importation from an intermediate country, the provisions of this Agreement~~ shall be fully applicable and the transaction or transactions shall, for the purposes of this Agreement, be regarded as having taken place between the country of origin and the country of importation.

---

[1] Under this Agreement the term "injury" shall, unless otherwise specified, be taken to mean material injury to a domestic industry, threat of material injury to a domestic industry or material retardation of the establishment of such an industry and shall be interpreted in accordance with the provisions of Article 15.

0053

- 48 -

UNDER PARAGRAPH 1

11.7 An application shall be rejected and an investigation shall be terminated promptly as soon as the authorities concerned are satisfied that there is not sufficient evidence of either subsidization or of injury to justify proceeding with the case.   There shall be immediate termination in cases where the amount of a subsidy is <u>de minimis</u> or where the volume of subsidized imports, actual or potential, or the injury, is negligible. For the purpose of this paragraph, the amount of the subsidy shall be considered to be negligible <u>de minimis</u> if the subsidy is less than 1 per cent <u>ad valorem</u>.

11.8 An investigation shall not hinder the procedure of customs clearance.

11.9 Investigations shall, except in special circumstances, be concluded within one year after their initiation.

SUBJECT TO THE REQUIREMENT

IN A COUNTERVAILIN DUTY INVESTIGATION

Article 12

Evidence

12.1 Interested ~~signatories~~ Members and interested parties[1,2] shall be given ample opportunity to present in writing all information and argument that they consider relevant in respect of the investigation in question. ~~Taking account of the need~~ to protect confidential information, written information and argument submitted by one interested ~~signatory~~ Member or interested party shall be made available promptly to other interested ~~signatories~~ Members or interested parties participating in the investigation.   Interested ~~signatories~~ Members and inter~~ested~~ parties also shall have the right, upon justification, to present *OTHER* information orally. ~~Where such information is provided orally, the interested parties subsequently shall be required to reduce such statements to writing.~~   Any decision of the investigating authorities can only be based on such information and arguments as were on the written record of ~~the authority~~ and which were available to interested ~~signatories~~ Members and interested parties participating in the investigation, due account having been given to the need to protect confidential information.

THE INVESTIGATION

---

[1] For the purpose of this Agreement "party" means any natural or juridical person resident in the territory of any ~~signatory~~ Member.

[2] Any "interested ~~signatory~~ Member" or "interested party" shall refer to a ~~signatory~~ Member or a party economically affected by the subsidy in question.

SUCH ORAL INFORMATION SHALL BE TAKEN INTO ACCOUNT BY THE AUTHORITIES ONLY INSOFAR AS IT IS SUBSEQUENTLY REPRODUCED IN WRITING AND MADE AVAILABLE TO THE OTHER INTERESTED PARTIES AS PROVIDED FOR ABOVE.

0054

- 49 -

12.2 Respondents to a countervailing duty questionnaire shall be given at least thirty days for reply.   As a general rule, the time-limit for exporters should be counted from the date of receipt of the questionnaire, which for this purpose shall be deemed to have been received one week from the day on which it was sent to the respondent or transmitted to the appropriate diplomatic representatives of the exporting country.   Due consideration should be given to any request for an extension of the thirty day period and, upon cause shown, such an extension should be granted whenever possible.

A-6.1.1 n.1

12.3 Any information which is by nature confidential, (for example, because its disclosure would be of significant competitive advantage to a competitor or because its disclosure would have a significantly adverse effect upon a person supplying the information or upon a person from whom he acquired the information) or which is provided on a confidential basis by parties to an investigation shall, upon good cause shown, be treated as such by the investigating authorities.   Such information shall not be disclosed without specific permission of the party submitting it.[1]   These authorities shall either require persons providing confidential information to furnish non-confidential summaries thereof or shall prepare such summaries.   These summaries shall be in sufficient detail to permit a reasonable understanding of the substance of the information submitted in confidence.   In the event such parties indicate that such information is not susceptible of summary, a statement of reasons why summarization is not possible must be provided.

THE　*THESE*
A-6.5

12.4 If the authorities find that a request for confidentiality is not warranted and if the supplier is unwilling to make the information public or to authorize its disclosure in generalized or summary form, the authorities may disregard such information.[2]

+6.5.2　*EITHER*

12.5 The investigating authorities may carry out investigations in the territory of other Members as required, provided that they have notified in good time the Member in question and unless the latter objects to the investigation.   Further, the investigating authorities may carry out investigations on the premises of a firm and may examine the records of a firm if (a) the firm so agrees and (b) the Member in question is notified and does not object.   The procedures set forth in Annex VI to this Agreement shall apply to investigations on the premises of a firm.

---

[1] Signatories Members are aware that in the territory of certain signatories Members disclosure pursuant to a narrowly-drawn protective order may be required.

[2] Signatories Members agree that requests for confidentiality should not be arbitrarily rejected.   Signatories Members further agree that the investigating authority may request the waiving of confidentiality only regarding information relevant to the proceedings.

[REPLACE w/ AD¶ 6.7 (PAGE 14), CHANGING ① "ARTICLE I" in AD TO "ARTICLE VI & ② "PARAGRAPH 9" in AD TO

0055

- 50 -

12.6 In cases in which any interested party or signatory Member refuses access to, or otherwise does not provide, necessary information within a reasonable period or significantly impedes the investigation, preliminary and final determinations[1], affirmative or negative, may be made on the basis of the facts available.

12.7 Before final determinations are made, investigating authorities shall inform all interested parties of the essential facts and considerations on the basis of which it is intended to apply definitive measures. Such disclosure should take place in sufficient time for the parties to defend their interests.

12.8 The procedures set out above are not intended to prevent the authorities of a signatory Member from proceeding expeditiously with regard to initiating an investigation, reaching preliminary or final determinations, whether affirmative or negative, or from applying provisional or final measures, in accordance with relevant provisions of this Agreement.

Article 13

Consultations

13.1 As soon as possible after a request for initiation of an investigation is accepted, and in any event before the initiation of any investigation, signatories Members the products of which may be subject to such investigation shall be invited for consultations with the aim of clarifying the situation as to the matters referred to in Article 11:1 above and arriving at a mutually agreed solution.

13.2 Furthermore, throughout the period of investigation, signatories Members the products of which are the subject of the investigation shall be afforded a reasonable opportunity to continue consultations, with a view to clarifying the factual situation and to arriving at a mutually agreed solution.[2]

---

[1] Because of different terms used under different systems in various countries the term 'determination' is hereinafter used to mean a formal decision or finding.

[2] It is particularly important, in accordance with the provisions of this paragraph, that no affirmative determination whether preliminary or final be made without reasonable opportunity for consultations having been given. Such consultations may establish the basis for proceeding under the provisions of Parts II and III X of this Agreement.

0056

- 51 -

13.3 Without prejudice to the obligation to afford reasonable opportunity for consultation, these provisions regarding consultations are not intended to prevent the authorities of a signatory Member from proceeding expeditiously with regard to initiating the investigation, reaching preliminary or final determinations, whether affirmative or negative, or from applying provisional or final measures, in accordance with the provisions of this Agreement.

13.4 The signatory Member which intends to initiate any investigation or is conducting such an investigation shall permit, upon request, the signatory Member or signatories Members the products of which are subject to such investigation access to non-confidential evidence including the non-confidential summary of confidential data being used for initiating or conducting the investigation.

Article 14

Calculation of the amount of a subsidy in terms
of the benefit to the recipient

For the purpose of Part V of this Agreement, any method used by the investigating authority to calculate the benefit to the recipient conferred pursuant to Article 1.1 above shall be provided for in the national legislation or implementing regulations of the signatory Member concerned and its application to each particular case shall be transparent and adequately explained. Furthermore any such method shall be consistent with the following guidelines:

(a) Government provision of equity capital shall not be considered as conferring a benefit, unless the investment decision can be regarded as inconsistent with the usual investment practice (including for the provision of risk capital) of private investors in the territory of that signatory Member;

(b) A loan by a government shall not be considered as conferring a benefit, unless there is a difference between the amount that the firm receiving the loan pays on the government loan and a comparable commercial loan which the firm could actually obtain on the market. In this case the benefit shall be the difference between these two amounts;

(c) A loan guarantee by a government shall not be considered as conferring a benefit, unless there is a difference between the amount that the firm receiving the guarantee pays on a loan guaranteed by the government and the amount that the firm would pay for a comparable commercial loan absent the government guarantee. In this case the benefit shall be the difference between these two amounts adjusted for any differences in fees;

0057

- 52 -

(d) The provision of goods or services or purchase of goods by a government shall not be considered as conferring a benefit unless the provision is made for less than adequate remuneration, or the purchase is made for more than adequate remuneration. The adequacy of remuneration shall be determined in relation to prevailing market conditions for the good or service in question in the country of provision or purchase (including price, quality, availability, marketability, transportation and other conditions of purchase or sale).

Article 15

Determination of injury

15.1 A determination of injury for purposes of Article VI of the General Agreement GATT 1993 shall be based on positive evidence and involve an objective examination of both (a) the volume of subsidized imports and the effect of the subsidized imports on prices in the domestic market for like products[1] and (b) the consequent impact of these imports on the domestic industry concerned.

15.2 With regard to the volume of subsidized imports, the investigating authorities shall consider whether there has been a significant increase in subsidized imports, either in absolute terms or relative to production or consumption in the importing signatory Member. With regard to the effect of the subsidized imports on prices, the investigating authorities shall consider whether there has been significant price undercutting by the subsidized imports as compared with price of a like domestic product, or whether the effect of such imports is otherwise to depress prices to a significant degree or to prevent price increases, which otherwise would have occurred to a significant degree. No one or several of these factors can necessarily give decisive guidance.

15.3 Where imports of a product from more than one country are simultaneously subject to countervailing duty investigations, the investigating authorities may cumulatively assess effects of such imports only if they determine that (1) the amount of subsidization established in relation to the imports from each country is more than de minimis as defined in Article 11.7 and that the volume of imports from each country is not negligible and (2) a cumulative assessment of the effects of the

---

[1] Throughout this Agreement the term "like product" ("produit similaire") shall be interpreted to mean a product which is identical, i.e., alike in all respects to the product under consideration or in the absence of such a product, another product which although not alike in all respects, has (a) physical, technical and/or chemical characteristics and (b) applications or uses closely resembling those of the product under consideration.

0058

- 53 -

> INCLUDING

imports is appropriate in light of the conditions of competition between imported products and the conditions of competition between the imported products and the like domestic product.

A-3.3 15.4 The examination of the impact on the domestic industry concerned shall include an evaluation of all relevant economic factors and indices having a bearing on the state of the industry including actual and potential decline **S** in output, sales, market share, profits, productivity, return on investments, or utilization of capacity; factors affecting domestic prices; actual and potential negative effects on cash flow, inventories, employment, wages, growth, ability to raise capital or investment and, in the case of agriculture, whether there has been an increased burden on Government support programmes. This list is not exhaustive, nor can one or several of these factors necessarily give decisive guidance.

A-3.4 15.5 It must be demonstrated that the subsidized imports are, through the effects[1] of subsidies, causing injury within the meaning of this Agreement. The authorities shall consider whether there are other factors[2] which at the same time are injuring the domestic industry, and the injuries caused by other factors must not be attributed to the subsidized imports. Determinations of injury shall contain explanations of how the authorities have considered such other factors.

15.6 A determination of threat of injury shall be based on facts and not merely on allegation, conjecture or remote possibility. The change in circumstances which would create a situation in which the subsidy would cause injury must be clearly foreseen and imminent. In making a determination regarding threat of material injury, the investigating authorities should consider, <u>inter alia</u>, such factors as: nature of the subsidy in question and the trade effects likely to rise therefrom; a significant rate of increase of subsidized imports into the domestic market **A-3.6** indicating the likelihood of substantially increased importation; sufficient freely disposable capacity of the exporter indicating the likelihood of substantially increased subsidized exports to the importing country's market, taking into account the availability of other export markets to absorb any additional exports; whether imports are entering at prices that will have a significant depressing or suppressing effect on domestic prices, and would likely increase demand for further imports, and inventories in the importing country of the product being investigated.

no one of these factors by itself can necessarily

IMPORTS   **IMPORTS.**

[1] As set forth in paragraphs 2 and 4 of this Article.
[2] Factors which may be relevant in this respect include inter alia, the volume and prices of **A-3.4** non-subsidized imports of the product in question, contraction in demand or changes in the pattern of consumption, trade restrictive practices of and competition between the foreign and domestic producers, developments in technology and the export performance and productivity of the domestic industry.

> S

- 54 -

give decisive guidance but ~~that~~ the totality of factors considered must lead to the conclusion that ~~further~~ subsidized imports are imminent and that unless protective action is taken, material injury would occur.

15.7 The effect of the subsidized imports shall **THAT** be assessed in relation to the domestic production of the like product when available data permit the separate identification of production **ON THE BASIS** of such criteria as: the production process, the producers' realization, profits. When the domestic production of the like product has no separate identity in these terms the effects of subsidized imports shall be assessed by the examination of the production of the narrowest group or range of products, which includes the like product, for which the necessary information can be provided.

A-3.5

Article 16

Definition of industry

16.1 For the purposes of this Agreement, the term "domestic industry" shall, except as provided in paragraph 2 below, be interpreted as referring to the domestic producers as a whole of the like products or to those of them whose collective output of the products constitutes a major proportion of the total domestic production of those products, except that when producers are related[1] to the exporters or importers or are themselves importers of the allegedly subsidized product or a like product from other countries, "domestic industry" may be interpreted as referring to the rest of the producers.

16.2 In exceptional circumstances the territory of a signatory Member may, for the production in question, be divided into two or more competitive markets and the producers within each market may be regarded as a separate industry if (a) the producers within such market sell all or almost all of their production of the product in question in that market, and (b) the demand in that market is not to any substantial degree supplied by producers of the product in question located elsewhere in the territory. In such

---

[1] For the purpose of this paragraph, producers shall be deemed to be related to exporters or importers only if (a) one of them directly or indirectly controls the other; or (b) both of them are directly or indirectly controlled by a third person; or (c) together they directly or indirectly control a third person, provided that there are grounds for believing or suspecting that the effect of the relationship is such as to cause the producer concerned to behave differently from non-related producers. For the purpose of this paragraph, one shall be deemed to control another when the former is legally or operationally in a position to exercise restraint or direction over the latter.

0060

- 55 -

circumstances injury may be found to exist even where a major portion of
the total domestic industry is not injured, provided there is a
concentration of subsidized imports into such an isolated market and
provided further that the subsidized imports are causing injury to the
producers of all or almost all of the production within such market.

i.e., A MARKET

16.3 When the industry has been interpreted as referring to the producers
in a certain area, as defined in paragraph 2 above, countervailing duties
shall be levied only on the products in question consigned for final
consumption to that area. When the constitutional law of the importing
signatory Member does not permit the levying of countervailing duties on
such a basis, the importing signatory Member may levy the countervailing
duties without limitation only if (a) the exporters shall have been given
an opportunity to cease exporting at subsidized prices to the area
concerned or otherwise give assurances pursuant to Article 19 of this
Agreement, and adequate assurances in this regard have not been promptly
given, and (b) such duties cannot be levied only on products of specific
producers which supply the area in question.

16.4 Where two or more countries have reached under the provisions of
Article XXIV:8(a) of the General Agreement GATT 1993 such a level of
integration that they have the characteristics of a single, unified market,
the industry in the entire area of integration shall be taken to be the
industry referred to in paragraphs 1 and 2 above.

Article 17

Imposition of countervailing duties

17.1 The decision whether or not to impose a countervailing duty in cases
where all requirements for the imposition have been fulfilled and the
decision whether the amount of the countervailing duty to be imposed shall
be the full amount of the subsidy or less are decisions to be made by the
authorities of the importing signatory Member. It is desirable that the
imposition should be permissive in the territory of all signatories
Members, that the duty should be less than the total amount of the subsidy
if such lesser duty would be adequate to remove injury to the domestic
industry, and that procedures should be established which would allow the
authorities concerned to take due account of representations made by
domestic interested parties[1] whose interests might be adversely affected by
the imposition of a countervailing duty.

---

[1] For the purpose of this paragraph, the term "domestic interested
parties" shall include consumers and industrial users of the imported
product subject to investigation.

- 56 -

17.2 No countervailing duty shall be levied[1] on any imported product in excess of the amount of the subsidy found to exist, calculated in terms of subsidization per unit of the subsidized and exported product.

COLLECTED, *IN EACH CASE,*

17.3 When a countervailing duty is imposed in respect of any product, such countervailing duty shall be ~~levied~~ in the appropriate amount, on a non-discriminatory basis on imports of such product from all sources found to be subsidized and ~~to be~~ causing injury, except as to imports from those sources which have renounced any subsidies in question or from which undertakings under the terms of this Agreement have been accepted.   Any exporter whose exports are subject to a definitive countervailing duty but who was not actually investigated for reasons other than a refusal to co-operate, shall be entitled to an expedited review in order that the investigating authorities promptly establish an individual countervailing duty rate for that exporter.

A-9.2

17.4 If, after reasonable efforts have been made to complete consultations, a ~~signatory~~ Member makes a final determination of the existence and amount of the subsidy and that, through the effects of the subsidy, the subsidized imports are causing injury, it may impose a countervailing duty in accordance with the provisions of this section unless the subsidy is withdrawn.

Article 18

IN ACCORDANCE WITH THE PROVISIONS OF ARTICLE 11, A PUBLIC NOTICE HAS BEEN GIVEN

Provisional measures and retroactivity

18.1 Provisional measures may be applied only if:

A-7.1

(a) ~~a~~ *AN* investigation has been initiated ~~in accordance published~~ to that effect and interested ~~signatories~~ Members and interested parties have been given adequate opportunities to submit information and make comments;

(b) a preliminary affirmative determination has been made ~~of~~ *OF* ~~subsidy exists and that there is material injury or threat thereof to a domestic industry caused by subsidized imports~~

(c) the authorities concerned judge that they are necessary to prevent injury being caused during the investigation.

---

[1] As used in this Agreement 'levy' shall mean the definitive or final legal assessment or collection of a duty or tax.   This definition is without prejudice to the meaning of the term 'levy' in Article VI of the ~~General Agreement~~ GATT ~~1993~~.

OF SUBSIDIZATION AND CONSEQUEN INJURY TO A DOMESTIC INDUSTRY, AND

0062

- 57 -

18.2 Provisional measures may take the form of provisional countervailing duties guaranteed by cash deposits or bonds equal to the amount of the provisionally calculated amount of subsidization.

18.3 Provisional measures shall not be applied sooner than 60 days from the date of initiation of the investigation.

A-7.4 18.4 The ~~application~~ APPLICATION of provisional measures shall be limited to as short a period as possible, not exceeding four months.

7-7.5 18.5 The relevant provisions of Article 17 shall be followed in the ~~imposition~~ APPLICATION of provisional measures.

7-10.2 18.6 Where a final determination of injury (but not of a threat thereof or of a material retardation of the establishment of an industry) is made, or in the case of a final determination of threat of injury, where the effect of the subsidized imports would, in the absence of the provisional measures, have led to a determination of injury, countervailing duties may be levied retroactively for the period for which provisional measures, if any, have been applied.

7-10.2 18.7 If the definitive countervailing duty is higher than the amount guaranteed by the cash deposit or bond, the difference shall not be collected. ~~If the definitive duty is less than the amount guaranteed by the cash deposit or bond, the excess amount shall be reimbursed or the bond released in an expeditious manner.~~

18.8 Except as provided in paragraph 6 above, where a determination of threat of injury or material retardation is made (but no injury has yet occurred), a definitive countervailing duty may be imposed only from the date of the determination of threat of injury or material retardation and any cash deposit made during the period of the application of provisional measures shall be refunded and any bonds released in an expeditious manner.

A-10.9 18.9 Where a final determination is negative, any cash deposit made during the period of the application of provisional measures shall be refunded and any bonds released in an expeditious manner.

18.10 In critical circumstances where for the subsidized product in question the authorities find that injury which is difficult to repair is caused by massive imports in a relatively short period of a product benefiting from subsidies paid or bestowed inconsistently with the provisions of the ~~General Agreement~~ GATT 1993 and of this Agreement and where it is deemed necessary, in order to preclude the recurrence of such injury, to assess countervailing duties retroactively on those imports, the definitive countervailing duties may be assessed on imports which were entered for consumption not more than ninety days prior to the date of application of provisional measures.

0063

IF THE DUTY FIXED IN THE FINAL DECISION IS LOWER THAN THE PROVISIONAL DUTY PAID OR PAYABLE, OR THE AMOUNT ESTIMATED FOR THE PURPOSE OF SECURITY, THE DIFFERENCE SHALL BE ~~...~~ AT THE CASE

- 58 -

UPON RECEIPT OF SATISFACTORY VOLUNTARY UNDERTAKINGS

Article 19

Undertakings

A-8.1

19.1 (a) Proceedings may[1] be suspended or terminated without the imposition of provisional measures or countervailing duties, ~~Undertakings are accepted~~ under which:

(i) the government of the exporting country agrees to eliminate or limit the subsidy or take other measures concerning its effects; or

A-8.2

(ii) the exporter agrees to revise its prices so that the ~~investigating~~ authorities are satisfied that the injurious ~~effect~~ of the subsidy is eliminated. *SUCH* Price increases under undertakings shall not be higher than necessary to eliminate the amount of the subsidy. Price undertakings shall not be sought or accepted from exporters unless the ~~importing signatory Member has (i) initiated an investigation in accordance with the provisions of Article 17 of this Agreement and~~ made preliminary determinations of subsidy and injury ~~resulting therefrom based on sufficient evidence in accordance with such investigation and (ii)~~ obtained the consent of the exporting signatory Member. Undertakings offered need not be accepted if the authorities ~~of the importing signatory Member~~ consider their acceptance impractical, for example if the number of actual or potential exporters is too great, or for other reasons.

AUTHORITIES OF THE IMPORTING COUNTRY HAVE

CAUSED BY SUCH SUBSIDIZATION AND

A-8.4

(b) If the undertakings are accepted, the investigation of injury shall nevertheless be completed if the exporting signatory Member so desires or the importing signatory Member so decides. In such a case, if a determination of no injury or threat thereof is made, the undertaking shall automatically lapse, except in cases where a determination of no threat of injury is due in large part to the existence of an undertaking. In such cases the authorities concerned may require ~~that~~ an undertaking be maintained for a reasonable period consistent with the provisions of this Agreement. ✓

A-8.5

(c) ~~Price~~ undertakings may be suggested by the authorities of the importing signatory Member, but no exporter shall be forced to enter into such an undertaking. The fact that governments or exporters do not offer such undertakings, or do not accept an invitation to do so, shall in no way prejudice the consideration of the case. However, the authorities are free to determine that a threat of injury is more likely to be realized if the subsidized imports continue.

---

[1] The word 'may' shall not be interpreted to allow the simultaneous continuation of proceedings with the implementation of price undertakings, except as provided in paragraph (b) of this Article.

IN THE EVENT THAT AN AFFIRMATIVE DETERMINATION OF SUBSIDIZATION AND INJURY IS MADE, THE UNDERTAKING SHALL ... PROVISIONS

0064

- 59 -

19.2 Authorities of an importing signatory Member may require any government or exporter from whom undertakings have been accepted to provide periodically information relevant to the fulfilment of such undertakings, and to permit verification of pertinent data. In case of violation of undertakings, the authorities of the importing signatory Member may take expeditious actions under this Agreement in conformity with its provisions which may constitute immediate application of provisional measures using the best information available. In such cases definitive duties may be levied in accordance with this Agreement on goods entered for consumption not more than ninety days before the application of such provisional measures, except that any such retroactive assessment shall not apply to imports entered before the violation of the undertaking.

19.3 Undertakings shall not remain in force any longer than countervailing duties could remain in force under this Agreement. The authorities of an importing signatory Member shall review the need for the continuation of any undertaking, where warranted, on their own initiative, or if interested exporters or importers of the product in question so request and submit positive information substantiating the need for such review.

Article 20

Duration of countervailing duties

20.1 A countervailing duty shall remain in force only as long as and to the extent necessary to counteract the subsidization which is causing injury. The authorities shall review the need for continued imposition of the duty, where warranted, on their own initiative or if any interested party so requests and submits positive information substantiating the need for review.

20.2 Notwithstanding the provisions of paragraph 1 above, any countervailing duty shall be terminated 5 years its imposition unless the authorities determine a review that there is 'good cause' for the continuation of the duty, after all interested parties have had a full opportunity to present their views.

Article 21

Measures to prevent circumvention of definitive countervailing duties

1.1 The authorities may include within the scope of application of a definitive countervailing duty on an imported product those parts or components destined for assembly or completion in the importing country, it has been established that:

(i)   the product assembled or completed from such parts or components in the importing country is a like product to a product which is subject to the definitive countervailing duty;

0065

[CONFORM TO TEXT
iP AD ART. 12].

- 60 -

(ii)   the assembly or completion of the like product in the importing
       country is carried out by a party which is related to or acting
       on behalf[1] of an exporter or producer whose exports of the like
       product are subject to a definitive countervailing duty;

(iii) the parts or components have been sourced in the country subject
       to the countervailing duty from the exporter or producer subject
       to the definitive countervailing duty, from suppliers in that
       country that have historically supplied the parts or components
       of the like product to the exporter or producer, or a party in
       the exporting country supplying parts of components of the like
       product on behalf of such an exporter or producer;

(iv)   the assembly operations in the importing country have started or
       expanded substantially and the imports of those parts of
       components have increased substantially since the initiation of
       the investigation which resulted in the definitive countervailing
       duty;

(v)   the total cost of parts or components imported is not less than
       70 per cent of the total cost of parts or components used in the
       assembly or completion operation, provided that in no case shall
       the parts and components be included within the scope of
       definitive measures if the value added by the assembly or
       completion operation is greater than 25 per cent of the
       ex-factory cost of the like product assembled or completed in the
       territory of the importing country;

(vi)   a determination is made that the inclusion of these parts or
       components within the scope of application of the definitive
       countervailing duty is necessary to prevent or offset the
       continuation or recurrence of the injury to the domestic industry
       producing a product like the product which is subject to the
       definitive countervailing duty.

21.2 The authorities may impose provisional measures in accordance with
Article 18 when they are satisfied that there is sufficient evidence that
the criteria set out in paragraphs 21.1(i-vi) are met. The authorities may
levy a definitive countervailing duty once all of the criteria in
paragraph 12.1 21.1 are fully satisfied. Any provisional or definitive
duty imposed under this paragraph shall not exceed the countervailing duty
in force on imports of the finished product in question.

---

[1] Such as when there is a contractual arrangement with the exporter or
producer in question (or with a party related to that exporter or producer)
covering the sale of the assembled product in the importing country.

0066

- 61 -

PURSUANT TO ARTICLE 11

Article 22

Public Notice and Explanation of
Countervailing Duty Determinations

INITIATION OF

A-13.1

22.1 When the ~~investigating~~ authorities are satisfied that there is sufficient evidence to justify ~~initiating~~ an investigation, the signatory Member or signatories Members, the products of which are subject to such investigation, other interested parties known to the investigating authorities to have an interest therein and the complainants shall be notified and a public notice shall be given.

[REPLACE W/ AD ¶ 6.1.3]

22.2 ~~Investigating authorities shall provide the full text of the complaint...~~ In cases where confidential information is provided in the complaint, investigating authorities shall require a non-confidential summary of such information in the non-confidential copy. The possibility of not providing a summary of confidential information shall be confined to extremely exceptional cases and in such cases the parties providing confidential information shall fully explain the reasons therefor.

~~Investigating authorities shall avoid...~~

[REPLACE W/ AD ¶ 5.5].

22.3 A public notice of the initiation of an investigation shall contain adequate information on the following: (i) the name of the exporting country and the product involved; (ii) the date of initiation of the investigation; (iii) a description of the subsidy practice or practices to be investigated; (iv) a summary of the factors on which the allegation of injury is based; (v) the address to which representations by interested parties should be directed; and (vi) the time-limits allowed to interested parties for making their views known.

22.4 Public notice shall be given of any preliminary or final determination, whether affirmative or negative, of any decision to accept an undertaking pursuant to Article 19, of the termination of such an undertaking, and of the revocation of a determination. Each such notice shall set forth the findings and conclusions reached on all issues of fact and law considered material by the investigating authorities *AND* in sufficient detail. All such notices shall be forwarded to the signatory Member or signatories Members the products of which are subject to such determination or undertaking and to other interested parties known to have an interest therein.

A-13.2

APPLICATION

THE NUMBER OF

¹It being understood that where ~~there are numerous~~ exporters ✓ the full text of the ~~complaint~~ should instead be provided only to the authorities of the exporting country or to the relevant trade association who then should forward copies to the exporters concerned.

INVOLVED IS PARTICULARLY

0067

- 62 -

[handwritten: ; THE NOTICE SHALL ... CONTAIN]

A-13.2.1

22.5 A public notice of the imposition of provisional measures shall set forth or otherwise make available adequate reasons for the preliminary determinations on the existence of a subsidy and injury (insofar as there is no separate preliminary injury determination and a notice thereof) and shall refer to the matters of fact and law which have led to arguments being accepted or rejected, due regard being paid to the requirement for the protection of confidential information, and in particular: (1) the names of the suppliers or when this is impracticable, the supplying countries involved; (ii) a description of the product which is sufficient for customs purposes; (iii) the amount of subsidy established and the basis on which the existence of a subsidy has been determined; (iv) factors which have led to the injury determination including factors other than subsidized imports which have been taken into account when the injury determination is made, insofar as there is no separate notice concerning such injury determination and including such information; (v) the main reasons leading to the determination.

A-13.2.2

[handwritten: PROVIDING FOR]

22.6 A public notice of suspension or conclusion of an investigation in the case of an affirmative determination providing for the imposition of a definitive duty or the acceptance of an undertaking shall contain or otherwise make available all relevant information on the matters of fact and law and reasons which have led to the imposition of final measures or to the acceptance of an undertaking, due regard being paid to the requirement for the protection of confidential information, and in particular: (i) the names of the suppliers or when this is impracticable, the supplying countries involved; (ii) a description of the product, which is sufficient for customs purposes; (iii) the amount of subsidy established and the basis on which the existence of a subsidy has been determined; (iv) factors which have led to the injury determination including information on factors other than dumping subsidies which have been taken into account when the injury determination is made, insofar as there is no separate notice concerning such injury determination and including such information; (v) the main reasons leading to the determination; (vi) the reasons for the acceptance or rejection of relevant arguments or claims made by the exporters and importers.

A-13.2.3

22.7 A public notice of the termination or suspension of an investigation following the acceptance of an undertaking pursuant to Article 19 shall include or otherwise make available the non-confidential part of *[handwritten: THIS]* undertaking.

A-13.3

22.8 The provisions of this Article ~~concerning notification and availability of information to parties~~ shall apply mutatis mutandis to the initiation and completion of administrative reviews pursuant to Article 20 and to decisions under Article 18 to apply duties retroactively.

0068

- 63 -

Article 23

Judicial Review

Each signatory Member shall maintain juridical, arbitral or administrative tribunals or procedures for the purpose, inter alia, of the prompt review of administrative action relating to final determinations and reviews of determinations within the meaning of Articles 17 and 20 of this Agreement. Such tribunals or procedures shall be independent of the authorities responsible for the determination or review in question, and shall provide all interested parties who participated in the administrative proceeding and are directly and individually affected by the administrative action with access to review.

A-14   S   AUTHORITIES

PART VI

Article 24

Committee on Subsidies and Countervailing Measures and other subsidiary bodies

24.1 There shall be established under this Agreement a Committee on Subsidies and Countervailing Measures composed of representatives from each of the signatories Members to this Agreement. The Committee shall elect its own Chairman and shall meet not less than twice a year and otherwise as envisaged by relevant provisions of this Agreement at the request of any signatory Member. The Committee shall carry out responsibilities as assigned to it under this Agreement or by the signatories Members and it shall afford signatories Members the opportunity of consulting on any matter relating to the operation of the Agreement or the furtherance of its objectives. The GATT MTO sSecretariat shall act as the secretariat to the Committee.

24.2 The Committee may set up subsidiary bodies as appropriate.

24.3 The Committee shall establish a Permanent Group of Experts composed of five independent persons, highly qualified in the fields of subsidies and trade relations. The experts will be elected by the Committee and one of them will rotate every year. The Committee may request the Group of Experts to prepare a proposed conclusion on the existence of a prohibited subsidy, as provided for in Article 4.5 above. The Committee may also seek an advisory opinion on the existence and nature of any subsidy.

24.4 The Group of Experts may be consulted by any signatory Member and give advisory opinions on the nature of any subsidy proposed to be introduced or currently maintained by that signatory Member. Such advisory opinions will be confidential and may not be invoked in proceedings under Article 7 of this Agreement.

0069

- 64 -

24.5 In carrying out their functions, the Committee and any subsidiary bodies may consult with and seek information from any source they deem appropriate.   However, before the Committee or a subsidiary body seeks such information from a source within the jurisdiction of a signatory Member, it shall inform the signatory Member involved.

PART VII

NOTIFICATION AND SURVEILLANCE

Article 25

Notifications

25.1 Signatories Members agree that, without prejudice to the provision of Article XVI:1 of the General Agreement GATT 1993, their notifications of subsidies shall be submitted not later than 30 June of each year and shall conform to the provisions of paragraphs 2 through 6 below.

25.2 Signatories Members shall notify any subsidy as defined in paragraphs 1 and 2 of Article 1 above, granted or maintained within their territory.

25.3 The content of notifications should be sufficiently specific to enable other signatories Members to evaluate the trade effects and to understand the operation of notified subsidy programmes.   In this connection and without prejudice to the contents and form of the questionnaire on subsidies[1], signatories Members shall ensure that their notifications contain the following information:

    (i)   form of a subsidy (i.e., grant, loan, tax concession, etc.);

    (ii)   subsidy per unit or, in cases where it is not possible, the total amount or the annual amount budgeted for that subsidy (indicating, if possible, the average subsidy per unit in the previous year);

    (iii) policy objective and/or purpose of a subsidy;

    (iv)   duration of a subsidy and/or any other time-limits attached to it;

    (v)   statistical data permitting an assessment of the trade effects of a subsidy.

---

[1]The Committee shall establish a Working Party to review the contents and form of the questionnaire as contained in BISD, 9S/193-194.

0070

외 무 부

종 별 :

번 호 : GVW-0834   일 시 : 92 0414 1800

수 신 : 장관(통기)

발 신 : 주 제네바 대사

제 목 : MTO 협정

대: WGV-0515

표제회정 2 조 3 항에 관한 GATT 사무국 ROESSLER 법률국장 의견을 아래 보고함.

1. GATT 93 이 GATT 47 과 법적으로 상이(LEGALLY DISTINCT) 하다고 규정한 MTO 협정 2 조 3 항은 일종의 경과 규정으로서, 각료회의(IMPLEMENTING CONFERENCE)가 결정하는 MTO 협정 발효시점까지 수락서를 기탁치못하는 국가, 상기 발효 시점부터 2 년내에 수락서를 기탁치 못하느 국가 및 동 2 년 경과 후에도 상당기간 수락서를 기탁못하는 국가들에 대해서는 현행 GATT(GATT 47)이 적용된다는 의미임.(상기 각시점내 수락서를 기탁하는 국가간에는 GATT 93 이 적용된다는 의미에서 구분 필요)

2. 상기 의미를 현행 문구와 같이 간접적으로 표현한 것은 (1) 수락서 미 기탁국에는 GATT 47 이 적용된다고 명시적으로 규정할 경우 GATT 47 과 GATT 93 간의 상당기간 병존을 암시하는 결과가 되므로 MTO 설립을 추진하는 입장에서는 바람직 하지 못하다는 점, (2) "LEGALLY DISTINCT"하다고 규정하는 것이 GATT 93에 대한 가입 INCENTIVE 효과가 높다는 점이 고려되었기 때문임.

3. 동규정은 GATT 47 하의 제결정, 양해, 패널 보고서의 법적 효과와는 아무런 관련이 없으며, 이문제는 16 조 1 항에 기존의 결정, 관행등을 승계하도록 명시적으로 규정하고 있음. 끝

(대사 박수길-국장)

예고 92.12.31. 까지

검 토 필 (1992.6 30.)

통상국   주주국

외 무 부

종 별 :

번 호 : GVW-0873   일 시 : 92 0424 1820

수 신 : 장관(통기, 경기원, 재무부, 농수산부, 상공부, 특허청)

발 신 : 주 제네바 대사

제 목 : UR/법제화 그룹 비공식 회의(개별 협정문, 4)

연: GVW-0822

1. TBT 협정문 사무국 수정안 (TEXT 611) 및 농산물 협정 PART C (위생 및 식물검역 조치, SPS) 사무국 수정안 (TEXT 707)에 대한 4.22-23간의 표제회의 요지를 아래 보고함.

가. 양 협정문의 적용 범위

- TBT 협정문 및 SPS TEXT 의 적용범위와 관련 (TBT 1조, SPS 4 항), 양협정의 관계를 분명히 하기 위해 TBT 협정 1조 5항 하단에 SPS 4 항의 취지를 추가하자고 미국이 제의함.

- 이에 대해 카나다는 TBT 협정 1조 3항 및 1조 5항을 종합한 별첨 수정문안을 제의하면서 SPS 4 항이 불요함을 지적한바, EC, 아르헨티나, 핀랜드등은 양협정은 동등한 지위를 가지므로 SPS 4항은 초안대로 유지할 것을 제의함.

나. 위생 및 검역 조치(SPS TEXT)

0 서문

- SPS TEXT 의 명칭과 관련, DECISION 을 AGREEMENT 로 바꾼 사무국 수정안에 대해 동수정은 T 3 의 MANDATE 를 벗어난다는 EC의 지적에 대해 카나다가 동조한 반면, 일본은 DECISION 의 법적 지위가 불분명한 점에 비추어 AGREEMENT 용어가 적절하다는 입장을 개진함.

0 8항 (SPS TEXT 에 따른 SPS 조치), 10항(국제기준에 합당한 SPS 조치)의 갓트상 법적 지위

- 8항 및 10항상의 SPS 조치는 갓트 규정상 합법적인 조치이므로, 8항 2줄 및 10항 3줄의 PRESUMED 는 DEEMED 로 수정할 것을 제의한바, 카나다는 동 조치가 갓트 7 규정에 반드시 합치한다고 볼수는 없으므로 PRESUMED 단어 존치를 주장함.

통상국   2차보   경기원   재무부   농수부   상공부   특허정

O 36 항, 37항(분쟁해결 절차)

- 통합 분쟁해결 절차와 제 36항 및 제 37항 절차와 관련, 동항의 특별 절차 문제여부가 제기되어 사무국이 검토의견을 추후 제시할 것을 요청한 가운데 36항 절차는특별 절차이나 37항절차는 특별절차가 아니라는 카나다의 의견제시가 있었음.(36 항절차는 각 협정문의 특별분쟁해결 절차에 대한 별도 논의시 재론하기로함)

O ANNEX B. 3,6 항(SPS 조치의 통보)

- SPS 조치의 통보와 관련, 홍콩이 동항의 문구 'ON THE NATIONAL LEVEL' 의 필요성에 대해 의문을 제기한바, EC 가 지방정부 차원의 조치는 통보의무가 없으므로 동문구는 필요하다는 의견을 개진함.

- 사무국은 모든 SPS 조치는 통보되어야 하므로 동문구는 필요하다는 의견을 제시한바, EC 가 이에 동조한 반면, 카나다는 추후 재론할 것을 희망함.

2. 한편 4.23 오전에는 MTO 설립 협정문 및 각개별 협정문안상의 용어 COUNTRY(COUNTRIES)에 대한 별첨 홍콩 제의를 논의하기위해 사무국 주재로 소규모 비공식 회의가 개최되었는바, 동제의 취지대로 협정문상의 COUNTRY 개념에는 MTO 회원국인 독립관세 영역이 포함되는 것으로 해석하기로 함.

(홍콩 제안중 INCLUDE 이하는 ANY SEPERATE CUPERATECUSTOMS TERRITORY MEMBER OF THE MTO 로 수정)

첨부: 1. TBT 협정문 및 SPS TEXT 관련 조항

2. COUNTRY 개념에 대한 홍콩 제안. 끝

(GVW(F)-275)

(대사 박수길-국장)

주 제 네 바 대 표 부

번 호 : GVE(F) - 0275   년월일 : 20424   시간 : 1820

수 신 : 장   판(등기, 경기원, 상중부, 재무부, 농림수산부)

발 신 : 주 제네바대사

제 목 : GVW-0813 첨부

총 9 매(표지포함)

보 안 통 제	

외신과 통 제	

0074

Proposal by Canada   **32**

Agreement on Technical Barriers to Trade

1.3   This Agreement applies to technical regulations, standards and
conformity assessment procedures used in relation to all products,
including industrial and agricultural products, with the exception of
sanitary and phytosanitary measures as defined in Annex 1A of the Agreement
on the Application of Sanitary and Phytosanitary Measures.

1dg92-49

0075

- 80 -

Article 1

General Provisions

1.1 General terms for standardization and procedures for assessment of conformity shall normally have the meaning given to them by definitions adopted within the United Nations system and by international standardizing bodies taking into account their context and in the light of the object and purpose of this Agreement.

1.2 However, for the purposes of this Agreement the meaning of the terms given in Annex 1 applies.

1.3 All products, including industrial and agricultural products, shall be subject to the provisions of this Agreement.

1.4 Purchasing specifications prepared by governmental bodies for production or consumption requirements of governmental bodies are not subject to the provisions of this Agreement but are addressed in the Agreement on Government Procurement, according to its coverage.

1.5 The provisions of this Agreement do not apply to sanitary and phytosanitary measures as defined in Annex A of the Decision of the CONTRACTING PARTIES Agreement on the Application of Sanitary and Phytosanitary Measures.

1.6 All references in this Agreement to technical regulations, standards and conformity assessment procedures shall be construed to include any amendments thereto and any additions to the rules or the product coverage thereof, except amendments and additions of an insignificant nature.

TECHNICAL REGULATIONS AND STANDARDS

Article 2

Preparation, Adoption and Application of Technical Regulations by Central Government Bodies

With respect to their central government bodies:

2.1 Parties Members shall ensure that in respect of technical regulations, products imported from the territory of any Party Member shall be accorded treatment no less favourable than that accorded to like products of national origin and to like products originating in any other country.

2.2 Parties Members shall ensure that technical regulations are not prepared, adopted or applied with a view to or with the effect of creating unnecessary obstacles to international trade. For this purpose, technical regulations shall not be more trade-restrictive than necessary to fulfil a

0076

- 21 -

PART-6

In respect of the following ~~Decision~~ Agreement on Sanitary and Phytosanitary Measures, it had been proposed that consumer concerns with relation to health, as well as animal welfare, should be fully addressed by this ~~{Decision}~~ Agreement. Most participants, however, were of the view that only some aspects of consumer concerns related to health were within the scope of the ~~Decision~~ Agreement, and insisted that other consumer concerns, along with animal welfare, could most appropriately be dealt with through other instruments.

~~DECISION-BY-CONTRACTING-PARTIES~~ AGREEMENT ON THE APPLICATION OF SANITARY AND PHYTOSANITARY MEASURES

~~The-CONTRACTING-PARTIES,~~

Reaffirming that no ~~contracting-party~~ Member should be prevented from adopting or enforcing measures necessary to protect human, animal or plant life or health, subject to the requirement that they are not applied in a manner which would constitute a means of arbitrary or unjustifiable discrimination between ~~countries~~ Members where the same conditions prevail or a disguised restriction on international trade;

Desiring to improve the human health, animal health and phytosanitary situation in all ~~contracting-parties~~ Members;

Noting that sanitary and phytosanitary measures are often applied on the basis of bilateral agreements or protocols;

Desiring the establishment of a multilateral framework of rules and disciplines to guide the adoption, development and the enforcement of sanitary and phytosanitary measures in order to minimize their negative effects on trade;

Recognising the important contribution that international standards, guidelines and recommendations can make in this regard;

Desiring to further the use of harmonized sanitary and phytosanitary measures between ~~contracting-parties~~ Members, on the basis of international standards, guidelines and recommendations developed by the relevant international organizations including the Codex Alimentarius Commission, the International Office of Epizootics, and the relevant international and regional organizations operating within the framework of the International Plant Protection Convention;

Recognising that developing ~~contracting-parties~~ Members may encounter special difficulties in complying with the sanitary or phytosanitary measures of importing ~~contracting-parties~~ Members, and as a consequence, in access to markets, and also in the formulation and application of sanitary or phytosanitary measures in their own territories, and desiring to assist them in their endeavours in this regard;

0077

- 22 -

<u>Desiring</u> therefore to elaborate rules for the application of the provisions of the ~~General Agreement~~ <u>GATT 1993</u> which relate to the use of sanitary or phytosanitary measures, in particular the provisions of Article XX(b)[*] ;

~~Decide~~ <u>It is agreed</u> as follows:

1.   This ~~decision~~ <u>Agreement</u> applies to all sanitary and phytosanitary measures which may, directly or indirectly, affect international trade. Such measures shall be developed and applied in accordance with the provisions of this ~~decision~~ <u>Agreement</u>.

2.   For the purposes of this ~~decision~~ <u>Agreement</u>, the definitions provided in Annex A shall apply.

3.   The annexes are an integral part of this ~~decision~~ <u>Agreement</u>.

4.   Nothing in this ~~decision~~ <u>Agreement</u> shall affect the rights of ~~parties~~ <u>Members</u> ~~to~~ <u>under</u> the Agreement on Technical Barriers to Trade with respect to measures not within the scope of this ~~decision~~ <u>Agreement</u>.

<u>Basic Rights and Obligations</u>

5.   ~~Contracting parties~~ <u>Members</u> have the right to take sanitary and phytosanitary measures necessary for the protection of human, animal or plant life or health, provided that such measures are not inconsistent with the provisions of this decision.

6.   ~~Contracting parties~~ <u>Members</u> shall ensure that sanitary and phytosanitary measures are applied only to the extent necessary to protect human, animal or plant life or health, are based on scientific principles and are not maintained against available scientific evidence.

7.   ~~Contracting parties~~ <u>Members</u> shall ensure that their sanitary and phytosanitary measures do not arbitrarily or unjustifiably discriminate between ~~contracting parties~~ <u>Members</u> where identical or similar conditions prevail, including between their own territory and other ~~contracting parties~~ <u>Members</u>. Sanitary and phytosanitary measures shall not be applied in a manner which would constitute a disguised restriction on international trade.

8.   Sanitary or phytosanitary measures which conform to the relevant provisions of this ~~decision~~ <u>Agreement</u> shall be presumed to be in accordance with the obligations of the ~~contracting parties~~ <u>Members</u> under the provisions of the ~~General Agreement~~ <u>GATT 1993</u> which relate to the use of sanitary or phytosanitary measures, in particular the provisions of Article XX(b).

---

[*]   In this ~~decision~~ <u>Agreement</u>, reference to Article XX(b) includes also the chapeau of that Article.

0078

- 23 -

Harmonization

9.   To harmonize sanitary and phytosanitary measures on as wide a basis as possible, ~~contracting-parties~~ Members shall base their sanitary or phytosanitary measures on international standards, guidelines or recommendations, where they exist, except as otherwise provided for in this ~~decision~~ Agreement.

10.   Sanitary or phytosanitary measures which conform to international standards, guidelines or recommendations shall be deemed to be necessary to protect human, animal or plant life or health, and presumed to be consistent with the relevant provisions of this ~~decision~~ Agreement and of the ~~General Agreement~~ GATT 1993.

11.   ~~Contracting-parties~~ Members may introduce or maintain sanitary or phytosanitary measures which result in a higher level of sanitary or phytosanitary protection than would be achieved by measures based on the relevant international standards, guidelines or recommendations, if there is a scientific justification, or as a consequence of the level of protection a ~~contracting-party~~ Member determines to be appropriate in accordance with the relevant provisions of paragraphs 16 through 23. Notwithstanding the above, all measures which result in a level of sanitary or phytosanitary protection different from that which would be achieved by measures based on international standards, guidelines or recommendations shall not be inconsistent with any other provision of this ~~decision~~ Agreement.

12.   ~~Contracting-parties~~ Members shall play a full part within the limits of their resources in the relevant international organizations and their subsidiary bodies, in particular the Codex Alimentarius Commission, the International Office of Epizootics, and in the international and regional organizations operating within the framework of the International Plant Protection Convention, to promote within these organizations the development and periodic review of standards, guidelines and recommendations with respect to all aspects of sanitary and phytosanitary measures.

13.   The Committee on Sanitary and Phytosanitary Measures, as provided for in paragraphs 38 and 41, shall develop a procedure to monitor the process of international harmonization and coordinate efforts in this regard with the relevant international organizations.

Equivalence

14.   ~~Contracting-parties~~ Members shall accept the sanitary or phytosanitary measures of other ~~contracting-parties~~ Members as equivalent, even if these measures differ from their own or from those used by other ~~contracting parties~~ Members trading in the same product, if the exporting ~~contracting party~~ Member objectively demonstrates to the importing ~~contracting-party~~ Member that its measures achieve the importing ~~contracting-party's~~ Member's appropriate level of sanitary or phytosanitary protection. For this purpose, reasonable access shall be given, upon request, to the importing ~~contracting-party~~ Member for inspection, testing and other relevant procedures.

0079

- 27 -

Sanitary and Phytosanitary Measures, provided for below, is enabled to grant to such countries, upon request, specified, time-limited exceptions in whole or in part from obligations under this decision Agreement, taking into account their financial, trade and development needs.

34. Contracting-parties Members should encourage and facilitate the active participation of developing countries Members in the relevant international organizations.

Consultations and Dispute Settlement

35. The provisions of Articles XXII and XXIII of the General-Agreement GATT 1993 and the as elaborated and applied by the MTO Understanding on Rules and Procedures Governing the Settlement of Disputes under-Articles XXII-and-XXIII-of-the-General-Agreement-on-Tariffs-and-Trade-as-adopted-by the-CONTRACTING-PARTIES shall apply to consultations and the settlement of disputes under this decision Agreement, except as otherwise specifically provided herein.

36. In a dispute under this decision Agreement involving scientific or technical issues, a panel should seek advice from experts chosen by the panel in consultation with the parties to the dispute. To this end, the panel may, when it deems it appropriate, establish an advisory technical experts group, or consult the relevant international organizations, at the request of either party to the dispute or on its own initiative.

37. Nothing in this decision Agreement shall impair the rights of contracting-parties Members under other international agreements, including the rights to resort to the good offices or dispute settlement mechanisms of other international organizations or established under any international agreement.

Administration

38. A Committee on Sanitary and Phytosanitary Measures shall be established to provide a regular forum for consultations. It shall carry out the functions necessary to implement the provisions of this decision Agreement and the furtherance of its objectives, in particular with respect to harmonization. The Committee shall reach its decisions by consensus.

39. The Committee shall encourage and facilitate ad hoc consultations or negotiations among its members on specific sanitary or phytosanitary issues. The Committee shall encourage the use of international standards, guidelines or recommendations by all contracting-parties Members and, in this regard, shall sponsor technical consultation and study with the objective of increasing coordination and integration between international and national systems and approaches for approving the use of food additives or for establishing tolerances for contaminants in foods, beverages and feedstuffs.

40. The Committee shall maintain close contact with the relevant international organizations in the field of sanitary and phytosanitary

0080

- 35 -

3.4 Developed contracting-parties Members shall, if requested by other contracting-parties Members, provide copies of the documents or, in case of voluminous documents, summaries of the documents covered by a specific notification in either English, French or Spanish.

3.5 The GATT MTO Secretariat shall promptly circulate copies of the notifications to all contracting-parties Members and interested international organizations and draw the attention of developing contracting-parties Members to any notifications relating to products of particular interest to them.

3.6 Contracting-parties Members shall designate one single central government authority as responsible for the implementation, on the national level, of the provisions concerning notification procedures according to paragraphs 3.1, 3.2, 3.3 and 3.4 of this Annex.

4.   General reservations

4.1 Nothing in this decision shall be construed as requiring:

   (a) the provision of particulars or copies of drafts or the publication of texts other than in the language of the contracting-party Member except as stated in paragraph 3.4 of this Annex; or

   (b) contracting-parties Members to disclose confidential information which would impede enforcement of sanitary or phytosanitary legislation or which would prejudice the legitimate commercial interests of particular enterprises.

0081

Hong Kong, 23 April 1992

Draft Explanatory Note

The terms "country" or "countries" as used in the Agreement
Establishing the MTO and the Multilateral Trade Agreements and
Plurilateral Trade Agreements in the Annexes to this Agreement are to be
understood to include any member of the MTO, which is either a State or
a separate customs territory.

0082

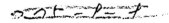

외　무　부

종　별 :

번　호 : GVW-0885　　　　　　　　　　일　시 : 92 0427 1600

수　신 : 장관(봉기,경기원,재무부,농수산부,상공부,특허청)

발　신 : 주 제네바 대사

제　목 : UR/법제화 그룹 비공식 회의(개별 협정문)

　　1. 농산물 협정 사무국 수정안(TEXT 707)에 대한 표제회의 4.23-24 논의
요지를아래보고함.(최농무관, 신서기관, 김농무관보 참석)

　　가. 사무국 수정안 INTRODUCTION

　　0 제 2항

　　- 비관세 조치의 감축 약속에 관한 PART B 의 법적 형태(농산물 협정의 부속서
또는 별도협정등)에 관한 논의는 추후 거론하자는 사무국 제안에 대해

　　- 미국, 호주, 뉴질랜드, 우루과이 등은 PART B 는 농산물 협정의 필수적 부분을
구성하므로 T-3에서 반드시 논의되어야 한다고 주장한 반면, EC,일본, 스위스, 북구,
멕시코 등은 PART B 는 협상 타결시 소멸할 절차 사항으로 이해된다고하면서
추후논의할 것은 제의한 PART 2 둘째문장에 유보입장을 표명하여, 의장이
현단계에서는 PART A 만 논의하되 추후 PART B 논의를 배제하지 않는 것으로
논의결과를 정리하였음.

　　0 제 4항(분해 해결 절차, 18조)

　　- PART A 18 조의 갓트 통합 분쟁해결 절차내지 위와 관련, 미국, 호주, 카나다등
은 18조 절차가 특별 절차가 아니라는 입장인 반면, 멕시코는 특별 절차임을 주장하여
통합 분쟁해결 절차의 예외에 관한 종합 토의시 재론키로 함.

　　0 농산물 협정과 보조금 협정과의 관계

　　- 국내 보조, 수출 보조에 관한 양협정문간의 상충부분에 대한 조화 문제는 T3 의
권한밖임을 인정한 가운데

　　- 미국, 카나다, 뉴질랜드등은 양협정문간의 조화 필요성을 지적한 반면

　　- EC, 멕시코, 북구등은 양협정문은 상호 독자적인 협정이라는 입장을 개진함.

　　나. 1조(개념 정의)

통상국	2차보	경기원	재무부	농수부	상공부	특허청	

외신 1과　통제관

0083

O F 항 이행기간의 개념과 관련, 동 기간을 <u>6년으로 명문화한 사무국 수정안</u>에 대해 필랜드는 <u>역년을 사용하는 경우에는 이행기간이 7년이 될수 있는 점을 감안하여이에 반대함</u>.

- 이에 대해 호주, 뉴질랜드, 알젠틴등이 협정문 내용에 충실하기 위해서는 사무국안대로 6년을 명문화할 것을 주장하였음.

O G 항 MARKET ACCESS CONCESSION 관련 CONCESSION의 개념이 4조 1항에서 명확하게 정의되고 있으므로 G 항은 삭제할 것을 일본이 제안하였으나, 호주, 뉴질랜드, 아르헨티나등은 동항의 의의는 4조 1항과 다르므로 존치해야 한다는 입장임.(이에 대해 사무국은 G 항은 양허의 개념을 규정한 조항이고 4조 1항은 양허 교섭결과에 관한조항으로 해석된다는 의견을 제시)

- EC 는 G 항과 관련, 기존 갓트 양허와 새로운 양허의 관계 즉 갓트 28조 절차에 있어서 기존 양허 세율과 수출 보조, 국내 보조 감축약속과의 관계에 대한 사무국의 명확한 해석을 요구한바, 사무국은 예비적 의견임을 전제로 새로운 양허 세율은 기존 갓트 양허세율보다 높일수 없는 것이 갓트의 일반적 원칙이므로 농산물 협상결과새로운 양허세율이 기존 세율보다 높아질 경우에는 이를 위한 새로운 규정이 필요할것이라고 함. 기존의 국내 보조, 수출보조금 감축을 양허하는 경우 기존 관세 양허와의 관계에 대하여는 분명한 결론없이 추후 재론하기로 하였음.

- G 항의 CONCESSION 개념에 대한 명확화가 필요하다는 제의가 있었으나 아르헨티나는 동항의 정의로 충분하다는 의견을 제시

다. 3조 (양허 및 감축약속의 포함)

O 미국은 각국의 양허 및 감축 약속을 C/S 에 명기할 의무를 명문화하는 3항의 신설을 제의한바, 의장은 미국제안의 취지를 살려 1항및 2항의 MEMBER 를 EACH MEMBER로 수정할것을 제의한데 대해 EC 는 3항 신설을 반대함.

O 1항(양허) 관련, MTO 협정 발효 이후 가입국(ACCEDING MEMBER) 의 양허표 첨부 의무가 불분명하다는 카나다 지적에 대해, 의장은 동항의 취지에 비추어 다음과 같이 수정할 것을 제안하였으나, 태국은 갓트 회원국중 MTO ACCEDING MEMBER 로 되는갓트 회원국의 기존 갓트양허표는 존중되어야 하므로 이에 반대한다는 입장제시

- THE SCHEDULES OF MARKET ACCESS CONCESSIONS RELATING TO EACH MEMBER SHALL BE PART OF THE SHCEDULES OF CONCESSIONS ANNEXED TO THE GATT 1993 IN ACCORDANCE WITH THE ARTICLE 2 PARAGRAPH 7 OF THE GATT 1993.

PAGE 2

0084

0 2항의 국내 보조 및 수출 보조 감축약속과 관련, 보조금 협정과 농산물 협정간의 상충가능성 여부에 대한 카나다의 의문제기에 양협정의 성격상 상충 가능성이 없다는 사무국의 해석이 있었음.

0 2항 감축 약속의 법적 지위에 대한 규정이 없다는 미국의 지적에 대해, 사무국측이 동항의 말미에 동 감축약속에도 1항의 양허에 대한 갓트의 관련 규정(2조 및 28조)이 해당된다는 취지의 문항이 추가될 필요성이 있다는 견해를 제시하였음.

라. 4조(양허)

0 미국은 2항의 취지가 비관세 조치를 제거하는데 있다고 언급하면서 이를 분명히 하기 위해 UNDERTAKE 를 SHALL 로 수정하고, 2줄 MEASURES뒤에 OF THE KIND 를 추가하자는 제의를 한 뒤,동 제안의 범위에 대한 EC 의 질문에 대해 갓트 11조 상의 수량제한 조치가 포함된다고 설명함.

- 일본, 카나다, EC, 멕시코등이 동 제안은 내용의 실질적 변화를 초래한다는 입장을 개진

마. 5조(특별 세이프가드 조치, SSG)

0 미국은 SSG 는 관세화 품목에만 적용된다는 것이 입안 취지이므로 이를 분명히 하기위해 1항 4줄 PRODUCT 뒤에 WHICH HAS BEEN SUBJECTED TO TARIFFICATION EXCERCISE 를 삽입하자고 제안함.

0 이에 대하여 뉴질랜드, 알젠틴, 브라질등은 지지하였고, 일본, 카나다, 멕시코는 농산물 협상시 SSG 의 COVERAGE 에 대한 합의가 없었으므로 동 제안은 실질 의미의 변화를 초래한다는 유보입장을 표명함.

0 뉴질랜드는 2줄 TAKE RECOURSE TO 를 APPLY AN ADDITIONAL DUTY IN ACCORDANCEWITH 로 수정할 것을 제안함.

0 일본, 카나다는 SSG 의 2가지 발동조건의 관계가 불분명하다고 하면서 1항 3줄BELOW 다음에 BUT NOT CONCURRENTLY(BOTH) 를 삽입하자고함.

바. 7조(국내 보조)

0 3항의 COUNTERVAILING MEASURE 의 범위에 대하여 EC, 일본, 카나다등이 보조금 협정상의 어느조치를 의미하느냐는 의문을 제기하였는바, 사무국은 상기 상계조치는 보조금 협정의 5부 상의 조치라고 언급함.

0 파키스탄, 인도등은 개도국 우대와 관련된 6조 2항의 국내 보조도 NON-ACTIONABLE 해야 한다고 하면서 3항 1줄 ANNEX 2 다음에 AND THOSE IN PARA 2

PAGE 3

0085

ARTICLE 6 를삽입하자고 제안함.

사. 10조(수출 보조 우회 규정)

0 EC, 일본, 인도등은 2항의 DISCIPLINE 의미가 불분명하다고 하면서 다자간 협정만을 의미하도록보다 구체적 규정이 필요하다고 하였음.

0 3항 관련, 농산물 뿐만 아니라 전 분야의 상품에 주어지는 보조금과 동 3항의관계가 분명치 않다는 인도, 카나다의 지적에 대해 아르헨티나는 농산물 협정과 보조금 협정은 별개의 협정이며 전분야의 상품에 주어지는 보조금은 보조금협정의 규율대상이므로 문제가 없다는 의견을 제시함.

아. 11조 (가공품 수출 보조)

0 카나다는 3조와 11조를 함께 해석할 경우 가공품수출 보조에 대한 기존 갓트 규정해석에 미치는 효과를 질문하였는바, 알제틴은 이에 대하여 농산물 협정상의 가공품에 대한 규정은 감축약속 이행기간중에만 적용되고, 그 이후는 갓트의 일반규정에적용된다고 하면서 8조의 문안수정에 반대하였음.

자. 12조(심각한 피해)

0 EC 는 동조하단의 의미가 불분명하므로 THE PRESUMPTION 이하를 THESE SUBSIDIES SHALL BE PRESUMED IN CONFORMITY WITH THE ARTICLES OF 16 AND 3 OF GATT '93으로 수정제의한데 대해, 호주, 뉴질랜드,아르헨티나 등이 동제안은 T3 에서 논의될사항이 아님을 지적함.(아르헨티나는 동 조항은 감축 약속에 관한 한시적 규정임을 지적)

차. 17조(감축약속에 대한 검토)

0 17조 5항의 REFORM PROGRAMME 의 의미가 분명하지 않다는 미국의 지적에 대해REFORM PROGRAMME 은 감축 약속에 따른 과도기간의 개혁 조치이고, 19조 REFORM PROCESS 는 과도기간 이후까지 포함하는 개혁 조치라는 사무국의 설명이 있었으나 미국은동 설명에 만족하지 않았음.

카. 제 19 조 (개혁조치에 대한 계속적인 검토)

0 동 조항에서 이행기간에 대한 개도국 우대원칙이 반영되어야 한다는 에집트의발언에대해, 뉴질랜드는 개도국에 대한 이행기간은 자동적으로 10 년이 되는것은 아니고 개도국의 감축약속 이행결과를 감안하여 10년 까지 연장할수 있는 것으로 해석된다 는 입장을 개진함.

타. 부속서 2(감축대상이 아닌 국내 보조)3항(식량안보)

0 동 항 1줄의 REVENUE FOREGONE 개념에 대한 미국의 질문에 대해
아르헨티나는예산   지출(BUDGETARY   OUTLAY)에   대응하는   개념이라는   의견을
제시하였으며, 한편으로 사무국은 GENERALTEXATION 은 제외하였음.

0 3줄의 NATIONAL LEGISLATION 과 관련, 인도는 규칙, 명령등을 포함한 개념인
NATIONAL MEASURES로 수정하는 것이 입안 취지에 맞는다는 견해를 제시함. 미국과
뉴질랜드는 동항의 입안 취지가 NATIONAL LEGISLATION 이라는 입장을 밝힘.

2. 차기 회의는 5.4 주간에 재개되어 FOG,정부조달협정, 서비스 협정, TRIPS
협정등을 논의할 예정임.

첨부: 농산물 협정 사무국 수정안 관련 부분. 끝

(GVW(F)-0276)

(대사 박수길-국장)

주 제 네 바 대 표 부

번 호 : GVF(F) - 0276   년원일 : 20527   시간 : 1600

수 신 : 장   관 (동기,경기원,재무부,농림수산부,상공부,특허청)

발 신 : 주 제네바대사

제 목 : UR 협상

총 8 매(표지포함)

외신관	
봉 제	

동향분석처	과기처	환경처	동자부	농수부	재무부	상공부	경기원	공보처	안기부	청와대	외연안	문합국	경제국	국기국	국학국	미주국	아주국	논석관	외경실	二차보	一차보	정보부처
1		1	1	1	1	1	1						0			1	1	1	1			

0088

707   15 April 1992

Review of Individual Texts in the Draft Final Act

(Texts on Agriculture)

Informal Note by the Secretariat

INTRODUCTION

1.   The present working paper has been prepared to assist the Legal
Drafting Group in its consideration of the following texts on Agriculture
in the Draft Final Act (MTN.TNC/W/FA):-

        Part A: Uruguay Round Agreement on Agriculture
        Part C: Decision by CONTRACTING PARTIES on the Application of
                  Sanitary and Phytosanitary Measures
        Part D: Declaration on Measures Concerning the Possible Negative
                  Effects of the Reform Programme on Net Food-Importing
                  Developing Countries

2.   Part B of the text on agriculture, which relates to the modalities for
the establishment of specific binding commitments to be incorporated in
Members' Schedules, is not proposed for specific review by the Legal
Drafting Group at this stage. At the appropriate stage consideration may
need to be given, inter alia, to whether particular sections of Part B
should be annexed to the Agreement on Agriculture, or be preserved in some
other form in a basic document.

3.   The terminology used in the individual texts has been rectified in the
following manner and where appropriate:

    (i)   References to "participant", "participants", "countries",
          "contracting parties" have been replaced by "Member" and
          "Members".

    (ii) References to "developing participants" or "developing countries"
          have been changed to "developing Members" and "developed
          participants" have been changed to "developed Members"

4.   The provisions on dispute settlement in the text of the Agreement on
Agriculture and Agreement on the Application of Sanitary and Phytosanitary
Measures will need to be examined in relation to those in the draft text of
the Understanding on Rules and Procedures Governing the Settlement of
Disputes in order that, inter alia, references in the Understanding to
special or additional rules or procedures contained in the covered
agreements can be finalized.

Agreement on the Application of Sanitary and Phytosanitary Measures

5.   Part C of the Text on Agriculture (Section L of MTN.TNC/W/FA) is
presently drafted in the form of a Decision by the CONTRACTING PARTIES.
Given that this text will be part of Annex 1A of the Agreement establishing

0089

- 5 -

(c)   "budgetary outlays" or "outlays" include revenue foregone;

(d)   "equivalent commitments" are as specified in the Schedules of domestic support commitments and the related supporting material;

(e)   "export subsidies" refer to subsidies contingent upon export performance including the export subsidies listed in Article 9 of this Agreement;

(f)   "implementation period" covers the ~~a six-year~~ period commencing in the year 1993 and ending in the year 1999;

(g)   "market access concessions" include all market access commitments undertaken pursuant to this Agreement;

(h)   "year" in (f) above and in relation to the specific commitments of a ~~participant~~ Member refers to the calendar, financial or marketing year specified in the Schedule of commitments relating to that ~~participant~~ Member.

Article 2 - Product Coverage

This Agreement applies to the products listed in Annex 1 to this Agreement, hereinafter referred to as agricultural products.

Part II

Article 3 - Incorporation of Concessions and Commitments

1.   The Schedules of market access concessions relating to ~~participants~~ Members shall be annexed to the Uruguay Round (1992) Protocol to the General Agreement on Tariffs and Trade.

2.   Schedules of domestic support and export competition commitments relating to ~~participants~~ Members shall be annexed to the aforementioned protocol as constituting commitments limiting subsidization.

Part III

Article 4 - Market Access Concessions

1.   Market access concessions contained in Schedules relate to bindings and reductions of tariffs, and to other market access commitments as specified therein.

2.   ~~Participants~~ Members undertake not to resort to, or revert to, any measures which have been converted into ordinary customs duties pursuant to concessions under this Agreement.

0090

- 6 -

Article 5 - Special Safeguard Provisions

1.   Notwithstanding the provisions of Article II:1(b) of the General Agreement GATT 1993, any participant Member may take recourse to the provisions of paragraphs 4 and 5 below in connection with the importation of an agricultural product which is specified in its Schedule as being the subject of a concession in respect of which the provisions of this Article may be invoked, if:

(i)   the volume of imports of that product entering the customs territory of the participant Member granting the concession during any year exceeds a trigger level equal to 125 per cent of the corresponding average quantity during the three preceding years for which data are available or 125 per cent of the minimum access opportunity, whichever is the greater[1]; or, but not concurrently,

(ii)   the price at which imports of that product may enter the customs territory of the participant Member granting the concession, as determined on the basis of the c.i.f. import price of the shipment concerned expressed in terms of its domestic currency, falls below a trigger price equal to the average 1986 to 1988 reference price[2], for the product concerned.

---

[1]Recourse to this provision requires that the average quantity or minimum access opportunities represent commercially significant levels of imports.

[2]The reference price used to invoke the provisions of this sub-paragraph shall, in general, be the average c.i.f. unit value of the product concerned or an appropriate price in terms of the quality of the product and its stage of processing. It shall, following its initial use, be publicly specified and available to the extent necessary to allow other participants Members to assess the additional duty that may be levied.

0091

3.   A participant Member shall be considered to be in compliance with its
domestic support reduction commitments in any year where the sector-wide
and product-specific product-specific and non-product-specific AMS values
for support, or the equivalent commitments, do not exceed the corresponding
annual commitment levels specified in the Schedule of domestic support
commitments of the participant Member concerned.

4.   As long as domestic support subject to reduction does not exceed 5 per
cent of the total value of production of a basic product in the case of
product-specific support, there shall be no requirement to undertake the
reduction of that support, and as long as domestic support subject to
reduction does not exceed 5 per cent of the value of total agricultural
production in the case of a sector-wide non-product-specific AMS, there
shall be no requirement to undertake the reduction of that support. For
developing countries Members the percentage under this paragraph shall be
10 per cent.

Article 7 - General Disciplines on Domestic Support

1.   Each participant Member shall ensure that any domestic support
measures in favour of agricultural producers which are not subject to
reduction commitments are maintained in conformity with the criteria set
out in Annex 2 to this Agreement.

2.   Any domestic support measure in favour of agricultural producers,
including any modification to such a measure, and any measure that is
subsequently introduced that cannot be shown to satisfy the criteria in
Annex 2 to this Agreement shall be included in the coverage of the
applicable AMS or equivalent commitment. Where no applicable AMS or
equivalent commitment exists the support in question shall not exceed the
de minimis level set out in Article 6(4).

3.   The domestic subsidies listed in Annex 2 to this Agreement shall be
considered as non-actionable for the purposes of countervailing measures,
but not otherwise, provided that such subsidies are in conformity with the
general and specific criteria relating thereto as prescribed in that Annex.

Part V

Article 8 - Export Competition Commitments

Each participant Member undertakes not to provide export subsidies
otherwise than in conformity with this Agreement and with its commitments
as specified in its Schedule of export competition commitments.

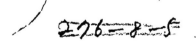

- 11 -

listed in sub-paragraphs (d) and (e) of paragraph 1 above provided that
these are not applied in a manner that would circumvent reduction
commitments.

Article 10 - Prevention of Circumvention
of Export Competition Commitments

1.   Export subsidies not listed in Article 9(1) of this Agreement shall
not be applied in a manner which results in, or which threatens to lead to,
circumvention of export subsidy commitments; nor shall non-commercial
transactions be used to circumvent such commitments.

2.   ~~Participants~~ **Members** undertake not to provide export credits, export
credit guarantees or insurance programmes otherwise than in conformity with
internationally agreed disciplines.

3.   Any ~~participant~~ **Member** which claims that any quantity exported in
excess of a reduction commitment level is not subsidized must establish
that no export subsidy, whether listed in Article 9 or not, has been
granted in respect of the quantity of exports in question.

4.   ~~Participants~~ **Members** donors of international food aid shall ensure:

    (a)   that the provision of international food aid is not tied directly
          or indirectly to commercial exports of agricultural products to
          recipient countries;

    (b)   that international food aid transactions, including bilateral
          food aid which is monetised, shall be carried out in accordance
          with the FAO "Principles of Surplus Disposal and Consultative
          Obligations" including, where appropriate, the system of Usual
          Marketing Requirements (UMRs);

    (c)   that such aid shall be provided to the extent possible in fully
          grant form or on terms no less concessional than those provided
          for in Article IV of the Food Aid Convention 1986.

Article 11 - Incorporated Products

    In no case may the per unit subsidy paid on an incorporated
agricultural primary product exceed the per unit export subsidy that would
be payable on exports of the primary product as such.

Part VI

Article 12 - Serious Prejudice

    Where reduction commitments on domestic support and export subsidies
are being applied in conformity with the terms of this Agreement, the
presumption will be that they do not cause serious prejudice in the sense
of Article XVI:1 of the ~~General Agreement~~ **GATT 1993**.

0093

- 13 -

for which exemption from the reduction commitment is claimed shall be notified promptly. This notification shall contain details of the new or modified measure and its conformity with the agreed criteria as set out in Annex 2 to this Agreement.

4. In the review process participants Members shall give due consideration to the influence of excessive rates of inflation on the ability of any participant Member to abide by its domestic support commitments.

5. The review process shall provide an opportunity for participants Members to raise any matter relevant to the implementation of commitments under the reform programme as set out in this Agreement.

6. Any participant Member may bring to the attention of participants Members any measure which it considers ought to have been notified by another participant Member.

Article 18 - Consultation and Conciliation

1. The provisions of Articles XXII and XXIII of the General Agreement GATT 1993, and the as elaborated and applied by the MTO Understanding on Rules and Procedures Governing the Settlement of Disputes under-Articles XXII-and-XXIII-of-the-General-Agreement-on-Tariffs-and-Trade-as-adopted-by the-CONTRACTING-PARTIES shall apply to consultations and the settlement of disputes under this Agreement.

2. On the basis of the commitments undertaken in the framework of this Agreement, participants Members will exercise due restraint in the application of their rights under the General Agreement GATT 1993 in relation to products included in the reform programme.

Part XI

Article 19 - Continuation of the Reform Process

1. Recognizing that the long-term objective of substantial progressive reductions in support and protection resulting in fundamental reform is an ongoing process, the participants Members agree that negotiations for continuing the process will be initiated one year before the end of the implementation period, taking into account: the experience to that date in implementing the reduction commitments; the effects of the reduction commitments on world trade in agriculture; and what further commitments are necessary to achieve the above mentioned long-term objectives.

PART XII

Article 20 - Final Provisions

0094

- 16 -

(v) inspection services, including general inspection services and
the inspection of particular products for health, safety, grading
or standardization purposes;

(vi) marketing and promotion services, including market information,
advice and promotion relating to particular products but
excluding expenditure for unspecified purposes that could be used
by sellers to reduce their selling price or confer a direct
economic benefit to purchasers; and

(vii) infrastructural services, including: electricity reticulation,
roads and other means of transport, market and port facilities,
water supply facilities, dams and drainage schemes, and
infrastructural works associated with environmental programmes.
In all cases the expenditure shall be directed to the provision
or construction of capital works only, and shall exclude the
subsidized provision of on-farm facilities other than for the
reticulation of generally-available public utilities. It shall
not include subsidies to inputs or operating costs, or
preferential user charges.

3.   Public stockholding for food security purposes

Expenditures (or revenue foregone) in relation to the
accumulation and holding of stocks of products which form an integral
part of a food security programme identified in national legislation.
This may include government aid to private storage of products as part
of such a programme.

The volume and accumulation of such stocks shall correspond to
predetermined targets related solely to food security. The
process of stock accumulation and disposal shall be financially
transparent. Food purchases by the government shall be made at
current market prices and sales from food security stocks shall
be made at no less than the current domestic market price for the
product and quality in question.

4.   Domestic Food Aid

Expenditures (or revenue foregone) in relation to the provision
of domestic food aid to sections of the population in need.

Eligibility to receive the food aid shall be subject to
clearly-defined criteria related to nutritional objectives. Such
aid shall be in the form of direct provision of food to those
concerned or the provision of means to allow eligible recipients
to buy food either at market or at subsidized prices. Food
purchases by the government shall be made at current market
prices and the financing and administration of the aid shall be
transparent.

0095

UR/법제화그룹 논의 현황

1992. 4. 28.

외 무 부 통 상 국

0096

- 목　　　　차 -

0097

Ⅰ. 개 요

1. 법제화그룹의 임무

○ 92.1.13 UR/무역협상위원회(TNC) 결정에 따라 Track 3하에 법제화그룹이
  구성되어 UR 협정 초안(draft Final Act)의 내부적 일관성 및 법적 합치성
  (internal consistency and legal conformity)을 확보하는 작업을
  수행하는 임무를 부여받음.

○ 따라서 법제화그룹의 작업은 중립적.기술적인 성격을 지니며, UR 협상
  참가국의 권리.의무의 균형에 변경을 초래하지 않는 범위내에서 UR 협정
  문안을 검토하는 것임.

  ※ to review the texts in the draft Final Act in order to ensure
     their internal consistency and legal conformity without changing
     the balance of rights and obligations established in the texts.

2. 현황 및 전망

○ 법제화그룹은 92.2.5 제1차 회의를 개최한 이래 지금까지 5차의 공식
  회의 및 수차례 비공식 회의를 개최하여, ①MTO 설립 협정문, ②통합
  분쟁해결 문안, ③개별 협정문 및 ④공통사항(cross-cutting issue)등을
  검토함.

○ 상기 공식, 비공식 회의를 통해 기술적인 세부사항에 대해 광범위한
  의견이 제시 되었으며, 특히 MTO 설립 협정문 및 통합 분쟁해결 문안과
  관련한 일부 쟁점들에 대해서는 참가국간 의견 대립도 있었음.

○ 현재까지 최종 확정된 문안은 없으며, 앞으로 추가적인 작업이 필요한
  상태임.
  - 현재 5월말까지의 작업일정이 제시되어 있음.

1

0098

o 법제화그룹의 작업은 제반 UR 협정문들간의 내부적 일관성 및 법적
  합치성을 확보하기 위한 UR 협상의 최종적인 문안정리 작업이므로
  UR 협상 타결에 필요한 주요쟁점(농산물 보조금, 서비스 MFN 일탈등)에
  대한 참가국들의 합의가 이루어진 연후에 마무리 될 수 있을 것으로
  전망됨.

3. 대응방향

o 기본적으로 UR 협상에 대한 기여의 차원에서 협정문의 다자주의적
  성격을 강화하는 방향으로 대응함.

o 각국의 실질적 입장이 대립하는 사항에 대하여 아국의 입장 개진이
  필요한 경우에는 기존 입장에 의해 대응함.

II. 분야별 현황

1. MTO 설립 협정

가. 현 황 (MTO 협정문안 주요내용 별첨)

o MTO가 UR 협상 결과 이행뿐 아니라 미래의 다자간 무역체제의
  운용을 위한 제도적인 틀을 제공하기 때문에 MTO 설립 협정 문안
  검토가 법제화그룹에서의 핵심적인 사안으로 대두되고 있음.

o 91.12.20자 초안이 실질내용 면에서 크게 변경되지는 않았으나,
  조문의 통폐합, 재배치 등으로 형태면에서는 상당한 변동이 있었음.

o 현재 MTO의 기본 목적 및 구조 관련 조문에 다소 진전이 있었으나,
  조부조항, 가입조건, 개정절차, Waiver, 부적용(non-application)등
  주요쟁점에 대하여는 추가적인 검토가 필요함.

2

0099

나. 주요쟁점 및 대응방향

1) 조부조항

갓트조문 및 규범제정 그룹에서 잠정 적용 의정서(PPA) 및 가입
의정서(PA)에 규정된 조부조항 폐지를 검토 하였으나 미국의
반대로 91.12.20자 최종의정서에는 조부조항을 철폐한다는
문안이 삭제됨.
이와관련, MTO 설립 협정문 Annex 1A에 잠정 적용의정서는
제외된다고 명시함으로써 잠정 적용 의정서에 근거하고 있는
조부조항이 철폐되는 것으로 되어 있으나, 미국은 연안해운에
있어서 미국내 건조선박만 사용토록한 Johns Act의 유지를
위해 조부조항의 계속적인 원용을 관철하려는 입장임.

o 미국 : UR/규범제정 그룹에서 조부조항 폐지 여부에 대한 결정이
없었으므로 조부조항은 계속 유효함.

o 이씨, 일본등 대다수
- 잠정 적용 의정서는 MTO 체제하에서는 계속 인정될 수 없으며
조부조항은 철폐되어야 함.

o 아국 : 조부조항이 유효하다는 주장은 Track 4에서 논의될 사항임.

2) Annex 4 협정의 지위 (2조 3항)

Annex 1, 2 및 3에 포함된 협정이 전체 MTO 회원국을 당사자로
하도록 상정하고 있는데 반해 Annex 4에 포함된 협정(민간항공
협정, 정부조달협정, 국제낙농협정 및 우유협정)은 일부
회원국만을 당사자로 하고 있음. 따라서 Annex 4 협정의
당사국이 아닌 MTO 회원국의 입장에서 볼때 Annex 4 협정이
MTO 설립 협정의 integral part가 될 수 있는지 여부가 논란의
대상이 됨.

o 이씨 및 카나다 : Annex 4 협정이 MTO 설립 협정의 integral
part임.

3

0100

o 홍콩, 싱가폴, 일본 : 웨이버, 개정, 탈퇴등에 관한 MTO 설립

　협정이 아닌 각각의 협정에 따르도록 규정되어 있으므로 integral

　part가 아님.

o 아　국 : Annex 4 협정이 회원국이 제한되어 있기는하나 MTO

　협정 Annex에 수록되므로 integral part로 보아야 하나 동 협정은

　당사국들간에만 적용되어야 함.

3) 투표권 (9조 1항)

> MTO 회원국은 1표의 투표권을 행사(MTO 설립 협정 제IX조 1항)
>
> 하며 EC에게도 회원국 자격을 부여(MTO 설립 협정 제XI조)
>
> 하도록 되어 있으므로 EC가 EC 회원국이 행사하는 투표권과
>
> 별도로 자체 투표권이 인정되는 것인지가 문제가 되고 있음.

o 미국, 일본, 뉴질랜드, 카나다, 태국 : 이씨가 자체의 투표권을

　갖지 않는다는 점을 명확히 규정해야 함.

o 이　씨 : 이씨는 이중 투표권을 향유할 의도는 없으나 이씨를

　적시하는데 반대

o 아　국 : 이씨의 MTO 회원국 자격은 인정되나 이씨에 대한

　이중 투표권 부여에는 반대

4) Waiver (9조 3항)

> UR 협정문중 일부 협정은 자체내에 Waiver 조항을 포함하고
>
> 있으나(예 : 서비스 협정 24조 4항) 일부협정은 Waiver 조항이
>
> 결여되어 있음 (예 : TRIPs 협정).
>
> 이와관련, Waiver 조항이 결여된 협정과 관련하여 Waiver를
>
> 획득코자 하는 경우 MTO 설립 협정내의 Waiver 조항(MTO 설립
>
> 협정문 IX조 3항)을 원용함으로써 가능하다는 입장과
>
> 각 협정문을 존중하여 자체 Waiver 조항이 없는 협정에
>
> 대하여는 Waiver를 부여하여서는 안된다는 입장이 대립

4

0101

ㅇ 이씨, 인도, 멕시코 : MTO 각료회의에 대해 일원적인 Waiver
   부여권을 인정

ㅇ 미국, 카나다, 일본 : Waiver 규정을 두고 있는 협정에 대해서만
   각료회의 Waiver 부여권 인정

ㅇ 아국 입장 : Waiver가 협정문상에 규정되지 않은 특별한 경우에
   부여하는 것이며, 개별협정에 Waiver 규정이 없더라도 Waiver를
   요청해야할 경우가 생길 수 있음을 감안, MTO 협정문내에 일원적인
   Waiver 조항을 마련하는 것이 바람직.

5) 개정 의결 정족수 (10조 1항)

┌───┐
│ MTO 설립 협정이나 다자간무역협정을 개정코자 하는 경우 이를   │
│ 만장일치에 의하도록 함으로써 개정 절차를 엄격히 할 것인지   │
│ 혹은 회원국 2/3 다수결로 함으로써 융통성을 부여할 것인지가   │
│ 쟁점이 되고 있음.   │
└───┘

ㅇ 아국, 이씨, 스웨덴, 브라질 : 협정의 단일성 유지를 위해
   컨센서스에 의한 수정안 채택

ㅇ 미국, 카나다, 뉴질랜드, 호주 : 협정 개정에 신축성 부여를 위해
   회원국 2/3에 의한 수정안 채택

6) 가입 의결 정족수 (12조 2항)

┌───┐
│ 신규 MTO 회원국 가입 요건을 현행 MTO 설립 협정 XII조 2항에   │
│ 규정된 회원국 과반수 이상 2/3 다수결로 할 것인지 아니면   │
│ 보다 엄격히 하여 회원국 2/3 이상 찬성으로 할 것인지가   │
│ 문제가 됨 (현행 갓트 33조는 전체 회원국 2/3의 찬성을 가입   │
│ 의결 요건으로 하고 있음).   │
└───┘

ㅇ 인도, 파키스탄, 카나다 : 회원국 과반수 이상 2/3 다수결

ㅇ 아국, 미국, 뉴질랜드, 홍콩 : 회원국 2/3 이상 찬성

5

2. 통합 분쟁해결 문안

가. 현 황 (통합 분쟁해결 문안 주요내용 별첨)

 o 최종의정서에 포함된 분쟁해결에 관한 3개 문안 (①UR/분쟁해결 협상
그룹 및 UR/제도분야 협상그룹에서 마련한 분쟁해결 규칙 및 절차에
관한 Understanding, ②통합 분쟁해결 체제 요소 (Elements of an
Integrated Dispute Settlement System), ③교차보복 관련 문안)을
단일화한 통합 분쟁해결 문안에 대한 검토 작업 진행중

 o 통합 분쟁해결 문안 마련에 상당한 진전이 있었으며, 통합문안
형태의 초안이 마련 되었으나 통합 분쟁해결 절차의 적용범위,
개도국 우대에 관한 1966년 결정, 보복조치 승인, non-violation
분쟁, 2개 이상의 관련 협정의 실질 규정이 상충되는 경우 처리
문제등이 쟁점으로 남아 있음.

나. 주요쟁점

1) 적용범위 (1조 1항)

> MTO 협정문 자체가 MTO 협정의 하부 규범인 통합 분쟁해결
> 절차의 적용 대상이 될 것인지 여부가 쟁점이 되고 있음.

 o 미국, 홍콩 : MTO 협정문에 권리.의무에 대한 실질 규정이
없으므로 MTO 협정문에 대한 분쟁이 통합 분쟁해결 절차의
대상이 아님.

 o 이씨, 카나다, 아국, 일본, 인도 : MTO 설립 협정문이 16조 4항
(국내법의 MTO 협정 일치), 9조(웨이버)등 실질 규정을 포함하고
있으므로 적용 대상으로 해야함.

6

0103

2) 개도국 우대에 관한 1966년 결정 (3조 11항)

개도국이 제소하는 경우 1966년도 절차(사무총장의 주선 및
협의 진행, 동 협의 실패시 즉각적인 패널 설치, 60일이내의
패널보고서 제출, 보고서 채택으로부터 90일이내에 패소국의
이행상황 보고, 패널 권고사항 불이행시 보복승인등)를
원용할 수 있도록 되어 있는바, 이와관련 1966년도 절차가
Annex 1A상의 동경라운드 협정에도 적용될 것인지 여부와
동 절차 원용개도국이 교차보복을 할 수 있도록 허용할
것인지 여부가 쟁점이 되고 있음.

o 미국, 이씨, 호주, 일본 : 개도국 우대에 관한 1966년 결정은
Annex 1A(동경라운드 협정)에 적용되지 않음. 또한 동 절차를
원용하는 개도국은 교차보복을 할 수 없음.

o 멕시코 : 79년 각료 결정 및 개별 동경라운드 협정이 분쟁해결에
관한 갓트의 관례를 존중하도록 규정하고 있으므로 동경라운드
협정에도 적용되며 교차보복도 인정되어야 함.

o 아 국 : 선진국 입장이 타당하나 입장 표명은 유보

3) 보복조치 승인의 제한 (22조 5항)

통합 분쟁해결 협정문(안) 22조 5항은 "개별 협정에 보복을
금지하는 규정이 있는 경우 분쟁해결기구가 보복을 승인하지
못한다"고 규정하고 있는바, 동항을 존치할 것인지 여부가
쟁점임.

o 미국, 인도 : 현재 MTO 부속 협정문안에 분쟁해결기구의 보복
승인을 제한하는 규정이 없으므로 동항은 삭제되어야 함.

o 이씨, 홍콩, 싱가폴 : 정부조달협정 확대 협상이 현재 진행중이며,
앞으로 체결될 협정이 여사한 금지 규정을 설정할 수 있으므로
22조 5항 존치가 필요

7

0104

4) 중재절차후 보복조치 승인 (22조 7항 마지막 문장)

> 22조 7항은 분쟁해결기구가 보복 수준의 적정성 여부에 대한
> 중재 결과를 통보받은후 일방 분쟁당사국 요청시 보복을
> 승인토록 하고 있는바, 일부 참가국들이 최종의정서 T text
> 5항에 동 문구가 포함되어 있지 않다는 점을 들어 이의 제기

o 인도, 브라질, 멕시코 : 중재 결과를 통보받은후 분쟁해결기구가
   보복을 승인한다는 문구 삭제
o 미국, 카나다 : 중재기간중에는 보복이 불가능하나 중재절차
   종료후에는 보복이 허용되어야 하므로 동 문구 유지
o 아 국 : 보복 수준의 적정성 여부 판단을 주목적으로 중재
   절차가 도입된 것이므로 중재절차 종료후 분쟁해결기구가
   보복을 허용할 수 있어야 함.

5) non-violation 분쟁 (26항)

> non-violation 조항이 93년도 갓트이외의 MTO 부속 협정에
> 의거한 분쟁에도 적용될 것인지 여부

o MTO 부속협정에 대한 non-violation 조항의 적용 여부는 동 협정
   검토후 결정할 문제라는데 대해 합의가 이루어짐으로써 실질적인
   토의가 이루어지지 않음.
o 단, TRIPs 및 서비스 협정과 관련 인도, 브라질이 적용 불가
   입장인 반면 이씨, 미국은 적용 가능하다는 입장 표명

6) 실질규정의 상충 (28항)

> 실질규정의 상충이라는 예외적인 경우 패널 또는 상소기구
> 절차를 여하히 할 것인지 여부

8

0105

o 미 국 : 상충되는 실질규정은 MTO 협정 발효이전에 모두 수정돼야
   하며, 만일 MTO 발효이후 상충되는 규정의 조화 문제는 패널이나
   상소기관의 해석에 의해 해결할 수 있으므로 28항(실질규정
   상충시 패널 또는 상소기구는 동 사실을 분쟁해결기구에 통보하여
   분쟁해결기구(이사회)가 적절한 조치를 취하도록 함) 삭제 필요
o 이씨, 인도 : 상충 규정의 존재에 대비하여 동 조항이 필요하며,
   상충 규정의 해석은 패널이 아닌 분쟁해결기구(이사회)의 권한임.

3. 개별 협정문 검토

o 개별 협정문 검토는 MTO 설립 협정문 및 통합 분쟁해결 문안 검토와
   관련된 사항으로서, 현재 MTO 설립 협정문 및 통합 분쟁해결 문안에
   대한 1-2차례 검토가 완료되었기 때문에 4.8부터 개별 협정문 검토가
   개시됨.

o 개별 협정문 검토에 있어서 용어를 통일하고 (예컨대 현행 UR 협정문들은
   회원국을 member, party, signatory 등으로 각각 달리 표현 함으로써
   일관성이 결여), MTO 설립 협정문 및 통합 분쟁해결 문안과의 불필요한
   중복을 피하거나 일관성을 확보하기 위하여 최종조항(final provisions :
   가입, 발효, 개정, 탈퇴, 유보조항등) 및 분쟁해결 관련조항을 수정 또는
   삭제하는데에 주안점을 두고 작업이 진행되고 있음.

4. 공통사항(Cross-cutting issues)

o 둘이상의 개별협정에서 사용되는 유사한 issue나 용어가 협정별로 달리
   취급되는 경우가 문제가 될 수 있기 때문에 cross-cutting issue가 일단
   법제화그룹의 검토 대상이 되고 있음.

o 일부 국가들은 원칙적으로 개별협정은 관련 context 하에서 자체적으로
   해석되어야 하므로 특정개념의 정의는 개별 협정이 결정할 문제라는
   입장임.

9

0106

o 그러나, 미국등 주요국가들은 동일한 조치에 대해 복수의 협정이 상충되는 의무를 부과 함으로써 회원국들이 공약을 이행하는데 있어서 어려움을 겪거나 불확실성이 발생할 가능성도 있을수 있다고 주장하고 있으며, 일단 개별협정에 대한 검토가 완료된 후에 종합적으로 cross-cutting issue에 대해 검토하기로 함.   끝.

외 무 부

종 별 :

번 호 : GVW-0905

일 시 : 92 0429 1950

수 신 : 장관(통기,상공부)

발 신 : 주제네바대사

제 목 : UR/법제화그룹(분쟁해결절차)

연: GVW-0822,0807

관세협정 및 반덤핑 협정문상의 분쟁해결절차를 가능한 범위내에서 MTO통합분쟁해결절차에 일치시키기 위한 카나다 수정안을 별첨 송부하니 동수정안에 대한 검토의견 회시바람.

첨부: 상기 카나다안(GVW(F)-286).끝

(대사 박수길-국장)

통상국   2차보   상공부

PAGE 1

주 제 네 바 대 표 부

번 호 : GVR(F) - 0286   년월일 : 204 2P   시간 : 1850

수 신 : 장 관(통계, 상공부)

발 신 : 주 제네바대사

제 목 : GVW-POS 첨부

종 5 매(프지프함)

보 안 통 제	

외신과 통 제	

0109

April 28, 1992

CUSTOMS VALUATION

Drafting Suggestions

Article 19

19.1   Except as otherwise provided herein, the provisions of Articles XXII and XXIII of the GATT 1993, as elaborated and applied by the MTO Understanding on Rules and Procedures Governing the Settlement of Disputes, are applicable to consultations under this Agreement.

[19.2   If any Member considers that any benefit accruing to it, directly or indirectly, under this Agreement is being nullified or impaired, or that the achievement of any objective of this Agreement is being impeded, as a result of the actions of another Member or of other Members it may, with a view to reaching a mutually satisfactory solution of this matter, request consultations with the Member or Members in question. Each Member shall afford sympathetic consideration to any request from another Member for consultations.]

19.3   The Technical Committee shall provide, upon request, advice and assistance to Members engaged in consultations.

Article 20

20.1   Except as otherwise provided in the provisions of this Agreement, the provisions of Articles XXII and XXIII of the GATT 1993, as elaborated and applied by the MTO Understanding on Rules and Procedures Governing the Settlement of Disputes, are applicable to settlement of disputes under this Agreement.

20.2   At the request of a party to the dispute, or on its own initiative, a panel established to examine a dispute relating to the provisions of this Agreement may request the Technical Committee to carry out an examination of any questions requiring detailed technical consideration. The panel shall determine terms-of-reference of the Technical Committee and set a time period for receipt of the report of the Technical Committee.

20.3   Confidential material provided to the panel shall not be disclosed without the specific permission of the person or government providing such information. Where such information is requested from the panel but release of such information by the panel is not authorized, a non-confidential summary of this information, authorized by the person or government providing the information, will

0110

be provided.

Annex II

para 3   The Technical Committee shall attempt to conclude its
            work on specific matters, especially those referred to it
            by Members, the Committee <u>or a panel</u>, in a reasonably
            short period of time.

para 9   (add an additional sentence at end)
            <u>Notwithstanding the provisions in sentence 1 of this
            paragraph, the Technical Committee shall meet as
            necessary to consider matters referred to it by a panel
            under the provisions of Article 20 of this Agreement.</u>

para 21   (add to para 21 the following two sentences)
            <u>On matters referred to it by a panel, the Technical
            Committee shall take decisions by consensus. Where
            consensus is not possible, the Technical Committee shall
            provide a report detailing the facts of the matter and
            indicating the views of the participants.</u>

Annex III

            – delete Annex, as special and additional provisions are
            incorporated into text

0111

ANTI-DUMPING

Drafting Suggestions

18.1   Except as modified herein, the provisions of Articles XXII and XXIII of the GATT 1993, as elaborated and applied by the MTO Understanding on Rules and Procedures Governing the Settlement of Disputes, are applicable to consultations and the settlement of disputes under this Agreement.

18.2   If any Member considers that any benefit accruing to it, directly or indirectly, under this Agreement is being nullified or impaired, or that the achievement of any objective is being impeded, by another Member or Members, it may, with a view to reaching a mutually satisfactory resolution of the matter, request in writing consultations with the Member or Members in question. Each Member shall afford sympathetic consideration to any request from another Member for consultation.

18.3   If any Member considers that the consultations have failed to achieve a mutually agreed solution and final action has been taken by the administering authorities of the importing country to levy definitive anti-dumping duties or to accept price undertakings, it may refer the matter to the DSB. When a provisional measure has a significant impact and the Member considers the measure was taken contrary to the provisions of paragraph 1 of Article 7 of this Agreement, a Member may also refer such matter to the DSB.

18.4   The DSB shall, at the request of any party to the dispute, establish a panel to examine the matter based upon:

    (a)   a written statement of the Member making the request indicating how a benefit accruing to it, directly or indirectly, under this Agreement has been nullified or impaired, or that the achieving of the objectives of the Agreement is being impeded,
          and

    (b)   the facts made available in conformity with appropriate domestic procedures to the authorities of the importing country.

18.5   Confidential information provided to the panel shall not be revealed without formal authorization from the person or authority providing the information. Where such

0112

information is requested from the panel but release of
such information by the panel is not authorized, a non-
confidential summary of the information, authorized by
the authority or person providing the information, will
be provided.

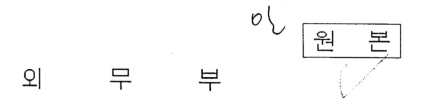

외 무 부

종 별 :

번 호 : GVW-0927   일   시 : 92 0505 1000

수 신 : 장 관(봉기, 경기원, 재무부, 농수산부, 상공부, 특허청)

발 신 : 주 제네바 대사

제 목 : UR/법제화 그룹 비공식 회의(개별 협정문)

연: 제네(경) 20644-371

연호, FOGS 및 TPRM 사무국 수정안(TEXT627)에 대한 5.4 표제회의 논의 요지를 아래 보고함.(신서기관 참석)

1. FOGSO FOGS TEXT 상의 통보조치 대상의 범위와 관련, 동 규정은 TPRM TEXT 과 같이 MTO 협정 부속서1A 협정뿐만 아니라 서비스 협정, TRIPS 협정 및 경우에 따라서는 부속서 4 협정(PTA)에도 적용되어야 한다는 미국, 뉴질랜드, 카나다 등 선진국의 견해와 동 규정은 통보조치에 대한 심의 절차에 관한 SECTION III(5P)에 비추어 부속서 1A 협정에만 적용된다는 싱가폴, 홍콩 등의 견해가 대두됨.

- FOGS TEXT 의 적용범위를 광범위하게 잡는 선진국측은 4P SECTION I 통보의 일반 의무중 첫째 문장 둘째줄 MTA 및 둘째단 9째줄 GATT 를 각각 MTA, WHERE APPROPRIATE, PTA 로 수정할 것을 제의함.

2. TPRM

O 목적에 관한 A 항(9P)과 관련, 뉴질랜드는 TPRM 12.20 초안의 F 항 7줄(12P)및 FOGS TEXT 12.20 초안 A3 항 6줄(3P)에 명기된 ENHANCED SURVEILLANCE 의 취지를 살려 A(I) 항 9째줄(9P)의 APPRECIATION 뒤에 SURVEILLANCE 를 추가하자는 제의를 한바

- 카나다, 미국 등이 이에 동조한 반면, 싱가폴은 SURVEILLANCE 의 추가는 A(I) 항 마지막 문장의 취지에 어긋남을 지적함. 끝

(대사 박수길-국장)

통상국   경기원   재무부   농수부   상공부   특허청   오치연

외 무 부

종 별 :

번 호 : GVW-0944 　　　　　　　　　　일 시 : 92 0507 1700

수 신 : 장 관(통기,경기원,재무부,농수산부,상공부,특허청)

발 신 : 주 제네바대사

제 목 : UR/법제화 그룹 비공식회의(개별협정문)

　　지적 재산권 협정 사무국 수정안(TEXT 790)에 대한 5.5-6 표제회의 논의 요지를 아래보고함.(김준규 서기관, 신서기관 참석)

　　1. 제 11조(대여권)- 영상저작물, 콤퓨터 프로그램 대여권에 관한 세째 문장 둘째줄 RIGHT 앞에 EXECLUSIVE를 추가하자는 미국의 제의가 있었으나, 카나다, 인도, 에집트등이 동 제의는 실질내용의 변경임을 들어 반대함.(미국은 상기 제의가 채택되지 않는 경우에는 13조 첫줄의 EXCLUSIVE 단어를 삭제할 것을 제의하였으나 다수국이이에 유보적인 입장이었음)

　　- 미국은 또한 세째문장(콤퓨터 프로그램에 대한 대여권 예외규정)에 관해서도 THE ESSENTIAL OBJECT를 AN ESSENTIAL OBJECT로 수정할 것을 제의했으나 다수국의 반대로 받아들여지지 않음.

　　2. 제 14조(공연자, 음반제작자, 방송기관 보호)

　　- 제 14조 TITLE 말미의 BROADCAST 를 BROADCAT ING ORG ANIZATION 으로 수정제안한 미국제의를 채택함.

　　- 제 4항 음반제작자에 대한 보호관련, 동 보호는 제11조 콤퓨터 프로그램 대여권의 보호에 관한 규정을 그대로 적용하는 것이 아니라 준용하자는 당초협정안(MUTATIS MUTANDIS)에 대해 미국은 MUTATIS MUTANDIS 삭제를 주장한 반면, 일본은 두개의 권리를 동일한 수준으로 보호하는 것은 타당하지 않다는 점을 들어 당초 협정안(준용)을지지 함.

　　3. 제 20조(기타요건)

　　- 미국은 동조의 첫째문장의 내용(1개 상표사용원칙)과 둘째문장의 내용(두개상표사용)이상치 된다고 주장하면서 이의 조화를 위해 6줄의 USE OF THE TRADE MARK INDENTIFYING 을 INDENTIF ICATION OF 로 수정하자는 제의를 한바, 브라질,

---

통상국　　경기원　　재무부　　농수부　　상공부　　특허정

PAGE 1 　　　　　　　　　　　　　　　　　92.05.08　　10:11 WH

　　　　　　　　　　　　　　　　　　　　　외신 1과 통제관

0115

아르헨티나가 둘째문장은 첫째문장에 대한 특별 규정으로서 둘째 문장의 취지는 문화적인차이등을 이유로 1개 이상의 상표 상용이 필요한 경우를 상정한 것이라고 주장함.

4. 제 23조(포도주 및 기타 주류의 지리표시에 대한 추가보호)- 포도주의 지리표시 보호를 위한 추가협상에 대한 이사회의 임무에 관한 4항 관련, 멕시코는동조의 TITLE 에 SPIRITS 가 있으므로 SPIRITS도 동 4항의 보호대상이 되어야 한다는 주장에대해 동 제안은 당초 협상 취지에 어긋남을 들어 다수국이 이에 반대

5. 제 24조(예외)

- 제 4항 포도주외에 기타 주류에 대한 유사한 지리적 명칭의 계속사용과 관련, EC 는 3줄 SPRITIS의 추가에 대해 이의를 제기했으나, 동 단어추가는 당초 협상시 사항이라는 사무국의 배경설명에 대해 미국, 카나다등이 동조함.,

6. 제25조(의장 보호 요 건)

- 제2항 말미의 COPYRIGHT 를 COPYRIGHT LAW 로 수정하는 것이 정확한 표현 이라는 미국이 제안을 채택함.

7. 제 27조(특허대상)

- 제1항 두번째 문장에 'PARAGRAPH 8 OF ARTICLE 70'이 새로이 추가된데 대해 인도가 동추가 의도를 사무국에 질의한바, 사무국은 제70조 8항의 의약, 화학물질의 특허에 관해서도 발명의 장소에 차별없이 적용하기 위한 것이라고 설명하고 미국은 사무국의 수정안이 보다 명백한 표현이라고 지지하였으나, 이집트는 이의 삭제를 주장함.

- 제 3항(A) 에 관해 스위스는 WIPO 모델법제 112조 3항(IV) 표현된 내용 'METHODS FOR TREATMENT OF THE HUMAN OR ANIMAL BODY BY SURGERY OR THERAPY,AS WELL AS DIAGNOSTIC METHODS PRACTICED ON THE HUMAN OR ANIMAL BODY' 이 더욱 구체적이고 명확한 표현이므로 동표현으로 대체할 것을 제안한바, 미국, EC등이 동조한 반면, 일본은유보입장을 개진함(스위스는 BODY 개념안에 정신이 포함되는 것으로 이해함)

8. 제 28조(특허권 내용)

- 제 1항(A) FOOT NOTE 와 관련 미국은 관련 규정인 제 6조의 내용이 명백히 결정 되었으므로 동 FOOT NOTE 는 삭제하자는 제의를 한바, 알젠틴, 인도, 브라질등은 제 28조상의 권리(IMPORTING)가 권리소지에 관한 제 6조의 적용대상임을 명문화한 FOOT

PAGE 2

0116

NOTE 를 그대로 유지할 것을 강력히 주장함.

9. 제 35조, 제 38조의 규정중 'HOLDER OF THE RIGHT' 대신 'RIGHT HOLDER'로 WORDING 를 통일하자는 미국 및 아국의 제안에 따라 이를 채택함.

10. 제 46조, 제 59조, 제 69조에 사용되고 있는 'COUNTERFEIT GOODS', 'PIRATEDGOODS' 표현과 일치시키기 위해 제 51조에 관한 FOOT NOTE 3 의 표현 'COUNTERFEIT TRADEMARK GOODS' 와 ' PRIRATED COPYRIGHTGOODS'을 앞서와 같이 표현하자는 미국의제안이 있었으나 뉴질랜드, 인도, 태국등이 이에 반대함.

11. 제 64조(분쟁해결)

- '동조의 내용은 MTO 의 통합분쟁 해결절차에 대한 협상결과에 따라 수정이 가능하다'는 FOOT NOTE 를 삭제한 사무국 수정안에 대해 카나다, 브라질등이 분쟁 해결절차의 내용이 아직 완결되지 않았음을 논거로 반대입장을 표명한 반면 미국은 동 주석의 삭제를 지지함.

12. 제 65조(경과 규정)

- 제 4항 'THE PROVISIONS ON PRODUCT PATENTS OF ' 의추가에 대해 인도, 파키스탄, 이집트는 강력히 이를 삭제할 것을 주장한 반면, 미국은 제4항과 규정 특히 물질특허에 관한 규정에만 적용되도록 제한하기 위한 것이라는 점에서 이의 삭제를 반대함.

13. 제 70조(현존하는 지적재산권 보호)

- 제4항 4줄의 용어 본협정 비준일(THE DATD OF RATIFICATION OF THIS AGREEMENT) 을 UR 최종의정서 채택일로 수정하자는 미국의 제의가 있었으나, 최종의정서 채택일 은 개별국의 협정비준일에 앞설 수 있으므로 별개의 개념이라는 다수국의 주장이 있 었음.(한편, 동 용어에 관한 TEXT 790WP 6항 사무국 해설과 관련, 미국이 7줄의 AGREEMENT 용어대신에 THIS AGREEMENT 용어사용을 선호한다는 점을 다시 언급한 반면,EC가 이에 대해 MTO AGREEMENT 용어 사용을 지지함)

14. 제 71조(검토 및 개정)

- 개정에 관한 2항 관련, 카나다는 동조항의 문안중 AND ACCEPTED BY 이하의 내용 이 분명하지 않음을 지적하면서 이사회에서의 콘센서스에 의한 개정안 채택 방식을제 의한 바, 아국, 미국등이 지지한 반면, 사무국은 동조항의 취지는 만장일치에 의한 개정방식이라는 의견을 제시하자, 일본, 홍콩등이 만장일치에 의한 개정방안의 취지가 존중되어야 함을 주장함.끝

(대사 박수길 - 국장)

PAGE 3

0117

외 무 부

110-760 서울 종로구 세종로 77번지   / (02)720-2188   / (02)725-1737 (FAX)

문서번호 통기 20644-**166** **1795H**

시행일자 1992. 5. 9.(   )

취급		장 관	
보존			
국 장	전 결		
심의관			
과 장			
기안	안 명 수		협조

수신   주 제네바 대사

참조

제목   UR/법제화그룹

─────────────────────────────

대 : GVW-0807

　　4.9 표제 그룹회의시 원산지 규정과 관련하여 제기된 사항에 대한 상공부 검토
의견을 별첨 송부하니 참고 바랍니다.

첨 부 : 동 검토 의견.　　　　　　　　　　　끝.

　　　　　　　　　외　무　부　장　관

0118

상 공 부

427-760 경기 과천시 중앙동 1번지 / 전화 (02) 503 - 9446 / 전송 (02) 503 - 9496, 3142

문서번호 국협 28143 - 258

시행일자 1992. 5. 6. (   )

수신 외무부

참조 통상기구과장

선결			지시	관기협의에 참조요함 검토바람 보고	
접수	일자 시간	92. 5. 7	결재 · 공 람		
	번호	15811			
처리과	·				
담당자	이명득				

제목 : 원산지 규정에 관한 각종제의에 대한 우리 입장 검토

'92. 4. 9 개최된 UR/법제화 그룹회의에서 원산지 협정문에 대한 각종 제의

사항에 대해 우리입장을 검토하여 송부합니다.

첨 부 : 원산지 규정에 관한 각종제의에 대한 우리입장 검토 1부.   끝.

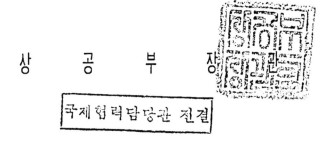

상 공 부 장

국제협력담당관 전결

0119

```
┌─────────────────────────────────────────────────────────┐
│  원산지 규정에 관한 각종제의에 대한 우리입장 검토           │
└─────────────────────────────────────────────────────────┘
```

('92. 4. 9 개최된 법제화 그룹회의)

1. 제 2조 (A)

o 현 규정내용

  - 과도기간중의 규율에 있어 명료성을 보장하여야 하는 대상에
    "administrative determinations" 만 있고 laws. regulations는 없음

o 일본의 제의 내용

  - 현 규정에 laws, regulations 을 추가하자고 제의

o 검 토

  - 상기 일본의 제의는 제 2조 (a) 의 3가지 요건이 행정결정 뿐만아니라
    법률. 규정에도 적용하게 함으로써 EC가 EC 이사회 규정 제 802/68호
    (REGULATION (EEC) NO 802/68 OF THE COUNCIL OF 27 JUNE 1968) 에 의한
    자의적 운용을 방지하고자 하는 의도로 보임.

  - 또한 "Rules of Origin" 의 정의 (제 1조 1) 에 laws, reugulations and
    administrative determinations 가 포함되어 있는 점을 감안하여 차기 UR/
    법제화그룹 회의시 일본 입장을 지지

0120

2. 제 8조 (분쟁해결절차)

o 현 규정 내용

- 분쟁해결협상 그룹에 의하여 개선된 일반 협정 제 23조의 규정을 본 협정에 적용할 수 있다.

o EC 의 제안 내용 (미국 동조)

- HS 제도가 마련된 후 발생하는 동제도 해석에 대한 분쟁은 GATT 23조 절차에 앞서 선절차로 CCC 의 HS 위원회에 회부한다는 내용을 동조 제 2항에 신설 하자고 제의

o 검 토

- CCC 는 각국의 관세제도의 국제적인 조화를 이루고 품목분류와 평가의 국제적인 통일을 기할 목적으로 설립된 기구로 HS 협약 (품목분류 협약임)을 제정하였고,

- HS 위원회는 동 협약에 따라 관세대상품목을 통일적으로 분류해석하는 기술적인 검토회의 인바, EC 의 제안은 동 위원회 전문성을 감안해 HS 제도의 해석에 대한 분쟁에 대해 동 위원회에서 선절차로 다루게 하여, 기술성.전문성을 높이고자 하는 의도로 분석됨

0121

- 그러나 현재 분야별로 상이한 분쟁해결 절차를 일원화하여 효율적으로 통합 시키기 위한 논의가 분쟁해결 협상그룹에서 진행되고 있으며

- 현 원산지 협정 부속서 I.1 (A) 에 의해 가입국의 원산지 규정의 일상적인 운영에서 발생하는 기술적인 문제의 검토 및 제시된 사실에 기초한 적절한 해결방안의 조언을 제공하는것 등을 담당하는 기술위원회를 구성토록 되어 있으므로 HS 제도 해석에 관한 분쟁해결에 대해 별도로 CCC의 HS 위원회의 선절차를 거치도록 할 실익이 없다고 판단됨

0122

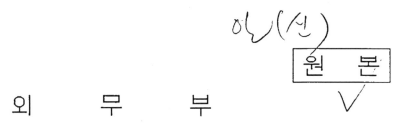

외 무 부

종 별 :

번 호 : GVW-0958   일 시 : 92 0508 1700

수 신 : 장관(통기, 경기원, 재무부, 농수산부, 상공부, 특허청)

발 신 : 주 제네바 대사

제 목 : UR/법제화 그룹 비공식회의

연: 제네(경) 20644-371

1. 연호 정부조달 협정에 관한 결정문(TEXT 626, K) 수입허가 절차 협정문(TEXT 611, H) 사무국 수정안에 대한 5.7 표제회의 논의 요지를 아래보고함.

(신서기관, 김상무관보 참석)

가. 정부 조달협정 결정문

0 동 문안의 내용에 비추어 타이블의 AGREEMENT 를 DICISION 으로 수정함.

0 UR 밖에서 개정작업이 이루어지고 있는 정부조달협정이 완성된후 그에 따라 해당 조항을 수정키로 함.(타이블, 1항(I), 2항의 제 9조를 제23조로)

나. 수입허가 절차 협정

0 제 1조

- 제 1조 4항 6줄의 GOVERNMENT 의 개념과 관련, 발효조항의 삭제에 따라 사무국이 삭제한 P 77의 주석 2(정부의 개념안에 EC 의 당국이 포함됨)를 살려 동 GOVERNMENT 의 주석으로 첨가키로 함.

0 제 2조 (자동적인 수입허가)

- 주석 2항(P.72) 관련, 1979 년 수입허가 절차협정의 당사국이었던 개도국에 까지 2년 유예를 주는 것이 당초 취지가 아니므로 이를 명확히 하기위해 첫줄 MEMBER뒤에 ' OTHER THAN DEVELOPPING COUNTRY MEMBERS WHICH WERE PARTIES TO THE IMPORT LICENSING AGREEMENT OF 1979' 를 추가하기로 함.

제 8조 (최종 조항)

- 사무국이 삭제한 5항 개정 조항 관련, 미국은 MTO 협정이 아직 완결되지 않은상태이므로 5항의 삭제에 반대한다는 입장을 개진함.

- 국내입법에 관한 2항 4(P.78) 관련, 카나다는(A) 항의 의무(MTO 발효일까지

통상국   2차보   경기원   재무부   농수부   상공부   특허청

PAGE 1   92.05.09   07:38 DQ

외신 1과 통제관 ✓

0123

국내법의 수입허가 절차 협정에의 일치)가 너무 엄격하다는 의견을 개진함. (A 항 첫줄 GEVERNMENT 는 B 항 PARTY 와 함께 MEMBER 로 수정키로함.)

2. 표제회의는 5.11 속개되어 서비스 협정문 GATT 93을 심의할 예정이며, 이로써개별 협정문 전체에 대한 1차 심의가 완료하게 되는바, 5.15 제6차 T3 공식회의를 개최하여 그간 논의현황을 확인할 예정임. 끝

   (대사 박수길-국장)

외 무 부

종 별 :

번 호 : GVW-0979   일 시 : 92 0512 1930

수 신 : 장관(통기, 경기원, 재무부, 농수산부, 상공부, 법무부, 문화부, 건설부, 교통부,

발 신 : 주 제네바 대사   체신부, 보사부, 과기처, 공보처, 항만청, 특허청)

제 목 : UR/법제화 그룹 비공식회의(개별협정문) ·

연: 제네(정) 20644-420(1)

GVW-873(2)

서비스 협정문 사무국 수정안(TEXT 769)에 대한 5.11 표제회의 논의 요지를 아래 보고함.

1. 서문

0 3항 5줄 및 4항 3줄의 NATIONAL POLICY OBJECTIVES 관련 당초 협상 취지가 중앙 정부의 정책뿐만 아니라 지방정부의 정책도 포함하는 것이므로 PUBLIC(또는 DOMESTIC) POLICY OBJECTIVES 로 수정하자는 카나다 제의에 대해 EC, 아르헨티나, 인도등이당초 취지보다 개념이 넓어진다는 점을 들어 이에 반대함.

2. 제 1조(범위 및 정의)

0 제 2항 및 3항은 12.20 초안의 주석에 따라 34조(개념) 논의후 검토키로 함.

(3P 7 항 참조)

3. 제 2조(MFN)

0 카나다는 브랏셀 TEXT 에 있었던 제 2조4항(ACQUIRED RIGHTS 에 대한 MFN 적용배제조항)이 아무런 토의없이 최종협정안에서 삭제된점에 대하여 이의를 제기한바, 사무국은 통상적으로 국제협정은 현존 규제제도에 대하여 적용되는것이며 명시적 규정이 없는한 소급효과가 없기때문에 구법률하에서 주어진 혜택은 MFN적용대상은 아니므로 이를 삭제하였다고 언급함.

0 미국은 (사법 및 행정공조 협정에 대한 MFN적용 배제를 규정한 주석에 대하여동협정등은 사실상 서비스 무역에 별다른 영향을 미치지 않는다는 이유를 들어 삭제할 것을 제의하였으나 기타 국가들은 추가 검토가 필요한 사항이라고 반대함.

0 홍콩은 연호 2(2항) 소규모 비공식 회의에서 잠정합의된 COUNTRY 개념에

통상국 농수부	2차보 상공부	법무부 건설부	보사부 과기처	문화부 해항정	교통부 특허청	체신부 공보저	경기원	재무부

대한사무국 정리문안을 배포해 줄것을 요청하면서(첨부 사무국문서 참조) 3항 4줄의 FRONTIER ZONES 의 개념이 홍콩과 같은 관세 영역에는 맞지 않으므로 BORDER ZONES 로 수정하자는 제의를 한바, EC 및 카나다가 FRONTIER 와 BORDER 개념은 차이가 없으며 FRONTIER 용어 사용에 문제가 없다는 의견 개진

4. 제 3조(공개주의)

0 카나다는 제 1항과 관련 사무국 수정안에 대하여 일반적으로 작용되는 조치만공표대상으로 하기보다는 구체적인 개별 결정, 조치들도 포함되어야한다고 하였으나EC 등 다른 나라들은 일반적으로 적용되는 조치만 공표대상으로 한정하는 것이 협상그룹의 의도였다고 반박함.

0 한편 EC 는 3항의 시장접근 약속을 한 분야에 있어서 규제 제도 변경의 통지 범위를 일반적 적용 효력을 가지는 조치로 한정하는 것은 원 협정 초안의 취지와 어긋나는 것이며, 특별한 경우에 효력이 한정되는 규제 조치의 통지 대상이 포함되어야하므로 단순히 MEASURES 라고 규정하자고 제의하였으며, 일본이 이에 동조하였으며,카나다 미국은 사무국 수정안을 지지함.

5. 제 5조 (경제통합)

0 6(B) 항의 법인 (JURIDICAL PERSON) 개념과관련, 동 개념은 제 34조에 서술되어 있으므로 CONSTITUTED 이하 PARAGRAPH 1 까지를 삭제하자는 멕시코 제의에 대해 EC는 동항의 법인개념은 34조와는 달리 모든 MTO 회원국이 아니라 경제 통합 협정 회원국내에서 영업 활동을하는 법인에 한정된다는 점을 지적하여 멕시코제의에 반대

6. 협정문 목차

0 목차(P7-8)에 협정문의 일부인 부속서를 명기하기로 함.(부속서 리스트가 명기된 5P 의 목차는 협정문이 완성될 때까지 협상의 목적을 위해 필요한 부분임)

0 협정문 목차의 괄호안에 있는 조항은 MTO협정문에 대한 논의결과에 따라 존치여부를 결정키로 함.(3P, 9 항 참조)

첨부: COUNTRY 용어에 대한 비공식 협의결과(사무국 문서) 1부.

(GVW(F)-313)

(대사 박수길-국장)

주 제 네 바 대 표 부

번 호 : GVE(F) - 0313   년월일 : 25/12/ʌ30시간 :

수 신 : 장   관 (동기, 경기원, 재무부, 농림수산부, 상공부, 특허청)

발 신 : 주 제네바대사

제 목 :

명무부, 문화부, 건설부, 교통부, 체신부, 보사부, 과기처, 공보처, 항만청

Guw - PTP 전 신

총 2 매(표지포함)

<table>
<tr><td>외신관</td><td></td></tr>
<tr><td>통 제</td><td></td></tr>
</table>

0127

Informal Consultations on the Term "Country" in the MTO Agreement

Informal consultations with interested delegations on the use of the term 'country' in the Agreement establishing the MTO were held on 23 April 1992.

The consultations resulted in an ad referendum agreement on the following two proposals:

(a) To include an explanatory note in the text of the MTO Agreement which would read as follows:

"The terms 'country' or 'countries' as used in the Agreement establishing the MTO and the Multilateral Trade Agreements and Plurilateral Trade Agreements in the annexes to this Agreement are to be understood to include any separate customs territory Member of the MTO."

(b) The terms 'developing Member', 'developed Member' and 'least-developed Member', which are used in the current drafts of the MTO Agreement and its Annexes, would be replaced by the terms 'developing country Member', 'developed country Member' and 'least-developed country Member'.

It was understood in the consultations that the consequences of this explanatory note for the references to 'country' in the anti-dumping and subsidy agreements, in particular the references to countries member of the EEC, would need to be examined in the review of these agreements by the Legal Drafting Group.

외 무 부

종 별 :

번 호 : GVW-0988   일 시 : 92 0513 1900

수 신 : 장 관(수신처 참조)

발 신 : 주 제네바대사

제 목 : UR/법제화그룹 비공식회의(개별협정문) ．

　　서비스 협정문 사무국 수정안(TEXT 769)에 대한 5.12. 논의 요지를 아래 보고함.(이경협관,신서기관, 한경협관보 참석)

　　1. 제 6조(국내규제)

　　O 아국은 5항 A)... 'SPECIFIC COMMITMENTS IN ACCORDANCEWITH ARTICLE XVI AND XVII OF THIS AGREEMENT...'에 대하여 서비스 협정 제 3부의 SPECIFIC COMMITMENTS 대 상인ARTICLE XVIII(ADDITIONAL COMMITMENTS)가 누락되었을뿐만 아니라 그표현도 제8 조 1항의...'SPECIFIC COMMITMENTS UNDER PART III OF THISAGREEMENT...' 제 6조 3항의 'SPECIFIC COMMITMENT'등과 일관성이 없다고 지적한 바, EC,스웨덴, 인도등이지지하여 SPECIFIC COMMITMENTS로 통일하기로 합의함.

　　2. 제 7조(인정)

　　O 미국은 자격인정을 국가간에 차별적인 방법으로 하지 않도록 규정한 제 3항과관련, 자격인정을 당연히 차별적으로 이루어지므로 자의적이거나 정당화될 수 없는차별만 금지하도록 규정할 것을 제의하였으나, (DISCRIMINIATION 앞에 UNJUSTIFIABLE OR ARBITRARY 추가) EC 등 기타국가는동 사항은 이미 협상 과정에서 집중적으로 토의된바 있으며 특정 표준 또는 기준을 충족하는 경우에만 차별하지 않도록 제한적으로 규정하였으므로 당초의 표현에 문제가 없다고 함.

　　O 서비스 협정 발효후 12개월이내에 현존인정 조치를 통지하도록 규정한 4항 A)와 관련, 사무국은 서비스 협정 단독으로 발효될 수는 없으므로 MTO 협정 발효이후 12개월이내로 통지한다는 문안으로 수정 제의하여 이를 채택함.

　　O 2항의 PARTY 를 MEMBER 로 수정한 것은 사무국 착오임을 확인함

　　3. 제 8조(독점)

　　O 미국은 SPECIFIC COMMITMENT 를 한분야에 새로이 독점 기업을 지정할 경우 제21

통상국	법무부	보사부	문화부	교통부	체신부	경기원	재무부	농수부
상공부	건설부	과기처	해항정	특허정	공보처			

PAGE 1

조(양허수정)를 적용하도록 한 4항에 제22조(협의), 23조(분쟁해결)도 적용토록 하자고 제의하였으나 22조 23조의 적용은 당연한 것이므로 굳이 추가할 필요가 없다는다수 의견에 따라 동제의를 철회함

4. 제12조(BOP 조항)

O MATHUR 의장은 본 조항 운영 관계기구의 기능을 MTO 협정의 구조에 비추어 다음과 같이 사무국이 정하였음을 설명함

- BOP 조항 원용국가의 협의 담당기구 : BOP위원회(5항 A 및 E)
- BOP 를 이유로한 제한조치의 통지처 : 일반이사회(4항)
- BOP 협의절차 제정기구 : 각료회의(5항 B)
- IMF 비회원국의 본조항 원용 절차 제정기구 : 각료회의(6항 : EC는 2년에 한번씩 개최되는 각료회의 보다는 일반 이사회가 적합하다고 지적

O 이에 대해, 4항 BOP 제한 조치의 통지처는 일반이사회보다는 BOP 위원회로 하자는 EC 의 의견이 제시되었으며, 한편 E항의 IMF 조사결과는 모든 개별MTO 회원국이수용하여야 한다는 취지로 규정하기로 합의함.

5. 제16조(시장접근)

O 1항의 OTHER MEMBERS 를 제2조 및 제17조 1항과 일관되게 ANY OTHER MEMBER로 통일하기로 합의함.

O 서비스의 국경간 공급에 자본이 동(유입, 유출)이필수적인 경우 당해 서비스의 국경간 공급에 시장접근 약속을 하였으면 관련 자본이동도 허용하도록 약속한 것이라고 규정한 제16조주석(P.25 첫째 주석)을 국경간 이동 이외의 서비스공급(특히 소비자 이동에 의한 공급형태)에도 해당하도록 규정하자고 스위스가 제의(THROUGH 이하OF ARTICLE I 까지 삭제) 하였으나 대부분의 나라가 반대함.

6. 2항의 OTHER MEMBER 를 1항의 ANY OTHER MEMBER로 통일함

7. 양허협상(제19조)

O 미국은 제3항의 후속 양허협상의 가인드라인 작성을 위한 국제 서비스 무역현황 평가담당기구로서 사무국초안의 각료회의 보다는 서비스이사회가 적합하다는 의견을 제시하였으며 인도는 가이드라인 작성 주체는 각료회의로 추정되는것인지 의문을 제시하였음.

8. 자유화약속 목록(제20조)

O 각국의 SCHEDULE 에 기재되어야 할 요소에 대하여제 16조, 17조, 18조 본문

내용등에 따라 다음과 같이 수정(동 항목들은 각국 SCHEDULE 의 각 COLUMN 의 제목이되게 됨) 하자는 제의에 대해 다수국이 동조하였으나 인도, 홍콩, 일본등이 당초안유지를 주장함.

- 1항 A) : LIMITATION AND CONDITIONS ON MARKET ACCESS
- 1 항 B : CONDITIONS AND QUALIFICATION ON NATIONALTREATMENT
- 1항 C) : ADDITIONAL COMMITMENTS.끝

  (대사   박수길-국장)수신처:통기, 경기원, 재무부, 법무부, 농수부, 상공부, 문화부, 건설부,교통부,체신부,보사부,과기처,공보처,항만청,특허청

외 무 부

종   별 :

번   호 : GVW-0996   일   시 : 92 0514 1930

수   신 : 장관(통기, 경기원, 재무부, 법무부, 농수부, 상공부, 문화부, 항만청, 특허청

발   신 : 주 제네바대사   건설부, 교통부, 체신부, 보사부, 과기처 공보처)

제   목 : UR/법제화그룹 비공식회의(개별협정문)   .

    서비스 협정문 사무국 수정안(TEXT 769)에 대한 5.13 논의 요지를 아래
보고함.(이경협관, 신서기관, 한경협관보 참석)

    1. 제 22조(협의), 23조(분쟁해결), 24조(공동행위)

    0 통합 분쟁해결 절차 및 MTO 협정의 토의가 진전된 이후에 추후 토의키로 함.

    2. 제 25조(이사회)

    0 제 1항의 서비스 이사회의 설치 및 권능의 근거는 MTO 협정의 해당 규정과 같이
서비스협정자체에서 찾아야 한다는 것(THERE SHALL BE) 이다수 의견이었음.

    0 제 2항 말미의 MEMBERS OF THIS AGREEMENT 는 MTO회원국을 의미하는 MEMBERS 로
변경함.

    3. 제 27조(타 국제 기구와의 관계)

    0 뉴질랜드는 동 조문의 MTO 협정문과 중복되므로 삭제하자고 주장하였으나 EC, 카
나다등은 타 국제기구와의 협력은 MTO 의 전체적인 차원에서의 협력뿐만 아니라 MTO
내여러 수준의 기구에서 이루어지는 협력도 상정할수 있으므로 서비스 협정에 별도
조항이 필요하다고 함.

    0 한편, EC 는 타국제기구와의 협력문제는 각료회의 보다는 일반 이사회가 취급하
는 것이 보다 적합하다고 지적함.

    4. 제 28조(수락 및 가입)

    0 사무국 초안은 본 조문을 모두 삭제하였으나 SCHEDULE 을 부속서에 포함시킨 국가
및 EC 에한하여 가입자격이 있다고 규정한 제 1항은 MTO협정 제
11조(원가맹국의양허표 제출의무 범위 관련 조항) 논의 결과에 따라 재생시킬수도
있다는 유보의사가 제기됨.(E.C)

    5. 제 30조(부적용)

| 통상국 | 법무부 | 보사부 | 문화부 | 교통부 | 체신부 | 경기원 | 재무부 | 농수부 |
| 상공부 | 건설부 | 과기처 | 해항청 | 특허청 | 공보처 | 2시10 | | |

외신 1과 통제관 ✓

0132

0 미국은 부적용 조항 MTO 협정 보다는 개별협정별로 규정하자는 것이 자국 기본입장이며, MTO협정에 규정한다 하더라도 MTO 협정상의 규정에 서비스 협정 제 30조 2 항과 같은 특수요건(부적용 이유 명시)이 주석등의 형식을 통해 MTO협정에 반영되지 않는한, MTO 협정상의 일반 규정이 개별 협정의 규정에 우선해서는 안된다는 입장을 개진함.

0 이에 인도는 MTO 상의 부적용 조항을 일반규정, 개별협정상의 조항을 특별규정으로 하는 2중 구조를 제시하였으나, EC 는 MTO 규정에 의한 일원적인 방법이나 또는 각 개별협정에 의한 부적용 규정중 양자 택일해야 한다는 의견을 개진함.

6. 제 31조(혜택부여 거부)

0 제 34조(용어의 정의)와 관련되므로 추후 토의키로함.

7. 제 32조(개정)

0 사무국 초안은 동 조문을 모두 삭제하였으나 미국, 일본, 카나다는 32조 1,2 항은 MTO 협정과 다른요소가 있으므로 당분간 유보하고 MTO 협정결과에 따라 결정하겠다고 함.(의장은 개정관련 조항은 기본적으로 MTO 차원에서 논의할 사항이므로 개별협정의 특수한 내용은 MTO 관련 규정에 반영되는 것이 바람직하다는 개인 의견을 피력)

8. 제 35조(부속서)

0 91.12.30 자 최종의정서안에는 없던 NATIONALSCHEDULE 양식(P.37) 이 삽입된데대하여 그 이유 및 법적 효력에 대한 의문이 제기되었는 바, 갓트법률국은 이는 최종의정서안에 누락되었던 것이며, 동 양식에 맞추어 SCHEDULE 을 제출할의무를 부과하는 것이라고 답변함.

0 이에 대하여 인도 및 EC 는 COMMITMENTS 의 명확성을 위하여 공통양식에 따라 SCHEDULE 을 제출할 필요성을 강조한 반면 스웨덴, 카나다, 호주등은 공통양식에 따를 필요성은 인정하나 SCHEDULE 양식 자체에 대해서 현재 협상이 진행중이기 때문에 이에 대한 토의는 시기상조라는 의견을 개진하면서 아무런 관련 본문없이 별도 PAGE 에 양식만 그려진 상태로법적 문서에 포함될수 있는지 의문을 표시함.

9. 제 21조(양허수정), 제34조(정의), 통신부속서, 항공부속서

0 기술적 과제가 남아 있는 분야이므로 토의하지 않음.

10. MFN 일탈에 관한 부속서

O 3항, 4항의 MFN 일탈 재검토 기구로서 사무국초안의 각료회의 보다는 서비스이사회가 적합하다는 의견(일본, 미국: 동 항의 검토대상으로서의 MFN일탈은 2항의 워이버와 다름을 지적함)과 MTO협정의 WAIVER 결정기구와 균형을 도모하여야 한다는 의견(EC, 카나다)이 대립됨.

11. DECISION CONCERNING ARTICLE 14(B) (P.56)

O 동 DECISION 의 법적 지위와 관련, 카나다 및 스위스는 MINISTERIAL DECISION으로 하는 것이 협상그룹의 의도였다고 한 반면 기타 국가들은 그와같은 이해가 없었다고 이의를 제기하여 합의를 도출하지 못함.

2. UNDERSTANDING ON COMMITMENTS IN FINANCIAL SERVICES

O 동 UNDERSTANDING 의 법적 지위와 관련,사무국 문서 제 6항(P.3) 이 현 상황을정확히 기술한 것이라는데는 이의가 없었으나 미국, EC, 스웨덴, 카나다등은 동 UNDERSTANDING 이 영구적지위를 가져야 한다고 주장한 반면, 인도, 브라질 등 개도국들은 동 UNDERSTANDING 은 NEGOTIATION GUIDELINE 에 불과하며, 영구적 성격을 가지는 것은 SPECIFIC COMMITMENTS 뿐이라고 주장함.

O MATHUR 의장은 동 UNDERSTANDING 과 DECISIONS CONCERNING ARTICLE 14(B) 의 법적 지위에 대하여 GATS 자체도 아니고 MINISTERIAL DECISION 도 아닌제 3의 형태를법률국에서 검토하도록 하고 협의를 종결함. 끝

(대사 박수길-국장)

PAGE 3

0134

외 무 부

종 별 :

번 호 : GVW-1004   일 시 : 92 0515 1200

수 신 : 장관(통기, 경기원, 재무부, 농림수산부, 상공부, 특허청)

발 신 : 주 제네바 대사

제 목 : UR/법제화 그룹

연: 제네(경) 20644-445

1. 표제그룹 6차 공식회의가 5.14 개최되어 3.23 제5차 공식회의 이후 진행된 비공식회의 결과를 공식적으로 확인한데 이어 의장제의로 향후 협의일정을 아래와 같이 정함.

0 통합분쟁 해결절차에 대한 사무국 수정안은 5월말경에 배포될 예정이며, 이어서 6월에 MTO 협정문, 개별협정문이 배포될 예정임.

0 통합 분쟁해결 절차에 대한 비공식 협의는 6.20 경에 재개하며, 이어서 MTO 협정문에 대한 논의를 가질 예정임.

0 기타 개별협정문에 대한 제 2차 논의 계획은 6월 말경 (필요한 경우 그이전에)에 동 필요성여부에 대한 논의를 거친후 확정키로함.

2. 한편 GATT 93 에 대한 5.13 비공식 논의에서는 조문별 논의를 하지 못하고 GATT 93 의 논의방향에 대한 일반적인 토의에 그친바, 동논의에서 미국 및 카나다는 GATT 47 협정문을 MTO 협정문의 체제와 일치시킬 뿐만 아니라 동협정문에 UR 협상의 성과를 반영하고(갓트2조에 농산물 협상 결과 반영), 또한 과거 갓트의 경험을 반영하여 사문화된 조항(제 3국산업 피해에 대한 반덤핑 상계관세 부과에관한 제 6조 6항 B 를 예로듦)의 삭제가능성, 부속서 상의 보충 규정을 본조항으로전환시키는 문제등도 함께 검토하는 방안을제시한 반면, 아국, 일본, 인도, EC 등 다수국이 GATT 93 에대한 논의는 중요한 사항이며, UR협상에서도 논의되지 않은점에 비추어 T3 권한내에서 극히 신중하게 접근해야 한다는 입장을 표명함.

3. GATT 93 사무국 수정안의 개별조문에 대한논의는 그 중요성에 비추어 각국의충분한 검토를실시한후 갖기로 한바 (검토일정은 확정되지않았으나 7월중에 검토될것으로 전망됨), 연호 동 사무국 수정안에 대한 본부 검토 의견회시 바람. 끝

통상국	2차보	외정실	분석관	경기원	재무부	농수부	상공부	특허청

(대사 박수길-국장)

0136

주 제 네 바 대 표 부

20, Route de Pre-Bois, POB 566 / (022) 791-0111 / (022) 791-0525(FAX)

문서번호 : 제네(경) 20644-757

시행일자 : 1992. 8. 21

수신 : 장관

참조 : 통상국장, 상공부장관

선결			지시	오섬교	
접수	일자시간		결재공람	대 사	
	번호	47776		차석대사	
처리자				참 사 관	
담당자	이재규			서 기 관	

제목 : UR/법제화 그룹(분쟁해결 절차)

    연 : GVW-905

    관세평가 협정 및 반덤핑 협정문의 분쟁해결절차와 MTO 통합분쟁 해결절차의
조화를 위한 카나다 비공식 수정안을 별첨 송부하니 업무에 참고 하시기 바랍니다.

    첨부 : 상기 카나다 수정안 1부. 끝.

92. 8. 21

    주   제   네   바   대   사

0137

CUSTOMS VALUATION

Drafting Suggestions

(restructure Articles 19 and 20 into one Article)
Consultations and Dispute Settlement

Article 19

19.1 Except as otherwise provided herein, the MTO Understanding on Rules and Procedures Governing the Settlement of Disputes, are applicable to consultations and the settlement of disputes under this Agreement.

19.2 If any Member considers that any benefit accruing to it, directly or indirectly, under this Agreement is being nullified or impaired, or that the achievement of any objective of this Agreement is being impeded, as a result of the actions of another Member or of other Members it may, with a view to reaching a mutually satisfactory solution of this matter, request consultations with the Member or Members in question. Each Member shall afford sympathetic consideration to any request from another Member for consultations.

19.3 The Technical Committee shall provide, upon request, advice and assistance to Members engaged in consultations.

*19.4 At the request of a party to the dispute, or on its own initiative, a panel established to examine a dispute relating to the provisions of this Agreement may request the Technical Committee to carry out an examination of any questions requiring ~~detailed~~ technical consideration. The panel shall determine the terms-of-reference of the Technical Committee for the particular dispute and set a time period for receipt of the report of the Technical Committee.

*19.5 Confidential material provided to the panel shall not be disclosed without the formal authorization from ~~specific permission of~~ the person or authority ~~government~~ providing such information. Where such information is requested from the panel but release of such information by the panel is not authorized, a non-confidential summary of this information, authorized by the person or authority ~~government~~ providing the information, shall be provided.

0138

Annex II

*para 2   (add an additional sub-paragraph - new (f) - and make
            consequential changes to text)

            (e) to facilitate, as requested, technical assistance to
            Members with a view to furthering the international
            acceptance of this Agreement; ~~and~~

            (f) to carry out an examination of a matter referred to
            it by a panel under Article 19 of this agreement; and

            (g f) to exercise such other responsibilities as the
            Committee may assign to it.

*para 3   The Technical Committee shall attempt to conclude its
            work on specific matters, especially those referred to it
            by Members, the Committee or a panel, in a reasonably
            short period of time. As provided in Article 19.4, a
            Panel shall ~~may~~ set a specific period time for receipt of
            a report of the Technical Committee and the Technical
            Committee shall provide its report within that period.

para 9   (add an additional sentence at end)
            Notwithstanding the provisions in sentence 1 of this
            paragraph, the Technical Committee shall meet as
            necessary to consider matters referred to it by a panel
            under the provisions of Article 19 of this Agreement.

*para 21   (add to para 21 the following two sentences)
            Notwithstanding the above provisions of this paragraph,
            on matters referred to it by a panel, the Technical
            Committee shall take decisions by consensus. Where no
            agreement is reached in the Technical Committee on the
            question referred to it by a panel ~~consensus is not
            possible~~, the Technical Committee shall provide a report
            detailing the facts of the matter and indicating the
            views of the members ~~participants~~.

Annex III

    - delete Annex, as special and additional provisions are
    incorporated into text

0139

June 22, 1992

ANTI-DUMPING

by special and additional provisions

Drafting Suggestions

*18.1   Except as otherwise provided ~~modified~~ herein, the MTO
         Understanding on Rules and Procedures Governing the
         Settlement of Disputes, are applicable to consultations
         and the settlement of disputes under this Agreement.

18.2   Each Member shall afford sympathetic consideration to,
         and shall afford adequate opportunity for consultation
         regarding, representations made by another member with
         respect to any matter affecting the operation of this
         Agreement.

18.3   If any Member considers that any benefit accruing to it,
         directly or indirectly, under this Agreement is being
         nullified or impaired, or that the achievement of any
         objective is being impeded, by another Member or Members,
         it may, with a view to reaching a mutually satisfactory
         resolution of the matter, request in writing
         consultations with the Member or Members in question.
         Each Member shall afford sympathetic consideration to any
         request from another Member for consultation.

*18.4   If the Member that requested consultations considers that
         the consultations pursuant to paragraph 18.3 have failed
         to achieve a mutually agreed solution and final action
         has been taken by the administering authorities of the
         importing Member ~~country~~ to levy definitive anti-dumping
         duties or to accept price undertakings, it may refer the
         matter to the Dispute Settlement Body (DSB). When a
         provisional measure has a significant impact and the
         Member considers the measure was taken contrary to the
         provisions of paragraph 1 of Article 7 of this Agreement,
         that Member may also refer such matter to the DSB.

*18.5   The DSB shall, at the request of the complaining party
         ~~any party to the dispute~~, establish a panel to examine
         the matter based upon:

         (a)   a written statement of the Member making the
                request indicating how a benefit accruing to it,
                directly or indirectly, under this Agreement has
                been nullified or impaired, or that the achieving
                of the objectives of the Agreement is being
                impeded,
                and

         (b)   the facts made available in conformity with

0140

appropriate domestic procedures to the authorities
of the importing Member ~~country~~.

*18.6   Confidential information provided to the panel shall not
be <u>disclosed</u> without formal authorization from the person
or authority providing such information. Where <u>such</u>
information is requested from the panel but release of
such information by the panel is not authorized, a non-
confidential summary of the information, authorized by
the <u>person</u> or <u>authority</u> providing the information, shall
~~will~~ be provided.

0141

외 무 부

종 별 :

번 호 : GVW-1775   일 시 : 92 0924 1730

수 신 : 장관(통기, 경기원, 재무부, 농수산부, 상공부)

발 신 : 주 제네바 대사

제 목 : UR/법제화 그룹 비공식 회의(GATT'93)

연: GVW-10041.

연호 3항 GATT '93(사무국안)에 대한 법제화 그룹 전체 차원에서의 논의에 앞서호주 대표부 주관으로 미국, EC, 일본, 카나다, 아국등 15여국이모여 법제화 차원에서 다루어야 할 동 갓트사무국안의 문제점을 파악하기 위해 지난 9.16 및 9.22 2차의 모임으로 갖고 15조 까지 검토 하였는바, 요지 아래 보고함. (신종원 서기관 참석)

가. 개별 조문

0 목차

- 잠정 적용 의정서의 MTO 협정상 지위(존폐여부)가 미정임 에 비추어 동 의정서의 갓트'93에서의 존치 여부 검토 필요(갓트 '93 의 84페이지에서는 PPA 가 삭제됨)

0 서문

- MTO 협정과 관련하여 재검토 필요 (MTO협정서문은 환경 요소를 감안, 자원의 적정한 이용을 추구하고 있는 반면, 갓트 '93 서문은 자원의 완전이용을 추구)

0 제 1조 (MFN)

- 2항에 열거된 MFN 원칙의 예외인 특혜중 현재도 유효한 특혜 현황 파악이 필요한바, 이를 갓트 사무국으로 하여금 정리키로 함.

0 제 2조(양허표)

- 4항: 수입독점과 갓트 '47 (현행갓트)의 제29조에 규정된 HAVANA CHARTER 와의관계 정립필요

- 6항: 양허표에 포함된 중량세, 과징금, 동 특혜폭의 표시 통화 액면가 (PAR VALVE) 개념과관련, 동 액면가 개념이 사용되고 있지 않는 현실을 감안, 대체 개념 정립 필요

통상국   경기원   재무부   농수부   상공부

PAGE 1   92.09.25 06:41 DZ

외신 1과 통제관

0142

0 제 3조(내국민 대우)

- 1항 주석(AD.I): 동 주석의 지방 정부 및 기관의 개념은 EC 의 경우 어디에 해당하는지 여부 검토 필요

0 제 4조 (영화 필름에 관한 특별 규정)

- 동 규정의 서비스 협정과의 관계 규명 필요

0 제 5조(통과 무역) 및 제 6조 (반덤핑 및상계관세)

- MTO 협정의 회원국 개념과 관련, EC 의경우 회원국(MEMBERSHIP)의 개념을 어떻게 적용할 것인가의 문제 (개별국 또는 EC 전체차원)

0 제 6조 6항

- 1줄과 8줄의 CONTRACTING PARTIES 를 사무국안처럼 상품 무역 이사회로 할것인지 아니면 반덤핑 위원회로 할 것인지 여부

0 제 7조(관세 평가)

- 1항: 9줄의 CONTRACTING PARTIES 를 상품 이사회,관세평가 위원회중 어느기관, 아니면 어떤 다른기관으로 해야 할 것인지 여부

0 제 10조(무역 규칙의 공표 및 적용)

- 2항 및 3항상의 단어 UNIFORM 이 적절한 용어인지 여부

0 제 13조(수량제한의 무차별 적용)

- 5항(동조의 모든 상품에의 확대 적용)과 농산물 협정 부속서 III 14조(최소시장 접근의 MFN 적용)와의 관계 명확화 필요

0 제 14조(수량 제한 무차별 적용의 예외)

- 동조의 24조(자유무역 협정, 관세 동맹) 와의관계 검토 필요

나. 공통사항

0 UR 협상 조문 그룹에서의 결정 수용 문제

- 조문그룹에서 합의된 결정의 법적성격(STATUS) 규명과 동 결정의 해당 조항에의 수용문제 (예 12조, 18조의 경우 BOP 조항에 관한 결정의 원조문에서 수용문제)

0 GATT '93 과 개별 협정간의 연계 언급 문제

- SINGLE-UNDERTAKING 의 원칙으로 MTO 협정의 1원 체제하에 들어온 GATT '93 과 개별협정또는 양해(UNDERSTANDING), 결정(DECISION) 간의관련 조항을 각 조항에서어떻게 기술적으로 CROSS-REFER 하는가의 문제 검토 필요

0 GATT '93 은 기본적으로 상품 무역을 규율하는 협정임에 비추어 GATT '47

상의CONTRACTINGPARTIES 를 일반 이사회(GENERAL COUNCIL) 또는 각료회의 (MINISTERIAL CONFERENCE)로 바꾸는 경우(예 : 12조) G.C. 또는 M. C 의 MTO 협정상의 기능에 비추어 볼때 기존 GATT 47상의 권리, 의무에 변동이 있는지 여부 검토 필요

2. 상기 검토시 제기된 특기 사항을 아래 보고함.

0 미국 대표는 상기 논의 과정에서 참석자의 참고로만 하기 바란다는 전제하에 MTO 기구의 기능에 따라 각각 MTO 해당기구 또는 MTO 자체로 용어를 바꾼 GATT '47 상의 CONTRACTING PARTIES 의 용어를 다시 사용하는 문제를 본국정부의 상당한 고위층 에서 검토중임을 언급하면서 동 배경을 아래와 같이 언급함.

- 첫째, GATT '47 상의 CONTRACTING PARTIES 의실제 기능은 조문에 따라 매우 다양한바, 동 역할이 정확히 MTO 의 어떤 기구에 해당하는지 결정하는 것은 쉽지 않음. 따라서 갓트 '47에서와 같은 CONTRACTING PARTIES 용어를 사용,융통성 있는 접근이 실제 운영에 있어서 효율적일 것임.

- 보다 기본적인 이유는 MTO 에 대한 미국내의 정서가 아직도 우호적 이라고 할수 없는바, 이는 미국인들이 자국의 주권을 MTO 에 상당부분 할양하는 것(참고로 MTO 협정 16조는 국내법 개정을 위해 노력해야 한다고 규정)을 달가와 하지 않는다는것이라면서 특히 15조의 MTO 는 MTO 사무국이 아니며 MTO 회원국으로 구성된 각료회의로 바꾸거나 CONTRACTING PARTIES 용어를 다시쓰는 방안도 고려할수 있음을 비춤(마스트리트조 약에 대한 불란서 국민 투표 과정에서 나타난 EC 집행위의 위상 강화에 대한 불란서국민의 거부감과의 유사성 언급)

0 이에 대해 상당수국이 MTO 설립은 SINGLE-UNDERTAKING 의 원칙에 따라 이미합의한 사항이며, 기술적으로도 CONTRACTING PARTIES 의용어는 MTO 라는 기구에는적합한 용어가 아님을 지적함.

(대사 박수길-국장)

1105

Legal Drafting Group   24 June 1992

REVIEW OF INDIVIDUAL TEXTS IN
THE DRAFT FINAL ACT

Informal Note by the Secretariat

        At informal meetings held in May 1992 the Legal Drafting Group
discussed rectifications to the text on Trade-Related Aspects of
Intellectual Property Rights, including Trade in Counterfeit Goods in
MTN.TNC/W/FA. The attached text reflects the rectifications agreed in
those meetings, including suggestions by the Secretariat contained in
document 790 and other suggestions made in the course of the discussion of
the text.

        When the Legal Drafting Group discussed the TRIPS text, there was a
general view that the terms "holder of the right" and "right holder" in
Section 6 of Part II of the TRIPS text should be harmonised (Article 36,
line 3; Article 37.1, line 12; Article 37.2, line 4). One view was that
this should be done by adopting the term "right holder" throughout, in
order to standardise usage with that in other parts of the TRIPS text.
Another view was that it would be preferable to use the term "holder of the
right" in this Section, since it was the term used and defined in the
Treaty on Intellectual Property in Respect of Integrated Circuits (IPIC
Treaty) that formed the basis of the commitments in the Section. Since the
two forms of harmonisation are mutually incompatible (at least without
changing the rest of the TRIPS text), the secretariat is suggesting in the
attached that the term "right holder" be used in Section 6 of Part II as in
other parts of the TRIPS Agreement, but with the addition of a footnote
stating that the term "right holder" in this Section shall be understood as
having the same meaning as the term "holder of the right" in the IPIC
Treaty.

        When the Legal Drafting Group discussed the TRIPS text, it was agreed
that the terminology referring to counterfeit and pirated goods in
Articles 46 (line 14), 51 (lines 3-4 and second footnote), 59 (line 5), 61
(lines 2 and 3) and 69 (line 7), should be harmonised. There were
different suggestions as to whether this should be done by referring to
"counterfeit trademark goods" and "pirated copyright goods" throughout or
by referring to "counterfeit goods" and "pirated goods" throughout. It
was, however, noted that, whichever set of terminology was chosen, the
meanings would not be affected since they would continue to be governed by
the definitions in the footnote to Article 51. Since that discussion, the
secretariat has looked into the drafting history of these terms. As
pointed out during the meeting, the definitions contained in a footnote to
Article 51 were derived from those in the Model for National Legislation to
Give Customs Powers to Implement Trademarks and Copyright Legislation
developed by the Customs Cooperation Council (see document
MTN.GNG/NG11/W/5/Add.5), which uses the terms "counterfeit goods" and

4-note18

0145

"pirated goods". The use of the more elaborate terms, "counterfeit trademark goods" and "pirated copyright goods", appears to have been a deliberate departure from the CCC language. Given this and that the meaning is not affected whichever terminology is used, the secretariat is suggesting in the attached text that these terms are used.

The rectifications have been marked by overstriking the words to be deleted; new text is in bold and underlined.

4-note18

TABLE OF CONTENTS

9fa-III   0147

<u>AGREEMENT ON TRADE-RELATED ASPECTS OF INTELLECTUAL</u>
<u>PROPERTY RIGHTS, INCLUDING TRADE IN COUNTERFEIT GOODS</u>

~~The-PARTIES-to-this-Agreement-(hereinafter-referred-to-as-"PARTIES"),~~
Members,

 <u>Desiring</u> to reduce distortions and impediments to international trade, and taking into account the need to promote effective and adequate protection of intellectual property rights, and to ensure that measures and procedures to enforce intellectual property rights do not themselves become barriers to legitimate trade;

 <u>Recognizing</u>, to this end, the need for new rules and disciplines concerning:

(a) the applicability of the basic principles of the GATT <u>1993</u> and of relevant international intellectual property agreements or conventions;

(b) the provision of adequate standards and principles concerning the availability, scope and use of trade-related intellectual property rights;

(c) the provision of effective and appropriate means for the enforcement of trade-related intellectual property rights, taking into account differences in national legal systems;

(d) the provision of effective and expeditious procedures for the multilateral prevention and settlement of disputes between governments; and

(e) transitional arrangements aiming at the fullest participation in the results of the negotiations;

 <u>Recognizing</u> the need for a multilateral framework of principles, rules and disciplines dealing with international trade in counterfeit goods;

 <u>Recognizing</u> that intellectual property rights are private rights;

 <u>Recognizing</u> the underlying public policy objectives of national systems for the protection of intellectual property, including developmental and technological objectives;

 <u>Recognizing</u> also the special needs of the least-developed ~~countries~~ **country Members** in respect of maximum flexibility in the domestic implementation of laws and regulations in order to enable them to create a sound and viable technological base;

 <u>Emphasizing</u> the importance of reducing tensions by reaching strengthened commitments to resolve disputes on trade-related intellectual property issues through multilateral procedures;

9fa-III   0148

Desiring to establish a mutually supportive relationship between GATT and the World Intellectual Property Organization (WIPO) as well as other relevant international organisations;

Hereby agree as follows:

PART I: GENERAL PROVISIONS AND BASIC PRINCIPLES

Article 1: Nature and Scope of Obligations

1.   ~~PARTIES~~ Members shall give effect to the provisions of this Agreement. ~~PARTIES~~ Members may, but shall not be obliged to, implement in their domestic law more extensive protection than is required by this Agreement, provided that such protection does not contravene the provisions of this Agreement. ~~PARTIES~~ Members shall be free to determine the appropriate method of implementing the provisions of this Agreement within their own legal system and practice.

2.   For the purposes of this Agreement, the term "intellectual property" refers to all categories of intellectual property that are the subject of Sections 1 to 7 of Part II.

3.   ~~PARTIES~~ Members shall accord the treatment provided for in this Agreement to the nationals of other ~~PARTIES~~ Members.[1] In respect of the relevant intellectual property right, the nationals of other ~~PARTIES~~ Members shall be understood as those natural or legal persons that would meet the criteria for eligibility for protection provided for in the Paris Convention (1967), the Berne Convention (1971), the Rome Convention and the Treaty on Intellectual Property in Respect of Integrated Circuits, were all ~~PARTIES~~ Members of the MTO members of those conventions.[2] Any ~~PARTY~~

---

[1] When "nationals" are referred to in this Agreement, they shall be deemed, in the case of Hong Kong, to mean persons, natural or legal, who are domiciled or who have a real and effective industrial or commercial establishment in Hong Kong.

[2] In this Agreement, "Paris Convention" refers to the Paris Convention for the Protection of Industrial Property; "Paris Convention (1967)" refers to the Stockholm Act of this Convention of 14 July 1967. "Berne Convention" refers to the Berne Convention for the Protection of Literary and Artistic Works; " Berne Convention (1971)" refers to the Paris Act of this Convention of 24 July 1971. "Rome Convention" refers to the International Convention for the Protection of Performers, Producers of Phonograms and Broadcasting Organisations, adopted at Rome on 26 October 1961. "Treaty on Intellectual Property in Respect of Integrated Circuits" (IPIC Treaty) refers to the Treaty on Intellectual Property in Respect of Integrated Circuits, adopted at Washington on 26 May 1989.

9fa-III

0149

Member availing itself of the possibilities provided in **paragraph** 3 **of** Article 5 or **paragraph** 2 **of Article** 6 of the Rome Convention shall make a notification as foreseen in those provisions to the Council ~~on~~ **for** Trade-Related Aspects of Intellectual Property Rights.

Article 2: Intellectual Property Conventions

1. In respect of Parts II, III and IV of this Agreement, ~~PARTIES~~ **Members** shall comply with Articles 1-12 and 19 of the Paris Convention (1967).

2. Nothing in Parts I to IV of this Agreement shall derogate from existing obligations that ~~PARTIES~~ **Members** may have to each other under the Paris Convention, the Berne Convention, the Rome Convention and the Treaty on Intellectual Property in Respect of Integrated Circuits.

Article 3: National Treatment

1. Each ~~PARTY~~ **Member** shall accord to the nationals of other ~~PARTIES~~ **Members** treatment no less favourable than that it accords to its own nationals with regard to the protection[1] of intellectual property, subject to the exceptions already provided in, respectively, the Paris Convention (1967), the Berne Convention (1971), the Rome Convention and the Treaty on Intellectual Property in Respect of Integrated Circuits. In respect of performers, producers of phonograms and broadcaster~~s~~**ing organizations**, this obligation only applies in respect of the rights provided under this Agreement. Any ~~PARTY~~ **Member** availing itself of the possibilities provided in Article 6 of the Berne Convention and **paragraph** 1(b) **of** Article 16 of the Rome Convention shall make a notification as foreseen in those provisions to the Council ~~on~~ **for** Trade-Related Aspects of Intellectual Property Rights.

2. ~~PARTIES~~ **Members** may avail themselves of the exceptions permitted under paragraph 1 above in relation to judicial and administrative procedures, including the designation of an address for service or the appointment of an agent within the jurisdiction of a ~~PARTY~~ **Member**, only where such exceptions are necessary to secure compliance with laws and regulations which are not inconsistent with the provisions of this Agreement and where such practices are not applied in a manner which would constitute a disguised restriction on trade.

Article 4: Most-Favoured-Nation Treatment

With regard to the protection of intellectual property, any advantage, favour, privilege or immunity granted by a ~~PARTY~~ **Member** to the nationals of any other country shall be accorded immediately and unconditionally to the

---

[1]For the purposes of Articles 3 and 4 of this Agreement, protection shall include matters affecting the availability, acquisition, scope, maintenance and enforcement of intellectual property rights as well as those matters affecting the use of intellectual property rights specifically addressed in ~~the~~ **this** Agreement.

9fa-III

0150

398 우루과이라운드 법제화 그룹 회의

nationals of all other ~~PARTIES~~ **Members**. Exempted from this obligation are any advantage, favour, privilege or immunity accorded by a ~~PARTY~~ **Member**:

(a) deriving from international agreements on judicial assistance and law enforcement of a general nature and not particularly confined to the protection of intellectual property ~~rights~~;

(b) granted in accordance with the provisions of the Berne Convention (1971) or the Rome Convention authorising that the treatment accorded be a function not of national treatment but of the treatment accorded in another country;

(c) in respect of the rights of performers, producers of phonograms and broadcaste~~rs~~**ing organizations** not provided under this Agreement;

(d) deriving from international agreements related to the protection of intellectual property which entered into force prior to the entry into force of [this Agreement] **[the Agreement Establishing the MTO]**, provided that such agreements are notified to the Council ~~on~~ **for** Trade-Related Aspects of Intellectual Property Rights and do not constitute an arbitrary or unjustifiable discrimination against nationals of other ~~PARTIES~~ **Members**.

Article 5: Multilateral Agreements on Acquisition or Maintenance of Protection

The obligations under Articles 3 and 4 above do not apply to procedures provided in multilateral agreements concluded under the auspices of the World Intellectual Property Organization relating to the acquisition or maintenance of intellectual property rights.

Article 6: Exhaustion

For the purposes of dispute settlement under this Agreement, subject to the provisions of Articles 3 and 4 above nothing in this Agreement shall be used to address the issue of the exhaustion of intellectual property rights.

Article 7: Objectives

The protection and enforcement of intellectual property rights should contribute to the promotion of technological innovation and to the transfer and dissemination of technology, to the mutual advantage of producers and users of technological knowledge and in a manner conducive to social and economic welfare, and to a balance of rights and obligations.

Article 8: Principles

1. ~~PARTIES~~ **Members** may, in formulating or amending their national laws and regulations, adopt measures necessary to protect public health and nutrition, and to promote the public interest in sectors of vital importance to their socio-economic and technological development, provided that such measures are consistent with the provisions of this Agreement.

9fa-III

0151

2. Appropriate measures, provided that they are consistent with the provisions of this Agreement, may be needed to prevent the abuse of intellectual property rights by right holders or the resort to practices which unreasonably restrain trade or adversely affect the international transfer of technology.

PART II: STANDARDS CONCERNING THE AVAILABILITY, SCOPE AND USE OF INTELLECTUAL PROPERTY RIGHTS

SECTION 1: COPYRIGHT AND RELATED RIGHTS

Article 9: Relation to Berne Convention

1. PARTIES Members shall comply with Articles 1-21 and the Appendix of the Berne Convention (1971). However, PARTIES Members shall not have rights or obligations under this Agreement in respect of the rights conferred under Article 6bis of that Convention or of the rights derived therefrom.

2. Copyright protection shall extend to expressions and not to ideas, procedures, methods of operation or mathematical concepts as such.

Article 10: Computer Programs and Compilations of Data

1. Computer programs, whether in source or object code, shall be protected as literary works under the Berne Convention (1971).

2. Compilations of data or other material, whether in machine readable or other form, which by reason of the selection or arrangement of their contents constitute intellectual creations shall be protected as such. Such protection, which shall not extend to the data or material itself, shall be without prejudice to any copyright subsisting in the data or material itself.

Article 11: Rental Rights

In respect of at least computer programs and cinematographic works, a PARTY Member shall provide authors and their successors in title the right to authorise or to prohibit the commercial rental to the public of originals or copies of their copyright works. A PARTY Member shall be excepted from this obligation in respect of cinematographic works unless such rental has led to widespread copying of such works which is materially impairing the exclusive right of reproduction conferred in that PARTY Member on authors and their successors in title. In respect of computer programs, this obligation does not apply to rentals where the program itself is not the essential object of the rental.

9fa-III

0152

Article 12: Term of Protection

Whenever the term of protection of a work, other than a photographic
work or a work of applied art, is calculated on a basis other than the life
of a natural person, such term shall be no less than fifty years from the
end of the calendar year of authorised publication, or, failing such
authorised publication within fifty years from the making of the work,
fifty years from the end of the calendar year of making.

Article 13: Limitations and Exceptions

PARTIES Members shall confine limitations or exceptions to exclusive
rights to certain special cases which do not conflict with a normal
exploitation of the work and do not unreasonably prejudice the legitimate
interests of the right holder.

Article 14: Protection of Performers, Producers of Phonograms
(Sound Recordings) and Broadeasts Broadcasing Organizations

1.   In respect of a fixation of their performance on a phonogram,
performers shall have the possibility of preventing the following acts when
undertaken without their authorisation: the fixation of their unfixed
performance and the reproduction of such fixation. Performers shall also
have the possibility of preventing the following acts when undertaken
without their authorisation: the broadcasting by wireless means and the
communication to the public of their live performance.

2.   Producers of phonograms shall enjoy the right to authorise or prohibit
the direct or indirect reproduction of their phonograms.

3.   Broadcasting organisations shall have the right to prohibit the
following acts when undertaken without their authorisation: the fixation,
the reproduction of fixations, and the rebroadcasting by wireless means of
broadcasts, as well as the communication to the public of television
broadcasts of the same. Where PARTIES Members do not grant such rights to
broadcasting organisations, they shall provide owners of copyright in the
subject matter of broadcasts with the possibility of preventing the above
acts, subject to the provisions of the Berne Convention (1971).

4.   The provisions of Article 11 in respect of computer programs shall
apply mutatis mutandis to producers of phonograms and any other right
holders in phonograms as determined in domestic law. If, on the date of
signature-of-this-Agreement adoption of the Final Act Establishing the
Results of the Uruguay Round of Multilateral Trade Negotiations a PARTY
Member has in force a system of equitable remuneration of right holders in
respect of the rental of phonograms, it may maintain such system provided
that the commercial rental of phonograms is not giving rise to the material
impairment of the exclusive rights of reproduction of right holders.

5.   The term of the protection available under this Agreement to
performers and producers of phonograms shall last at least until the end of
a period of fifty years computed from the end of the calendar year in which

9fa-III

the fixation was made or the performance ~~or broadcast~~ took place. The term of protection granted pursuant to paragraph 3 above shall last for at least twenty years from the end of the calendar year in which the broadcast took place.

6.   Any ~~PARTY~~ **Member** ~~to this Agreement~~ may, in relation to the rights conferred under paragraphs 1-3 above, provide for conditions, limitations, exceptions and reservations to the extent permitted by the Rome Convention. However, the provisions of Article 18 of the Berne Convention (1971) shall also apply, _mutatis mutandis_, to the rights of performers and producers of phonograms in phonograms.

<h3 align="center">SECTION 2: TRADEMARKS</h3>

<h4 align="center">Article 15: Protectable Subject Matter</h4>

1.   Any sign, or any combination of signs, capable of distinguishing the goods or services of one undertaking from those of other undertakings, shall be capable of constituting a trademark. Such signs, in particular words including personal names, letters, numerals, figurative elements and combinations of colours as well as any combination of such signs, shall be eligible for registration as trademarks. Where signs are not inherently capable of distinguishing the relevant goods or services, ~~PARTIES~~ **Members** may make registrability depend on distinctiveness acquired through use. ~~PARTIES~~ **Members** may require, as a condition of registration, that signs be visually perceptible.

2.   Paragraph 1 above shall not be understood to prevent a ~~PARTY~~ **Member** from denying registration of a trademark on other grounds, provided that they do not derogate from the provisions of the Paris Convention (1967).

3.   ~~PARTIES~~ **Members** may make registrability depend on use. However, actual use of a trademark shall not be a condition for filing an application for registration.   An application shall not be refused solely on the ground that intended use has not taken place before the expiry of a period of three years from the date of application.

4.   The nature of the goods or services to which a trademark is to be applied shall in no case form an obstacle to registration of the trademark.

5.   ~~PARTIES~~ **Members** shall publish each trademark either before it is registered or promptly after it is registered and shall afford a reasonable opportunity for petitions to cancel the registration. In addition, ~~PARTIES~~ **Members** may afford an opportunity for the registration of a trademark to be opposed.

<h4 align="center">Article 16: Rights Conferred</h4>

1.   The owner of a registered trademark shall have the exclusive right to prevent all third parties not having his consent from using in the course of trade identical or similar signs for goods or services which are

identical or similar to those in respect of which the trademark is registered where such use would result in a likelihood of confusion. In case of the use of an identical sign for identical goods or services, a likelihood of confusion shall be presumed. The rights described above shall not prejudice any existing prior rights, nor shall they affect the possibility of ~~PARTIES~~ Members making rights available on the basis of use.

2.   Article 6bis of the Paris Convention (1967) shall apply, mutatis mutandis, to services. In determining whether a trademark is well-known, account shall be taken of the knowledge of the trademark in the relevant sector of the public, including knowledge in that ~~PARTY~~ Member obtained as a result of the promotion of the trademark.

3.   Article 6bis of the Paris Convention (1967)) shall apply, mutatis mutandis, to goods or services which are not similar to those in respect of which a trademark is registered, provided that use of that trademark in relation to those goods or services would indicate a connection between those goods or services and the owner of the registered trademark and provided that the interests of the owner of the registered trademark are likely to be damaged by such use.

Article 17: Exceptions

~~PARTIES~~ Members may provide limited exceptions to the rights conferred by a trademark, such as fair use of descriptive terms, provided that such exceptions take account of the legitimate interests of the owner of the trademark and of third parties.

Article 18: Term of Protection

Initial registration, and each renewal of registration, of a trademark shall be for a term of no less than seven years. The registration of a trademark shall be renewable indefinitely.

Article 19: Requirement of Use

1.   If use is required to maintain a registration, the registration may be cancelled only after an uninterrupted period of at least three years of non-use, unless valid reasons based on the existence of obstacles to such use are shown by the trademark owner. Circumstances arising independently of the will of the owner of the trademark which constitute an obstacle to the use of the trademark, such as import restrictions on or other government requirements for goods or services protected by the trademark, shall be recognised as valid reasons for non-use.

2.   When subject to the control of its owner, use of a trademark by another person shall be recognised as use of the trademark for the purpose of maintaining the registration.

9fa-III

0155

UR(우루과이라운드)-법제화 그룹회의, 1992. 전2권(V.2 4-12월) 403

Article 20: Other Requirements

The use of a trademark in ~~commerce~~ **the course of trade** shall not be unjustifiably encumbered by special requirements, such as use with another trademark, use in a special form or use in a manner detrimental to its capability to distinguish the goods or services of one undertaking from those of other undertakings. This will not preclude a requirement prescribing the use of the trademark identifying the undertaking producing the goods or services along with, but without linking it to, the trademark distinguishing the specific goods or services in question of that undertaking.

Article 21: Licensing and Assignment

~~PARTIES~~ **Members** may determine conditions on the licensing and assignment of trademarks, it being understood that the compulsory licensing of trademarks shall not be permitted and that the owner of a registered trademark shall have the right to assign his trademark with or without the transfer of the business to which the trademark belongs.

SECTION 3: GEOGRAPHICAL INDICATIONS

Article 22: Protection of Geographical Indications

1. Geographical indications are, for the purposes of this Agreement, indications which identify a good as originating in the territory of a ~~PARTY~~ **Member**, or a region or locality in that territory, where a given quality, reputation or other characteristic of the good is essentially attributable to its geographical origin.

2. In respect of geographical indications, ~~PARTIES~~ **Members** shall provide the legal means for interested parties to prevent:

   (a) the use of any means in the designation or presentation of a good that indicates or suggests that the good in question originates in a geographical area other than the true place of origin in a manner which misleads the public as to the geographical origin of the good;

   (b) any use which constitutes an act of unfair competition within the meaning of Article 10bis of the Paris Convention (1967).

3. A ~~PARTY~~ **Member** shall, ex officio if its legislation so permits or at the request of an interested party, refuse or invalidate the registration of a trademark which contains or consists of a geographical indication with respect to goods not originating in the territory indicated, if use of the indication in the trademark for such goods in that ~~PARTY~~ **Member** is of such a nature as to mislead the public as to the true place of origin.

4. The provisions of the preceding paragraphs of this Article shall apply to a geographical indication which, although literally true as to the territory, region or locality in which the goods originate, falsely represents to the public that the goods originate in another territory.

9fa-III

Article 23: Additional Protection for Geographical Indications for Wines and Spirits

1.   Each PARTY Member shall provide the legal means for interested parties to prevent use of a geographical indication identifying wines for wines not originating in the place indicated by the geographical indication in question or identifying spirits for spirits not originating in the place indicated by the geographical indication in question, even where the true origin of the goods is indicated or the geographical indication is used in translation or accompanied by expressions such as "kind", "type", "style", "imitation" or the like.[1]

2.   The registration of a trademark for wines which contains or consists of a geographical indication identifying wines or for spirits which contains or consists of a geographical indication identifying spirits shall be refused or invalidated, _ex officio_ if domestic legislation so permits or at the request of an interested party, with respect to such wines or spirits not having this origin.

3.   In the case of homonymous geographical indications for wines, protection shall be accorded to each indication, subject to the provisions of paragraph 4 of Article 22 above. Each PARTY Member shall determine the practical conditions under which the homonymous indications in question will be differentiated from each other, taking into account the need to ensure equitable treatment of the producers concerned and that consumers are not misled.

4.   In order to facilitate the protection of geographical indications for wines, negotiations shall be undertaken in the Council on for Trade-Related Aspects of Intellectual Property Rights concerning the establishment of a multilateral system of notification and registration of geographical indications for wines eligible for protection in those PARTIES Members participating in the system.

Article 24: International Negotiations; Exceptions

1.   PARTIES Members agree to enter into negotiations aimed at increasing the protection of individual geographical indications under Article 23. The provisions of paragraphs 4-8 below shall not be used by a PARTYMember to refuse to conduct negotiations or to conclude bilateral or multilateral agreements. In the context of such negotiations, PARTIES Members shall be willing to consider the continued applicability of these provisions to individual geographical indications whose use was the subject of such negotiations.

2.   The Council on for Trade-Related Aspects of Intellectual Property Rights shall keep under review the application of the provisions of this

---

[1]Notwithstanding the first sentence of Article 42, PARTIES Members may, with respect to these obligations, instead provide for enforcement by administrative action.

9fa-III

0157

Section; the first such review shall take place within two years of the entry into force of [this Agreement] [the Agreement Establishing the MTO]. Any matter affecting the compliance with the obligations under these provisions may be drawn to the attention of the Council, which, at the request of a PARTY Member, shall consult with any PARTY Member or PARTIES Members in respect of such matter in respect of which it has not been possible to find a satisfactory solution through bilateral or plurilateral consultations between the PARTIES Members concerned. The Council shall take such action as may be agreed to facilitate the operation and further the objectives of this Section.

3. In implementing this Section, a PARTY Member shall not diminish the protection of geographical indications that existed in that PARTY Member immediately prior to the date of entry into force of [this Agreement] [the Agreement Establishing the MTO].

4. Nothing in this Section shall require a PARTY Member to prevent continued and similar use of a particular geographical indication of another PARTY Member identifying wines or spirits in connection with goods or services by any of its nationals or domiciliaries who have used that geographical indication in a continuous manner with regard to the same or related goods or services in the territory of that PARTY Member either (a) for at least ten years preceding its signature of this Agreement the date of adoption of the Final Act Embodying the Results of the Uruguay Round of Multilateral Trade Negotiations or (b) in good faith preceding its signature of this Agreement that date.

5. Where a trademark has been applied for or registered in good faith, or where rights to a trademark have been acquired through use in good faith either:

   (a) before the date of application of these provisions in that PARTY Member as defined in Part VI below; or

   (b) before the geographical indication is protected in its country of origin;

measures adopted to implement this Section shall not prejudice eligibility for or the validity of the registration of a trademark, or the right to use a trademark, on the basis that such a trademark is identical with, or similar to, a geographical indication.

6. Nothing in this Section shall require a PARTY Member to apply its provisions in respect of a geographical indication of any other PARTY Member with respect to goods or services for which the relevant indication is identical with the term customary in common language as the common name for such goods or services in the territory of that PARTY Member. Nothing in this Section shall require a PARTY Member to apply its provisions in respect of a geographical indication of any other PARTY Member with respect to products of the vine for which the relevant indication is identical with the customary name of a grape variety existing in the territory of that PARTY Member as of the date of entry into force of [this Agreement] [the Agreement Establishing the MTO].

9fa-III

0158

- 13 -

7. A ~~PARTY~~ **Member** may provide that any request made under this Section in connection with the use or registration of a trademark must be presented within five years after the adverse use of the protected indication has become generally known in that ~~PARTY~~ **Member** or after the date of registration of the trademark in that ~~PARTY~~ **Member** provided that the trademark has been published by that date, if such date is earlier than the date on which the adverse use became generally known in that ~~PARTY~~ **Member**, provided that the geographical indication is not used or registered in bad faith.

8. The provisions of this Section shall in no way prejudice the right of any person to use, in the course of trade, his name or the name of his predecessor in business, except where such name is used in such a manner as to mislead the public.

9. There shall be no obligation under this Agreement to protect geographical indications which are not or cease to be protected in their country of origin, or which have fallen into disuse in that country.

SECTION 4: INDUSTRIAL DESIGNS

Article 25: Requirements for Protection

1. ~~PARTIES~~ **Members** shall provide for the protection of independently created industrial designs that are new or original. ~~PARTIES~~ **Members** may provide that designs are not new or original if they do not significantly differ from known designs or combinations of known design features. ~~PARTIES~~ **Members** may provide that such protection shall not extend to designs dictated essentially by technical or functional considerations.

2. Each ~~PARTY~~ **Member** shall ensure that requirements for securing protection for textile designs, in particular in regard to any cost, examination or publication, do not unreasonably impair the opportunity to seek and obtain such protection. ~~PARTIES~~ **Members** shall be free to meet this obligation through industrial design law or through copyright **law**.

Article 26: Protection

1. The owner of a protected industrial design shall have the right to prevent third parties not having his consent from making, selling or importing articles bearing or embodying a design which is a copy, or substantially a copy, of the protected design, when such acts are undertaken for commercial purposes.

2. ~~PARTIES~~ **Members** may provide limited exceptions to the protection of industrial designs, provided that such exceptions do not unreasonably conflict with the normal exploitation of protected industrial designs and do not unreasonably prejudice the legitimate interests of the owner of the protected design, taking account of the legitimate interests of third parties.

3. The duration of protection available shall amount to at least ten years.

9fa-III

0159

SECTION 5: PATENTS

Article 27: Patentable Subject Matter

1.   Subject to the provisions of paragraphs 2 and 3 below, patents shall be available for any inventions, whether products or processes, in all fields of technology, provided that they are new, involve an inventive step and are capable of industrial application.[1] Subject to paragraph 4 of Article 65, **paragraph 8 of Article 70** and paragraph 3 of this Article, patents shall be available and patent rights enjoyable without discrimination as to the place of invention, the field of technology and whether products are imported or locally produced.

2.   ~~PARTIES~~ **Members** may exclude from patentability inventions, the prevention within their territory of the commercial exploitation of which is necessary to protect ordre public or morality, including to protect human, animal or plant life or health or to avoid serious prejudice to the environment, provided that such exclusion is not made merely because the exploitation is prohibited by domestic law.

3.   ~~PARTIES~~ **Members** may also exclude from patentability:

   (a) diagnostic, therapeutic and surgical methods for the treatment of humans or animals;

   (b) plants and animals other than microorganisms, and essentially biological processes for the production of plants or animals other than non-biological and microbiological processes. However, ~~PARTIES~~ **Members** shall provide for the protection of plant varieties either by patents or by an effective sui generis system or by any combination thereof. ~~This~~ **The** provision**s of this sub-paragraph** shall be reviewed four years after the entry into force of [this Agreement] **[the Agreement Establishing the MTO]**.

Article 28: Rights Conferred

1.   A patent shall confer on its owner the following exclusive rights:

   (a) where the subject matter of a patent is a product, to prevent third parties not having his consent from the acts of: making, using, offering for sale, selling, or importing[2] for these purposes that product;

---

[1]For the purposes of this Article, the terms "inventive step" and "capable of industrial application" may be deemed by a ~~PARTY~~ **Member** to be synonymous with the terms "non-obvious" and "useful" respectively.

[2]This right, like all other rights conferred under this Agreement in respect of the use, sale, importation or other distribution of goods, is subject to the provisions of Article 6 above.

(b) where the subject matter of a patent is a process, to prevent
third parties not having his consent from the act of using the
process, and from the acts of: using, offering for sale,
selling, or importing for these purposes at least the product
obtained directly by that process.

2.   Patent owners shall also have the right to assign, or transfer by
succession, the patent and to conclude licensing contracts.

Article 29: Conditions on Patent Applicants

1.   PARTIES Members shall require that an applicant for a patent shall
disclose the invention in a manner sufficiently clear and complete for the
invention to be carried out by a person skilled in the art and may require
the applicant to indicate the best mode for carrying out the invention
known to the inventor at the filing date or, where priority is claimed, at
the priority date of the application.

2.   PARTIES Members may require an applicant for a patent to provide
information concerning his corresponding foreign applications and grants.

Article 30: Exceptions to Rights Conferred

PARTIES Members may provide limited exceptions to the exclusive rights
conferred by a patent, provided that such exceptions do not unreasonably
conflict with a normal exploitation of the patent and do not unreasonably
prejudice the legitimate interests of the patent owner, taking account of
the legitimate interests of third parties.

Article 31: Other Use Without Authorisation of the Right Holder

Where the law of a PARTY Member allows for other use[1] of the subject
matter of a patent without the authorisation of the right holder, including
use by the government or third parties authorised by the government, the
following provisions shall be respected:

(a) authorisation of such use shall be considered on its individual
merits;

(b) such use may only be permitted if, prior to such use, the
proposed user has made efforts to obtain authorisation from the
right holder on reasonable commercial terms and conditions and
that such efforts have not been successful within a reasonable
period of time. This requirement may be waived by a PARTY Member
in the case of a national emergency or other circumstances of
extreme urgency or in cases of public non-commercial use. In
situations of national emergency or other circumstances of
extreme urgency, the right holder shall, nevertheless, be
notified as soon as reasonably practicable. In the case of
public non-commercial use, where the government or contractor,

---

[1]"Other use" refers to use other than that allowed under Article 30.

9fa-III

without making a patent search, knows or has demonstrable grounds to know that a valid patent is or will be used by or for the government, the right holder shall be informed promptly;

(c) the scope and duration of such use shall be limited to the purpose for which it was authorised;

(d) such use shall be non-exclusive;

(e) such use shall be non-assignable, except with that part of the enterprise or goodwill which enjoys such use;

(f) any such use shall be authorised predominantly for the supply of the domestic market of the ~~PARTY~~ Member authorising such use;

(g) authorisation for such use shall be liable, subject to adequate protection of the legitimate interests of the persons so authorised, to be terminated if and when the circumstances which led to it cease to exist and are unlikely to recur. The competent authority shall have the authority to review, upon motivated request, the continued existence of these circumstances;

(h) the right holder shall be paid adequate remuneration in the circumstances of each case, taking into account the economic value of the authorisation; ~~reasonably-practicable.--In-the-case-of-public-non-commercial use,-where-the-government-or-contractor,-without-making-a-patent search,-knows-or-has-demonstrable-grounds-to-know-that-a-valid patent-is-or-will-be-used-by-or-for-the-government,-the-right holder-shall-be-informed-promptly;~~

(i) the legal validity of any decision relating to the authorisation of such use shall be subject to judicial review or other independent review by a distinct higher authority in that ~~PARTY~~ Member;

(j) any decision relating to the remuneration provided in respect of such use shall be subject to judicial review or other independent review by a distinct higher authority in that ~~PARTY~~ Member;

(k) ~~PARTIES~~ Members are not obliged to apply the conditions set forth in sub-paragraphs (b) and (f) above where such use is permitted to remedy a practice determined after judicial or administrative process to be anti-competitive. The need to correct anti-competitive practices may be taken into account in determining the amount of remuneration in such cases. Competent authorities shall have the authority to refuse termination of authorisation if and when the conditions which led to such authorisation are likely to recur;

(l) where such use is authorised to permit the exploitation of a patent ("the second patent") which cannot be exploited without

9fa-III

0162

infringing another patent ("the first patent"), the following additional conditions shall apply:

(i)   the invention claimed in the second patent shall involve an important technical advance of considerable economic significance in relation to the invention claimed in the first patent;

(ii)   the owner of the first patent shall be entitled to a cross-licence on reasonable terms to use the invention claimed in the second patent; and

(iii)   the use authorised in respect of the first patent shall be non-assignable except with the assignment of the second patent.

Article 32: Revocation/Forfeiture

An opportunity for judicial review of any decision to revoke or forfeit a patent shall be available.

Article 33: Term of Protection

The term of protection available shall not end before the expiration of a period of twenty years counted from the filing date.[1]

Article 34: Process Patents: Burden of Proof

1.   For the purposes of civil proceedings in respect of the infringement of the rights of the owner referred to in **paragraph 1(b) of** Article 28 **above**, if the subject matter of a patent is a process for obtaining a product, the judicial authorities shall have the authority to order the defendant to prove that the process to obtain an identical product is different from the patented process. Therefore, PARTIES **Members** shall provide, in at least one of the following circumstances, that any identical product when produced without the consent of the patent owner shall, in the absence of proof to the contrary, be deemed to have been obtained by the patented process:

(a)   if the product obtained by the patented process is new;

(b)   if there is a substantial likelihood that the identical product was made by the process and the owner of the patent has been unable through reasonable efforts to determine the process actually used.

2.   Any PARTY **Member** shall be free to provide that the burden of proof indicated in paragraph 1 shall be on the alleged infringer only if the

---

[1] It is understood that those PARTIES **Members** which do not have a system of original grant may provide that the term of protection shall be computed from the filing date in the system of original grant.

9fa-III

0163

condition referred to in sub-paragraph (a) is fulfilled or only if the condition referred to in sub-paragraph (b) is fulfilled.

3.   In the adduction of proof to the contrary, the legitimate interests of the defendant in protecting his manufacturing and business secrets shall be taken into account.

SECTION 6: LAYOUT-DESIGNS (TOPOGRAPHIES) OF INTEGRATED CIRCUITS

Article 35: Relation to IPIC Treaty

PARTIES Members agree to provide protection to the layout-designs (topographies) of integrated circuits (hereinafter referred to as "layout-designs") in accordance with Articles 2-7 (other than paragraph 3 of Article 6), Article 12 and paragraph 3 of Article 16 of the Treaty on Intellectual Property in Respect of Integrated Circuits as-opened-for signature-on-26-May-1989 and, in addition, to comply with the following provisions.

Article 36: Scope of the Protection

Subject to the provisions of paragraph 1 of Article 37 below, PARTIES Members shall consider unlawful the following acts if performed without the authorisation of the right holder[1] of-the-right: importing, selling, or otherwise distributing for commercial purposes a protected layout-design, an integrated circuit in which a protected layout-design is incorporated, or an article incorporating such an integrated circuit only insofar as it continues to contain an unlawfully reproduced layout-design.

Article 37: Acts not Requiring the Authorisation of the Holder of the Right

1.   Notwithstanding Article 36 above, no PARTY Members shall consider unlawful the performance of any of the acts referred to in that Article in respect of an integrated circuit incorporating an unlawfully reproduced layout-design or any article incorporating such an integrated circuit where the person performing or ordering such acts did not know and had no reasonable ground to know, when acquiring the integrated circuit or article incorporating such an integrated circuit, that it incorporated an unlawfully reproduced layout-design. PARTIES Members shall provide that, after the time that such person has received sufficient notice that the layout-design was unlawfully reproduced, he may perform any of the acts with respect to the stock on hand or ordered before such time, but shall be liable to pay to the right holder of-the-right a sum equivalent to a reasonable royalty such as would be payable under a freely negotiated licence in respect of such a layout-design.

2.   The conditions set out in sub-paragraphs (a)-(k) of Article 31 above shall apply mutatis mutandis in the event of any non-voluntary licensing of

---

[1]The term "right holder" in this Section shall be understood as having the same meaning as the term "holder of the right" in the IPIC Treaty.

9fa-III

a layout-design or of its use by or for the government without the
authorisation of the right holder.

Article 38: Term of Protection

1.   In PARTIES Members requiring registration as a condition of
protection, the term of protection of layout-designs shall not end before
the expiration of a period of ten years counted from the date of filing an
application for registration or from the first commercial exploitation
wherever in the world it occurs.

2.   In PARTIES Members not requiring registration as a condition for
protection, layout-designs shall be protected for a term of no less than
ten years from the date of the first commercial exploitation wherever in
the world it occurs.

3.   Notwithstanding paragraphs 1 and 2 above, a PARTY Member may provide
that protection shall lapse fifteen years after the creation of the
layout-design.

SECTION 7: PROTECTION OF UNDISCLOSED INFORMATION

Article 39

1.   In the course of ensuring effective protection against unfair
competition as provided in Article 10bis of the Paris Convention (1967),
PARTIES Members shall protect undisclosed information in accordance with
paragraph 2 below and data submitted to governments or governmental
agencies in accordance with paragraph 3 below.

2.   Natural and legal persons shall have the possibility of preventing
information lawfully within their control from being disclosed to, acquired
by, or used by others without their consent in a manner contrary to honest
commercial practices[1] so long as such information:

-    is secret in the sense that it is not, as a body or in the precise
     configuration and assembly of its components, generally known among or
     readily accessible to persons within the circles that normally deal
     with the kind of information in question;

-    has commercial value because it is secret; and

-    has been subject to reasonable steps under the circumstances, by the
     person lawfully in control of the information, to keep it secret.

---

[1]For the purpose of this provision, "a manner contrary to honest
commercial practices" shall mean at least practices such as breach of
contract, breach of confidence and inducement to breach, and includes the
acquisition of undisclosed information by third parties who knew, or were
grossly negligent in failing to know, that such practices were involved in
the acquisition.

9fa-III

3. PARTIES Members, when requiring, as a condition of approving the
marketing of pharmaceutical or of agricultural chemical products which
utilise new chemical entities, the submission of undisclosed test or other
data, the origination of which involves a considerable effort, shall
protect such data against unfair commercial use. In addition, PARTIES
Members shall protect such data against disclosure, except where necessary
to protect the public, or unless steps are taken to ensure that the data
are protected against unfair commercial use.

SECTION 8: CONTROL OF ANTI-COMPETITIVE PRACTICES IN CONTRACTUAL LICENCES

Article 40

1. PARTIES Members agree that some licensing practices or conditions
pertaining to intellectual property rights which restrain competition may
have adverse effects on trade and may impede the transfer and dissemination
of technology.

2. Nothing in this Agreement shall prevent PARTIES Members from
specifying in their national legislation licensing practices or conditions
that may in particular cases constitute an abuse of intellectual property
rights having an adverse effect on competition in the relevant market. As
provided above, a PARTY Member may adopt, consistently with the other
provisions of this Agreement, appropriate measures to prevent or control
such practices, which may include for example exclusive grantback
conditions, conditions preventing challenges to validity and coercive
package licensing, in the light of the relevant laws and regulations of
that PARTY Member.

3. Each PARTY Member shall enter, upon request, into consultations with
any other PARTY Member which has cause to believe that an intellectual
property right owner that is a national or domiciliary of the PARTY Member
to which the request for consultations has been addressed is undertaking
practices in violation of the requesting PARTY's Member's laws and
regulations on the subject matter of this Section, and which wishes to
secure compliance with such legislation, without prejudice to any action
under the law and to the full freedom of an ultimate decision of either
PARTY Member. The PARTY Member addressed shall accord full and sympathetic
consideration to, and shall afford adequate opportunity for, consultations
with the requesting PARTY Member, and shall cooperate through supply of
publicly available non-confidential information of relevance to the matter
in question and of other information available to the PARTY Member, subject
to domestic law and to the conclusion of mutually satisfactory agreements
concerning the safeguarding of its confidentiality by the requesting PARTY
Member.

4. A PARTY Member whose nationals or domiciliaries are subject to
proceedings in another PARTY Member concerning alleged violation of that
other PARTY's Member's laws and regulations on the subject matter of this
Section shall, upon request, be granted an opportunity for consultations by
the other PARTY Member under the same conditions as those foreseen in
paragraph 3 above.

9fa-III

0166

PART III: ENFORCEMENT OF INTELLECTUAL PROPERTY RIGHTS

SECTION 1: GENERAL OBLIGATIONS

Article 41

1. ~~PARTIES~~ **Members** shall ensure that enforcement procedures as specified in this Part are available under their national laws so as to permit effective action against any act of infringement of intellectual property rights covered by this Agreement, including expeditious remedies to prevent infringements and remedies which constitute a deterrent to further infringements. These procedures shall be applied in such a manner as to avoid the creation of barriers to legitimate trade and to provide for safeguards against their abuse.

2. Procedures concerning the enforcement of intellectual property rights shall be fair and equitable. They shall not be unnecessarily complicated or costly, or entail unreasonable time-limits or unwarranted delays.

3. Decisions on the merits of a case shall preferably be in writing and reasoned. They shall be made available at least to the parties to the ~~dispute~~ **proceeding** without undue delay. Decisions on the merits of a case shall be based only on evidence in respect of which parties were offered the opportunity to be heard.

4. Parties to a ~~dispute~~ **proceeding** shall have an opportunity for review by a judicial authority of final administrative decisions and, subject to jurisdictional provisions in national laws concerning the importance of a case, of at least the legal aspects of initial judicial decisions on the merits of a case. However, there shall be no obligation to provide an opportunity for review of acquittals in criminal cases.

5. It is understood that this Part does not create any obligation to put in place a judicial system for the enforcement of intellectual property rights distinct from that for the enforcement of laws in general, nor does it affect the capacity of ~~PARTIES~~ **Members** to enforce their laws in general. Nothing in this Part creates any obligation with respect to the distribution of resources as between enforcement of intellectual property rights and the enforcement of laws in general.

SECTION 2: CIVIL AND ADMINISTRATIVE PROCEDURES AND REMEDIES

Article 42: Fair and Equitable Procedures

~~PARTIES~~ **Members** shall make available to right holders[1] civil judicial procedures concerning the enforcement of any intellectual property right

---

[1] For the purpose of this Part, the term "right holder" includes federations and associations having legal standing to assert such rights.

9fa-III

covered by this Agreement. Defendants shall have the right to written notice which is timely and contains sufficient detail, including the basis of the claims. Parties shall be allowed to be represented by independent legal counsel, and procedures shall not impose overly burdensome requirements concerning mandatory personal appearances. All parties to such procedures shall be duly entitled to substantiate their claims and to present all relevant evidence. The procedure shall provide a means to identify and protect confidential information, unless this would be contrary to existing constitutional requirements.

Article 43:   Evidence of Proof

1.   The judicial authorities shall have the authority, where a party has presented reasonably available evidence sufficient to support its claims and has specified evidence relevant to substantiation of its claims which lies in the control of the opposing party, to order that this evidence be produced by the opposing party, subject in appropriate cases to conditions which ensure the protection of confidential information.

2.   In cases in which a party to a proceeding voluntarily and without good reason refuses access to, or otherwise does not provide necessary information within a reasonable period, or significantly impedes a procedure relating to an enforcement action, a PARTY Member may accord judicial authorities the authority to make preliminary and final determinations, affirmative or negative, on the basis of the information presented to them, including the complaint or the allegation presented by the party adversely affected by the denial of access to information, subject to providing the parties an opportunity to be heard on the allegations or evidence.

Article 44:   Injunctions

1.   The judicial authorities shall have the authority to order a party to desist from an infringement, _inter alia_ to prevent the entry into the channels of commerce in their jurisdiction of imported goods that involve the infringement of an intellectual property right, immediately after customs clearance of such goods. PARTIES Members are not obliged to accord such authority in respect of protected subject matter acquired or ordered by a person prior to knowing or having reasonable grounds to know that dealing in such subject matter would entail the infringement of an intellectual property right.

2.   Notwithstanding the other provisions of this Part and provided that the provisions of Part II specifically addressing use by governments, or by third parties authorised by a government, without the authorisation of the right holder are complied with, PARTIES Members may limit the remedies available against such use to payment of remuneration in accordance with sub-paragraph (h) of Article 31 above. In other cases, the remedies under this Part shall apply or, where these remedies are inconsistent with national law, declaratory judgments and adequate compensation shall be available.

9fa-III

Article 45: Damages

1.   The judicial authorities shall have the authority to order the
infringer to pay the right holder damages adequate to compensate for the
injury the right holder has suffered because of an infringement of his
intellectual property right by an infringer who knew or had reasonable
grounds to know that he was engaged in infringing activity.

2.   The judicial authorities shall also have the authority to order the
infringer to pay the right holder expenses, which may include appropriate
attorney's fees. In appropriate cases, PARTIES Members may authorise the
judicial authorities to order recovery of profits and/or payment of
pre-established damages even where the infringer did not know or had no
reasonable grounds to know that he was engaged in infringing activity.

Article 46: Other Remedies

In order to create an effective deterrent to infringement, the
judicial authorities shall have the authority to order that goods that they
have found to be infringing be, without compensation of any sort, disposed
of outside the channels of commerce in such a manner as to avoid any harm
caused to the right holder, or, unless this would be contrary to existing
constitutional requirements, destroyed. The judicial authorities shall
also have the authority to order that materials and implements the
predominant use of which has been in the creation of the infringing goods
be, without compensation of any sort, disposed of outside the channels of
commerce in such a manner as to minimise the risks of further
infringements. In considering such requests, the need for proportionality
between the seriousness of the infringement and the remedies ordered as
well as the interests of third parties shall be taken into account. In
regard to counterfeit trademark goods, the simple removal of the trademark
unlawfully affixed shall not be sufficient, other than in exceptional
cases, to permit release of the goods into the channels of commerce.

Article 47: Right of Information

PARTIES Members may provide that the judicial authorities shall have
the authority, unless this would be out of proportion to the seriousness of
the infringement, to order the infringer to inform the right holder of the
identity of third persons involved in the production and distribution of
the infringing goods or services and of their channels of distribution.

Article 48: Indemnification of the Defendant

1.   The judicial authorities shall have the authority to order a party at
whose request measures were taken and who has abused enforcement procedures
to provide to a party wrongfully enjoined or restrained adequate
compensation for the injury suffered because of such abuse. The judicial
authorities shall also have the authority to order the applicant to pay the
defendant expenses, which may include appropriate attorney's fees.

9fa-III

0169

2.   In respect of the administration of any law pertaining to the protection or enforcement of intellectual property rights, ~~PARTIES~~ **Members** shall only exempt both public authorities and officials from liability to appropriate remedial measures where actions are taken or intended in good faith in the course of the administration of such laws.

Article 49: Administrative Procedures

To the extent that any civil remedy can be ordered as a result of administrative procedures on the merits of a case, such procedures shall conform to principles equivalent in substance to those set forth in this Section.

SECTION 3: PROVISIONAL MEASURES

Article 50

1.   The judicial authorities shall have the authority to order prompt and effective provisional measures:

   (a)   to prevent an infringement of any intellectual property right from occurring, and in particular to prevent the entry into the channels of commerce in their jurisdiction of goods, including imported goods immediately after customs clearance;

   (b)   to preserve relevant evidence in regard to the alleged infringement.

2.   The judicial authorities shall have the authority to adopt provisional measures *inaudita altera parte* where appropriate, in particular where any delay is likely to cause irreparable harm to the right holder, or where there is a demonstrable risk of evidence being destroyed.

3.   The judicial authorities shall have the authority to require the applicant to provide any reasonably available evidence in order to satisfy themselves with a sufficient degree of certainty that the applicant is the right holder and that his right is being infringed or that such infringement is imminent, and to order the applicant to provide a security or equivalent assurance sufficient to protect the defendant and to prevent abuse.

4.   Where provisional measures have been adopted *inaudita altera parte*, the parties affected shall be given notice, without delay after the execution of the measures at the latest. A review, including a right to be heard, shall take place upon request of the defendant with a view to deciding, within a reasonable period after the notification of the measures, whether these measures shall be modified, revoked or confirmed.

5.   The applicant may be required to supply other information necessary for the identification of the goods concerned by the authority that will execute the provisional measures.

9fa-III

6.   Without prejudice to paragraph 4 above, provisional measures taken on the basis of paragraphs 1 and 2 above shall, upon request by the defendant, be revoked or otherwise cease to have effect, if proceedings leading to a decision on the merits of the case are not initiated within a reasonable period, to be determined by the judicial authority ordering the measures where national law so permits or, in the absence of such a determination, not to exceed twenty working days or thirty-one calendar days, whichever is the longer.

7.   Where the provisional measures are revoked or where they lapse due to any act or omission by the applicant, or where it is subsequently found that there has been no infringement or threat of infringement of an intellectual property right, the judicial authorities shall have the authority to order the applicant, upon request of the defendant, to provide the defendant appropriate compensation for any injury caused by these measures.

8.   To the extent that any provisional measure can be ordered as a result of administrative procedures, such procedures shall conform to principles equivalent in substance to those set forth in this Section.

SECTION 4:   SPECIAL REQUIREMENTS RELATED TO BORDER MEASURES[1]

Article 51:   Suspension of Release by Customs Authorities

PARTIES Members shall, in conformity with the provisions set out below, adopt procedures[2] to enable a right holder, who has valid grounds for suspecting that the importation of counterfeit trademark or pirated

---

[1] Where a PARTY Member has dismantled substantially all controls over movement of goods across its border with another PARTY Member with which it forms part of a customs union, it shall not be required to apply the provisions of this Section at that border.

[2] It is understood that there shall be no obligation to apply such procedures to imports of goods put on the market in another country by or with the consent of the right holder, or to goods in transit.

9fa-III

copyright goods[1] may take place, to lodge an application in writing with competent authorities, administrative or judicial, for the suspension by the customs authorities of the release into free circulation of such goods. ~~PARTIES~~ Members may enable such an application to be made in respect of goods which involve other infringements of intellectual property rights, provided that the requirements of this Section are met. ~~PARTIES~~ Members may also provide for corresponding procedures concerning the suspension by the customs authorities of the release of infringing goods destined for exportation from their territories.

Article 52: Application

Any right holder initiating the procedures under Article 51 above shall be required to provide adequate evidence to satisfy the competent authorities that, under the laws of the country of importation, there is _prima facie_ an infringement of his intellectual property right and to supply a sufficiently detailed description of the goods to make them readily recognisable by the customs authorities. The competent authorities shall inform the applicant within a reasonable period whether they have accepted the application and, where determined by the competent authorities, the period for which the customs authorities will take action.

Article 53: Security or Equivalent Assurance

1.   The competent authorities shall have the authority to require an applicant to provide a security or equivalent assurance sufficient to protect the defendant and the competent authorities and to prevent abuse. Such security or equivalent assurance shall not unreasonably deter recourse to these procedures.

2.   Where pursuant to an application under this Section the release of goods involving industrial designs, patents, ~~integrated-circuits~~ **layout-designs** or undisclosed information into free circulation has been

---

[1]For the purposes of this Agreement:

- counterfeit trademark goods shall mean any goods, including packaging, bearing without authorisation a trademark which is identical to the trademark validly registered in respect of such goods, or which cannot be distinguished in its essential aspects from such a trademark, and which thereby infringes the rights of the owner of the trademark in question under the law of the country of importation;

- pirated copyright goods shall mean any goods which are copies made without the consent of the right holder or person duly authorised by him in the country of production and which are made directly or indirectly from an article where the making of that copy would have constituted an infringement of a copyright or a related right under the law of the country of importation.

suspended by customs authorities on the basis of a decision other than by a judicial or other independent authority, and the period provided for in Article 55 has expired without the granting of provisional relief by the duly empowered authority, and provided that all other conditions for importation have been complied with, the owner, importer, or consignee of such goods shall be entitled to their release on the posting of a security in an amount sufficient to protect the right holder for any infringement. Payment of such security shall not prejudice any other remedy available to the right holder, it being understood that the security shall be released if the right holder fails to pursue his right of action within a reasonable period of time.

Article 54: Notice of Suspension

The importer and the applicant shall be promptly notified of the suspension of the release of goods according to Article 51 above.

Article 55: Duration of Suspension

If, within a period not exceeding ten working days after the applicant has been served notice of the suspension, the customs authorities have not been informed that proceedings leading to a decision on the merits of the case have been initiated by a party other than the defendant, or that the duly empowered authority has taken provisional measures prolonging the suspension of the release of the goods, the goods shall be released, provided that all other conditions for importation or exportation have been complied with; in appropriate cases, this time-limit may be extended by another ten working days. If proceedings leading to a decision on the merits of the case have been initiated, a review, including a right to be heard, shall take place upon request of the defendant with a view to deciding, within a reasonable period, whether these measures shall be modified, revoked or confirmed. Notwithstanding the above, where the suspension of the release of goods is carried out or continued in accordance with a provisional judicial measure, the provisions of Article 50, paragraph 6 above shall apply.

Article 56: Indemnification of the Importer
and of the Owner of the Goods

Relevant authorities shall have the authority to order the applicant to pay the importer, the consignee and the owner of the goods appropriate compensation for any injury caused to them through the wrongful detention of goods or through the detention of goods released pursuant to Article 55 above.

Article 57: Right of Inspection and Information

Without prejudice to the protection of confidential information, PARTIES Members shall provide the competent authorities the authority to give the right holder sufficient opportunity to have any product detained by the customs authorities inspected in order to substantiate his claims.

9fa-III

The competent authorities shall also have authority to give the importer an equivalent opportunity to have any such product inspected. Where a positive determination has been made on the merits of a case, ~~PARTIES~~ Members may provide the competent authorities the authority to inform the right holder of the names and addresses of the consignor, the importer and the consignee and of the quantity of the goods in question.

Article 58: Ex Officio Action

Where ~~PARTIES~~ Members require competent authorities to act upon their own initiative and to suspend the release of goods in respect of which they have acquired prima facie evidence that an intellectual property right is being infringed:

(a) the competent authorities may at any time seek from the right holder any information that may assist them to exercise these powers;

(b) the importer and the right holder shall be promptly notified of the suspension. Where the importer has lodged an appeal against the suspension with the competent authorities, the suspension shall be subject to the conditions, mutatis mutandis, set out at Article 55 above;

(c) ~~PARTIES~~ Members shall only exempt both public authorities and officials from liability to appropriate remedial measures where actions are taken or intended in good faith.

Article 59: Remedies

Without prejudice to other rights of action open to the right holder and subject to the right of the defendant to seek review by a judicial authority, competent authorities shall have the authority to order the destruction or disposal of infringing goods in accordance with the principles set out in Article 46 above. In regard to counterfeit trademark goods, the authorities shall not allow the re-exportation of the infringing goods in an unaltered state or subject them to a different customs procedure, other than in exceptional circumstances.

Article 60: De Minimis Imports

~~PARTIES~~ Members may exclude from the application of the above provisions small quantities of goods of a non-commercial nature contained in travellers' personal luggage or sent in small consignments.

SECTION 5: CRIMINAL PROCEDURES

Article 61

~~PARTIES~~ Members shall provide for criminal procedures and penalties to be applied at least in cases of wilful trademark counterfeiting or

9fa-III

0174

copyright piracy on a commercial scale. Remedies available shall include imprisonment and/or monetary fines sufficient to provide a deterrent, consistently with the level of penalties applied for crimes of a corresponding gravity. In appropriate cases, remedies available shall also include the seizure, forfeiture and destruction of the infringing goods and of any materials and implements the predominant use of which has been in the commission of the offence. PARTIES Members may provide for criminal procedures and penalties to be applied in other cases of infringement of intellectual property rights, in particular where they are committed wilfully and on a commercial scale.

PART IV: ACQUISITION AND MAINTENANCE OF INTELLECTUAL PROPERTY RIGHTS AND RELATED INTER-PARTES PROCEDURES

Article 62

1. PARTIES Members may require, as a condition of the acquisition or maintenance of the intellectual property rights provided for under Sections 2-6 of Part II of this Agreement, compliance with reasonable procedures and formalities. Such procedures and formalities shall be consistent with the provisions of this Agreement.

2. Where the acquisition of an intellectual property right is subject to the right being granted or registered, PARTIES Members shall ensure that the procedures for grant or registration, subject to compliance with the substantive conditions for acquisition of the right, permit the granting or registration of the right within a reasonable period of time so as to avoid unwarranted curtailment of the period of protection.

3. Article 4 of the Paris Convention (1967) shall apply mutatis mutandis to service marks.

4. Procedures concerning the acquisition or maintenance of intellectual property rights and, where the national law provides for such procedures, administrative revocation and inter partes procedures such as opposition, revocation and cancellation, shall be governed by the general principles set out in paragraphs 2 and 3 of Article 41.

5. Final administrative decisions in any of the procedures referred to under paragraph 4 above shall be subject to review by a judicial or quasi-judicial authority. However, there shall be no obligation to provide an opportunity for such review of decisions in cases of unsuccessful opposition or administrative revocation, provided that the grounds for such procedures can be the subject of invalidation procedures.

9fa-III

PART V: DISPUTE PREVENTION AND SETTLEMENT

Article 63: Transparency

1.   Laws and regulations, and final judicial decisions and administrative rulings of general application, made effective by any PARTY **Member** pertaining to the subject matter of this Agreement (the availability, scope, acquisition, enforcement and prevention of the abuse of intellectual property rights) shall be published, or where such publication is not practicable made publicly available, in a national language, in such a manner as to enable governments and right holders to become acquainted with them.   Agreements concerning the subject matter of this Agreement which are in force between the government or a governmental agency of any PARTY **Member** and the government or a governmental agency of any other PARTY **Member** shall also be published.

2.   PARTIES **Members** shall notify the laws and regulations referred to in paragraph 1 above to the Council on Trade-Related Aspects of Intellectual Property Rights in order to assist that Council in its review of the operation of this Agreement.   The Council shall attempt to minimise the burden on PARTIES **Members** in carrying out this obligation and may decide to waive the obligation to notify such laws and regulations directly to the Council if consultations with the World Intellectual Property Organisation on the establishment of a common register containing these laws and regulations are successful.   The Council shall also consider in this connection any action required regarding notifications pursuant to the obligations under this Agreement stemming from the provisions of Article 6*ter* of the Paris Convention (1967).

3.   Each PARTY **Member** shall be prepared to supply, in response to a written request from another PARTY **Member**, information of the sort referred to in paragraph 1 above.   A PARTY **Member**, having reason to believe that a specific judicial decision or administrative ruling or bilateral agreement in the area of intellectual property rights affects its rights under this Agreement, may also request in writing to be given access to or be informed in sufficient detail of such specific judicial decisions or administrative rulings or bilateral agreements.

4.   Nothing in paragraphs 1 to 3 above shall require PARTIES **Members** to disclose confidential information which would impede law enforcement or otherwise be contrary to the public interest or would prejudice the legitimate commercial interests of particular enterprises, public or private.

Article 64: Dispute Settlement

The provisions of Articles XXII and XXIII of the General Agreement on Tariffs and Trade **1993 as elaborated and applied by the MTO** and the Understanding on Rules and Procedures Governing the Settlement of Disputes under Articles XXII and XXIII of the General Agreement on Tariffs and Trade as adopted by the CONTRACTING PARTIES shall apply to consultations and the

9fa-III

settlement of disputes under this Agreement except as otherwise
specifically provided herein.[1]

PART VI: TRANSITIONAL ARRANGEMENTS

Article 65: Transitional Arrangements

1.   Subject to the provisions of paragraphs 2, 3 and 4 below, no PARTY
Member shall be obliged to apply the provisions of this Agreement before
the expiry of a general period of one year following the date of entry into
force of [this Agreement] **[the Agreement Establishing the MTO]**.

2.   Any developing country PARTY **Member** is entitled to delay for a further
period of four years the date of application, as defined in paragraph 1
above, of the provisions of this Agreement other than Articles 3, 4 and 5
of Part I.

3.   Any other PARTY **Member** which is in the process of transformation from
a centrally-planned into a market, free-enterprise economy and which is
undertaking structural reform of its intellectual property system and
facing special problems in the preparation and implementation of
intellectual property laws, may also benefit from a period of delay as
foreseen in paragraph 2 above.

4.   To the extent that a developing country PARTY **Member** is obliged by
this Agreement to extend product patent protection to areas of technology
not **so** protectable in its territory on the general date of application of
this Agreement for that PARTY **Member**, as defined in paragraph 2 above, it
may delay the application of **the provisions on product patents of** Section 5
of Part II of this Agreement to such areas of technology for an additional
period of five years.

5.   Any PARTY **Member** availing itself of a transitional period under
paragraphs 1, 2, 3 or 4 **above** shall ensure that any changes in its domestic
laws, regulations and practice made during that period do not result in a
lesser degree of consistency with the provisions of this Agreement.

Article 66: Least-Developed ~~Countries~~ **Country** Members

1.   In view of their special needs and requirements, their economic,
financial and administrative constraints, and their need for flexibility to
create a viable technological base, least-developed country ~~PARTIES~~ **Members**
shall not be required to apply the provisions of this Agreement, other than
Articles 3, 4 and 5, for a period of 10 years from the date of

---

[1]This provision may need to be revised in the light of the outcome of
work on the establishment of an Integrated Dispute Settlement Understanding
under the Agreement Establishing the Multilateral Trade Organisation.

application as defined under paragraph 1 of Article 65 above. The Council shall, upon duly motivated request by a least-developed ~~country-PARTY~~ **Member**, accord extensions of this period.

2.   Developed country ~~PARTIES~~ **Members** shall provide incentives to enterprises and institutions in their territories for the purpose of promoting and encouraging technology transfer to least-developed country ~~PARTIES~~ **Members** in order to enable them to create a sound and viable technological base.

Article 67: Technical Cooperation

In order to facilitate the implementation of this Agreement, developed country ~~PARTIES~~ **Members** shall provide, on request and on mutually agreed terms and conditions, technical and financial cooperation in favour of developing and least-developed country ~~PARTIES~~ **Members**. Such cooperation shall include assistance in the preparation of domestic legislation on the protection and enforcement of intellectual property rights as well as on the prevention of their abuse, and shall include support regarding the establishment or reinforcement of domestic offices and agencies relevant to these matters, including the training of personnel.

PART VII: INSTITUTIONAL ARRANGEMENTS; FINAL PROVISIONS

Article 68: Council ~~on~~ for Trade-Related Aspects of Intellectual Property Rights

The Council ~~on~~ **for** Trade-Related Aspects of Intellectual Property Rights shall monitor the operation of this Agreement and, in particular, ~~PARTIES~~ **Members'** compliance with their obligations hereunder, and shall afford ~~PARTIES~~ **Members** the opportunity of consulting on matters relating to the trade-related aspects of intellectual property rights. It shall carry out such other responsibilities as assigned to it by the ~~PARTIES~~ **Members**, and it shall, in particular, provide any assistance requested by them in the context of dispute settlement procedures. In carrying out its functions, the Council may consult with and seek information from any source it deems appropriate. In consultation with the World Intellectual Property Organization, the Council shall seek to establish, within one year of its first meeting, appropriate arrangements for cooperation with bodies of that Organization.

Article 69: International Cooperation

~~PARTIES~~ **Members** agree to cooperate with each other with a view to eliminating international trade in goods infringing intellectual property rights. For this purpose, they shall establish and notify contact points in their national administrations and be ready to exchange information on trade in infringing goods. They shall, in particular, promote the exchange of information and cooperation between customs authorities with regard to trade in counterfeit **trademark goods** and pirated **copyright** goods.

9fa-III   0178

Article 70: Protection of Existing Subject Matter

1. This Agreement does not give rise to obligations in respect of acts which occurred before the date of application of the Agreement for the PARTY Member in question.

2. Except as otherwise provided for in this Agreement, this Agreement gives rise to obligations in respect of all subject matter existing at the date of application of this Agreement for the PARTY Member in question, and which is protected in that PARTY Member on the said date, or which meets or comes subsequently to meet the criteria for protection under the terms of this Agreement. In respect of this paragraph and paragraphs 3 and 4 below, copyright obligations with respect to existing copyrighted works shall be solely determined under Article 18 of the Berne Convention (1971), and obligations with respect to the rights of producers of phonograms and performers in existing phonograms shall be determined solely under Article 18 of the Berne Convention (1971) as made applicable under paragraph 6 of Article 14 of this Agreement.

3. There shall be no obligation to restore protection to subject matter which on the date of application of this Agreement for the PARTY Member in question has fallen into the public domain.

4. In respect of any acts in respect of specific objects embodying protected subject matter which become infringing under the terms of legislation in conformity with this Agreement, and which were commenced, or in respect of which a significant investment was made, before the date of ratification acceptance of [this Agreement] the Agreement Establishing the MTO] by that PARTY Member, any PARTY Member may provide for a limitation of the remedies available to the right holder as to the continued performance of such acts after the date of application of the Agreement for that PARTY Member. In such cases the PARTY Member shall, however, at least provide for the payment of equitable remuneration.

5. A PARTY Member is not obliged to apply the provisions of Article 11 and of paragraph 4 of Article 14 with respect to originals or copies purchased prior to the date of application of this Agreement for that PARTY Member.

6. PARTIES Members shall not be required to apply Article 31, or the requirement in paragraph 1 of Article 27 that patent rights shall be enjoyable without discrimination as to the field of technology, to use without the authorisation of the right holder where authorisation for such use was granted by the government before the date this Agreement became known.

7. In the case of intellectual property rights for which protection is conditional upon registration, applications for protection which are pending on the date of application of this Agreement for the PARTY Member in question shall be permitted to be amended to claim any enhanced protection provided under the provisions of this Agreement. Such amendments shall not include new matter.

9fa-III

0179

8. Where a PARTY Member does not make available as of the date of entry into force of [this Agreement] [the Agreement establishing the MTO] patent protection for pharmaceutical and agricultural chemical products commensurate with its obligations under Article 27, that PARTY Member shall:

  (i) notwithstanding the provisions of Part VI above, provide as from the date of entry into force of [the this Agreement] [the Agreement Establishing the MTO] a means by which applications for patents for such inventions can be filed;

  (ii) apply to these applications, as of the date of application of this Agreement, the criteria for patentability as laid down in this Agreement as if those criteria were being applied on the date of filing in that PARTY Member or, where priority is available and claimed, the priority date of the application;

  (iii) provide patent protection in accordance with this Agreement as from the grant of the patent and for the remainder of the patent term, counted from the filing date in accordance with Article 33 of this Agreement, for those of these applications that meet the criteria for protection referred to in sub-paragraph (ii) above.

9. Where a product is the subject of a patent application in a PARTY Member in accordance with paragraph 8(i) above, exclusive marketing rights shall be granted, notwithstanding the provisions of Part VI above, for a period of five years after obtaining market approval in that PARTY Member or until a product patent is granted or rejected in that PARTY Member, whichever period is shorter, provided that, subsequent to the entry into force of [this Agreement] [the Agreement Establishing the MTO], a patent application has been filed and a patent granted for that product in another PARTY Member and marketing approval obtained in such other PARTY Member.

Article 71: Review and Amendment

1. PARTIES The Council for Trade-Related Aspects of Intellectual Property Rights shall review the implementation of this Agreement after the expiration of the transitional period referred to in paragraph 2 of Article 65 above. They The Council shall, having regard to the experience gained in its implementation, review it two years after that date, and at identical intervals thereafter. The PARTIES Council may also undertake reviews in the light of any relevant new developments which might warrant modification or amendment of this Agreement.

2. Amendments merely serving the purpose of adjusting to higher levels of protection of intellectual property rights achieved, and in force, in other multilateral agreements and accepted by all PARTIES Members may be adopted by the Council.

Article 72: Reservations

Reservations may not be entered in respect of any of the provisions of this Agreement without the consent of the other PARTIES Members.

9fa-III

0180

Article 73: Security Exceptions

Nothing in this Agreement shall be construed:

(a) to require any ~~PARTY~~ **Member** to furnish any information the disclosure of which it considers contrary to its essential security interests; or

(b) to prevent any ~~PARTY~~ **Member** from taking any action which it considers necessary for the protection of its essential security interests;

    (i) relating to fissionable materials or the materials from which they are derived;

    (ii) relating to the traffic in arms, ammunition and implements of war and to such traffic in other goods and materials as is carried on directly or indirectly for the purpose of supplying a military establishment;

    (iii) taken in time of war or other emergency in international relations; or

(c) to prevent any ~~PARTY~~ **Member** from taking any action in pursuance of its obligations under the United Nations Charter for the maintenance of international peace and security.

Legal Drafting Group   24 June 1992

Agreement on Trade-Related Aspects of Intellectual Property Rights, including Trade in Counterfeit Goods

Specific points and drafting suggestions to which the Group may wish to revert in the course of its further consideration of the text are listed below.

Preamble

It was suggested that, in line 3 of sub-paragraph (c) of the second indent and in line 1 of the fifth indent, the word "national" might be changed to "domestic", there being no intent to make a distinction between national legal systems or national systems for the protection of intellectual property and domestic ones. (See also note on Article 8.1 below.)

Article 6

It was suggested that the following footnote, which had appeared in earlier drafts of the TRIPS Agreement, be reinserted:

"For the purposes of exhaustion, the European Communities shall be considered a single Member."

Articles 8.1 (line 1), 40.2 (line 2), 41.1 (line 2), 41.4 (line 3), 44.2 (line 8), 50.6 (line 6) and 62.4 (line 2)

It was suggested that, regardless of any general solution that might be found in the MTO to the issue of the applicability of the adjective "national" to Members that were not nation states, it would be desirable to replace the word "national" where references are made to national legislation, regulations or law in these provisions by "domestic" in order to standardise usage with other parts of the Agreement which refer to domestic legislation, regulations or law without intending to make a distinction in meaning.

Article 11

It was suggested that, in the last line, the words "the essential object" be changed to "an essential object".

Articles 11 and 13

It was suggested that, in line 2 of Article 11, the word "exclusive" be added before "right". In order to allow for applicability of the provisions of Article 13 on limitations and exceptions to rental rights under Article 11, it was alternatively suggested that the word "exclusive" be deleted in the first line of Article 13.

4-note19

Article 14, paragraph 4

It was suggested that the first five words of this paragraph be altered to read: "The provisions of the first sentence of Article 11", in order to make it clear that the last sentence of Article 11 would not apply to phonograms.

Article 23, paragraph 2

It was suggested that the words at the end of the sentence "not having this origin" be replaced by "not originating in the place indicated by the geographical indication in question", in order to align the language with that used in paragraph 1.

Article 24, paragraph 2

It was suggested that more thought might need to be given to the relation of this provision to Article 64.

Article 24, paragraph 4

A participant reserved its position on the inclusion of the words "or spirits" in the third line. The Legal Drafting Group noted the secretariat's explanation that this addition had been made in the corrigenda circulated in document 155 in January 1992 in order to reflect accurately the intention of the Chairman of the TRIPS Negotiating Group in adding, in the draft Final Act, spirits to the products benefiting from additional protection under Article 23 of the TRIPS text.

Article 27, paragraph 1

Some participants said that they might revert to the drafting of the second sentence.

Article 27, paragraph 3(a)

It was suggested that this provision be redrafted along the lines of the corresponding provision in the WIPO Model Law for Developing Countries on Inventions (Patents), Section 112 (3)(iv), so that the text would read:

"Methods for treatment of the human or animal body by surgery or therapy, as well as diagnostic methods practised on the human or animal body.".

Article 41, paragraphs 3 and 4

One participant reserved its position on the suggestion that, in line 3 of paragraph 2 and line 1 of paragraph 4, the term "dispute" be replaced by "proceeding", in order to avoid any risk of confusion with terminology used in the Understanding on Rules and Procedures Governing the Settlement of Disputes and in order to align usage with that in the rest of Part III of the TRIPS text.

4-note19

0183

Article 56

It was suggested that, in line 1, the word "Relevant" be changed to "Competent".

Article 64

It was suggested that it should be made clear that Articles XXII and XXIII of the GATT 1993 would be applied *mutatis mutandis*, not literally, since the obligations and benefits accruing under the TRIPS Agreement were different from those under the GATT.

Different views were expressed on the desirability of retaining the footnote. In the end, it was noted that the footnote would be retained for the time being, given that the work on the Understanding on Rules and Procedures Governing the Settlement of Disputes had not yet been completed.

Article 65, paragraph 4

The Legal Drafting Group noted the secretariat's explanation that the two corrections made in January clarified the intention of the Chairman in putting forward the text that the paragraph should deal with product patent protection only. Some participants reserved their position regarding the second correction.

Article 68

The question was raised as to whether it should be made clear that this provision would be without prejudice to the functions of the Dispute Settlement Body.

Article 69

It was suggested that, in line 4, "national administrations" be changed to "central governments". It was also suggested that a generic solution should be found for the problem underlying the suggestion.

Article 70, paragraph 6

The question was raised as to whether the date referred to in this provision might be clarified.

Article 70, paragraph 8

It was suggested that, in sub-paragraph (ii), "the date of application of this Agreement" be replaced by "the relevant date of application of this Agreement in accordance with Part VI above".

Article 71, paragraph 2

It was suggested that the requirement that amendments of the sort referred to in this provision must have been "accepted by all Members" be

4-note19

replaced by language reflecting a requirement that such amendments must
have received the positive agreement of all Members without requiring
formal acceptance as such. For example, it was suggested that the words
"and accepted by all Members may be adopted by the Council" might be
replaced by "may be adopted unanimously by the Council".

4-note19

FROM: EPB 통상조정3과 이성학 사무관

URUGUAY ROUND: TRACK 3; AUSTRALIAN APPROACHES TO MTO AND INTEGRATED DISPUTE SETTLEMENT ISSUES

1. **Multilateral Trade Organisation**

The Track 3 Group is charged with the task of completing work on the legal/institutional framework for the Final Act through elaborating the Agreement on Establishment of the Multilateral Trade Organisation (MTO). Useful progress has been made but a number of issues remain to be resolved. Issues on which Australia has formulated views are listed below.

Non-application

In Australia's view there is an unintended loophole in the current text which would enable countries to circumvent the obligation of the Single Undertaking. At the moment, the text would allow a country to refuse to apply the new TRIPS or Services Agreements but another member would not be permitted to non-apply GATT to that country by way of retaliation unless it was already "non-applying" GATT to that member.

This has been considered by the Track 3 Group and the following solutions have been considered:

- permitting non-application of other Goods Agreements by the injured member, e.g. textiles, agriculture, anti-dumping, in response to non-application of TRIPS or Services by another member

- allowing 'retaliatory' non-application by removing the prohibition on non-application of GATT unless the MTO member has already been doing so

- a provision requiring countries to announce non-application intentions at the time the Uruguay Round texts are initialled

- a provision stating that non-application be in respect of all agreements under the new MTO only, i.e. reject or accept and apply the whole package: this would seem the best means of protecting the Single Undertaking.

Given our strong desire to protect the Single Undertaking, Australia's preference would be for a solution along the lines of the last two options, ie. the intention to accept and apply or to reject should be made clear from an early stage.

0186

CH019257/5

2.

Amendment procedures

. The key agreements (GATT, GATS, TRIPS) have different amendment provisions and Australia takes the view that it is desirable to have a single MTO-wide amendment provision.

. The key issue to be addressed would appear to be the numbers required for amendment and whether, having achieved the minimum number for amendment, that amendment should be binding on all MTO members or only on those which accept the amendment (the latter being GATT Article XXX:1 practice)

. The Australian position is to seek a workable MTO-wide amendment procedure, i.e. one flexible enough to be used in practice. We are inclined to favour the drafting of provisions in the MTO agreement which would allow an amendment to take effect for the Members which ratify the amendment upon acceptance by two-thirds of Members, and thereafter for each Member which ratifies the amendment;

> with the safeguard that an amendment may be judged by the Ministerial Council of the MTO as of such importance that a Member not accepting it could only remain a Member with the express consent of the Council (i.e. peer group leverage for important amendments). Australia would also like to see certain fundamental provisions such as the MFN (Article I of GATT) to have a unanimity requirement for amendment (essentially to ensure that these cannot be amended without the consent of all members).

Grandfather legislation

There is a general assumption that the Uruguay Round will result in the abolition of the 'grandfather clause' in the GATT Protocol of Provisional Application which protects national legislation existing at the time of accession which would otherwise be contrary to the GATT.

. The U.S. has expressed the strong desire to keep grandfather coverage for its Jones Act, which contravenes national treatment obligations in respect of shipbuilding, operations and crewing. As an alternative to grandfather coverage, the U.S. wishes to maintain a permanent reservation from its GATT obligations for measures maintained under the Jones Act.

. Australia is opposed to either course of action. We would not like to see the 'grandfather clause' abolished only to be replaced by reservations used to perpetuate the most trade-distorting grandfathered measures while also allowing non-grandfathered measures to become similarly protected.

0187

CH01925716

3.

Schedules

The view has been expressed that in order to shore up the value of the Uruguay Round package a clause should be added to Article XI stating that those countries eligible to become original members of the MTO, being those GATT Contracting Parties which accept the Round package, should also have presented schedules for both GATT and GATS. This would ensure countries fully meet their Round obligations in respect of tariff cuts and bindings, agriculture commitments and services.

- We support the objective behind this view but recognise that there will probably need to be a less onerous requirement for the least developed group.

2. GATT 1993

- Some states see value in the GATT (which goes into the MTO) undergoing textual rectification.

- There are three main approaches which have been discussed in relation to this issue

  - thoroughly recast it so that the Goods Annex agreements become 'chapters' of GATT, so GATT 1993 is textually as well as legally different to GATT 1947;

  - modify the text in a strictly technical sense to harmonise MTO terminology, (delete 'obsolete' clauses, etc, as per the Secretariat draft);

  - leave the text of GATT alone;

- Australia would prefer to leave the text of GATT 1947 alone but would be prepared to consider the second option.

- There is also a need to define how the Agreements in the Goods Annex relate to GATT, and in some cases to each other, so that overlapping obligations are clarified.

- If GATT 1993 is to be a separate legal/textual instrument from the (existing) GATT 1947, it is also necessary to clarify whether those Contracting Parties which join the MTO need simultaneously to withdraw from GATT 1947.

0188

CH019207/7

4.

4.   "Crosscutting" Issues

The main 'crosscutting' work involves harmonisation
across texts of institutional, decision-making, waiver
and final provisions. One way to do this is to delete
all such provisions from individual texts and have the
MTO provisions apply across the board.

Australia takes the view that technical (non-substantive)
harmonisation of the Anti-Dumping and Countervail texts
should also be a priority, but little has been done to
date.

Other crosscutting work which needs to be done but which
will be complex, politically-edged and involve substance,
is working out the relationship between the Subsidies and
Agriculture Agreements.

5.   Integrated Dispute Settlement System

The Track 3 Group has achieved considerable progress on
the integrated dispute settlement (IDS) text and work has
continued in informal discussions in Geneva.

The IDS text, which is the product of the "amalgamation"
of Sections 'S' and 'T' of the Dunkel package, consists
of

  —   Section 'S' - the negotiated outcome of the Dispute
      Settlement negotiation group on the elaboration of
      GATT Article XXII and XXIII procedures, and

  —   Section 'T' - the "Elements of an Integrated Dispute
      Settlement System" put together in the Institutions
      Group process in the last few weeks of 1991.

The Track 3 Group is required to produce a text which
pulls 'S' and 'T' together

  —   As the detailed product of negotiation, an "'S' is
      best" philosophy is prevalent, but not all aspects
      of 'S' may be appropriate to all Agreements

  —   For example, if negotiators wrote in special dispute
      procedures to an Agreement, they obviously wanted
      those to prevail (e.g., different time-frames or
      arbitral procedures). The Track 3 Group will have
      to integrate others as far as possible to the
      overall system, whilst respecting negotiators'
      intentions

  —   Similarly, some aspects which are integral to GATT
      dispute settlement (e.g., non-violation) may not be
      relevant for other Agreements.

.0189

5.

The Group is thus refining a single text with these
considerations in mind

- and examining a listing of the 'special or
  additional' dispute procedures in individual texts
  to establish the extent to which these depart from
  IDS procedures

  : and whether technical redrafting is
    possible/useful to clarify at which point
    special procedures cut in to the IDS for that
    Agreement

The Integrated Dispute Settlement system is a key feature
of the Multilateral Trade Organisation (MTO).

- It is Australia's hope (and the hope of a number of
  other countries) that an IDS system will end 'forum-
  shopping' facilitate more efficient dispute
  settlement processes and end delays

- The IDS will enable the same rules of procedure to
  be applied to all disputes brought under Agreements
  covered by the MTO

- This would enable the rules of procedure elaborated
  for GATT in the 'S' text, including more automatic
  time-frames, appeals, review, no blockage at
  adoption stage, arbitration, compensation,
  retaliation, no unilateral action, etc, to be
  extended to the new 'Codes' and to TRIPS and
  services

- The 'T' text contains procedures for cross-
  retaliation and provisions on handling disputes
  involving more than one Agreement (where both
  procedural and substantive conflict may arise)

- Several of the texts in the Dunkel package also
  contain their own dispute settlement procedures, and
  these depart from 'S' text procedures in certain
  instances

Link with GATT Articles XXII and XXIII

We also take the view that references in the 'S' text to
the IDS being derived from GATT Articles XXII and XXIII
should be retained. This is linked to maintaining the
full scope of substantive GATT rights under those
Articles notwithstanding the procedural elaboration of
the IDS.

0190

6.

Issues that Need to be Revisited Later

. We take the view that a number of aspects of the current text will have to be considered again after work on special procedures in individual texts has progressed

- e.g. Paragraph 1.2 on handling of cases where more than one Agreement is involved and there is a conflict between procedures in these Agreements

- Paragraph 2.1: Coverage of Annex 4 Agreements (Aircraft, Procurement, Meat, Dairy) by the IDS procedures. (This is linked to the general issue of these Agreements' role under the MTO.)

Disputes in Transition

. The process for "disputes in transition" between GATT and the MTO (and implicitly, as yet unimplemented GATT cases) needs further work.

GATT 1993

. Throughout the text, various references to "GATT 1993" need to be considered as to whether these are too narrow, i.e., are all or some of the other Annex 1A Goods texts also meant to be covered by the original references "GATT"?

Non-violation

. Our goal is to ensure existing GATT Article XXIII:1(b) and (c) rights are maintained through the IDS system. (The IDS text treats non-violation cases differently to violation cases in some procedural respects, e.g., arbitration). Application of XXIII:1(b) to all Goods Agreements appears not in doubt (subject to clarifying aspects of green boxes and peace clause in Subsidies/Agriculture text)

- The issues cannot be resolved at this time, pending consideration of individual texts and resolution of some substantive aspect of the Dunkel package e.g., TRIPS.

Department of Foreign Affairs and Trade
Canberra

1? September 1992

0191

외 무 부

종 별 :

번 호 : GVW-1867   일 시 : 92 1006 1800

수 신 : 장관(통기, 경기원, 재무부, 농수산부, 상공부)

발 신 : 주 제네바대사

제 목 : UR/법제화 그룹 비공식 회의 (GATT'93)

연: GVW - 1775

1. 연호 호주 대표부 주관하의 GATT'93 검토를 위한 소그룹은 9.25 및 10.5추가모임을 갖고 GATT '93(사무국안)의 1회독을 완료 하였는바, 동 검토에서 제기된 문제점을 MATHUR 의장 주재로 법제화 그룹(T3)의 추후일정 논의를 위해 10.8 개최될 동그룹 비공식 회의에 보고하되 (법제화 그룹 전체 차원에서의 GATT '93에 대한 논의문제는 동 소그룹에서 GATT '93을 추가 1회독한뒤 검토하기로 하고, 필요한 경우 갓트 사무국 직원을 소그룹 검토에초청하여 TRANSPARENCY를 제고하기로 함 (신종원 서기관 참석)

2. 상기 검토 작업에서 제기된 문제점은 아레임

가 개별조문

O 16조(보조금)

- 현행 GATT(GATT '47) 체제하에서는 수출 보조금에 대한 SECTION B를 수락하지않은 국가가 상당수 있음에 반하여 UR에서는 MTO협정 16조 2항에 따라 개별조문에 대한 유보가 금지되어 있어 GATT '47을 GATT '93이 승계함에 있어 특정국가의 경우에는 권리 의무의 상충가능성이 있음

- UR 보조금. 상계관세 협정문과의 CROSS REFERENCE가 필요함

- 5항과 관련, 동조항 운용의 검토를 구체적으로어느 기구(상품 무역이사회 또는 보조금. 상계 관세위원회)에서 할 것인지 여부 O 18조 (및12조) (BOP)

- 2,3,7,13 및 22항의 ESTABLISHMENT OF INDUSTRY의 개념에 대한 주석 (P.76) 과 관련, EC의 MTO MEMBERSHIP 개념의 구체화 필요 (개별국 또는 EC전체)

√ - BOP조치에 관한 1979년 결정, URBOP 협정문과의 관계 및 CROSS-REFERENCE문제

- 각 항(특히 12항)의 체약국단을 구체적으로 MTO의 어느기구로 결정할 것인가의

통상국   경기원   재무부   농수부   상공부

PAGE 1   92.10.07   07:52 CR

외신 1과 통제관 /

0192

문제.

  0 19조(세이프가드)

  - UR 세이프가드 협정문과의 CROSS-REFERENCE 문제

  - 2항 3항과관련, CONTRACTING PARTIES 의 상품무역 이사회(CTG)에 의한
대체의적정 여부

  0 20조(일반적인 예외)

  - 동 20조가 MTO 협정 ANNEX 1A(상품무역 분야협정)상의 타협정에 적용되는지 여부

  - B항 (사람, 동.식물의 생명 및 건강에 관한 예외)과 UR SPS협정, D항
(특허권보호)과 TRIPS 협정과의 CROSS- REFERENCE 문제

  0 22조,23조

  - 22조2항 첫줄 및 23조2항 4줄, 8줄의 MTO기구 지정문제 (DSB, CTG, GC등)

  0 24조

  - 1항 4-5줄의 '26조, 33조 및 PPA(잠정 적용 의정서)' 삭제여부

  - 1항3줄, 11줄의 'MTO설립 협정'과 '본협정'의 선택문제

  - 1항8줄 PROVIEDED 이하, 12항과 관련 EC회원국의 개념의 구체화 필요.

  - CUSTOMS TERRITORY개념의 명확화 필요(1항2-3줄)

  - 3항 B(TRIESTE 자유 무역지대)의 존치 필요 여부

  - 7항 지역협정 관리기구 지정문제 (CTG 또는 GE)

  - 12항과 분쟁해결절차와의 CROSS - REFERENCE필요

  0 25조 (정책결정)

  - 5항 (웨이버)삭제여부 : MTO 협정이 일원적으로 웨이버제도를

  규율 하느냐의 여부에 따른 동항의 삭제 여부

  - 3항,4항의 MTO협정과의 일치문제 (1국 1투표권과 EC의 투표권 문제)

  0 27조(양허철회)

  - UR협상에 따라 INR(직접교섭국 지위)가 영향을 받는지의 여부

  0 28조(양허 재교섭)

  - 1항 9줄 PSI(주공급국 지위)의 개념에 관한주석 (P.80 4항 마지막 및 5항)과관련
EC의 MTO MEMBERSHIP 개념의 명확화 필요

  0 29조(HAVANA 헌장과의 관계), 30조(수정), 31조(발회), 32조(체약국)

  33조(가입)의 삭제여부

- MTO 협정과의 연 계하에 검토

0 35조(부적용)

- MTO협정과의 연계 하에 검토 (삭제여부)

0 37조(개도국 우대 : 약속)

- 2항(B)(I)의 개도국 우대 운용기구 지정문제 :GC (일반이사회)또는 CTG

0 38조(공동행동)

- 동조 제목에서 MTO삭제 여부

- 공동행동 주체와 관련, 2항 1줄의 MTO적정여부 (MC(각료회의)또는 CTG에 의한대체 여부)

나. 공통문제

0 현행 GATT상의 체약국단 (CONTRACTING PARTIES) 용어를 봉상 임무를 수행하는적절한 MTO 내의 기구로 대체하는 경우 해당 임무를 수행하는 최상급 기관을 적시하고 권한 위임방식을 채택할 것인지 (AUTHORITY APPROACH)아니면 최하급 기관을 적시하고 권고방식을 채택할 것인지 여부(OPERATIONAL ARPPROACH)

0 GATT '93과 세이프가드 협정문, 보조금 상계 관세 협정문등 타 협정문과의 관계 설정문제

0 수개 조항의 삭제에 따른 각 조항의 재배열과 주요조항의 본래 번호 유지문재(애 28조 양허 재협상)

0 GATT '47상의 역사적인 날짜에 대한 처리문제

0 각 조항의 주석 (AD ARTICLE)과 UR 결정의 해당 조항내 수용 여부 및 방법

(대 사 박수길 -국장)

외 무 부

종 별 :

번 호 : GVW-1918 일 시 : 92 1013 1840

수 신 : 장관(통기, 경기원, 재무부, 농수산부, 상공부)

발 신 : 주제네바대사

제 목 : 법제화 그룹 비공식 회의(GATT'93)

연: GVW-1775, 1867

연호 호주대표부 주관으로 개최된 GATT '93에대한 비공식 소그룹의 검토과정에서 제기된 사항들을 호주 대표부가 별첨과 같이 정리하여 동검토 참가국 및 갓트사무국에 회람하였는바, GATT'93에 대한 검토시 참고바람.

첨부: GATT'93 요 검토사항(호주 대표부정리)(GVW(F)-0607).끝

(대사 박수길-국장)

통상국   경기원   재무부   농수부   상공부

92.10.14   06:58 FX
외신 1과 통제관

0195

주 제 네 바 대 표 부

번호 : GVW(F) - *607*   년월일 : *2/0/3*   시간 : *1840*

수신 : 장   관(중기, 경기원, 재무부, 농림수산부, 상공부)

발신 : 주제네바대사

제목 : *GVW-1P18 첨부*

총 *5* 매(표지포함)

보안통제	

의신관통제	

0196

AUSTRALIAN PERMANENT MISSION TO THE GATT, GENEVA

56 RUE DE MOILLEBEAU, GENEVA, TELEPHONE 734 6200

DATE: 6 October 1992

NO OF PAGES INCLUDING COVER: 4

FROM FAX No   : Geneva, 733 6586

Authorised by : M. Borthwick
Section   : Geneva GATT
Telephone   : 734 6200
Auth. Officer's signature: *S.C. Hartmann*

TO: MR A. PRATES, BRAZIL   (2)
       MR B. JANSEN, EC   (24)
       MR P. CHEUNG, HONG KONG   (18)
       MR M. KUMAR, INDIA   (738 4548)
       MR M. TSUJI, JAPAN   (6)
       MS C. HERNANDEZ, MEXICO   (20)
       MR K. LILLERUD, NORWAY   (733 9979)
       MR M. TRAINOR, NEW ZEALAND   (16)
       MR H. ERNST, SWITZERLAND   (22)
       MS R. RASTAPANA, THAILAND   (29)
       MR C. PARLIN, USTR   (749 4885)
       MR D. GEORGE, CANADA   (12)
       MS P. FABRO, ARGENTINA   (13)
       MR M. LINDSTROM, SWEDEN   (21)
       MR J. SHIN, KOREA   (19)

FROM: MEREDITH BORTHWICK

Please find attached an 'Indicative List' of issues passed to
Mr Mathur, for your information, as discussed.

1666G

'Indicative list' of issues passed to Mr Mather, & for your information, as discussed.

Kenneth Buckle 6/10

GATT 1993

2/4

Generic issues identified:

1. Approaches to change.

- three approaches covering positions of no change, change only where necessary, and change where required to update the text

2. 'Contracting parties' substitutions (appropriate level of body)

- alternative approaches are through reference to the source of authority or to the operational body (at committee level)
- whichever approach is adopted, there will be a need to clarify the linkage through the MTO (Article IV)

3. 'Contracting parties' substitutions (General Council/Council for Trade in Goods)

- General Council or Council for Trade in Goods, depending on the applicability of certain provisions of the GATT (eg Articles XX, XXI) to the TRIPS and Services Agreements

4. Applicability of GATT Articles

- to other Annex IA Agreements. This is specified in some cases, not in others. The setting out of the MTO Annex IA currently gives no indication that the GATT 93 would apply to other Agreements in that Annex.

5. Schedule of Concessions

- Article II is to go beyond tariff schedules, and full coverage needs to be specified either in the text of the GATT 1993 or in each relevant specific Agreement in Annex 1A, or both

6. MTO/Members

- need for distinction between the institution/secretariat and its members.
- establish where there is a legal need to refer to the corporate identity rather than the collectivity of members

0198

3/H

2.

7. Dispute Settlement Body/other relevant body

.   whether the Dispute Settlement Body, as a procedural body,
     should take on the function of a political body (General
     Council) in overseeing consultations under Article XXII

8. EC/member states

.   identification of points where this issue is relevant

9. Preamble

.   whether to align with changes in MTO preamble (and to
     incorporate further changes which may be made there,
     particularly with regard to language on the environment)

.   whether a separate preamble is appropriate

10. Relationship of Articles XXV, XXVI to the MTO Agreement

.   Whether Articles XXV and XXVI should be retained separately

.   if XXV should, whether it should be brought into line with
     MTO text (XXV.3, XXV.4)

.   if XXVI should, need to see whether dates are consistent
     with referenced Articles, and whether there would be a
     need to retain XXVI if dates could simply be changed in
     the referenced articles

11. Relationship of Articles XXX-XXXIII to the MTO Agreement

.   Deletion from the GATT 1993 will depend on resolution in
     the MTO

12. Relationship of Article XXXV to the MTO Agreement

.   retention here depends on resolution of this issue in the
     MTO context

13. Outmoded references places/dates/arrangements

.   identification of such references

.   establish which are still relevant/need to be retained

14. Outmoded references - par value

.   identification of references related to par value which no
     longer make sense and need updating

15. Cross-referencing

.   to make text more operational and for greater ease of
     reference, need to establish a mechanism for alerting user
     to other relevant Agreements which would have bearing on
     each Article

0199

4/4

3.

. options would be to cross reference from the GATT 1993 text, or in each relevant Agreement, or both.

. such a mechanism would not have legal status

16. Ad Articles/GATT Articles decisions

. mechanism for greater ease of reference to relevant Ad Articles or Articles decisions (eg footnote, placement immediately pursuant to relevant Article)

17. Renumbering of Articles

. whether Articles should be renumbered if some are deleted

18. Associated legal instruments

. list full set as specified in Annex 1A 1(a)-(f)

19. Typographical Errors

. identify, circulate list

ENDS

0200

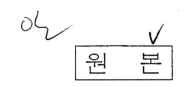

외 무 부

종 별 :

번 호 : GVW-1951   일 시 : 92 1016 1800

수 신 : 장 관(통기,경기원,재무부,농수산부,상공부)

발 신 : 주 제네바 대사

제 목 : 법제화 그룹 비공식 회의 (GATT '93)

연 : GVW - 1918

1. GATT '93에 대한 <u>비공식 검토 그룹</u> 10.15(목) 모임을 갖고 호주 대표부가 정리한 GATT '93 상의 연호 쟁점중 정책적 결정을 요하는 사항(1항의 갓트 TEXT 수정 여부 및 방법에 대한 접근방식)과 MTO 관련사항(10-13항)을 제외한 나머지 쟁점에 대해 논의를 가짐(신종원 서기관 참석)

2. 상기 논의의 요지는 아래임.

가. 실질사항

1) 2,3항(CONTACTING PARTIES의 MTO 해당 기구에 의한 대체)

- AUTHORITY APPROACH(북구)와 OPERATIONAL APPROACH(인도,홍콩,아국)간의 의견차가 있는 가운데 미국은 CONTRACTING PARTIES에 로의 복귀 검토방안을 언급함.

- 상기 양 접근 방법중 어느 쪽을 택하느냐는 문제는 <u>정책적 결정</u> 사항인바, 양접근방안 을 보완하는 GATT '93의 실제 운용방안에 대한 검토를 착수할 필요성도 지적됨.

2) 4항 (갓트 조문의 MTO 협정 부속서 1A상의 타협정문에의 적용 여부)

- 갓트 '93을 상품분야 개별협정 (MTO 협정문 3차 수정안 P.28 및 29상의 부속서 1A 협정의 2-13)에 <u>일반적으로 적용</u>되며 다만 개별 협정문에 <u>특별 조항이 있는 경우에는 동 특별조항의 우선</u> 적용 된다는 것이 지배적인 의견 이었음(예 :갓트 20조 및21조의 상품 분야 개별 협정에의 적용)

3) 5항(양허율표)

- UR 결과 추가되는 관세양허 이외의 양자협의 결과 (예: 비관세 장벽에 대한 약속) 에 대한 근거를 제공하기 위해 갓트 2조(및 28조의 양허 재교섭)를 수정하면 갓트 '47 상의 권리.의무의 균형이 변경될 가능성이 있으므로 2조(및28조)의 수정에

통상국   경기원   재무부   농수부   상공부

반대하는 의견 (일본,EC)이 제시 되었음.

- 상기 2조(및 28조)를 수정하지 않는 경우 비관세 장벽에 대한 약속들에 관한양허표의 첨부 형태(해당 협정문의 별도 부속서에 첨부 되는지 여부)의 문제가 제기됨.

4) 6항(CONTRACTING PARTIES의 MTO에 의한 대체의 경우)

- 외환협약 (제15조) 체결의 경우 CONTRACTING PARTIES를 법인격을 가지는 MTO (MTO 협정문 8조 1항)에 의해 대체하는 사무국안을 지지하는 의견 (인도)와 MTO 자체에 대해 거부감을 표명 (미국) 하는 의견이 있었으나 동 MTO가 실제운용에 있어서 MTO 사무국이 될 가능성을 방지할 필요성에 대해서는 공감대가 있었음

5) 7항 (22조 양자협의)

- 23조 양자협의는 단순히 패널 절차상의 양자협의 이나 22조 양자협의는 보다광범위한 협의의 성격을 가지므로 22조의 협의 관장 기구는 정치적 성격을 띄는 상품무역 이사회 (또는 상기'1)'항의 접근방법에 따라서는 일반 이사회)로 대체 하자는의견(미국)과 동22조 협의도 DSB 관장 사항이라는 의견이 제시됨.

6) 8항 (EC의 회원국 개념문제)

- 동문제 (개별국 또는 EC전체가 MTO 회원국으로 가입 하는지 문제)은 브랏셀에서 아직 결론이 나지 않았음을 EC측이 언급함.

7) 9항(서문)

- MTO협정 서문 상의 환경관련 사항 (SUSTAINABLE DEVELOPMENT)의 반영 필요성언급(호주)

라. 기술적인 사항

1) 15항(CROSS-REFERENCING)

- 갓트 '93과 개별협정간 및 개별협정들 간의 상호 연관성을 일목 요연하게 정리할 필요성과 동 CROSS - REFERENCIOG은 법적효력을 가지지 않는다는 점이 강조됨.

- 동 CROSS-REFERENCING 준비작업은 현 소규모 검토그룹과 갓트 사무국간의 협력이 요하는 사항임이 지적됨.

2) 16항(보충규정 및 관련결정 위치)

- 준거 (REFERENCE)의 편의를 위해 이들을 주석으로 위치를 변경 하자는 의견이(EC)이 제시됨.

3) 17항(조문의 RENUMBERING)

PAGE 2

0202

- 28조등 주요조항의 원래 번호의 유지를 위한 방안 강구가 필요함이 지적됨 (미국)

(대사 박수길 - 국장)

외 무 부

110-760 서울 종로구 세종로 77번지 / (02)720-2188 / (02)720-2686 (FAX)

문서번호 통기 20644-388

시행일자 1992.11.10.( )

42181

수신 주 제네바 대사

참조

취급		장 관	
보존			
국 장	전 결		
심의관			
과 장			
기안	안 명 수		협조

제목 UR/MTO 협정

        주한 호주대사관은 11.4. 다자간 무역기구설립 협정관련 자국입장을 전달하여

온바 이를 별첨 송부하니, 귀업무에 참고하시기 바랍니다.

        첨부 : 동 자료 1부. 끝.

검인
1992. 11. 10
공지관

외 무 부 장 관

0204

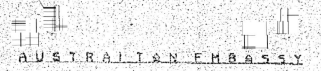

S E O U L

11th Floor, Kyobo Building   Tel: 730 6490
1, Chongno 1-ka, Chongno-ku   Fax: 722 9264
Seoul 110-714

FACSIMILE MESSAGE

TO: Mr Hong Jong Ki
           Director
           Multilateral Trade Organisations Division
           Ministry of Foreign Affairs
           FAX No: 7202686

FROM: Ms Elizabeth Toohey
           Second Secretary
           Australian Embassy
           Seoul

DATE: 4 November 1992

PAGES: 5

SUBJECT: MULTILATERAL TRADE ORGANISATION : DRAFT TEXT

Dear Director Hong

Australia has been further considering its position on a
number of issues arising from the Multilateral Treaty
Organisation (MTO).

Please find attached a paper outlining Australia's current
views on some issues which have been raised in the context of
the work of the Track 3 Grouup in Geneva. We would be most
interested in any response you may have to these views, or any
other areas of concern to the ROK which we have not covered
specifically.

Regards,

Elizabeth Toohey
Second Secretary

0205

MULTILATERAL TREATY ORGANISATION : DRAFT TEXT

The Track 3 Group is charged with the task of completing work on the legal/institutional framework for the Final Act through elaborating the Agreement on Establishment of the Multilateral Trade Organisation (MTO). Useful progress has been made but a number of issues remain to be resolved. Issues on which Australia has formulated views are as follows:

Grandfather Legislation

Australia is opposed to the retention of Grandfather coverage being sought by the U.S. to protect its legislation contravening national treatment obligations in respect of shipbuilding, operations and crewing (Jones Act). Australia is also opposed to the U.S. proposed alternative measure of maintaining a permanent reservation from its GATT obligations in respect of this legislation.

The E.C. has adopted a similar approach to that of Australia. However, given the U.S. attachment to the retention of the Grandfather clause, we are interested in any views or proposals which may further prospects of resolving the issue.

Non-Application

In Australia's view there is a loophole in the current draft of Article 13 of the MTO which would enable countries to circumvent the single undertaking obligation. For instance, a country could refuse to apply the new TRIPS or Services Agreements, but another member could not non-apply GATT to that country in retaliation (unless it was already non-applying GATT to that member).

The Track 3 Group has discussed various proposals to deal with this possibility. Australia's preference would be for a solution that required countries to state their intention to: accept and apply in full or to reject from an early stage (eg. at the initialling of the Uruguay Round texts).

Schedules

In order to shore up the value of the U.R. package, there is some support for the view that a clause should be added to Article 11 to the effect that those countries eligible to become original members of the MTO should also have presented schedules for both the GATT and the GATS. This would ensure that countries fully meet their Round obligations in respect of tariff cuts and bindings, agriculture commitments and services. While this would be a desirable outcome, Australia recognises that there may need to be a less onerous requirement for the least developed group.

0206

Voting Majorities

The power of the Ministerial Conference and the General Council to make decisions by simple majority vote has caused some concern, particularly in NGO circles. (For instance, the WWF has expressed its concern to the Australian Minister for Trade and Overseas Development).

While more detailed provisions on decision making may be more ideal, Australia can accept the text in its present form. It is not unusual for International Organisations to be given the power to make decisions by simple majority. In light of the history of GATT, the complex nature of international trade relations, the difficulties associated with implementing majority decisions in the international plane and the consensus approach GATT has favoured in decision making, Australia considers it unlikely that this power would be abused by the MTO. Australia also notes that for admission of new members (Article 12) a two-thirds majority of votes cast is required and that this majority should comprise more than half the MTO membership.

Powers of Interpretation

Some concern has also been expressed about the lack of constraints on the interpretation of the provisions of the Agreements attached to the MTO by the Ministerial Conference and the General Council. For the same reasons outlined in the previous paragraph, Australia does not consider the risk of consequences unintended by the drafters arising to be a major concern at this stage.

Amendments Procedures

Two options are currently under discussion. The first requires consensus for proposed amendments prior to submission to members which would become binding on all members if accepted by a majority of two-thirds of the members. The Ministerial Conference could suspend the effect of the amendment in relation to a requesting country for a specified period. The second option requires adoption of the amendment by a majority of two-thirds of members prior to its submission to the members, which would then make it binding on all members. Amendment to this Article of the MTO would require a unanimous vote under both options.

The key issue appears to be the numbers required for amendment and whether the amendment should be binding on all members once the numbers have been satisfied. Australia believes it is important to achieve an MTO-wide amendment procedure which is effective in practice. To this end, we favour a provision which would allow an amendment to take effect for members which accept it (after it has satisfied the two-thirds requirement) and for each member which thereafter ratifies the amendment. We would also favour a safeguard to the effect that if the Ministerial Council judged the amendment to the MTO to be of major importance, a member which did not accept

0207

the amendment could only remain a member with the express
consent of the Council.

In addition, amendments to fundamental provisions (such as
Article 1 of GATT on MFN) would ideally require unanimous
support.

Legal Personality, Privileges and Immunities

As with the Voting and Powers of Interpretation provisions,
concern has been expressed by some at the brevity and lack of
specificity of draft provisions conferring legal personality,
privileges and immunities on the MTO. Australia is of the
view that the MTO will express the will of its members through
the Ministerial Conference and the General Council, which, as
referred to above, we do not regard as containing significant
risk factor. Privileges and immunities of the MTO will be
determined to some extent by its Headquarters Agreement and
other Agreements it concludes with member states. The GATT
has been under close scrutiny by members since its inception
and there is no reason to believe members will adopt a
different position in respect of the MTO.

Environment Provisions

Environment groups have actively put forward their views about
the absence of substantive references to the environment in
the MTO text (eg. on environment impact assessments,
polluter-pays principle). Australia understands that the U.S.
is supportive of introducing minor changes to the preamble of
the MTO to accommodate environment concerns. If general
agreement on this emerged, Australia could also be prepared to
support the introduction of minor changes to the preamble
which would be designed to bring it into line with UNCED
language. However, we realise that achieving such consensus
could prove difficult and we are most concerned that even
minor changes to the Preamble could give rise to calls for
other modifications to the Preamble.

We would anticipate considerable resistance to any attempt to
introduce major changes to the main text, which has already
been the subject of lengthy negotiation and considerable
bilateral concessions by members. Australia considers it
preferable that any substantive proposals relating to
environment and trade issues be left to a future review.

Consultation with NGOs

NGOs, and the WWF in particular, have complained that
Article 4, which provides for the MTO to consult and cooperate
with NGOs as appropriate, does not give NGOs a "legitimate
expectation of consultation". Australia is of the view that
the current provision allows adequate scope for MTO
consultation with NGOs. Article 4 is broadly similar in
effect to the provisions for consulting agencies (including
NGOs) in the environment-specific Conventions concluded
recently, the Framework Conventions on Climate Change and
Biological Diversity. Bearing in mind the complexity and the

0208

technical nature of a large part of the U.R. texts, the
practical value of formal consultative structures with NGOs is
lessened.

Each country has the right to include NGOs in their national
delegations should they choose. Australia itself has well
established processes for consulting NGOs but our preference
remains that in the international trade context, NGOs should
not formally participate in negotiating groups.

Dispute Resolution

Although Article 9.2 permits the Ministerial Conference or the
General Council to interpret the provisions of the MTO text,
there is no specific provision dealing with dispute settlement
mechanisms. In the event of a dispute relating to the
interpretation and implementation of the MTO text. The outcome
would depend on the views of a simple majority. An E.C.
proposal that the MTO be made a covered text has received
little support thus far, although a more formal dispute
settlement provision than the elementary procedure currently
proposed may be more effective. Australia has generally
supported more formal international dispute resolution
procedures.

Unilateralism

The present Article 16.4, requiring members to endeavour to
take all necessary steps to bring domestic laws into line with
the annexed Agreements, does not accord with the expectations
of a number of negotiating parties. In the long term it
would serve the MTO well if members accepted an obligation to
bring their domestic legislation into line with these
Agreements.

0209

주 제 네 바 대 표 부

20, Route de Pre-Bois, POB 566 / (022) 791-0111 / (022) 791-0525(FAX)

문서번호 제네(경) 20644 - 1025

시행일자 1992.11.19.

수신 장관

참조 통상국장

선결			지시		
접수	일자시간		결재공람		
	번호	66063			
	처리과				
	담당자	이병구			

제목 UR/법제화 그룹

92. 11. 20

대 : WGV-515(92. 4. 3)

　　WGV-481(92. 3.30)

　　통기 20644-388(92.11.10)

1. MTO 협정문 3차 수정안(docu. 945, 92. 5. 29)과 통합분쟁 해결절차 1차 수정안 (docu 513, 92.3.19) 상의 주요쟁점을 별첨 송부합니다.

2. UR 협상의 본격화에 대비, 동 쟁점에 대한 본부 검토의견을 가능한 조기에 회시 바랍니다.

첨부 : 상기 MTO 협정안 및 MTO 통합 분쟁해결 절차상의 주요 쟁점 1부. 끝.

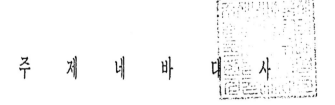

주 제 네 바 대 사

0210

MTO 협정 3차 수정안상의 주요쟁점 사항

O grandfather clause (2조 주석)

- MTO 범위(2조) 주석에 조부조항 관련 문구 포함 여부

- 미국 포함 찬성, EC등 대다수국 포함 반대

O EC의 투표권(9조)

- 1국 1투표권과 관련, EC 자체의 독자적인 투표권 향유 문제는 미결
  (11조에 의하면 EC는 MTO원 회원국 자격이 있는바, 미국은 EC의 2 중
  투표권 금지를 명문화 하자는 입장)

O 협정 해석(9조)

- MTO 협정 및 부속서 1,2,3 협정에 대한 해석 채택 정족수 관련,
  콘센서스에 의한 결정 방식과 투표국 2/3이상인 동시에 회원국
  과반수인 찬성 투표에 의한 결정 방식이 대립하고 있음. (아국은
  콘센서스 입장)

- 부속서 1,2,3 협정 해석권과 관련, 각료이사회가 독자적인 해석권을
  갖는다는 견해 (미국, 키나다)와 분야별 협정에 대한 해석권은 해당
  특별이사회의 권고에 기초해서 제한적으로 사용되어야 한다는 견해
  (EC, 인도등)가 대립

O 웨이버(9조)

- 각료이사회의 웨이버 부여권을 웨이버 규정이 있는 협정에 한정하자는
  입장 (미국, 일본 : TRIPS 협정은 웨이버 규정이 없음)과 웨이버 규정이
  없는 협정에 한정하자는 입장(인도, 홍콩등), 전체 협정에 대한 각료
  이사회의 웨이버 부여권을 인정하자는 입장(EC, 아국)이 있음.

0211

0 협정 개정(10조) (협정의 단일성 또는 개정의 신축성)

  - 개정안 채택 정족수

    . 콘센서스(아국, EC, 스웨덴등)

    . 회원국의 2/3(미국, 카나다, 호주등)

  - 채택된 개정안 발효

    . 회원국의 2/3 수락

      〈전체회원국에 적용 : 아국, EC, 스웨덴

       수락국에게만 적용 : 미, 카, 뉴, 호〉

      (단 MFN등 기본원칙에 대해서는 개정안의 채택이 회원국 2/3로

      이루어지는 경우 동 개정안의 발효는 전회원국의 수락으로 하자는

      제안이 있음)

0 개도국의 양허표 제출 의무(11조)

  - 원가맹국의 지위와 관련, 양허표를 제출하지 않고도 가입할 수 있었던
    GATT '47의 관행을 유지하자는 인도, 방글라데시등 개도국의 입장과
    GATT '93은 GATT '47과 별개이며, MTO에는 서비스 협정이 새로이 포합
    되므로 양허표 제출을 모든 원가맹국의 의무로 하자는 입장(미.카나다등)
    이 대립

0 협정 부적용(13조)

  - 미국은 MTO 협정에 부적용 조항을 설치하는 것에 반대(개별 협정상의
    부적용 조항으로 규율하자는 입장), EC는 MTO 협정에서 일원적으로
    규정하고 개별 부적용조항 삭제 주장

  - GATT '47에 대한 부적용 범위는 현재 이상으로 확대되는 것은 방지함.

0 국내법일치 의무(16조 4항)

  - 국내법의 MTO 협정에의 일치를 권고사항으로 규정

  - 미국 : 수정반대(EC는 동조항 찬성), 기타국은 동 조항의 강화 또는
           유지, 싱가폴은 동조항 삭제 주장(당연히 일치시켜야 한다는 입장)

0212

통합분쟁 해결절차(1차 수정안)에 관한 주요 쟁점

1. 1항(적용범위)

(MTO 협정, 통합분쟁 해결절차, TPRM 협정문의 적용 여부)

0 MTO 협정문

- 적용인정 : MTO 협정문상의 실질 규정(국내법의 MTO 협정문 일치, 웨이버 조항등)을 근거로 듬. : EC, 카나다, 아국, 인도, 일본등

- 적용불인정 : MTO 협정문은 실질 규정이 없다는 논거(미국), 부속 협정이 모협정인 MTO 협정에 대한 분쟁을 규율할 수는 없으며 MTO 협정에 대한 분쟁은 동 협정의 해석 조항의 규율대상이라는 논거(홍콩)

0 분쟁해결 절차 양해 및 TPRM 협정문

- 적용 불인정 : T Text상에 적용 근거가 없음(미국)

- 적용여부 검토 필요 : EC, 인도(분쟁해결 절차의 2항 일방 조치에 대한 분쟁능)

2. Appendix II (특별절차 범위)

0 개별 협정 검토 필요

3. 2.1항(MTO 협정의 Annex 4 협정에 대한 통합 분쟁해결 절차 적용 여부)

0 부속서 4 협정의 기구에서 적용여부 결정할 것인지의 문제

- 해당협정 기구에서 결정 : 향후 진전 사항에 대비해서 동방안을 지지 (홍콩, 미국, 아국, 일본등)

0213

- 당연적용 : 해당 협정 기구에서 적용여부를 결정하는 경우 동 결정은
  콘센서스에 의하게 되므로 사실상 적용이 불가능하게 됨
  (EC, 스위스)

4. 3.11항(개도국 우대에 관한 1966년 결정)

0 개도국이 제소국인 경우 적용되는 1966년 갓트 분쟁해결절차가 Annex 1A의
  동경라운드 협정에도 적용되는지 여부에 대해

  - 미국, EC, 호주, 일본등 선진국은 '66년 절차가 동경라운드 협정에도
    적용된다는 결정은 어디에서도 찾아볼수 없으므로(동 문안에 대한 합의
    부재)갓트 '47에만 적용된다는 입장

  - 맥시코, 브라질, 칠레, 인도등은 '79년 각료결정 및 개별 동경협정이
    갓트의 관례를 존중한다라고 되어 있으므로 동경라운드 협정에도 적용된
    다는 입장.

0 '66년 절차에 의한 패널 결정(상품분야)의 불이행시 통합 분쟁해결 절차에
  따라 서비스, TRIPs 분야에서의 보복을 할 수 있는지 여부

  - 선진국 : 교차보복 불가

  - 후진국 : 교차 보복이 가능

    (미국이 개도국에 대하여 패널 구성 절차 및 패널 결정 이행절차에
    이중으로 특혜를 주는 것은 곤란하다는 강경 입장)

5. 25.4항(중재결과 이행절차)

0 동항관련, 보조금.상계관세 협정문(I text)의 제 8조 5항에 언급된
  중재절차와 동항과의 관계에 대한 심의 필요성이 제기되어 I text 논의시
  재론 예정

0214

6. 26항(non-violation 분쟁)

o 26.1 및 26.2항 관련, non-violation 분쟁에 대한 갓트 제 23조 1(b) 및 제 23조 1(c) 절차가 갓트 '93이외 기타 MTO 부속협정에 대해서도 적용되는지 여부는 동항의 주석 1(27P 및 28P)대로 각협정에 대한 추가 검토를 통해 결정할 사항이라는 점을 확인함.

o 주요국 입장

  - 부속서 1(A)에 대한 적용

    . 23 1(b)의 적용에 대해서 특별히 이의를 제기한 국가는 없었으나 23 1(c)는 보조금 협정 및 반덤핑 협정에는 적용될 수 없다는 입장이 지배적.

    . 서비스 협정에 대한 적용

    부정적 입장 : 서비스협정상의 관련 절차가 통합분쟁해결 절차의
                  내용과 상이한 점이 많으므로 원 협상자의 취지에
                  따라 자동적인 적용은 곤란(태국, 인도, 브라질등)

    . 적극적인 입장 : 서비스 협정은 MTO 협정의 integral part라는
       점에서 다소 상이한 규정이 있더라도 이는 해석 또는 수정을 통해
       적용될 사항(미국, 카나다, EC등)

  - TRIPs 협정에 대한 적용

    . 부정적인 입장 : 동 협정에 non-violation 절차가 없으므로 적용불가
       (카나다, 태국, 인도, 일본, 브라질등)

    . 적극적인 입장 : MTO 협정과의 구조상 적용금지 규정이 없으므로
       적용(미국, EC, 뉴질랜드등)

0215

외 무 부

종 별 : 지 급

번 호 : GVW-2272 일 시 : 92 1204 1730

수 신 : 장 관 (봉기, 경기원, 재무부, 농수산부, 상공부, 특허청)

발 신 : 주 제네바 대사

제 목 : UR/법제화 그룹 비공식 회의

연: GVW-1918

1. 11.26 개최된 제 23차 TNC 결정에 따라 DFA에 대한 금년내의 정치적 타결을 위해 필요한연말까지의 T3 작업 계획 논의를 위해 금12.4(금) 10:00 에 MATHUR 의장방에서 15여국이비공식 회합을 가졌는바, 동 논의 요지 아래보고함. (이성주 참사관, 신종원 서기관 참석가) T3 에서 우선 검토할 협정이 GATT('93), MTO협정, 통합분쟁해결 절차(특히 개별협정의특별분쟁 해결 절차에 관한 APPENDIX II)라는점에 의견이일치하였음.

- MTO 협정과 GATT ('93)중 어느것을 먼저논의하 것인지에 대해서는 견해차가 있었으나 MATHUR 의장은 GATT ('93) 우선 논 의 방안을제시나. 상기 협정에 대한 검토 방식으로는 주요 쟁점중심으로 검토하자는 데에는 의견이 일치하였으나,구체적으로어떤 검토 방식을 취할 것인가에대해서는 상당수국이 FLEXIBLE 한 APPROACH 를취하여 T4 에 넘길 문제를 가급적 줄이자는원론적 인 방안을 제시하는 정도에서그쳤음. (태국 및 카나다등은 가급적 T4 에문제를 넘기지 않기를 희망)

- 검토 방식과 관련, 호주는 검토 작업의효율화를 위해 소규모의 비공식 그룹을별도운용하는 방안을 제의했으나 호응을 얻지못함. (홍콩등이 TRANSPARENCY 강조)

다. 상기 작업을 위한 구체적인 일정에 대해서는논의가 이루어지지 못하였는바,동일정은 상기 가,나항과 함께 12.8(화) 개최된 전체 차원의 T3비공식 회의에서 논의 예정임.

2. 동 회의 벽두에 호주대표는 동국 중심으로 소규모그룹에서 정리한 연호 GATT('93)에 대한 요검토사항 목록을 별첨과 같이 사안별로 정리하여MATHUR 의장에게

통상국 경기원 재무부 농수부 상공부 특허정

PAGE 1 92.12.05 05:43 DX

외신 1과 통제관 ✓

0216

제출하면서 향후 검토 작업의참고자료로 활용할 것을 희망한바, 동 쟁점등GATT('93)에 대한 본부 검토의견 회시 바람.

　　첨부: GATT 요검토 사항(GVW(F)-728)

　　(대사 박수길-국장)

주 제 네 바 대 표 부

번 호 : GVW(F)-0728　　년월일 : 2/2°04　　시간 : 17∞

수 신 : 장 관

발 신 : 주 제네바대사 (통기, 경기반, 재무부, 농수산부, 상공부, 동자처)

제 목 : 'GVW-2272 첨부

총 5 매(표지포함)

보안 등 재	

과신관 등 재	

0218

C234   1 December 1992

POINTS ON GATT 1993

Generic issues identified:

Approaches:

1.   Approaches to change

-    three approaches covering positions of no change, change only where
     necessary, and change where desirable in order to update the text.

Institutional

2.   "Contracting parties" substitutions (appropriate level of body)

-    alternative approaches are through reference to the source of
     authority or to the operational body (at committee/Council level)

-    whichever approach is adopted, there will be a need to clarify the
     linkage through the MTO (Article IV).

3.   "Contracting parties" substitutions (General Council/Council for Trade
in Goods)

-    General Council or Council for Trade in Goods, depending on the
     applicability of certain provisions of the GATT (e.g. Articles XX,
     XXI) to the TRIPS and Services Agreements. Even so, there may be
     instances where General Council is required.

4.   MTO/Members

-    need for distinction between the institution/secretariat and its
     members

-    establish where there is a legal need to refer to the corporate
     identity rather than the collectivity of members

-    on withdrawal, "withdrawal from the Agreement establishing the MTO"
     may need to replace "withdraw from the MTO".

Relationships under the MTO

5.   Applicability of GATT Articles

-    to other Annex 1A Agreements. This is specified in some cases, not in
     others. The setting out of the MTO Annex 1A currently gives no
     indication that the GATT 1993 would apply to other Agreements in that
     Annex.

6.   Relationship of Articles XXV, XXVI to the MTO Agreement

-    whether Articles XXV and XXVI should be retained separately

0219

- : -

- if Article XXV should, whether it should be brought into line with MTO text (Article XXV:3, Article XXV:4)

- if Article XXVI should, need to see whether dates are consistent with referenced Articles, and whether there would be a need to retain Article XXVI if dates could simply be changed in the referenced Articles.

7. Relationship of Articles XXX-XXXIII to the MTO Agreement

- deletion from the GATT 1993 will depend on resolution in the MTO

8 Relationship of Article XXXV to the MTO Agreement

- retention here depends on resolution of this issue in the MTO context.

Other issues

9. Preamble

- whether to align with changes in MTO preamble (and to incorporate further changes which may be made there, particularly with regard to language on the environment)

- where a separate preamble is appropriate.

10. Dispute Settlement Body/other relevant body

- whether the Dispute Settlement Body, as a procedural body, should oversee consultations under Article XXII:2.

11. EC/Member States

- identification of points where this issue is relevant.

12. Schedule of Concessions

- Article II is to go beyond tariff schedules, and full coverage needs to be specified either in the text of the GATT 1993 or in each relevant specific Agreement in Annex 1A, or both.

13. Outmoded references places/dates/arrangements

- identification of such references

- establish which are still relevant/need to be retained.

14. Outmoded references - par value

- identification of references related to par value which no longer make sense and need updating.

0220

- 3 -

15. Cross-referencing

- to make text more operational and for greater ease of reference, need to establish a mechanism for alerting user to other relevant Agreements which would have bearing on each Article

- options would be to cross reference from the GATT 1993 text, or in each relevant Agreement, or both

- such a mechanism would not have legal status.

16. Ad Articles/GATT Articles decisions

- mechanism for greater ease of reference to relevant Ad Articles or Articles decisions (e.g. footnote, placement immediately pursuant to relevant Article).

17. Renumbering of Articles

- whether Articles should be renumbered if some are deleted.

18. Associated legal instruments

- list full set as specified in Annex 1A 1(a)-(f).

19. Typographical Errors

- identify, circulate list.

0221

- .. -

<u>GATT 1993</u>

Secretariat text 838 of 6 May 1992 - typographical errors in transcript of the text of GATT 1947:

p.9   Article I:4, last paragraph, 1st line: Annexe
         Article I:4, last paragraph, 2nd line: sub-paragraph<u>s</u>
         Article II:1(b), 6th line: provide <u>for</u> therein

p.11   Article II:6(a), 10th line: <u>P</u>rovided

p.20   Article IX:1, 2nd line: their <u>other</u>

p.22   Article XI:2(ii), 1st line: product<u>.</u>

p.25   Article XII:4(c)(i), 4th line: with <u>the</u> provisions

p.26   Article XIII:2, 1st paragraph, 4th line: restrictions<u>.</u>
         Article XIII:2(d), 1st line: countries.

p.32   Article XVII:1(c), 4th line: sub-paragraph<u>s</u>

p.33   Article XVII:4(c), 3rd line: interest<u>s</u>

p.35   Article XVIII:7(b), 10th line: find<u>s</u>

p.45   Article XXIV:1, 13th line: by <u>a</u> single

p.51   Article XXVIII:4, 1st paragraph, 3rd line: negotiation<u>s</u> for <u>modification or</u> withdrawal.

p.60   Article XXXVII:5, 1st line: paragraph<u>s</u> 1 to 4
         Article XXXVIII:1, 1st line: with<u>in</u>

p.68   Ad Article III, paragraph 1, 2nd line: with<u>in</u>

p.70   Ad Article VI, paragraphs 2 and 3, 1, 1st line: ma<u>ny</u>

p.72   Ad Article XII, paragraph 3(c)(i), 1st line: restriction<u>s</u>

p.75   Ad Article XVII, paragraph 1(a), 1st line: <u>e</u>nsure

p.80   Ad Article XXVIII, paragraph 1, 4, 2nd line: principle <u>principal</u>

Additionally, there are three places where the phrase "Member or parties" should be changed to "Member or Members":

p.31   Article XVI:1, 12th line
p.43   Article XXII:2, 3rd line
p.44   Article XXIII:1, 13th line

We noted also that all words appearing in italics in the General Agreement have been replaced by bold type in this text.

0222

발 신 전 보

분류번호	보존기간

번   호 : WGV-1923   921208 1610 FO 종별 : 지급

수   신 : 주 제네바   대사.//충영사

발   신 : 장 관(통 기)

제   목 : UR 법제화그룹 비공식회의

    대 : GVW-2272

    대호 GATT '93 관련 사항에 대한 검토 의견을 별첨(FAX) 송부하니 참고바람.

    첨 부(FAX) : 동 검토의견.   끝.

                                    (통상국장 대리   오 행 겸)

보 안 통 제	扯

앙 고 재	92 년 상 12 월 기 구 7 일 과	기안자 성 명 안명여	과 장	심의관 扯	국 장 전결	차 관	장 관	/	扯

외신과통제

0223

외 무 부

종 별 :

번 호 : GVW-2300　　　　　　　　　　일 시 : 92 1208 1830

수 신 : 장관(봉기, 경기원, 재무부, 농수산부, 상공부, 특허청)

발 신 : 주제네바대사

제 목 : UR 법제화 그룹

연: GVW-2272

11.26 TNC 결정에 따른 연말까지의 T3 작업일정 논의를 위해 T3 전체 비공식회의가 MATHUR 의장 주재로 12.8(화)개최되어 MTO 협정에 대해서는 금일 제기된 쟁점을 TNC 의장에게 보고하여 GUIDELINE 를 받아 추후 세부작업을 하기로 하고, 우선은 GATT('93)과 통합 분쟁해결 절차 협정문을 검토하기로 하였는바, 요지 아래 보고함. (이성주참사관, 김봉주, 신종원서기관참석)

1. 의장은 벽두에 향후 T3 에서 검토할 4개분야에서 대한 주요쟁점을 아래와 같이 예시한뒤, 동 4개 분야는 전체로 한꺼번에 검토해야할 문제(TOTAL PACKAGE) 라른 점을 지적하고 향후 T3 작업 방안에 대한 각국의의견을 요청하면서 MTO 협정문안상의쟁점은 주로 정책적 결정을 요하는 사항이어서 당장 T3에서 논의하기가 어렵지 않겠느냐는 개인적인 의견을 제시함.

가. MTO 협정문

- 개정조항, 웨이버, 부적용 저항등

나. 분쟁해결 절차

- 1966년 결정의 적용범위, NON-VIOLATION 분쟁의 적용 범위, 중재 절차에서의 중재자의 역할, ANNEX II 상의 특별절차

다. GATT('93)

- 갓트 협정문과 MTO 협정문 ANNEX IA 상의기타 협정문과의 관계

라. 개별협정문

- 협정문간의 상충문제 해결

2. 이에 대해 각국은 향후 검토숫서, 검토작업등에대 해 아래 의견을 개진함.

가. 검토순서

통상국　　경기원　　재무부　　농수부　　상공부　　특허정

92.12.09　　07:34 CJ

외신 1과 통제관

0224

- 미국은 T3 전체회의에서 아직 논의하지 못한 GATT'(93)와 분쟁해결 절차의 APPENDIXII(특별 분쟁해결절차)를 먼저 논의하고 MTO 협정문 쟁점은 T3 차원에서는 당장해 결할 전망이밝지 않음에 비추어 T1,T2 의 결과를 보고한뒤 논의할 것을 희망함.(특히 부적용 문제를 언급하면서 T1, T2 의 결과가 가시화 되지않은 상황에서 입장을정하기 곤란하다고 언급)

- 이에 대해 카나다, EC가 동조(EC는 소극적동조)한 반면, 아국,일본, 멕시코등대다수 국가는 MTO 협정문 쟁점 해결이 정치적 합의의 관건이라는 점에 비추어 MTO협정문 우선검토를 선호한 반면, 태국, 인도등은 우선순위에 대해 유동적인 자세를취함.

나. 검토방법등 기타

- 아국 포함 다수국이 향후 검토과정에서 T3 MANDATE의 유지, TRANSPARENCY 유지및 구체적인 검토계획(TIME-TABLE) 필요성을 강조함.

- 기타, 우루과이, 칠레는 농산물 협정의 PART B도 검토대상이라는 점을 지적함.

3. 한편, 미국은 상기 의견 제시 과정에서 무역과 환경관련 부문이 보완될 필요성이 있다고하면서 관련 협정으로 TBT 협정과 SPS(위생검역) 협정을 제시한데 대해 각국은 미국의 의도를 좀더 자세히 밝힐 것을 요구하면서 1차적인 의견을 아래와 같이밝힌바,미국은 비공식 협의를 통해 동건을 논의할것을 제의함.

- 긍정반응: 환경문제는 MTO 차원에서 논의할수 있을 것임.(EC, 스웨덴(북구))

- 부정반응: TBT 협정문, SPS 협정문은 일괄 협상의 결과로서 이에대한 변경은 협상결과의 균형을 파괴하는 것임.

- 유보적반응: TE MANDATE 를 지켜야함.(아국,인도, 콜롬비아,말련등 다수국)

4. MATHUR 의장은 상기 논의를 아래와 같이종합함.

0 향후 T3 검토작업의 TIME-FRAME 은 11.26 TNC회의의 MANDATE 에 따르며 현재로서 구체적인 검토 계획(WORK PROGRAMME) 제시는 유익하지 않은것으로 봄.

0 검토범위 관련, 각 협정문은 상호 불가분한 관계(INTEGRAL WHOLE) 에 있으므로 모든협정문을 대상으로 하며, 검토 쟁점은 T3 MANDATE에 따라 법률적, 기술적 문제에 국한함.

0 검토 순서관련, MTO 협정문에 대해서는 금일논의결과를 TNC 의장에게 보고하고GUIDELINE를 받기로 하고, 우선은 12.9 부터 GATT('93),분쟁해결 절차, 이어서 개별협정문을 검토하기로 함.

PAGE 2

5. 한편,호주는 GATT('93) 상의 쟁점에 대한 연호 자국주관의 소규모 그룹 검토결과를 간략히 소개하엿으며, 홍콩은 독자관세영으로서의 자국의 지위문제와 관련 WTO협정의 부속협정에서 사용되고 있는 'NATIONAL' 이라는 용어에 대한별첨 'EXPLANATORY NOTE' 초안을 소개함.

첨부: 상기 홍콩 INFORMAL NOTE(2251)1부.(GVW(F)-0735).끝

(대사 박수길-국장)

주 제 네 바 대 표 부

번 호 : GVW(F) - 735   년월일 : 2/208   시간 : 1:00

수 신 : 장 관

발 신 : 주 제네바대사 (통제, 경기천, 재무부, 총단부, 상공부, 특허청)

제 목 :

총 P 매(표지포함)

보 안 봉 제	

외신규 봉 제	

배부처	장관실	차관실	一차보	二차보	외경실	분석관	아주국	미주국	구주국	중아국	국기국	경제국	통상국	문협국	외연원	청와대	안기부처	공기보원	경기원	상공부	재무부	농수부	동자부	환경처	과기처	특등성청
												0				1	1	1					1		

0227

735 P 1

2251   ＊ 사무총장 친서 누각 부분은 번역수 숙독 예정임.

7.12.92

"National" in the Final Act

Informal Note by the Secretariat

In the course of the Legal Drafting Group, the point has been raised
that the use of the word "national" in the texts to be attached to the MTO
(or otherwise included in the Final Act) entails a lack of precision, and
could engender legal uncertainty, with regard to the legal position of
separate customs territories Members of the MTO. Following informal
consultations held with interested delegations, this Note proposes a
possible solution to this question.

Discussion

The word "national" appears in various contexts in the Draft Final Act
texts, which can be classified into seven categories.

1.   The first four categories would be dealt with as follows:

An explanatory note would be added in an appropriate place in the text
of the MTO, together with the explanatory note already agreed to on
the word "country"; it would be indicated that this note refers to
Annex 1 of the MTO.

> "In the case of a separate customs territory Member of the MTO,
> where an expression in the agreements and associated legal
> instruments in the annexes to the MTO is qualified by the term
> "national", such expression shall be read as pertaining to that
> customs territory unless otherwise specified."

This note would apply only in the case of separate customs territories
members of the MTO, and would not affect the text in respect of any
other Member of the MTO.

The references to "national" covered by this note would be the following:

(1)   "National" in the sense of goods and services "of national
        origin": References to goods of "national origin", or to
        "national treatment" in the sense of treatment accorded to
        goods, services and persons of national origin;

(2)   "National legislation"; "national law"; "national policy",
        "national economies," "national regulations", "national systems"
        or "national regulatory bodies"; "on/at the national level";
        "national publication" or "national language"; and

(3)   "National" in the sense of "of a Member" or "representing a
        Member"; and

(4)   "National security" (TBT) or "national emergency" (TRIPs).

0228

1

ANNOTATED LIST OF EXAMPLES

List of contents

Index

0229

A-1

PROVISIONS TO BE COVERED GENERALLY BY THE EXPLANATORY NOTE TO ANNEX 1 OF THE MTO AGREEMENT:

(1)   "National" in the sense of "goods of national origin", "national treatment" for goods of national origin and "national treatment" for persons

General Agreement on Tariffs and Trade (1993)

Article III
National Treatment on Internal Taxation and Regulation

III:4. The products of the territory of any contracting party imported into the territory of any other contracting party shall be accorded treatment no less favourable than that accorded to like products of national origin in respect of all laws, regulations and requirements affecting their internal sale, offering for sale, purchase, transportation, distribution or use. The provisions of this paragraph shall not prevent the application of differential internal transportation charges which are based exclusively on the economic operation of the means of transport and not on the nationality of the product.

...

IV:(a) Screen quotas may require the exhibition of cinematograph films of national origin during a specified minimum proportion of the total screen time actually utilized,...

IV:(b) With the exception of screen time reserved for films of national origin under a screen quota, screen time including that released by administrative action from screen time reserved for films of national origin, shall not be allocated formally or in effect among sources of supply;

VII:2.(a) The value for customs purposes of imported merchandise should be based on the actual value of the imported merchandise on which duty is assessed, or of like merchandise, and should not be based on the value of merchandise of national origin or on arbitrary or fictitious values.*

XX(f)   imposed for the protection of national treasures of artistic, historic or archaeological value;

Note Ad Paragraph 1 (a) Article XVII

Governmental measures imposed to insure standards of quality and efficiency in the operation of external trade, or privileges granted for the exploitation of national natural resources ...

Agreement on Technical Barriers to Trade

2.   With respect to their central government bodies:

2.1 Parties shall ensure that in respect of technical regulations, products imported from the territory of any Party shall be accorded treatment no less favourable than that accorded to like products of national origin and to like products originating in any other country.

...

5.1.1   conformity assessment procedures are prepared, adopted and applied so as to grant access for suppliers of like products originating in the territories of other Parties under conditions no less favourable than those accorded to suppliers of like products of national origin or originating in any other country, in a comparable situation; ....

5.2.5   any fees imposed for assessing the conformity of products originating in the territories of other Parties are equitable in relation to any fees chargeable for assessing the conformity of like products of national origin or originating in any other country,

0230

A-3

3. Each Party shall permit non-resident providers of financial services to provide, as a principal, as a principal through an intermediary or as an intermediary, and under terms and conditions that accord national treatment, the following services:...

National Treatment

1. Under terms and conditions that accord national treatment, each Party shall grant to financial service providers of any other Party established in its territory access to payment and clearing systems...

2. When membership or participation in, or access to, any self-regulatory body... is required by a Party ... the Party shall ensure that such entities accord national treatment to financial service providers of any other Party resident in the territory of the Party.

(2) 'National legislation'; "national law"; "national policy", "national economies," "national regulations", "national systems" or "national regulatory bodies"; "on/at the national level"; "national publication" or "national language"

In these provisions, "national" is used to refer to domestic implementation of international commitments, or to domestic policy, legislation, regulations, economies or systems in contrast with their international counterparts, to the domestic level in contrast to the international level, or to publication domestically or in a domestic language (as opposed to publication internationally or in a GATT official language).

a. 'National legislation'

General Agreement on Tariffs and Trade (1993)

Note Ad Paragraph 1 Article III

The application of paragraph 1 to internal taxes imposed by local governments and authorities with the territory of a contracting party is subject to the provisions of the final paragraph of Article XXIV. The term "reasonable measures" in the last-mentioned paragraph would not require, for example, the repeal of existing national legislation authorizing local governments to impose internal taxes...

Agreement on Implementation of Article VI of the GATT

Article 14
Judicial Review

Each Party, whose national legislation contains provisions on anti-dumping measures, shall maintain judicial, arbitral or administrative tribunals or procedures...

Agreement on Import Licensing

Article 8: Final provisions

8.4. National Legislation

(no reference to "national" in the provision for which this is the title)

Agreement on Implementation of Article VII

Article 26: National Legislation

(no reference to "national" in the provision for which this is the title)

0231

A-5

SECTION 1: GENERAL OBLIGATIONS

Article 41

1. PARTIES shall ensure that enforcement procedures as specified in this Part are available under their national laws ...

4. Parties to a dispute shall have an opportunity for review by a judicial authority of final administrative decisions and, subject to jurisdictional provisions in national laws concerning the importance of a case, of at least the legal aspects of initial judicial decisions on the merits of a case.

Article 44: Injunctions

2. ....In other cases, the remedies under this Part shall apply or, where these remedies are inconsistent with national law, declaratory judgments and adequate compensation shall be available.

SECTION 3: PROVISIONAL MEASURES

Article 50

6. ... to be determined by the judicial authority ordering the measures where national law so permits ...

PART IV: ACQUISITION AND MAINTENANCE OF INTELLECTUAL PROPERTY RIGHTS AND RELATED INTER-PARTES PROCEDURES

Article 62

4. Procedures concerning the acquisition or maintenance of intellectual property rights and, where the national law provides for such procedures, administrative revocation and inter partes procedures ...

c. "National policy", "national consensus", "national regulations", "national economies", "national taxes", "national systems", "national administrations" or "national bodies"

General Agreement on Tariffs and Trade

Article XXXVIII:2

(e) collaborate in seeking feasible methods to expand trade for the purpose of economic development, through international harmonization and adjustment of national policies and regulations, through technical and commercial standards affecting production, transportation and marketing, and through export promotion by the establishment of facilities for the increased flow of trade information and the development of market research;...

Agreement on Implementation of Article VII

5.1(a)(iv) the customs duties and other national taxes payable in the country of importation by reason of the importation or sale of the goods.

Agreement on Technical Barriers to Trade

11.2 Parties shall, if requested, advise other Parties, especially the developing countries, and shall grant them technical assistance on mutually agreed terms and conditions regarding the establishment of national standardizing bodies, and participation in the international standardizing bodies, and shall encourage their national standardizing bodies to do likewise.

TBT Code of Good Practice for the Preparation, Adoption and Application of Standards

0232

A-7

The CONTRACTING PARTIES,

Desiring to improve the operation of notification procedures under the General Agreement, and thereby to contribute to the transparency of national trade policies and to the effectiveness of surveillance arrangements established to that end,...

The terms of reference of the working group will be:

- to undertake a thorough review of all existing notification obligations of contracting parties established under the General Agreement, with a view to simplifying, standardizing and consolidating these obligations to the greatest extent practicable, as well as to improving compliance with these obligations, bearing in mind the overall objective of improving the transparency of national trade policies and the effectiveness of surveillance arrangements established to this end, and also bearing in mind the possible need of some developing contracting parties for assistance in meeting their notification obligations; ...

General Agreement on Trade in Services

(Preamble)

Desiring the early achievement of progressively higher levels of liberalization of trade in services....while giving due respect to national policy objectives;

Recognizing the right of Parties to regulate ...in order to meet national policy objectives,...

Article XIX
Negotiation of Commitments

2. The process of liberalization shall take place with due respect for national policy objectives ...

Agreement on Trade Related Aspects of Intellectual Property Rights

(Preamble)

... Recognising, to this end, the need for new rules and disciplines concerning: ...

(c) the provision of effective and appropriate means for the enforcement of trade-related intellectual property rights, taking into account differences in national legal systems; ...

Recognising the underlying public policy objectives of national systems for the protection of intellectual property, including developmental and technological objectives;

Article 69: International Cooperation

PARTIES agree to cooperate with each other with a view to eliminating international trade in goods infringing intellectual property rights. For this purpose, they shall establish and notify contact points in their national administrations and be ready to exchange information on trade in infringing goods....

d.	"On/at the national level"

Agreement on Technical Barriers to Trade

10.10 Parties shall designate a single central government authority that is responsible for the implementation on the national level of the provisions concerning notification procedures under this Agreement except those included in Annex 3.

0233

A-9

... The ~~CONTRACTING PARTIES~~ Council for Trade in Goods shall be informed immediately of all changes in national tariffs resulting from recourse to this Article.

TBT Code of Good Practice for the Preparation, Adoption and Application of Standards

H.   The standardizing body within the territory of a ~~Party~~ Member shall make every effort to avoid duplication of, or overlap with, the work of other standardizing bodies in the national territory or with the work of relevant international or regional standardizing bodies...

(4)   "National security" or "national emergency"

Agreement on Technical Barriers to Trade

2.2   ... technical regulations shall not be more trade-restrictive than necessary to fulfil a legitimate objective, taking account of the risks non-fulfilment would create. Such legitimate objectives are, inter alia, **national security** requirements; ...

2.10 Subject to the provisions in the lead-in to Article 2, paragraph 9, where urgent problems of safety, health, environmental protection or national security arise or threaten to arise for a Party, ...

5.4   ... Parties shall ensure that central government bodies use [relevant guides or recommendations issued by international standardizing bodies], or the relevant parts of them, as a basis for their conformity assessment procedures, except where, as duly explained upon request, such guides or recommendations or relevant parts are inappropriate for the Parties concerned, for, inter alia, such reasons as national security requirements; ...

5.7 Where urgent problems of safety, health, environmental protection or national security arise or threaten to arise for a Party, ...

Agreement on Trade Related Aspects of Intellectual Property Rights

Article 31: Other Use Without Authorisation of the Right Holder

(b) .... This requirement may be waived by a PARTY in the case of a national emergency or other circumstances of extreme urgency or in cases of public non-commercial use. In situations of national emergency or other circumstances of extreme urgency, the right holder shall, nevertheless, be notified ...

0234

A-11

With regard to the protection of intellectual property, any advantage, favour, privilege or immunity granted by a PARTY to the nationals of any other country shall be accorded immediately and unconditionally to the nationals of all other PARTIES. Exempted from this obligation are any advantage, favour, privilege or immunity accorded by a PARTY: ...

(b)   granted in accordance with the provisions of the Berne Convention (1971) or the Rome Convention authorising that the treatment accorded be a function not of national treatment but of the treatment accorded in another country; ...

(d)   deriving from international agreements related to the protection of intellectual property which entered into force prior to the entry into force of this Agreement, provided that such agreements are notified to the Council on Trade-Related Aspects of Intellectual Property Rights and do not constitute an arbitrary or unjustifiable discrimination against nationals of other PARTIES.

Article 24: International Negotiations; Exceptions

4.   Nothing in this Section shall require a PARTY to prevent continued and similar use of a particular geographical indication of another PARTY identifying wines in connection with goods or services by any of its nationals or domiciliaries who have used that geographical indication in a continuous manner with regard to the same or related goods or services in the territory of that PARTY either (a) for at least ten years preceding its signature of this Agreement or (b) in good faith preceding its signature of this Agreement.

Article 40

3.   Each PARTY shall enter, upon request, into consultations with any other PARTY which has cause to believe that an intellectual property right owner that is a national or domiciliary of the PARTY to which the request for consultations has been addressed is undertaking practices in violation of the requesting PARTY's laws and regulations on the subject matter of this Section, ...

4.   A PARTY whose nationals or domiciliaries are subject to proceedings in another PARTY concerning alleged violation of that other PARTY's laws and regulations on the subject matter of this Section shall, upon request, be granted an opportunity for consultations by the other PARTY under the same conditions as those foreseen in paragraph 3 above.

0235

외   무   부

10

110-760 서울 종로구 세종로 77번지   / (02)720-2188   / (02)720-2686 (FAX)

문서번호 통기 20644-

시행일자 1992.12.11.(   )

수신   내부결재

참조

취급		차 관	장 관
보존		전결	
국 장	(서명)		
심의관		기획관리실장	
과 장	(서명)	총무과장	
기안	안 명 수	기획운영담당관	협조

제목   UR/법제화 그룹회의 참가 정부대표 임명

      스위스 제네바에서 개최되는 UR/법제화 그룹 회의(12.14-18)에 참석할 정부
대표를 "정부대표 및 특별사절의 임명에 관한 법률"에 의거, 아래와 같이 임명할
것을 건의합니다.

                    -    아   래   -

    1. 회 의 명 : UR/법제화 그룹 회의

    2. 기간 및 장소 : 92.12.14-18, 스위스 제네바

    3. 정부대표 : 통상기구과장 홍 종 기

    4. 출장기간 : 92.12.14-20. (6박 7일)

    5. 훈 령 : 별 첨

    6. 소요경비

        가. 항 공 료 : $2,111

        나. 체 재 비 : $66 X 6박 = $396

        다. 일 식 비 : ($20 + $42) X 7일 = $434

                    (총액 : $2,941)

        라. 지변항목 : 경제활동, 국외여비

    첨부 : 훈령. 끝.

                                    0236

훈 령
=========

1. UR/법제화 그룹은 92.1.13. UR/무역협상위원회(TNC)에서 결정된 mandate에
   따라 UR 협정 초안(Draft Final Act)의 내부적 일관성과 법적 합치성을 확보
   하는 작업을 수행하도록 임부를 부여받음.

2. UR/법제화 그룹에서의 작업이 중립적이며 기술적인 성격을 갖는 점을 감안하여,
   동 그룹에서의 작업이 UR 협상 참가국의 권리.의무의 균형에 변경을 초래하지
   않도록 하는 범위내에서 진행되도록 유의하면서 회의에 임함.

3. 금번 UR/법제화 그룹회의에서는 GATT '93협정, 통합분쟁해결절차 협정 및 여타
   협정문을 검토할 예정인바 협정문 상호간에 일관성이 유지되도록 문안을 검토하고
   기타 용어상의 통일을 기하는 방향으로 회의가 진행되도록 기여함.

4. 금번 회의에서 제기되는 쟁점에 대한 각 참가국의 동향을 면밀히 파악하고
   MTO 설립 협정문에 대한 미국.EC등 주요국의 입장을 파악하여 향후 UR/법제화
   그룹회의에 대한 대책을 수립함. 끝.

0237

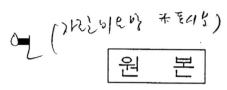

외 무 부

종 별 :

번 호 : GVW-2342   일   시 : 92 1211 1700

수 신 : 장 관(통기,경기원,재무부,농수산부,상공부,특허청)

발 신 : 주 제네바 대사

제 목 : UR/ 법제화 그룹(GATT '93)

연: GVW-2300

1. 표제그룹 회의는 12.10 MATHUR 의장 주재로 개최되어 연호 결정에 따라 GATT ('93)을 검토한바, 쟁점은 MTO 에 대한 정치적 지침이 나온뒤에 논의 하기로 하고 우선은 기술적인 문제에 국한하여 논의함. (신종원 서기관 참석)

2. 갓트 ('93)에 대한 검토 방법은 MTO 설립을 전제로 필요한 경우에 한하여 GATT '47 를 수정하는 방안을 잠정 채택하였음.

3. 동 검토는 사무국 문서 (92.5.6 자 838) 를 기초로 이루어 졌으며, 동 검토시 호주 그룹 문서 (92.12.3 자 2234)를 활용 하였는바, 동 검토시 논의된 조항은 아래임.

O 전문(PREAMBLE) 첫째 문안, 1조 주석 (ADARTICLE), 2조 1항(C) (양허표 문제) 2조 6항 (PARVALUE 용어 사용 문제), 3조 3항 (내국세에 대한특별 협정), 12조 4항B(BOP 제한 조치 검토), 14조4항 C (BOP 협의 절차), 14조 5항 B (특혜 협정에 관한 ANNEX A), 16조 4항 (보조금 경과규정), 20조 J항, 22조 2항 (협의), 25조 2항 (1차총회 개최), 26조 1항 (협정일자), 29조 (하바나헌장), 36조 8항 및 37 1항 A 의 주석(29조와의 관계)

- 상기 사항중 2조 1항 12조 4항 C, 16조 4항, 22조2항은 추가 협의가 필요한 사항임을 확인하고, 2조6항, 3조 3항, 14조 5항 B, 16조 4항, 26조 1항은 동조항의 적용 여부 상황에 대한 보충 자료를 사무국이 관계국과 협의를 봉해 준비하여 내주에추가 검토키로 하였으며, 기타 사항은 사무국 수정안에 따르기로 잠정 합의함.

- 한편 카나다는 29조 (하바나 헌장)이 삭제되더라도 하바나 헌장의 취지를 적용 하도록 되어 있는 1조4항 주석 (AD ARTICLE 1 (4))은 존치가 필요함을 강조함.

4. 동 법제화 그룹은 12.14 주간에는 상기 보충 자료가 필요한 사항과 통합

통상국   경기원   농수부   상공부   특허정   재무부

92.12.12   05:35 FO

외신 1과 통제관

0238

분쟁해결 절차중 APPENDIX II＊ (개별 협정 문상의 특별 또는 추가분쟁해결 절차)을
검토키로 함.

    끝

    (대사 박수길-국장)

관리번호 92-969   발 신 전 보

번 호 : **WGV-1971**   **921214 1828** 티 종별 : 지급

수 신 : 주 제네바   대사. 총영사

발 신 : 장 관 (통 기)

제 목 : MTO 설립 문제

대 : GVW-2351

아래 사항을 MTO 관련 협의에 참고 바람.

1. 미국의 MTO 설립 협정문에 대한 대안 비공식 문서에 대한 평가.

   ㅇ 대호 미측이 MTO 대안관련 비공식 문서를 배포한 것은 MTO 설립시 동 협정문에
   포함된 국내법의 다자간 무역규범 일치, 다수결에 의한 의사결정, 조부조항
   등에 대해 미 의회가 반대하고 있기 때문에 MTO 설립협정 초안을 수락하기
   어렵기 때문인 것으로 판단됨.

   ㅇ 동 대안 문서에 따르면 미국은 MTO를 설립치 않고 기존 갓트의 컨센서스
   관행을 유지하며 현 MTO 설립협정 초안중 UR 협상결과 이행에 필요한 요소들
   (일괄수락조항, 원회원국 및 가입요건조항, 제반협정의 부속서 수록등)만을
   취사 선택하여 UR 의정서 형식으로 채택한다는 입장으로서 동건관련 상당한
   논란이 있을 것으로 예상됨.

2. 19개 주요국 수석대표 비공식 회의 대책

   ㅇ 아국은 MTO 설립으로 다자간 무역체제가 강화된다는 점에서 MTO 설립협정
   초안을 수락하는데 별다른 문제가 없다는 입장인 바, 19개 주요국 수석대표
   비공식 회의에서 미측이 연호 대안문서에 따라 UR 의정서 방식을 주장할 경우
   하기와 같이 대처 바람.   /계속

보 안 통 제

앙 고 재	92 년 12 월 14 일	통상기구과	기안자 성명 안명수	과 장	심의관	국 장	차 관	장 관	외신과통제
						전결			

0240

가. MTO 설립은 UR 협상결과의 이행뿐 아니라 다자간 무역체제의 강화를 위해 필요함.

나. 91.12.20 최종의정서안이 제시된 이래 MTO 설립을 전제로 법제화 그룹의 작업이 진행되어 오는등 MTO 설립은 UR 협상에서 핵심적인 요소인 바, 현단계에서 MTO 설립이 무산되는 경우 실질사항의 변화를 초래(잠정적용 의정서 존치 및 국내법의 다자간 무역협정 합치 조항 삭제등)할 우려가 있음.

다. 기존 갓트 협정의 규율 대상 뿐아니라 신분야까지 대상으로 하고 있는 UR 협상결과 이행을 위해서는 포괄적인 기능이 부여된 항구적인 제도적 틀(MTO)이 필요한 바, 미국이 상정하고 있는 각료급 무역위원회를 정점으로 하는 계약적 성격의 체제로는 UR 협상결과 이행 및 다자간 무역 체제유지 기능을 효율적으로 수행하기 어려움.

라. 절차적인 측면에서도 MTO 설립문제는 오랜기간 논의를 거쳐 UR 협상 참가국간에 컨센서스가 이루어진 사항이며, 현재 MTO 설립협정 제2차 수정안까지 나온 상태에서 미국이 MTO 설립에 반대한다는 것은 이해하기 어려움. 끝.

(통상국장   홍 정 표)

0241

외 무 부

종 별 :

번 호 : GVW-2365

일 시 : 92 1215 1530

수 신 : 장관(봉기, 경기원, 재무부, 농림수산부, 상공부)

발 신 : 주제네바대사

제 목 : UR 동향/법제화 그룹

당관 신종원서기관은 금 12.15 MATHUR 법제화 그룹의장을 보좌하고 있는 J.CROOME 갓트지역협력 협정국장을 접촉, 금주초에 T3 회의를 속개하며 통합 분쟁 해결 절차 APPENDIX II(통합절차와 개별협정 분쟁 해결절차와의 관계) 와 GATT('93) 중 기타 기술적사항을 계속 논의키로한 일정과 관련, 금주 T3 일정을 문의한바, 동인은 MTO 협정에대한 정치적 타결이 선행되지 않는한 T3 작업의 계속은 무의미하다는 MATHUR 의장의생각을 다시 확인하면서 통합분쟁 해결절차 APPENDIX II 및 GATT('93) 세부사항에 대한 T3 논의 준비가되어 있지 않다고 말함으로써 금주에는 T3회의가 개최될 가능성이크지 않다는 점을 시사함.끝

(대사 박수길-국장)

통상국   경기원   재무부   농수부   상공부

PAGE 1

92.12.16   04:06 EI

외신 1과 통제관 ✓

0242

외 무 부

종 별 : 지 급

번 호 : GVW-2389 일 시 : 92 1217 1900

수 신 : 장 관(봉기, 경기원, 재무부, 농수산부, 상공부, 특허청)

발 신 : 주 제네바 대사

제 목 : UR/ 법제화 그룹

12.16(수) ROESSLER 갓트법률 국장이 홍종기 통상기구 과장과의 오찬 협의에서 UR 결과 이행에 관한 미국 제안 (각료설정, UR의정서), MTO 협정에 대한 대안으로 각료회의 결정과 UR 의정서의 형태로 UR 협상결과를 수용, 이행하는 방안을 제안한바, 본인 으로서는 SINGLE UNDERTAKING 이행기구 설치등 MTO 협정의 기본 요소가 미국의 새로운 제안에도 포함되어 있는점에 비추어 MTO 의 설립에 반대하는 이유를 이해할수없음.

0 미국법 체계상 어떤 형태의 국제법도 연방법의 하위 (미국 헌법에 대한 이해 부족 인듯)에 있으므로 UR 협상의 결과를 수용하는 법적 형식이 결정 (DECISION) 이든의정서 (PROTOCOL) 이든 협정 (AGREEMENT) 또는 조약 (TREATY) 이든 이행을 위한 미국내 입법 을 전제로 하는 경우 똑같은 법적 효력을 가지는바 미국이 '각료결정'을제의한 의도를 명확히 알수는 없지만 무역 정책상의 이유보다는 국내 홍보와 관련한고려라고 봄.

0 다만, 미국은 MTO 를 설치하지 않고 상기와같은 법적 이행구조를 취함 으로써기존 MTO 협정 문안 중에서 불만을 가지고 있는 사항을 이행 대상에서 제외할 가능성이 있는바, 이런점에서 MTO 협정의 SINGLE-UNDERTAKING 의원칙이 손상될 우려가 있음.

나. MTO 협정문

0 던켈 초안의 FINAL ACT 에 MTO 설립이 상정되어 있으나 동 의정서가 합의된 문서는 아니므로 MTO 설립 자체에 대해 참가국이 합의했다고 볼수는 없음.

0 UR 협상은 결과를 DEFINITIVE 한 BASIS에서 이행할 것을 목표로 진행한 만큼 GRANDFATHER CLAUSE 를 계속 원용할려는 시도는 협상의 취지와 맞지 않다고 봄.

0 국내법의 갓트 합치 노력조항과 관련, 참가국이 MTO 협정을 준수하는 것은 당연

통상국   경기원   재무부   농수부   상공부   특허청

PAGE 1 92.12.18   05:09 FO

외신 1과 통제관

0243

한 것이며, 오히려 SHALL ENDEAVOUR CLAUSE 는 갓트와 일치하지않은 국내법에 대한구실이 되어다자 통상 체제를 약화시킬 가능성이 있음.

다. 분쟁해결

0 23항 (분쟁 절차는 오로지 갓트 분쟁해결 절차를 따른다는 조항)은 TAUTOLOGY로서 동항이 없더라도 관련 조항의 의무를 지키는 것은 당연하므로 동조항은 새로운권리 의무를 창조하는 것이 아닌바, 정치적 으로는 의미가 있을 지 모르나 법적으로는 아무런 의미가 없는 사항임.

- 동항이 일방 조치의 금지를 규율한다는 견해도 있으나 일방 조치는 차별 조치이므로 기본적으로 갓트1조 위반이며 23항은 이를 재확인 하는외에 별다른 의미는 없음.

0 NON-VIOLATION 분쟁해결 절차 (26항)의 적용범위

✱ 갓트상 NON-VIOLATION 의 개념은 갓트 규정이 상품 무역에 있어서 관세 양허효과가 보조금등 비국경 조치로 인해 저해되는 것을 방지하고 양허 당시의 기대 이익을 보존하자는데 그취지가 있음.

0 따라서, 국경 조치외에 국내조치 까지도 완벽하게 규율하고 있거나 양허 절차가 없는 협정 (TRIPS, 반덤핑, 보조금, 상계관세 협정등)에 NON-VIOLATION) 분쟁 절차를 적용 하려는 시도는 무리한 점이 있으며

- 같은 맥락에서 갓트 23조 1항(C) 가 상정하고 있는 어떤 상황의 존재에 기인한 분쟁은 서비스 협정에는 적용됬 않는 것으로 해석하는 것이 타당함.끝

(대사 박수길-국장)

주 제 네 바 대 표 부

문서번호 : 제네(경) 20644-*1100*

시행일자 : 1992. 12.18.

수신 : 외무부장관
참조 : 통상국장

설				지시		
접수	일자시간			결재	대　사	
	번호	71330			차석대사	
	처리자			공람	참사관	
	담당자	이병호			서기관	

제목 : MTO 관련 미국대안에 대한 분석

대 : WGV-1971

92. 12. 12 대사급 비공식 회의시 제시된 미국의 표제 제안에 대한 당관 분석을 별첨 송부합니다. 끝.

주　제　네　바　대

0245

MTO 관련 미국 제안 분석

'92. 12. 13
경 제 과

1. 미국 제안의 요지(첨부)

O UR 협상 결과(MTO 협정 제외) 이행을 위한 각료회의 결정 채택

O 각료회의 결정 포함 내용

  - 다자통상체계 범위 설정 : MTO 협정(3차 수정)상의 모든 부속협정

  - UR 결과 이행기관 설치 : 각료회의(MC), 일반이사회(GC), 3개 분야
                           (상품, 서비스, TRIPs)이사회, 통합분쟁
                           해결기구, TPRM기구, 기타위원회

  - 다자통상체제의 정책결정방법 : 갓트의 Consensus에 의한 정책결정관행
                                유지

  - UR 결과의 국내 비준절차 회부 약속

  - 국내절차 종료시 UR결과 시행을 위한 의정서(Protocol) 문안 채택

O UR 의정서 내용

  - 수락(Acceptance), 가입(accession) 조항 규정

  - Single-undertaking 임을 명시하는 규정(전체협정에 대한 수락, 발효,
    탈퇴등)

  - GATT 93에 의한 갓트 47의 승계를 선언하는 규정

  - MTO 협정(3차 수정안)상의 부속협정 첨부(MTA'S 및 PTA'S)

2. MTO 협정문과 미국제안의 공통점

O UR 결과의 이행 수단

  - 대상협정(Annex 1-4)의 범위 및 설치될 각기관이 동일(단, 환경위원회
    는 예외)

0246

- 부속협정에 대해 single-undertaking 원칙이 적용된다는 점도 동일

- 수락전 국내 절차를 요하는 점에서도 동일

3. MTO 협정문과 미국 제안의 차이점

	MTO 협정안	미국 제안
채택	Final Act채택 또는 서명을/통해 UR 협상 결과 채택(MTO 협정문 포함)	UR결과 채택(TNC)후, 갓트측별 총회에서 UR협상결과 이행을 위한 각료회의 결정 채택(UR 의정서 포함)
UR 결과 이행 방법	국내절차후 MTO 협정문에 서명등을 통해 수락	국내 절차후 UR의정서(protocol)에 서명등을 통해 수락
기속력 정도	법적 기속력이 강한 협정문	법적 기속력이 약한 UR 의정서 (Protocol)
기구설치여부	국제법인격을 갖는 기구설치	기구 불설치(현 사무국의 모든 부속협정 이행 관장)
주요 실제 내용의 차이	※ 내용 별첨	※ 하기 MTO 쟁점이 빠져 있음. (주로 미국 불만사항) - grandfather clause 철폐규정 약화(Decision에 포함) - 국내법 일치 노력 조항 - 웨이버 부여 조항 - 부적용 조항 - 개정, 해석 조항

0247

4. 미국 제안의 배경 분석

O MTO에 대한 미국내(특히 의회)의 거부감

- 국제법 인격을 갖는 MTO가 창설되고 동 기구가 국제통상 문제를 포괄적으로 관할하는 경우 통상에 관한 미의회의 입법권이 제약되는 결과가 되어 전체 UR 결과를 Cover하는 MTO 협정이 미의회에서 거부될 가능성

O MTO 협정 내용에 대한 불만

- 더우기, MTO 협정에는 Grandfather 조항의 지위가 불분명하고 국내법 일치 노력조항이 있으며, 또한 부적용 조항, 웨이버 조항, 투표관련 조항(EC의 2중 투표권 인정 여지가 있음)등이 미국의 불만 사항이어서 이들 조항을 수정하지 않고서는 MTO 협정이 미의회를 통과하기가 더욱 어렵다는 판단을 했을 가능성도 있음.

O UR 결과 이행을 위한 대안 강구

- MTO 협정의 미의회 통과 가능성이 낮음에 비추어 UR 결과 이행을 위한 대안 강구 필요
- 통합분쟁해결 절차의 패널결과의 강제이행(21항), 교차보복 인정(22항)이 UR 결과의 이행을 실질적으로 보장하고 있으므로 UR 결과의 모협정은 어떤 법적 형태를 띠더라도 무방하다는 판단을 했을 가능성

5. UR 협상 과정에 비추어본 미국 제안의 타당성 여부와 예상 반응

O Punta 선언과의 관계

- Punta 선언은 최종 Paragaph에서 모든 분야의 협상이 확정(establish)된 뒤에 각료급 갓트 특별총회를 개최하여 UR 결과의 이행 문제를 논의하기로 결정하였음에 비추어, 논리면에서 미국 제안인 각료결정의 채택 절차 에는 문제가 없음. (오히려 타분야 협상결과와 한꺼번에 MTO 협정을 채택 키로 되어 있는 DFA가 문제가 있어 MTO 협정 근거에 의문을 제기하고 있는 소수 개도국들로부터 지지를 받을 가능성도 있음)

0248

- 그러나, 실제 UR 협상의 진행 경과와 협상자의 의도를 밝혀주고 있는 DFA의 최종 의정서(Final Act)에는 MTO 협정을 협상의 integral part로 명기되어(1항) 있으며, 이는 punta 선언을 발전시킨 것으로 해석되고 있음에 비추어 미국 제안에 반대할 국가도 상당 예상됨.

O 미국제안 내용에 대한 타당성 여부
  - grandfather clause 포함 문제 :
    . Final Act에서 UR 결과를 definitive basis로 하는 것이 바람직(agree on the desirability of the application...... on a definitive basis) 하다고 합의한 점에 비추어 미국의 grandfather 조항 부활시도는 무리한 점이 많아 다수국의 반발이 예상됨.
  - 국내법 일치 노력 조항 :
    . 동 조항은 통합분쟁 해결 절차의 패널 절차의 강제 이행 조항 도입 (21항)에 비추어 존속내지 강화되어야 하는바, 이에 대한 삭제는 상당수국의 반발이 예상됨.
    . 다만, 분쟁에 관한 모든 결정 및 이행을 분쟁해결 규율에 의해서만 한다는 통합분쟁해결절차 23항에 의해 국내법 일치 의무가 발생하므로 endeavour clause를 없애는 것이 오히려 국내법 일치 의무를 더욱 강화 하는 것이라고 해석하는 일부 국가도 있음
  - 기타, 웨이버, 부적용, 개정.해석 조항
    . 전체협상의 consistent한 운용을 위해 필요한 사항이므로 UR 결과를 이행하기 위한 총괄문서에 반드시 필요하며 이러한 사항은 Protocol 이라는 법적 기속력이 약한 문서에서는 규정하기 곤란하므로 UR결과의 총괄문서는 협정이 되어야 할 것이라는 논리를 제기할 국가가 상당수 예상됨. (EC 및 개도국등)
  - 한편, UR 결과 이행을 위해 각료회의, 일반이사회, 개별협정 이사회등의 권한과 기능등을 규율할 협정문의 필요성이 제기됨.

0249

6. 미국제안이 아국 이익에 미치는 부문

O Grandfather clase : 아국 조선업계의 미국 연안운항 선박 건조 가능성에
비추어 검토 필요 (아국 양곡법)

O 국내법 일치 노력 : 슈퍼 301조에 대한 견계 장치 감안 검토 필요

O 부적용 : TRIPs 협정에 대한 특정국(예 : 일본)에 대한 부적용 가능성등
검토 필요

O 웨이버 : TRIPs 협정 일부 조항에 대한 웨이버 필요성 및 가능성에 대한
검토 필요

0250

UR 결과 이행을 위한 미국제안(각료결정 및 UR 의정서) 평가

92. 12. 15
경 제 과

1. 긍정 평가 부분

0 Single-Undertaking 원칙 유지

- Coverage, 수락(acceptance), 가입(accession) 발효(entry into force), 탈퇴(withdrawal) 관련 규정에 동 원칙 유지

0 Single-undertaking 원칙 실현을 위한 기관 설치

- 각료무역위원회(Ministeral Tracde Committee)

- 일반이사회(General council)

- 기타 기관설치

0 따라서 UR 결과를 이행하는데 커다란 문제는 없다고 봄.

2. 부정 평가 부분

가. Single-undertaking 원칙 관련

0 Single-undertaking 원칙 실현기관(MTC 또는 GC)의 권한과 기능에 대한 규정이 미흡

- 미국 제안에는 MTC (또는 GC)는 전부속 협정을 관할하며, 필요한 하위기관을 두고, 결정은 콘센서스에 의한다고만 되어 있음.

0 전체협정 총괄기관으로서의 MTC 또는 GC의 주요 미흡한 사항은 아래임.

- 협정간의 불일치가 발생하는 경우를 대비한 해석조항이 없음. (통합분쟁해결 절차에 의한 해석은 구체적인 분쟁을 전제로 함)

- 웨이버 조항, 부적용 조항이 없음으로써 UR 협상당시 MTO 설립을 전제로 논의가 미흡하게 이루어진 부분이 있는 개별협정(TRIPS)상의 내용을 최종적인 것으로 확정하게 되어 협상분야 또는 국가간의 이익 불균형 초래

0251

예 : TRIPS에만 웨이버 조항, 부적용 조항이 없음.

(웨이버 조항은 장래의 불확실한 경우를 위해, 부적용 조항은
다자협정의 경우에는 특정국간의 특별관계를 감안 필요한 조항
들임)

나. Definitive basis에 의한 UR 결과 적용 취지 약화

- 미국 제안은 GATT II의 Coverage에 Grandfather clause의 부활을
기도하여 다자 통상 체제의 주요 원칙의 적용을 제한하려 하고 있음.
(예 : Jones Act의 경우 내국민 대우 원칙 배제)

다. 국내법의 GATT 합치 노력 조항의 약화

- 갓트기능의 강화를 위해 도입된 패널결과의 강계이행(통합 분쟁해결
절차의 21항)과 교차보복인정(동 22항)에 대한 대전제 또는 반대급
부인 국내법의 갓트합치 조항이 포함은 되어 있으나 법적 구속력이
약한 Decesion(주로 절차적인 사항 규정)에 포함되어 있음.

라. 환경관련 사항의 추가

- 각료결정 사항에 UR 협상에서 논의되지 않은 "Sustainable Development"
개념을 도입하고 있으며, Protocol에서는 무역과 환경위원회(Committee
On Trade and the Environment)룰 설치

3. 아국 대응 방향

- 상기 부정평가 부분중 아국과 상당한 이해 관계가 있는 부분은 grand father
clause 부활기도, 국내법의 갓트합치 일치 노력 조항의 약화, 환경관련
사항의 추가 부문임. (기타 사항은 원칙관련 조항으로 장래의 기대 이익과
관련됨)
- 상기 3개 분야에 대한 아국의 입장은 아국의 관세화 문제에 대한 미국의
태도에 따라 신축적으로 대처할 수도 있다고 봄.

0252

UR/결과 이행 Mechanism에 관한 미국제안 평가

1992. 12. 16
경 제 과

1. 긍정평가

- Single Underataking의 원칙을 그대로 유지

- UR 협상 결과 이행을 위해 필요한 기관 설치

    O   MTO 협정에서 예정된 제기관을 그대로 존치

- 따라서 UR 결과 이행에 큰 문제 없음.

2. 문제점

- 법적 지위가 상대적으로 약한 Protocol 형식을 통한 UR 결과 이행을 예정

    O   계약적(contractual) 성격의 현행 GATT 체제를 그대로 답습(GATT II)

- 각료위원회(Ministerial Trade Committee) 및 일반이사회(General Council)의
  존재 근거는 Protocol에 규정할 사항이 아님(개별협정상 근거 없음)

- Grandfather Clause 존치로 UR 협상 참가국의 여망인 UR 결과의 definistive
  besis에 의한 이행 불가능

- 국내법의 GATT 합치 노력 조항 약화

    O   법적 구속력이 약한 Ministerial Decision에 포함

- 환경관련 사항 추가

    O   UR에서 세부적 토의가 없었던 사항

    O   무역고 환경위원회(Committee on Trade and Env.)의 권능 모호

3. 아국입장

- 아국은 기본적으로 MTO 설립 선호하나

- Single Undertaking 원칙등 UR의 기본정신이 유지되고,

- 상기 2항 제문제점이 적절히 수용되며,

- 통합분쟁 해결절차(특히 23항, 일방조치 금지)의 핵심적 요소가 존중된다면

- 아국은 contractnal arrangement에 의한 UR 결과 이행 신축성 있게 고려가능

0253

외교문서 비밀해제: 우루과이라운드2 18
우루과이라운드 법제화 그룹 회의

초판인쇄 2024년 03월 15일
초판발행 2024년 03월 15일

지은이 한국학술정보(주)
펴낸이 채종준
펴낸곳 한국학술정보(주)
주 소 경기도 파주시 회동길 230(문발동)
전 화 031-908-3181(대표)
팩 스 031-908-3189
홈페이지 http://ebook.kstudy.com
E-mail 출판사업부 publish@kstudy.com
등 록 제일산-115호(2000. 6. 19)

ISBN   979-11-7217-120-9 94340
       979-11-7217-102-5 94340 (set)